MASTER DATA MANAGEMENT

&

ENTERPRISE ENGINEERING

Dr. Eng. M. Naoulo

Master, Transactional, & Process Data Management
& Enterprise Engineering

Foreword

Compared to other professions, the world of data management and technology is quite immature. Go to the walls of Rome and marvel at the civil engineering feats of the Romans that are more than two millennia old. Look at the walls of the pyramids in Egypt and read how some accountant has calculated how much grain is owed the Pharaoh a thousand years ago. Go to the high cliffs of Chile and enter some of the caves there, and you will find bones that suggest that medicine was being practiced over 10,000 years ago.

So when you compare the professional maturity of technology and information engineering with that of civil engineering, accounting and medicine, it is no contest. Other professions have been around for thousands of years while computer technology has been around since the early 1960's.

It is in the context of maturity that one needs to read the book – Master Data Management and Enterprise Engineering by Dr. M. Naoulo. The world of technology has several related yet distinct approaches – Martin's and Finklestein's information engineering, Ted Codd's relational technology, Inmon's data warehouse, and others.

This book takes these approaches and others and does two important things – it blends them together and it takes the bodies of thought and turns them into an engineering approach. As such this book is another important step in the evolution of computer science.

This is a next step in the maturation of computer science. I recommend it to any serious student of computer science or to any serious practitioner.

Bill Inmon

May 21, 2012

Dr. Eng. M. Naoulo

Master, Transactional, & Process Data Management & Enterprise Engineering

Table of Contents

Dr. Eng. M. Naoulo

Dr. Eng. M. Naoulo

Dr. Eng. M. Naoulo

Dr. Eng. M. Naoulo

Dr. Eng. M. Naoulo

Dr. Eng. M. Naoulo

11

Dr. Eng. M. Naoulo

13

Dr. Eng. M. Naoulo

Dr. Eng. M. Naoulo

13

Acknowledgement

First, I would like to thank my wife Ghenwa who provided me with constructive remarks and feedback. She encouraged me to write the book and endured the time alone while I was working hard to complete it. Second, I attribute many thanks to my sons Omar who reviewed the book and Sammy who developed diagrams and art work needed to assure its professional presentation.

Furthermore I thank IBM, Texas Instruments, Hitachi Consulting, and Gavroshe USA that presented me with opportunities to provide Best of Practice Consulting and Training Services to major US and International enterprises.

Dr. Eng. M. Naoulo

Prologue

Based on the work of Dr. E. F. Codd's Relational Technology, James Martin and Clive Finklestein's Information Engineering, and Bill Inmon's Data Warehousing, the discipline of Data Modeling using Relational and Multidimensional techniques started to emerge as a reliable instrument to design and structure the databases. Major technical weaknesses, non-technical hindrances, and obstructions affected the Data Architecture and Data Modeling disciplines. They are:

1. There was no cohesive connect between the Relational and Multidimensional techniques.
2. These two techniques are applied independently in the areas of the Enterprise Data Architecture: the Relational technique in the Operational Systems and the ODS and the Multidimensional technique in the Business Data Marts.
3. Data Architecture and Data Modeling require qualified staff to carry them out. Currently many individuals and corporations without the proper education, skills, and experience are pretending to be experts in these disciplines, and many enterprises are requesting their consulting services without verifying their credentials. The hiring directors and mangers of these enterprises should acquire the knowledge about the essence and features of Data Architecture and Data Modeling to properly conduct their selection and hiring tasks.
4. Many IT staff having their education and skills in Data Base Administration pretend to be Data Architect and Data Modelers. These persons' pretense is similar to the pretense of the Programmers in the early stages of IT to be Business and Enterprise Analyst, or the Accountants pretense to be Financial Experts, or the Midwifes pretense to be Obstetricians MD. This deception drastically hindered the cohesion of IT systems and resulted in many incorrect and unstructured databases.
5. Many enterprises are selecting the consulting services of individuals and corporations based on the dollar figures. They have no idea about Knowledge, Expertise, and Quality/Cost ratio. Many hundreds of millions of dollars projects were wasted due to improperly selecting incompetent and cheap consulting services.
6. Data Architecture and Data Modeling still lack the credence and credentials to be considered as an Engineering Curriculum.

This book rectifies the technical weaknesses and alleviates the non-technical hindrances and obstructions. It institutes an Enterprise Engineering Curriculum covering the Enterprise Data Architecture and Modeling, the Business Process Re-engineering, and the Enterprise Re-Engineering and Improvement.

1. It aggregates the Relational and Multidimensional techniques and incorporates them in an innovative, comprehensive, and cohesive: SAM O NAOULO Enterprise Data Modeling Technique. This technique would be applied across the Enterprise: Operational Systems, Central Data Repositories, and Business and Enterprise Data Marts.
2. It institutes an Enterprise Engineering Curriculum with syllabus, credence, and credentials. Enterprise Engineers can follow this curriculum to acquire the necessary skills to undertake the Data Architecture, Data Modeling, and Enterprise Improvements. This Curriculum would provide also the criteria to hire Data Architects, Data Modelers, Enterprise Architects and Engineers and to select proper Enterprise Data individuals and corporations consultants.

Dr. Eng. M. Naoulo

Introduction

This book covers two major areas:

A - The Information Technology evolved thru many stages since the dawn of computers in the mid of the twentieth century. In the first decade of the twenty first century additional requirements were encountered due to the persistent and intense needs for integration of different systems of the enterprises as a result of the inception and development of many disconnected applications and their databases by different departments of an enterprise, and from mergers and acquisitions. This put tremendous emphasis on the Architecture, Consolidation, Integration, Quality Assurance, and Synchronization of data.

These needs necessitate the conception of Techniques, Standards, and Tools to:
1. Conceive and Develop approaches and techniques for Data Architecture, Data Consolidation, and Data Integration across the Enterprise using Data Modeling, Data Standards, Data Dictionaries, and Metadata.
2. Conceive and Develop approaches and techniques for Data Quality and Data Governance.
3. Conceive and Develop approaches and techniques for Data Propagation, Data Migration, and Data Synchronization across the Enterprise using Data Mapping, ETL, Data Conversion, and Service Oriented Architecture.

The first part of the book lay out the blueprint for the **Enterprise Data Framework.** This Framework establishes the groundwork to fulfill the needs for Data Integration and Consolidation across the Enterprise. It encompasses the **System of Apparatus, Machinery, and Operation,** the **Enterprise Engineering Model,** the **On-Line Mechanical Processing,** the **Enterprise Intelligence,** and the **Enterprise Data Architecture.** Their implementation involves Data Modeling, Data Standards, Data Dictionaries, Metadata, Data Quality, Data Governance, Data Propagation, Data Migration, and Data Synchronization.

The **System of Apparatus, Machinery, and Operation** comprises the building blocks of the Enterprise, their structure, and their interlinks. The information pertinent to these building blocks are analyzed, classified, and evaluated to provide the data groundwork for building the **Enterprise Engineering Model** and the infrastructure of the **Enterprise Data Architecture.** The **System of Apparatus, Machinery, and Operation** encompasses an innovative technique for grouping, classifying, and development of the Master Data and separates it from the Transactional and Process Data.

The **Enterprise Engineering Model** reflects and details in a data architecture milieu the Information pertinent to the **System of Apparatus, Machinery, and Operation** using elegant new comprehensive methods and techniques which are dramatically lacking in this field. It carries the foundation of comprehensive Data Architecture, Data Consolidation, and Data Integration across the Enterprise.

The Enterprise Data Framework depicts and describes a new Modeling technique: **On-Line Mechanical Processing** (OLMP). The OLMP encompasses the streaming of the Enterprise Processes to capture the time and cost of handling the enterprise's activities.

The aggregation of the streamed results forms the base for **Enterprise Intelligence** (EI). The Enterprise Intelligence emphasizes the design and construction of EI Data Marts. Query and Reporting from the EI Data Marts provide the information needed for **Enterprise Engineering.**

The **Enterprise Data Architecture** outlines and depicts the conception and design of the overall Data Architecture of the Enterprise and the mapping from the Legacy Systems thru the Central Data Repository to the Business and Enterprise Data Marts.

B - The globalization that evolved in the last decade of the twentieth century and went into full thrust in the first decade of the twenty first century added additional needs for Consolidation, Integration, and Synchronization of data. It also emphasized the need for efficiency and effectiveness of the enterprises' functioning as the competition from different regions of the world affected the bottom line cost of operations and therefore the profit of enterprises.

In this very competitive world and cut-throat market, if the efficiency and effectiveness of an enterprise are not improved, it is certain that this enterprise will lose income and market share therefore will lose major strengths that contribute to its survival. This will put tremendous importance on the need for Business Process Improvement. This need induced the conception of techniques and development of Enterprise Engineering and Reengineering. The current techniques in this area: Activity Based Costing (ABC), Business Process Management (BPM), Reengineering the Corporation, and Reengineering Management lack comprehensive and solid approach and techniques necessary to be part of Engineering or Reengineering curriculum.

The second part of the book concentrates on the development of the **Enterprise Engineering Framework.** This Framework includes Methodology, Guidelines, Deliverables, and Techniques for Enterprise Engineering and Reengineering. It utilizes the **Enterprise Data Framework,** the **System of Apparatus, Machinery, and Operation,** the **Enterprise Engineering Model,** the **On-Line Mechanical Processing,** and the **Enterprise Intelligence** developed in the first part of the book as its technical foundation.

Enterprise Engineering provides the infrastructure and information analysis base to re-conceive, revitalize, and re-engineer the Enterprise's Operation to improve its efficiency and effectiveness and aiming to accomplish the main objective of Business Operation Management.

Abstract

The Master, Transactional, & Process Data Management comprise Framework, Techniques, Best of Practice, and Architecture to design and manage the Master, Transactional, & Process Data reflecting the Information of the Enterprise.

The Enterprise Engineering comprises Framework, Methodology, Guidelines, Deliverables, and Techniques to engineer the Enterprises and improve their Performance.

The book establishes the Fundamentals of design, modeling, and management of Master, Transactional, and Process Data and the Principles of Enterprise Engineering.

The Foundation of Enterprise Information is the System of Apparatus, Machinery, and Operation. The technical depiction reflecting this System is the Enterprise Engineering Model. This Model encompasses the Master Data, Mechanism, and Mechanics which reflect in an IT data architecture milieu the Apparatus, Machinery, and Operation.

The book includes two parts:

The first part encompasses the **Enterprise Data Framework** and its new Modeling Techniques supporting the analysis, design, and management of the Master, Transactional, and Process Data. The Enterprise Data Framework illustrates and depicts the Data Architecture across the enterprise covering the integration and consolidation of the data of the Legacy Systems in a Central Data Repository, and the propagation of this data into the Business and Enterprise Intelligence Data Marts. It elucidates the essentials of the design and architecture of the Enterprise Engineering Model which illustrates a clear and concise view depicting the operational aspects of the Enterprise and their relations to the Enterprise's needs.

This part provides the principles and techniques for the analysis and design of the:
- ➢ Master Data representing the main objects of an enterprise,
- ➢ Transactional Data detailing the results of transactions occurring in an enterprise, and
- ➢ Process Data capturing the data pertinent to the functioning of an enterprise.

The first part comprises the following chapters:

1. **An Introduction** specifying the classification and arrangement of Data.

2. **The Enterprise Data Framework** for analyzing the System of Apparatus, Machinery, and Operation of the enterprise. The components of the Apparatus encompass the Needs, Activities, Operators, Utilities, Locations, and Occurrences. These components are

involved in the Enterprise Operation and answer respectively the questions: Why, How, Who, What, Where, and When of the Enterprise's functioning. The Machinery covers the Procedures regulating the Transactions and the Operation covers the functioning Sessions and Transactions.

The essentials of the analysis and design of the **Enterprise Engineering Model** are established. The Master, Mechanism, and Mechanics Data reflect in the Enterprise Engineering Model the Apparatus, Machinery, and Operation. This Model illustrates in a Data milieu the Enterprise functioning.

3. **The Modeling Technique supporting the design of the Enterprise Engineering Model.** This technique: SAM O NAOULO Modeling Technique is explained and elaborated in detail. It is used in the design of the Enterprise Engineering Model, the Enterprise Data Architecture, and Enterprise Engineering. It establishes the technical base for the design and separation of Master, Mechanism, and Mechanics Transactional and Process Data. This sophisticated technique is erected on top of the Relational Normalization Data Modeling technique developed by Dr. E. F. Codd [2] and the Multidimensional Data Modeling technique developed by Bill Inmon [9] and detailed by Ralph Kimball [13].

4. **The principles of Enterprise Intelligence (EI)**. It elaborates the design and construction of the Enterprise Intelligence Data Marts. These Data Marts promulgate the same concepts as the Business Intelligence (BI) Data Marts and handle Process Data instead of Transactional Data. The technique used is the multidimensional Facts and Dimension Entities with Star and Snowflake schemas.

Building the Data Marts based on the Enterprise Engineering Model is illustrated. The design and construction of the Enterprise Intelligence Data Marts Fact and Dimension entities are elaborated.

5. The **Correlation and Mapping of the data from the Legacy Systems to the Central Data Repository and then further to the Business and Enterprise Intelligence Data Marts** are detailed. This data involves:
   ▪ The Master Data identified in the Legacy Systems, the Master Data Entities of the Central Data Repository, and the Dimension Entities of the Data Marts.
   ▪ The Transactional Data identified in the Legacy Systems, the Transactional Data Entities of the Central Data Repository, and the Fact Entities of the Business Intelligence Data Marts.
   ▪ The Process (functioning) Data – if any – identified in the Legacy Systems, the Process Data Entities of the Central Data Repository, and the Fact Entities of the Enterprise Intelligence Data Marts.

6. **The Master, Transactional, and Process Data Integration, Consolidation, and Architecture** are elaborated. The ODS and different Central Data Repositories architecture are analyzed and their advantages and disadvantages are detailed. The

Enterprise Data Architectures involving Master, Transactional, and Process Data are elaborated. Transitions and roadmaps between the different architectures are described. The directions for the Integration, Consolidation, Propagation, Synchronization, and Consistency of the Master, Transactional, and Process Data across the enterprise architecture are evaluated and detailed.

The second part encompasses the **Enterprise Engineering Framework**, Methodology, Guidelines, Deliverables, and Techniques. It bestows the blueprint of the functioning of enterprises. Detailed Case Studies are presented supporting the theoretical aspect of Enterprise Engineering. These Case Studies provide clear and practical hands-on exercises reflecting the functioning of the Enterprises and illustrating the implementation of Enterprise Engineering. It is remarkable that the Improvement and Revitalization of similar enterprises depend drastically on the Enterprises' guiding strategies and this would impact their Enterprise Engineering Model and Business Model.

This part details the basics of Enterprise Engineering and its implementation thru the processing of the Enterprise Engineering Model. It provides the cost data (materiel cost, labor cost, time) reflecting the functioning of the Enterprise and point out the efficiency, performance, strengths, and weaknesses of its operation.

The second part comprises the following chapters:

7. The Outline of **Enterprise Engineering Framework** is delineated.

8. A comprehensive **Methodology** that provides the steps to perform the analysis and design of the **Enterprise Engineering System** of Apparatus, Machinery, and Operation (SAM O NAOULO). It provides the path to follow and tasks to implement in order to execute each step of the Enterprise Engineering exercise. The Enterprise Engineering building blocks and their participation in the Global Enterprise Engineering are stated.

9. **The Guidelines and Deliverables** supporting the Enterprise Engineering endeavor. These Guidelines enable the completion of the Enterprise Engineering Methodology's steps using Best-of-Practice.

10. **Case Studies** illustrating the design of the Enterprise Engineering System of Apparatus, Machinery, and Operation and the processing of the Enterprise Engineering Model to improve the enterprise's performance. These Case Studies elucidate and clarify the implementation of the Enterprise Engineering System. The objective of the exercises is the optimization of the value and impact of additional cost that ABC and XYZ Airlines (fictitious airlines) would charge theirs customers to cover part of the airlines' operation cost for performing Flight Reservation and/or Ticket Purchasing (FR&TP) responding to the customers' contact with the airlines' staff by telephone or personally at the airline's offices on top of the cost of the ticket; no charges are added if the customers perform these tasks themselves on the Internet. This optimization is implemented thru the engineering of the airlines' FR&TP Operation. These Case Studies exemplify how the

Dr. Eng. M. Naoulo

Enterprise Engineering System of Apparatus, Machinery, and Operation can support the improvement of the business operation thru pursuing the Enterprise's Needs, Missions, Strategies, and Business Models.

- ➤ ABC Airline aims to serve high class clientele and preserve the quality and reputation of its services.
- ➤ XYZ Airline aims to serve bargain hunting clientele while trying to keep adequate services quality.

Four appendices are included:

Appendix A. **The Interlink of the System of Apparatus, Machinery & Operation.**

Appendix B. **The Resolution of Relationships between the Entities of the Enterprise Engineering Model.**

Appendix C. **Enterprise Engineering Model's Associative Entities.** The Associative Entities encountered in the Enterprise Engineering Model are examined, analyzed, and resolved.

Appendix D. **Transactional Data Models**. It elaborates how to derive the Transactional Data Models from the Enterprise Engineering Models.

This book underscores three major innovations:

1. A new framework and technique to design and consolidate the Master Data. This is very important especially for getting a single version of truth thru consolidating the Master Data of the enterprises, getting accurate and up-to-date Master Data, responding to the requests for the integration of many Legacy Systems and/or from Merger and Acquisition.

2. Establishing a comprehensive Enterprise Data Architecture: ODS, Central Data Repository, Business and Intelligence Data Marts.

3. Establishing an Enterprise Engineering System of Apparatus, Machinery, and Operation (SAM O NAOULO) to measure the performance of the Enterprise's Operation, to introduce improvement and revitalization, and to assess the impact of introducing changes into the operational tactics and strategies of the Enterprise.

It is important to stress that:

1. This book provides the basis for a comprehensive **Master Data Management and Enterprise Engineering Curriculum** thru:
   - ➤ Guiding the Enterprise Data Modelers and Architects to implement the grouping, integration, and consolidation of the Master Data in an elegant manner.
   - ➤ Leading the Business and Technical Analysts and Engineers to model the operation of the Enterprise and measure the functioning of the operational Business Processes.
   - ➤ Directing and guiding the Business Process Analysts to assess, evaluate, and decrease the Operational Cost.
   - ➤ Steering the Top Management to understand the features and capabilities of

Dr. Eng. M. Naoulo

Enterprise Engineering and engage them to incite the use and implementation of Enterprise Engineering. Top Management can skim the details of the Modeling Techniques as they are not required to be expert in these techniques.

2. The book comprises innovative techniques and elegant approach and design, which were not instituted in any previous study, to address:

   ➢ **Master Data Management** thru grouping and classifying the Master Data in an innovative way that can be implemented across the Enterprise Data Architecture: Central Data Repository and Business and Intelligence (BI & EI) Data Marts. This data classification is based on the questions: Why, How, Who, What, Where and When.

   ➢ **Separating the Master Data, Transactional Data, and Process Data**. This separation enables the easiness in dealing with MDM, BI, and EI. The separation approach enormously facilitates the mapping and propagation between the Central Data Repository and the Business and Enterprise Data Marts.

   ➢ **Enterprise Engineering System of Apparatus, Machinery, and Operation (SAM O NAOULO).** It details the basics and techniques of the design of the Enterprise Engineering Model including the interaction of the Master, Transactional, and Process Data. This data supports the Transactional Systems, Business Intelligence, Business Process Management, Enterprise Intelligence, and Enterprise Engineering.

   ➢ **Synchronization and Integration** of Master, Transactional, and Process Data across the enterprise: Legacy Systems, Central Data Repository, and Business and Intelligence Data Marts.

   ➢ **Building and processing the Enterprise Engineering System of Apparatus, Machinery, and Operation.** Building this system provides the necessary groundwork to achieve the enterprises' functioning improvement. The Enterprise Engineering System establishes the base for assessing and evaluating the enterprises operation and improving their performance.

Note: The book could be used as Users' Manual for Master Data Management and Enterprise Engineering. It contains technical details affecting the design of the Enterprise Engineering Model and its implementation. However due to the elaborated technical details and in order to clarify and simplify the use of these details and to alleviate the references between the sections of the book (already tremendous), several repetitions were hosted.

Note: I appreciate the reader's feedback related to the details of this book and any possible enhancements. You can email me at DrNaoulo@EnterpriseEngineering.org with your comments and evaluation.

Dr. Eng. M. Naoulo

PART I – Enterprise Master, Transactional, & Process Data Architecture & Management

This part of the book establishes the principles and fundamentals of Enterprise Data Architecture and Management. It encompasses:

- ➤ Definition and Classification of Data.
- ➤ The Enterprise Data Framework including the System of Apparatus, Machinery, and Operation and the Enterprise Engineering Model.
- ➤ The SAM O NAOULO Modeling Technique covering the Master, Transactional, and Process Data.
- ➤ The Enterprise Intelligence and its Data Marts.
- ➤ The Enterprise Data Mapping between the Legacy Systems, Central Data Repository, and the Business and Enterprise Intelligence Data Marts.
- ➤ Enterprise Data Architecture including Master, Transactional, and Process Data Integration, Consolidation, Synchronization, and Consistency.

1.   Introduction to Data

Since the dawn of enterprises' book keeping, the scribes, accountants, financial officers, directors, etc. toiled to document the transactions involved in the running and functioning of the enterprises. In the early civilizations, the financial and operational book keeping tasks were rudimentary and used tablets, clays, and stones to store this data. In later civilizations, the financial and operational book keeping tasks became very complex. They used papers, tapes, disks, and electronics storage. The complexity was driven by many factors: volume of transactions, complexity of market sophistication, increase in the number of different Lines of Business in the same enterprise, number of branches/divisions keeping their own books for the same and/or different Lines of Business, abundance of cheap storage, fast processing of data, complexity of query, reporting, and business intelligence requirements.

The complexity, arising from the reconciliation, integration, and consolidation of all the data of an enterprise, plus the additional complexity resulting from mergers and acquisitions, made the Enterprise Data Management task an enormous endeavor. To implement these integration and consolidation, there were recently incomplete attempts to classify the data in use and to separate this data in a logical approach. Many authors divided the data into two classes: Master Data and Transactional Data. This data was segregated in the Data Marts which are based on multidimensional data modeling technique but still intertwined in the ODS and the Central data Repositories that are based on Relational Normalization Data Modeling Technique. So far there was no comprehensive technical approach to separate the Master Data from the Transactional Data.

1.1   INFORMATION & DATA

The Webster Dictionary [22] defines Data as:

"Information, esp. information organized for analysis or used as the basis for decision-making."

and:

"Numerical information suitable for computer processing".

And it defines Information as:

"Knowledge derived from study, experience, or instruction."

And it defines Knowledge as:

"The sum or range of what has been perceived, discovered, or learned."

This book defines Data as:

Dr. Eng. M. Naoulo

"A set of alphanumerical, symbols, and figures that are meaningless in themselves, and need processing by electronic and/or non-electronic devices: computers, etc., and interpretation by human beings (using logic, linguistics, dictionaries, etc.) to deduce Information from them."

It defines Information as:

"A set of data that after processing by electronic and/or non-electronic devices and interpretation by human beings become suitable for meaning and understandable deduction; the Information is used as the basis for Knowledge."

It defines Knowledge as:

"The analysis and analytics of Information and the proceeding of reasoning process on its results to achieve decision-making and other purposes."

1.2 CLASSIFICATION OF DATA

The data of the enterprise could be classified into three constituents:

➤ **Master Data**: The descriptive (alphanumeric and some numeric data e.g. unit price) pertinent to the objects of interest of an enterprise (Client, Product, Account, etc.). This data is illustrative in nature and it portrays, depicts, and directly related to the objects of interest. It includes Reference and External Data (Ref. Section 2.2.8).

➤ **Mechanism Data**: Data that regulates the transactions occurring in an enterprise (Cash withdraw limit in an ATM, Minimum wages for a new employee, etc.). This data is illustrative in nature; it regulates and directly related to the Operation Transactions.

➤ **Mechanics Data**: This data reflects the operation of the enterprise. It includes:
- **Process Data:** Sometimes called Business Process Data. It is the data of the Operation Sessions reflecting the functioning of the mechanics of the enterprises and includes the measures pertinent to their performance (Time spent answering a telephone call, Start Date-Time of an Airline flight, etc.). This data is factual in nature and contains figures quantifying the operation, running, and functioning of the enterprise. It also includes the figures useful to Activity Based Costing.
- **Transactional Data**: Data detailing the transactions of the enterprise including the measures pertinent to these transactions (Amount transferred in a bank wiring transaction, Cash received as payment for a product sold, etc.). It is stating the data of the Operation Transactions. This data is factual in nature and contains figures quantifying the transactions that the enterprise incurs during its functioning.

The Process Data is different from the Transactional Data as the former is related to the Activities' time and cost while the latter is related to the figures relevant to the transactions.

Dr. Eng. M. Naoulo

This data reflects the features of the three constituents: Apparatus, Machinery, and Operation (Ref Section 2.1). It forms the foundation for all Data processing: Transactional Processing, Business Intelligence, Enterprise Intelligence, and Enterprise Engineering.

1.3 DEFINITION OF ENTERPRISE DATA ARCHITECTURE & ENTERPRISE DATA MANAGEMENT

The Enterprise Data milieu encompasses the Legacy Systems (sometimes called Operational Systems or Source Systems), the ODS, the Central Data Repository, and the Business and Intelligence Data Marts. The Enterprise Data Architecture comprises:

"Design, distribution, structure, modeling techniques, integration, metadata and data dictionary, consolidation, matching, referential integrity, propagation, mapping, links and relations, conversion, synchronization, Extraction, Transformation, and Loading (ETL and ELT), traceability, lineage, and standards of the enterprise data."

The Enterprise Data Management includes in addition to the Enterprise Data Architecture:

"Data governance, quality assurance (completeness, validity, consistency, timeliness/freshness, accuracy/precision, reliability, availability, and uniqueness), collection, aggregation, security, profiling, cleansing, stewardship, storage, archiving, and backup and recovery of the enterprise data."

It is important to note that very often in the IT literature the terms Enterprise Data Architecture and Enterprise Data Management are used interchangeably to cover all above mentioned undertakings (E.g.: Master Data Management (MDM)).

1.4 CURRENT & HISTORICAL DATA

The data of the enterprises include current and historical data. The Enterprises would certainly want to keep both data. For storage and data retrieval performance, the enterprises might keep these data in separate environments.

> **Current Master Data** provides the picture of the current status of the Master Data and it is stored in the Legacy Systems, ODS, and/or the Central Data Repository.

> **Historical Master Data** depicts the changes affecting the Master Data. This is very important when there are needs to produce queries and reports spanning historical data as needed by the Business. In the Legacy Systems, ODS, or the Central Data Repository the historical Master Data is very limited and is often kept thru additional tables were the relationships between the current Master Data main tables and the historical Master Data tables are One-to-Many. In the Data Marts serving Business and Enterprise Intelligence the historical Master Data is kept thru Slowly Changing Dimensions Type 2, and sometimes Type 3.

> **Current Transactional Data** provides the daily transactions and it is stored in the Legacy Systems, ODS, and/or the Central Data Repository.

> **Historical Transactional Data** are usually kept thru archive storage. Sometimes few

27

weeks or few months of Transactional Data is kept online and is stored in the Legacy Systems, ODS, and/or the Central Data Repository, or additional storage very closely associated with them. In the Business Intelligence Data Marts, the Transactional Data is aggregated to provide queries and reports that sometimes are spanning many years of the enterprise's operation.

➢ **Current Process Data** reflects the daily functioning of the enterprise. It is stored in the Legacy Systems, ODS, and/or the Central Data Repository.

➢ **Historical Process Data** are dealing mostly with historical data spanning from days to few months. Sometimes few weeks or few months of Process Data is kept online and is stored in the Legacy Systems and/or the Central Data Repository, or additional storage very closely associated with them. In the Enterprise Intelligence Data Marts (Ref. Section 4.1.1) the Process Data is stored to provide operational queries and reports related to the cost and performance of the enterprise. This data is very often spanning limited time (few months) of the enterprise's operation. The queries and reports aim to support the engineering and re-engineering of the enterprise.

1.5   HISTORY OF DATA STRUCTURES' DESIGN

The design of the Data Structure of databases evolved so far thru three major phases:

➢ **Flat files** supporting the Analysts and Programmers' immediate data storage needs. These files were mostly implemented in VSAM files without comprehensive design techniques. They included Master Data, Transactional Data, Process Data, and Historical Data (sometimes this data is stored in specific files) arranged in non-structured layout.

➢ **Relational Data Design** to store the enterprises' current data. This design was initiated and consolidated by Dr. E. F. Codd [2] and C. Date [3] based on Relational Normalization Data Modeling Technique. This technique was further elaborated by other scientists. Clive Finkelstein and James Martin contributed to make this technique accessible to large IT audience. This technique ensued Information Engineering discipline. It served mainly Transactional Data. Extending its scope to include Historical Data engendered performance difficulties in the data retrieval: historical data designed in a Relational Approach causes the creation of One-to-Many relationship between the main entities and the historical entities. Additional complexity arises from the Modifiable Data Instances (Ref. Section 3.7).

➢ **Business Intelligence**. Data Warehousing and Data Marts' design was initiated by Bill Inmon and was elaborated by Ralph Kimball. It is based on Multidimensional Modeling Technique. Data Warehousing is the base for Business Intelligence.

This book covers the fourth phase:

➢ **Enterprise Intelligence**. This concept is based on SAM M NAOULO Modeling Technique. This technique is elaborated in this book. Enterprise Intelligence supports Enterprise Engineering and Re-engineering.

Dr. Eng. M. Naoulo

1.6 ARRANGEMENT & ALIGNMENT OF DATA

This book aims to provide an elegant approach for Data Management thru the grouping, design, integration, and consolidation of the Master, Mechanism, and Mechanics' Transactional and Process Data. It also comprises features that were not addressed before to respond to Data Architecture and Enterprise Operation Analysis' needs.

1. In all previously designed and almost in all current **Enterprise Data Architectures** there is no separation between the Master and Transactional Data in the Legacy Systems, the ODS, and the Central Data Repositories. The trend now is to perform this separation; however, the technique to implement this separation is not mature. This book provides an innovative approach to separate the Master Data from the Transactional and process Data in the Central Data Repositories and propagate this data to the Business and Enterprise Intelligence Data Marts.

2. All current **Master Data Management** are based on chaotic selection and design of the Master Data objects needed by the applications. Any grouping and analysis of these Master Data objects is currently based on disorderly rules. This book provides an innovative, logical, and easy to implement approach to group, classify, and design the Master Data objects used in the Enterprises. This grouping and design can be used in the Central Data Repository, Business and Intelligence Data Marts, and across the Enterprise Data Architecture and Enterprise Engineering. This book provides an innovative modeling technique to implement the design of the Master Data.

3. All current **Transactional Data** designs are based on non-orderly selection of transactional entities supporting the transactional data needed by the analysis of the applications in hand, and their relations to the Master Data Entities. The technique used in many Legacy Systems follow the Flat Files design indicated in Section 1.5, and recently most operational systems and the ODS follow the relational modeling technique and stopping very often at the 3rd NF. This book provides an innovative, logical, and easy to implement approach to design the transactional data and to implement their relation to the Master Data.

4. **Business Intelligence (BI) Data Marts** provide historical data aggregating the transactional facts of the enterprises. The modeling design is based on the Fact and Dimension Entities/Tables. The technique used in the BI Data Marts follows the multidimensional modeling technique. Since the infrastructure of the Enterprise Engineering System of Apparatus, Machinery, and Operation (SAM O NAOULO) supports the separation of Master, Transactional, and Process Data, this book provides a straightforward approach to design the BI Dimension Entities based on the design of the Master Data and the design the BI Fact Entities based on the design of the Transactional Data.

5. The Data Modeling design of the **Process Data** is currently non-existent. Business

Dr. Eng. M. Naoulo

Process Management (BPM) is based on Business Process Modeling technique but provides very little information to engineer and/or re-engineer the enterprises. Activity Based Costing (ABC) is using Business Process Modeling and not Data Modeling. Furthermore it does not provide a comprehensive approach that includes modeling and techniques to perform Enterprise Engineering or Re-engineering. This book provides an innovative, logical, comprehensive, elaborated, and easy to implement approach to analyze and design the Process Data in a Data Modeling milieu.

6. **Enterprise Intelligence (EI) Data Marts** provide data aggregating the functioning facts cost of the functioning of the enterprises. As in the BI, the modeling design is based on the Fact and Dimension Entities/Tables and the technique used in the EI Data Marts follows the multidimensional modeling technique. Also the design the EI Dimension Entities is based on the design of the Master Data and the design the EI Fact Entities is based on the design of the Process Data.

In addition, this book helps resolving two major problems:

1. Inconsistencies in the propagation and dissemination of Master Data across the Enterprises including Legacy Systems, ODS, Central Data Repository, and Data Marts.

2. Lineage and Traceability of Data as part of Data Governance and ETL architecture.

Note: Activity Based Costing emphasizes Cost Allocation which includes: Fixed Cost: expenses which are independent of the volume of produced goods and services and Variable Cost: expenses that change (sometimes quasi-linearly) in proportion to the functioning of the business. The Enterprise Engineering Case Studies provided in this book are dealing with services not incorporating physical products. The same approach could be applied to deal with physical products. Fixed and variable costs were assessed to evaluate the cost and judge the options for improvement and revitalization of the enterprises.

Dr. Eng. M. Naoulo

2.   The Enterprise Data Framework

The objectives of the Enterprise Data Framework cover the establishment of a Technical Data Infrastructure supporting the Information needed by the enterprise. The span of the Enterprise Data Framework comprises:

- Information and Data Strategy
- Enterprise Data Architecture
- Legacy Systems
- Structure and Quality of the Legacy Systems Data
- Central Data Repository
- Enterprise Engineering Data Model
- Enterprise Data Propagation and Aggregation
- Enterprise Data Consolidation and Integration
- Enterprise Data Quality
- Enterprise Data Extraction, Transformation, and Loading (ETL)
- Business Intelligence Data Marts
- Enterprise Intelligence Data Marts
- Transactional Data Query and Reporting Requirements
- Business Intelligence Query and Reporting Requirements
- Enterprise Intelligence and Engineering Query and Reporting Requirements
- Implementation of Query and Reporting from the Central Data Repository, Business and Enterprise Intelligence Data Marts.

The extent of the Enterprise Data Framework includes the creation, construction, and detail of the Enterprise Engineering Data Model that would serve Transactional Data Reporting, Business Intelligence, and Enterprise Intelligence and Engineering. The Enterprise Engineering Data Model illustrates in a Data Modeling milieu the three constituents of the Enterprise Data: the Master Data, the Mechanism, and the Mechanics that reflect respectively in a Data Architecture milieu the Apparatus, Machinery, and Operation of the Enterprise.

This chapter outlines the Enterprise Data Framework. It lists and describes the structure of the Enterprise building blocks that contribute and participate in the construction and implementation of the Enterprise Data Architecture and Enterprise Engineering. These building blocks are classified into three constituents: the Apparatus, the Machinery, and the Operation.

The Enterprise Data Framework aims to implement, in an IT milieu, the Information pertinent to the System of Apparatus, Machinery (SAM), and their Operation (O). This System and its three constituents: the Apparatus, the Machinery, and the Operation are explained in details in this chapter.

The structure of the Master, Transactional, and Process Data and the processing and results interpretation of the System of Apparatus, Machinery, and their Operation provide the source for Business Intelligence, Enterprise Intelligence, and Enterprise Engineering and Re-engineering. The Data Modeling Technique developed to support the Enterprise Engineering System of

31

Apparatus, Machinery, and Operation (**SAM O NAOULO**) is detailed in Chapters 2, 3, 4, 5, 12, 13 & 14. This technique handles the On-Line Mechanical Processing (**OLMP**).

2.1 THE THREE CONSTITUENTS OF THE ENTERPRISE INFORMATION ARCHITECTURE

The Enterprise's Information has three constituents that interlink to enable the functioning of the Enterprise:

1. **The Apparatus**. It includes the main players and objects that intervene in the operation of Enterprises. The Apparatus is partitioned into six components that encompass the members involved in the operation. Example: Customers, Products, Countries, etc.

2. **The Machinery**. It embodies the procedures that encompass the Enterprise internal and external rules and regulations, guidelines, techniques, etc. governing the Operation Transactions of the Enterprise. It regulates the transactions resulting from the implementation of the Business Functions and their Processes. Example: Ticket Purchasing Rules, Auto Insurance Rules, etc.

3. **The Operation**. It comprises the Sessions and Transactions that are triggered by the events or happenings. The Operation carries the Enterprise functioning. Example: Telephone call, ATM Money withdrawal, etc.

These three constituents must be analyzed and modeled in order to establish the Enterprise Information Architecture. The data details of this architecture will constitute the foundation of the Enterprise Engineering Model. This model would be the base to facilitate and support the improvement and revitalization of the Enterprises.

2.2 THE ENTERPRISE'S APPARATUS

The Webster Dictionary [22] defines Apparatus as:

"The totality of means by which a designated function is performed or a specific task executed."

The Apparatus includes the materiel and material needed for the functioning of the enterprise.

The Enterprise Apparatus is subdivided into six Components: **N**eeds, **A**ctivities, **O**perators, **U**tilities, **L**ocations, and **O**ccurrences (**NAOULO**) that answer the six famous questions identified and established as a base in Journalism: Ref. James G. Stovall [17]: WHY, HOW, WHO, WHAT, WHERE, and WHEN.

Each Apparatus Component contains Members: Customer, Airplane, Flight, Airport, Client, passenger, etc. An Apparatus Member is a building block about which information is needed and

Dr. Eng. M. Naoulo

gathered. Each Apparatus Component includes at least one Apparatus Member and an Apparatus Member belongs to only one Apparatus Component. Examples of Apparatus Members are provided hereafter for each Component.

The Enterprise Apparatus is illustrated in the Enterprise Engineering Model by the Master Data of the Enterprise. This Master Data would be used for Transactional applications as well as for BI and EI Data Marts, Analytical and Business Intelligence applications, Enterprise Intelligence, and Enterprise Engineering and Re-engineering.

Depending on the requirements of the Transactional, Analytical, and Enterprise Engineering exercises, the Enterprise Apparatus would include past, current, and/or planned/future Apparatus' Members.

Associative links exist between the Members of the same Apparatus Component or different Apparatus Components. Section 2.9.1.2 elaborates this concept.

Note: John Zachman [27] used the Journalism questions to define an Enterprise Architecture Framework but took a different approach for analyzing the Enterprise Data Architecture and its details (which is much less comprehensive than Bill Inmon's approach) and did not elaborate the Operation and Engineering of the Enterprises.

2.2.1 The Needs

The Apparatus Needs include at a high level the reason d'être for the existence of the Enterprise, the reasons behind the functioning of the Enterprise, the financial needs of shareholders and employees, the needs of the customers, the needs of the society and environment, etc. Examples: Customer Satisfaction, Regional Revenue... At more detailed levels, they include Line of Business needs, regional needs, etc.

The Apparatus Needs incorporate the business requirements to be satisfied by the Enterprise functioning. These needs include objectives and goals. Very often these objectives and goals are measured by Key Performance Indicators (KPI) and Metrics and are expressed in figures: Return-On-Investment (ROI), Market Share, Price Earning (PE) Ratio, Profit = Earning − Cost, FR&TP Customer Satisfaction, etc.

The Apparatus Needs are the answer to the question **WHY.** They include the reasons for the enterprise survival, prosperity, and thriving:
- At a high level: Why the Enterprise exists? Why the Enterprise functions? The answers would encompass increase the enterprise revenue, decrease the enterprise cost, improve the customers' satisfaction, etc. Measures would be used to assess the functioning of the Enterprise and address its performance in order for the Enterprise to survive.
- At a low level: Why the Customer Satisfaction related to a specific business function is important and needs to be improved, Why the Operation Cost of certain regions impacts the Enterprise and needs to be decreased, etc. Measures encompass customers' satisfaction pertinent to a specific business function, etc.

2.2.2 The Activities

The Apparatus Activities embody the Enterprise Business Functions and their Processes. The Apparatus Activities control the Operation Sessions that the Enterprise performs to function. These Activities empower and facilitate the functioning of the Enterprise.

H. James Harrington [15] defines a Business Process as:

"A business process consists of a group of logically related tasks that use the resources of the organization to provide defined results in support of the organization's objectives."

It is important to note that in the definition of Mr. Harrington, tasks correspond to the Activities' of this book, resources are the Operators and Utilities, and organization's objectives are the Needs. This book provides a more complete definition of the Business Process by incorporating also the Locations, and Occurrences. The definition of a Business Process becomes:

"A business process consists of a group of logically related **A**ctivities, actuated by **O**ccurrence events, performed by internal and external **O**perators, use in-house and outside **U**tilities, performed in and across **L**ocations, in order to provide results in support of the Enterprise's **N**eeds."

The Enterprise Business Functions are the main undertaking of Enterprises and include the Enterprise Business Processes: Manufacturing, Services Generation, Material Handling, Information Processing, Development, Marketing, Production, etc. Each Business Process encapsulates and performs a part of a specific Business Function. Example: Ticket Purchasing, Satisfaction Survey, Merchandise Advertising, etc. An Enterprise Business Process could include more granular Enterprise Business Processes:
  ➢ The Marketing Process includes the following Business Processes: Campaign Management, Marketing Survey Analysis, etc.
  ➢ The Car Servicing Process includes the following Business Processes: Car Transmission Checking, Oil Changing, etc.

The Apparatus Activities include the Business Functions, their Processes, and Tasks and control the Operation Sessions resulting from their functioning. The Apparatus Activities encompass the Enterprise internal and external directives, instructions, guidelines, techniques, etc. to control the Operation Sessions of the Enterprise. Examples: Survey Gathering, Class Attending, etc.

An Apparatus Activity could include other Apparatus Activities. The Activity directly interacting with the Operation Sessions is denoted by Elementary Activity. It is very often the lowest level of Activities. The Apparatus Activities control the Operation Sessions: E.g.: Car Servicing controls the following Sessions: Car Transmission Checking Session, Oil Changing Session, etc. An Apparatus Activity could be implemented thru one or many Operation Sessions.

The Apparatus Activities are the answer to the question **HOW:**
  ➢ How this Enterprise functions?

In Information Engineering, Object Oriented Analysis and Design, and in many Business and Management literature there are no clear distinction between Business Functions, Functions, Business Processes, Processes, Procedures, Tasks, and Activities and these terms are very often used interchangeably. This document provides clear and distinct definition to these terms:

➤ An Activity is the global word used for Business Function, Function, Business Process, and Process. Its objective is to control the Operation Sessions.

➤ Business Functions or Functions identify the major functions within an Enterprise.

➤ A Business Process or Processes identify the minor functions within an Enterprise.

➤ A Business Function is composed of other Business Functions and/or Business Processes and/or Elementary Activities.

➤ A Business Process is composed of other Business Processes and/or Elementary Activities.

➤ A Business Task or Task is a set of Activities realizing a minor business objective.

➤ A Business Scenario is a set of Tasks realizing a major business objective.

➤ A Procedure is defined as part of the Machinery (Ref. Section 2.3).

2.2.3 The Operators

The Apparatus Operators designate the parties, agents, systems, organization units, or representatives involved in the Operation of the enterprise. The Apparatus Operators include physical or virtual operators: Customer, Person, Supplier, Employee, Competitor, Government Agency, Shareholder, System, Equipment, Tools, etc. and could be internal or external Operators.

The Apparatus Operators are the answer to the question **WHO:**

➤ Who affects and/or is affected by this Enterprise functioning?

➤ With whom this Enterprise deals with?

➤ Who is participating in the Sessions?

➤ Who provides input and/or receives output from this Enterprise?

2.2.4 The Utilities

The Apparatus Utilities include all the materiel and materials that the Enterprise uses to function. They are the ingredients affected by the Activities' tasks thru the Operation Sessions and Transactions. The Apparatus Utilities could be physical ingredients: Supply, Commodity, Spare Part, Lottery Ticket, etc. or virtual ingredients: Airline Flight, Taxi Ride, Data, etc.

The Apparatus Utilities are the answer to the question **WHAT:**

➤ What are the things the Enterprise utilizes, handles, employs, make use of, or deals with?

2.2.5 The Locations

The Apparatus Locations include the milieu, environment, areas, etc. This encompasses physical locations: Building, Region, Zipcode, Address, Airport, etc. and virtual locations: Telephone Area Code, Web Site, URL, Telephone Number, Internet Address, etc.

The Apparatus Locations are the answer to the question **WHERE:**

➤ Where this Enterprise functions or operates?

➤ Where the Operation Session is taking place or happening?

Dr. Eng. M. Naoulo

2.2.6 The Occurrences

The Apparatus Occurrences include the date, time, time intervals, chronological periods, and the Events. The Apparatus Occurrences specify the timeframe of the Sessions and indicate the time of the Enterprise Transactions. An Occurrence event or happening triggers one or many Operation Sessions.

The Apparatus Occurrences are the answer to the question **WHEN:**
  ➢ When the Sessions and Transactions of the Enterprise occurred.

The Apparatus Occurrences provide the time analysis for Sessions and Transactions. They also provide timeframe for the rules governing the Sessions and Transactions and for aggregation for historical data.

2.2.7 Multiple Roles of an Object

The Apparatus Object could be part of different Apparatus Components depending on the role it assumes, even in the same Enterprise Engineering Model. Example: Telephone Number would be part of the Location Component if it does play the role of location of a contact. It would be part of the Utility Component if it plays the role of an item of interest for repair or billing. In this case, the definition of the object would certainly be different, and the names of the Apparatus Objects should be different. By using the Best of Practice elaborated in Section 3.3, the entities' name in the model would differ (at least) by the first three letters indicating the Component of the Entity (**UTL** for Utility and **LOC** for Location).

2.2.8 External & Reference Data

External Data is Master Data that is defined and controlled by external organizations: government organizations, international organizations, etc. Example: Currency, State, Social Security Number, etc. This data has similar characteristics to the Master Data and is analyzed and treated as part of the Master Data.

Reference Data has similar characteristics to the Master Data and is analyzed and treated as part of the Master Data. Detailed descriptions of External and Reference Data are provided by Bill Inmon in [11 pp. 16-21].

2.3   THE ENTERPRISE MACHINERY

The Enterprise Machinery regulates the Transactions resulting from the execution of the Business Functions and their Processes. It is represented in the Enterprise Engineering Model (Ref. Section 2.8.2) by the Mechanism.

The Enterprise Machinery is composed of Machinery Procedures. The Machinery Procedures encompass the rules and regulations governing the Operation Transactions. A Machinery Procedure could include other Machinery Procedures. The Machinery Procedure directly interacting with the Operation Transactions is denoted by Elementary Procedure. It is very often the lowest level of Procedures.

Dr. Eng. M. Naoulo

The analysis of the Machinery Procedures is best performed using the Use Cases of UML. These Use Cases are examined and analyzed. They contribute to the design of the Mechanism (Ref. Section 2.8.2).

2.4   THE ENTERPRISE OPERATION

The Enterprise Operation embodies the execution of the Enterprise Activities. It manifests the functioning of the enterprise's objects: industrial machines, tools, cars, communications, connections, etc. An Operation Session could serve one or many specific business Needs. It might generate and/or modify one or many Operation Transactions. The Enterprise Operation Constituent includes all the Operation Sessions and their Transactions. The Enterprise Operation is illustrated in the Enterprise Engineering Model by the Mechanics.

The objective of the Operation Sessions is to carry out the Functioning of the Enterprise. The analysis of the processing of the Operation Sessions provides the base to improve and revitalize the Enterprise's performance. The data reflecting the functioning of the enterprise and expressing the Operation Sessions is the **Process Data**.

The Transactions are the record of the execution of Sessions, their input and results data. The Operation Transactions are the lowest level of details in the whole System of Apparatus, Machinery, and Operation. The data of the Operation Transactions is the **Transactional Data**.

The Enterprise Operation would include past, current, and/or planned or future Operation Sessions and Transactions as required by the Enterprise Engineering exercise. The planned or future Operation Sessions and Transactions would be used for the Target Mechanics Processing and Results' Generation & Interpretation (Ref. Section 8.15).

2.4.1 The Operation Sessions
The Operation Sessions perform the Operation of the Enterprise. They are illustrated in the Enterprise Engineering Model by the Mechanics Sessions. The Mechanics Sessions reveal and exhibit the Operation of the Enterprise. They register the time of the Operation Sessions.

The Operation Sessions interlink One-to-One, One-to-Many, Many-to-One, and Many-to-Many with the Apparatus Members:
- To reach or satisfy the **Needs**
- **Are controlled by t**he Apparatus Activities
- To be affected by or affect the **Operators**
- To handle the **Utilities**
- To be performed in the **Locations**
- To be performed during the **Occurrences** and triggered by their **Events.**

The Operation Sessions generate Operation Transactions. An Operation Session could generate or modify zero, one or many Operation Transactions. The Operation Sessions are triggered by events or happenings that take place during the functioning of the Enterprise. These Sessions are

Dr. Eng. M. Naoulo

part of the mechanics of the enterprise, carry out its functioning, and are controlled by its Activities. They consume and utilize ingredients and time and produce products and results.

An episode of an Operation Session is the Operation Session Incidence. It occurs once and has Start and End Timestamps. The Operation Session Incidence should not be modified unless there are errors. It is implemented in the Enterprise Engineering Model by the Mechanics Session Instance.

2.4.2 The Operation Transactions

The Machinery Procedures regulate the Operation Transactions: Example: The Banking Teller procedures regulate the following Transactions: Check Deposit, Cash withdrawal, etc. The Operation Transaction could be created/generated or modified in the Enterprise by one or many Operation Sessions. It incorporates the transactional information of the functioning of the Enterprise.

An episode of an Operation Transaction is the Operation Transaction Incidence. The Operation Transaction Incidence occurs once but could be modified many times. It has timestamp(s). Historical data of the creation and modification of Transactions could also be stored if needed by using additional historical transaction entities where the relationship between the transaction entity and the historical transaction entities is One-to-Many. The Operation Transaction Incidence is implemented in the Enterprise Engineering Model by the Mechanics Transaction Instance.

The Operation Transaction is illustrated in the Enterprise Engineering Model by the Mechanics Transaction. The Mechanics Transactions hold all the Transactional Data of the Operation of the Enterprise.

2.5 SYSTEM OF APPARATUS, MACHINERY, & OPERATION

The System of Apparatus and Machinery (**SAM**) and their Operation (**O**) embodies the functioning of the Enterprises and serves analyzing it. It encompasses:

> The **A**pparatus which includes the Components: **N**eeds of the Enterprise, **A**ctivities that control the Functioning of the Enterprise, **O**perators from within and outside of the Enterprise, **U**tilities handled by the Enterprise, **L**ocations of operation of the Enterprise, and **O**ccurrences that indicate time and events.

> The **M**achinery which includes the rules regulating the Operation Transactions of the Enterprise.

> The **O**peration that epitomizes the functioning of the Enterprise.

The System of Apparatus, Machinery, and Operation is denoted by the acronym **SAM O NAOULO**. It is illustrated in a Data Modeling milieu by the Enterprise Engineering Model,

The Apparatus, Machinery, and Operation interlink with each other. Diagram 2.1 illustrates the

Dr. Eng. M. Naoulo

Apparatus and its Components: Needs, Activities, Operators, Utilities, Locations, and Occurrences, the Machinery, and the Operation which includes Sessions and Transactions. This diagram also exhibits the interlinks between them.

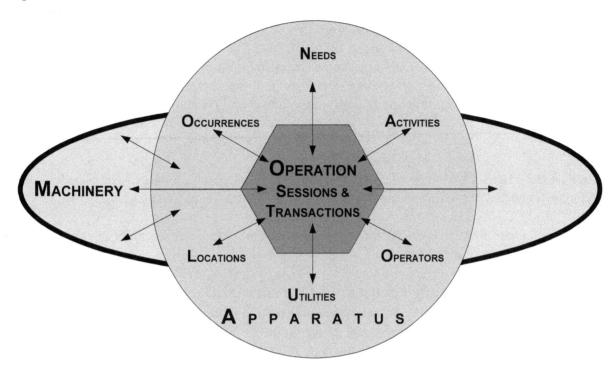

Diagram 2.1: The Apparatus, Machinery, & Operation interlink with each other

The Apparatus, Machinery, and Operation are reflected respectively in a Data Modeling milieu by the Master Data, Mechanism, and Mechanics.

2.6 THE INTERLINKS OF THE SYSTEM OF APPARATUS, MACHINERY, & OPERATION

The Interlinks of the Apparatus, Machinery, and Operation are provided hereafter. This Interlinks denote the connections between and within the building blocks of the Enterprise Constituents. The detailed technical analysis and examples of this Interlinks would be provided in Chapters 2, 3, 4, 5, 12, 13 & 14. Table 2.1 summarizes this Interlinks.

From>> >>To	Apparatus Members	Machinery Procedures	Operation Sessions	Operation Transactions
Apparatus Members	OK	OK	OK	OK
Machinery Procedures	OK	OK	Not Valid	Mandatory
Operation Sessions	Mandatory	Not Valid	OK	Mandatory
Operation Transactions	OK	Mandatory	Mandatory	OK

Dr. Eng. M. Naoulo

Table 2.1: Summary of Interlinks of Apparatus, Machinery, & Operation

It is important to note that:
- ➢ Since the Apparatus Activities control the Operation Sessions, an Operation Session must interlink to at least one Apparatus Activity.
- ➢ Since the Apparatus Occurrence Events trigger the Operation Sessions, an Operation Session must interlink to at least one Occurrence Event.
- ➢ Since the Mechanism Procedures regulate the Operation Transactions, an Operation Transaction must interlink to at least one Mechanism Procedure.
- ➢ Since the Operation Sessions generate the Operation Transactions, an Operation Transaction must interlink to at least one Operation Session.

2.6.1 The Main Theorem of Enterprise Information Architecture
The main Theorem of the Enterprise Information Architecture is:

"An Operation Session Incidence must interlink with at least one Member of each Component of the Apparatus."

2.6.2 Proof for the Main Theorem of Enterprise Information Architecture
The proof for the Main Theorem of Enterprise Information Architecture is as follows:
1. An operation session is performed to accomplish a **Need** (profit, reduction of cost, etc. or at least to satisfy certain performance); otherwise this operation session does not add value and could be eliminated completely without affecting the objectives of the enterprise.
2. An operation session should be controlled; a non-controlled operation session is unjustifiable in an enterprise. The control of the operation sessions is achieved by the **Activities**.
3. An operation session is performed by **O**perator(s). This is obvious.
4. An operation session uses **U**tilities (ingredients, materials, etc.).
5. An operation session is performed in **L**ocation(s): Physical and/or virtual (Building, Website, Telephone Number used in a connection or Fax, etc.).
6. An operation session is triggered by an Event and has Start and End Timestamps.

2.6.3 The Second Theorem of Enterprise Information Architecture
The second Theorem of the Enterprise Information Architecture is:

"An Operation Transaction Incidence must interlink, directly or indirectly, with at least one Member of each Component of the Apparatus."

2.6.4 Proof for the Second Theorem of Enterprise Information Architecture
From the Main Theorem of Enterprise Information Architecture, since an Operation Session Incidence must interlink to at least one Member of each Component of the Apparatus, and since an Operation Transaction must interlink to at least one Operation Session (Ref. Section 2.6), therefore an Operation Transaction interlinks thru the Operation Sessions to at least one Member of each Component of the Apparatus. This is besides the possibility of direct links (not thru the

Operation Sessions) from the Operation Transactions to the Apparatus or indirect links thru the Machinery Procedures.

2.7 DECOMPOSITION DIAGRAMS

In Information Engineering the structure of Process Modeling follows the generic tree shape as indicated in the Information Engineering Decomposition or "Composed-of" Diagrams (Ref. James Martin [5], Information Engineering, Book II, Planning & Analysis, Page 258). In these structures each node could be composed into one or multiple nodes.

Information Engineering (Ref. James Martin [5], Information Engineering, Book II, Planning & Analysis, Page 258) defines the Decomposition Diagram as:

"Function decomposition is the breakdown of the activities of the enterprise into progressively greater detail."

He also defines the Elementary Business Process (in the same page of his book) as:

"The smallest unit of activity of meaning to the end user, and which when complete leaves the information area in a self-consistent state."

The structure of the Enterprise Engineering Apparatus Activities and the structure of the Machinery Procedures follow similar structure with the addition of Associations between the nodes. In addition a child Apparatus Activity could have many parent Apparatus Activities and a child Machinery Procedure could have many parent Machinery Procedures.

The Information Engineering modeling did not differentiate between processes, procedures, and activities. Furthermore confusion was introduced in Object Oriented Analysis where the Activity Diagram is similar to the Process Dependency Diagram in Information Engineering. The Enterprise Engineering's approach detailed in this book differentiates between Function, Process, Procedure and Activity: Ref. Section 2.2.2.

Note: It is very important to differentiate the Apparatus Activities from the Machinery Procedures. The Apparatus Activities control the Enterprise Operation Sessions; their objective is to manage and govern the Mechanics Sessions of the Enterprise. The Machinery Procedures regulate the Enterprise Operation Transactions; their objective is to validate the Mechanics Transactions of the Enterprise.

2.7.1 Business Functions, Processes, & Activities Decomposition

The Business Functions could be decomposed into Business Functions and/or Business Processes. A Business Process could be decomposed into other Business Processes. The Activity Entities resulting from the resolution of the Many-to-Many relationships encountered between the Activity Entities or between the Activity Entities and other Master Data Entities (Ref. Section 13.1), and which directly interact with the Operation Sessions are also denoted as Elementary Activities.

Dr. Eng. M. Naoulo

2.7.2 Machinery Procedures Decomposition

The Machinery Procedure could be decomposed into other Machinery Procedures. The Mechanism Associative Entities resulting from the resolution of the Many-to-Many relationships encountered between the Mechanism Entities (Ref. Section 13.2), or between the Mechanism Entities and Master Data Entities (Ref. Section 13.5), and which directly interact with the Operation Transactions are also denoted as Elementary Procedures.

2.8 THE ENTERPRISE ENGINEERING MODEL

The Enterprise Engineering Model represents the data structure of the Central Data Repository. It reflects the System of Apparatus, Machinery, and Operation (**SAM O NAOULO**). The Apparatus, Machinery, and Operation are represented in The Enterprise Engineering Model by the Master Data, Mechanism, and Mechanics. The Apparatus, Machinery, and Operation interlink between each other (Ref. Section 2.1) and these Interlinks are reflected/modeled in the Enterprise Engineering Model by the Interactions between the Master Data, Mechanism, and Mechanics. These Interactions are illustrated thru relationships in the Enterprise Engineering Model Entity-Relationship Diagram.

The Enterprise Engineering Model is a Data Model that includes the entities of Master Data, Mechanism, and Mechanics and their relationships. It is designed by the Enterprise Engineers to capture the data related to the functioning of the Enterprise. It reflects the enterprise functioning in a Data Architecture milieu. The processing or running of the Enterprise Engineering Model provides the time and cost of the enterprise operation and enables the engineering and/or re-engineering of the enterprise functioning in order to improve the efficiency, effectiveness, and performance of the Enterprise.

2.8.1 The Master Data

The Master Data represents/reflects/models the business information pertinent to the Apparatus Members. These Members are Objects of Interest of the Enterprise and their information is non-transactional. Therefore the Master Data includes only non-transactional data: data about customers, products, employees, materials, suppliers, etc.
1. The Master Data of the Enterprise illustrates in the Enterprise Engineering Model the Enterprise Apparatus.
2. A Master Data Dimension represents/reflects/models in the Enterprise Engineering Model an Apparatus Member.
3. The Master Data Dimension Profile is a group of entities that completely represent the Apparatus Member. It holds the detail data about a Master Data Dimension. It is illustrated in the Enterprise Engineering Model's Entity-Relationship Diagram by a set of entities and their relationships.
4. The Master Data Component, which groups all Master Data Dimension Profiles pertinent to one Apparatus Component, represents in the Enterprise Engineering Model the Apparatus Component. This is very useful to get a high level view of the Enterprise Component's Members during the global improvement and revitalization of the Enterprise.

5. There would be relationships between the Master Data Entities within and across different Master Data Components. These relationships are detailed and resolved as per Sections 2.9.1, 2.9.1.1, & 2.9.1.2 and Chapters 3, 4, 5, 12, 13 & 14.
6. A Master Data Dimension Instance represents in the Enterprise Engineering Model an Apparatus Member Incidence.
7. The data pertinent to the Master Data would change with time. For more detailed analysis about modifiable Master Data Dimensions please refer to Section 3.7.1.

2.8.2 The Mechanism

The Mechanism represents/reflects/models the business information pertinent to the Machinery Procedures. The information about these procedures is non-transactional. Therefore the Mechanism includes only non-transactional data. The Mechanism Procedures regulate the transactions and their data: payment, purchases, etc.

1. The Mechanism of the Enterprise illustrates in the Enterprise Engineering Model the Enterprise Machinery.
2. A Mechanism Procedure represents/reflects/models in the Enterprise Engineering Model a Machinery Procedure.
3. The basis of the Mechanism Procedures design is the Use Cases developed during the analysis of the Machinery (Ref. Section 2.3).
4. The Mechanism Procedure Profile holds in the Enterprise Engineering Model the detail data about a Mechanism Procedure. It is a group of entities that completely represent the Machinery Procedure. It is illustrated in the Enterprise Engineering Model's Entity-Relationship Diagram by a set of entities and their relationships.
5. There would be relationships between the Mechanism Entities. These relationships are detailed and resolved as per Sections 2.9.2, 2.9.2.1, & 2.9.2.2 and Chapters 3, 4, 5, 12, 13 & 14.
6. A Mechanism Procedure Instance represents in the Enterprise Engineering Model a Machinery Procedure Incidence.
7. The data pertinent to the Mechanism Procedures would change with time. For more detailed analysis about modifiable Mechanism Procedures please refer to Section 3.7.2.

2.8.3 The Mechanics

The Mechanics comprises the business data that portrays the Enterprise Operation. It incorporates data that depicts the Sessions triggered by the Enterprise Events: Customer Satisfaction Survey Sessions, Call Center Calls, etc. and their resulting transactional data: Payments, Student Class Attendance, etc. The Mechanics data includes time related figures.

The Mechanics represents in the Enterprise Engineering Model the Enterprise Operation. It includes two domains: the Mechanics Sessions Domain and the Mechanics Transactions Domain. The execution of the Mechanics is triggered by the Events, sustained by the interaction of the Mechanics Sessions and Transactions with the Mechanism and Master Data, and implemented thru the processing of the Enterprise Engineering Model. The execution of the Mechanics would result in creating/reading/writing/modifying/deleting of IT data. The Mechanics of the Enterprise illustrates in the Enterprise Engineering Model the Enterprise Operation.

Dr. Eng. M. Naoulo

2.8.3.1 The Mechanics Sessions

1. A Mechanics Session represents/reflects/models in the Enterprise Engineering Model an Operation Session.
2. The Mechanics Session Profile holds in the Enterprise Engineering Model the detail data about a Mechanics Session. It is a group of entities that completely represent the Operation Session. It is illustrated in the Enterprise Engineering Model's Entity-Relationship Diagram by a set of entities and their relationships.
3. The Mechanics Session is triggered in the Enterprise Engineering Model by one or many Master Data Occurrence Events.
4. A Mechanics Session could have subtypes.
5. The Mechanics Session includes the Start and End Timestamps for the Session and references to the Master Data. It might also include additional measures.
6. There would be relationships between the Mechanics Session Entities. These relationships are detailed and resolved as per Sections 2.9.3, 2.9.3.1, & 2.9.3.2 and Chapters 3, 4, 5, 12, 13 & 14.
7. A Mechanics Session Instance represents in the Enterprise Engineering Model an Operation Session Incidence. It is not modifiable (unless there are errors); Ref. Section 2.4.1. For more detailed analysis about modification of Mechanics Sessions please refer to Section 3.7.3.

2.8.3.2 The Mechanics Transactions

1. A Mechanics Transaction represents/reflects/models in the Enterprise Engineering Model an Operation Transaction.
2. The Mechanics Transaction Profile holds in the Enterprise Engineering Model the detail data about a Mechanics Transaction. It is a group of entities that completely represent the Operation Transaction. It is illustrated in the Enterprise Engineering Model's Entity-Relationship Diagram by a set of entities and their relationships.
3. A Mechanics Transaction could have One-to-Many relationships with Mechanics Transaction Detail Entities as part of the Mechanics Transaction Profile. These children entities would capture data related to the modifications of the transactions, historical data, etc.
4. The Mechanics Transaction is instigated in the Enterprise Engineering Model by one or many Mechanics Sessions.
5. The Mechanics Transaction includes measures, occurrence timestamp(s), and references to the Master Data, Mechanism, and Mechanics Sessions.
6. A Mechanics Transaction Instance represents in the Enterprise Engineering Model an Operation Transaction Incidence. It is created once but could be modified many times and has an occurrence timestamp(s); Ref. Section 2.4.2. For more detailed analysis about modifiable Mechanics Transactions please refer to Section 3.7.4.

Diagram 2.2 illustrates the Master Data and its Components: Needs, Activities, Operators, Utilities, Locations, and Occurrences, the Mechanism, and the Mechanics which includes Sessions and Transactions, and represents the interaction between them.

Dr. Eng. M. Naoulo

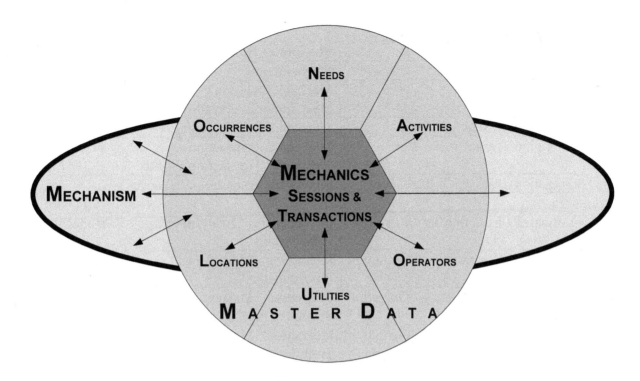

Diagram 2.2: The Master Data, Mechanism, & Mechanics interact with each other

2.8.4 Summary Table

The following table illustrates the three constituents of Enterprise Engineering and their Interlinks and how they are represented/reflected/modeled in the Enterprise Engineering Model:

Enterprise Functioning	Enterprise Engineering Model
Apparatus, Machinery, & Operation	Master Data, Mechanism & Mechanics

Apparatus Constituent	Master Data Constituent
Apparatus	Master Data
Apparatus Component	Master Data Component
Apparatus Member	Master Data Dimension Master Data Dimension Profile
Apparatus Member Incidence	Master Data Dimension Instance
Apparatus Incidence	Master Data Instance
Apparatus Elementary Activity	Master Data Elementary Activity

Machinery Constituent	Mechanism Constituent
Machinery	Mechanism
Machinery Procedure	Mechanism Procedure Mechanism Procedure Profile
Machinery Procedure Incidence	Mechanism Procedure Instance
Machinery Elementary Procedure	Mechanism Elementary Procedure

Dr. Eng. M. Naoulo

Operation Constituent	Mechanics Constituent
Operation	Mechanics
Operation Session	Mechanics Session Mechanics Session Profile
Operation Session Incidence	Mechanics Session Instance
Operation Transaction	Mechanics Transaction Mechanics Transaction Profile
Operation Transaction Incidence	Mechanics Transaction Instance

Enterprise Functioning Interlinks	Enterprise Engineering Model Interactions
Interlinks Apparatus – Machinery Procedures	Interaction Master Data – Mechanism Procedures
Interlinks Apparatus – Operation Sessions	Interaction Master Data – Mechanics Sessions
Interlinks Apparatus – Operation Transactions	Interaction Master Data – Mechanics Transactions
No Interlinks between Machinery Procedures & Operation Sessions	No Interaction between Mechanism Procedures & Mechanics Sessions
Interlinks Machinery Procedures – Operation Transactions	Interaction Mechanism Procedures – Mechanics Transactions
Interlinks Operation Sessions – Operation Transactions	Interaction Mechanics Sessions – Mechanics Transactions

Table 2.2: The Enterprise Constituents & Interlinks & their representation in the Enterprise Engineering Model

Note: If the Data Vault technique is used for the data modeling, the concept of profile would include the Data Vault Hub and its Satellite Entities [19].

2.9   THE STRUCTURE OF THE ENTERPRISE ENGINEERING MODEL

The Enterprise Engineering Model includes the three constituents: Master Data, Mechanism Procedures, and Mechanics Sessions and Transactions. Also there are Associative Entities within these constituents and between them. This section provides the analysis of the structure details of the Constituents and their interrelations.

The Enterprise Engineering Model includes non-Associative Entities and Associative Entities. The non-Associative Entities exist within the Constituents while the Associative Entities exist within and across the Constituents. Table 14.1 indicates the source and destination realms of these Associative Entities.

2.9.1 The Structure of the Master Data

The Master Data includes six components (Ref. Section 2.2). Each component includes Master Data Dimensions and Master Data Associative Entities that reflect the Apparatus Members and their Interlinks. The data captured in the Master Data is descriptive and non-transactional. This data might change with time due to modifications, etc. and the technique governing the modeling of this change is described in Sections 3.7 & 3.7.1.

A Master Data Entity profile holds the detail data about a Master Data Dimension or a Master Data Associative Entity. A Master Data profile forms a group of entities that completely represent an Apparatus Member or an association between Apparatus Members.

The Master Data includes Dimensions with their profiles and Master Data Associative Entities with their profiles. Section 2.8.1 defines the Master Data Dimension Profile; similar definition would be applied to the Master Data Associative Entity Profile. Sections 14.1, 14.2, & 14.3 provide additional details related to the Master Data Associative Entities.

2.9.1.1 The Structure of the Master Data Dimensions

The structure of the Master Data Dimension is composed of a main entity exhibiting the Member and additional entities that together completely represent the Apparatus Member. The main entity and its additional entities form the Master Data Dimension Profile. The structure of the Entity-Relationship of the Master Data Dimension Profile follows the Relational Normalization Data Modeling Technique.

Note: During the Integration and Consolidation of Master Data Entities (Dimensions and Associative Entities) resulting from the metadata coming from the Legacy Systems, there would be the need to create Hierarchies and Nodes. The approach and techniques governing the creation of these Hierarchies and Nodes would follow the MDM directions pertinent to this subject and the MDM tools' documentation available in the market.

2.9.1.2 The Structure of the Master Data Associative Entities

A Master Data Associative Entity could have Profile Entities the same way as a Master Data Dimension Entity.

2.9.2 The Structure of the Mechanism Data

The Mechanism Procedures (Ref. Section 2.8.2) reflect the Machinery Procedures. The data captured in the Mechanism Procedure is descriptive and non-transactional. This data might change with time due to modifications, etc. and the technique governing the modeling of this change is described in Sections 3.7 & 3.7.2.

A Mechanism Procedure profile holds the detail data about a Mechanism Procedure or a Mechanism Procedure Associative Entity. A Mechanism Procedure profile forms a group of entities that completely represent a Machinery Procedure, or an association between Machinery Procedures, or an association between Machinery Procedures and the Apparatus.

Dr. Eng. M. Naoulo

The Mechanism includes Procedures with their profiles and Procedures Associative Entities with their profiles. Section 2.8.2 defines the Mechanism Procedure Profile; similar definition would be applied to the Mechanism Procedure Associative Entity Profile. Sections 14.4, 14.5, & 14.6 provide additional details related to the Mechanism Procedure Associative Entities.

2.9.2.1 The Structure of the Mechanism Procedures
Similar to the structure of the Master Data Dimensions, the structure of the Mechanism Procedure is composed of a main entity exhibiting the Machinery Procedure and additional entities that together completely represent the Machinery Procedure. The main entity and its additional entities form the Mechanism Procedure Profile. The structure of the Entity-Relationship of the Mechanism Procedure Profile follows the Relational Normalization Data Modeling Technique.

2.9.2.2 The Structure of the Mechanism Procedure Associative Entities
A Mechanism Procedure Associative Entity could have Profile Entities the same way as a Mechanism Procedure Entity.

2.9.3 The Structure of the Mechanics Session Data
The Mechanics Sessions (Ref. Section 2.8.3.1) reflects the Operation Sessions. The data captured in the Mechanics Session depicts the functioning Process measures occurring in the Enterprise (Ref. Sections 2.8.3 & 2.8.3.1). This data would not change with time (unless there are errors to be rectified) Ref. Sections 3.7 & 3.7.3.

A Mechanics Session profile holds the detail data about a Mechanics Session or a Mechanics Session Associative Entity. A Mechanics Session profile forms a group of entities that completely represent an Operation Session, or an association between Operation Sessions, or an association between Operation Sessions and the Apparatus.

The Mechanics Session Domain includes Sessions with their profiles and Mechanics Session Associative Entities with their profiles. Section 2.8.3.1 defines the Mechanics Session Profile; similar definition would be applied to the Mechanics Session Associative Entity Profile. Sections 14.7, 14.8, & 14.9 provide additional details related to the Mechanics Session Associative Entities.

2.9.3.1 The Structure of the Mechanics Sessions
Similar to the structure of the Master Data dimensions, the structure of the Mechanics Session is composed of a main entity exhibiting the Operation Session and additional entities that together completely represent the Operation Session. The main entity and its additional entities form the Mechanics Session Profile. The structure of the Entity-Relationship of the Mechanics Session Profile follows the Relational Normalization Data Modeling Technique.

2.9.3.2 The Structure of the Mechanics Session Associative Entities
A Mechanics Session Associative Entity could have Profile Entities the same way as a Mechanics Session Entity.

Dr. Eng. M. Naoulo

2.9.4 The Structure of the Mechanics Transaction Data

The Mechanics Transactions (Ref. Section 2.8.3.2) reflects the Operation Transactions. The data captured in the Mechanics Transaction is transactional and depicts the Transaction figures occurring in the Enterprise (Ref. Sections 2.8.3 & 2.8.3.2). This data might change with time due to modifications, etc. and the technique governing the modeling of this change is described in Sections 3.7 & 3.7.4.

A Mechanics Transaction profile holds the detail data about a Mechanics Transaction or a Mechanics Transaction Associative Entity. A Mechanics Transaction profile forms a group of entities that completely represent an Operation Transaction, or an association between Operation Transactions, or an association between Operation Transactions and Operation Sessions, or an association between Operation Transactions and the Mechanism, or an association between Operation Transactions and the Apparatus.

The Mechanics Transaction Domain includes Transactions with their profiles and Mechanics Transaction Associative Entities with their profiles. Section 2.8.3.2 defines the Mechanics Transaction Profile; similar definition would be applied to the Mechanics Transaction Associative Entity Profile. Sections 14.10, 14.11, & 14.12 provide additional details related to the Mechanics Transaction Associative Entities.

2.9.4.1 The Structure of the Mechanics Transactions

Similar to the structure of the Master Data dimensions, the structure of the Mechanics Transaction is composed of a main entity exhibiting the Operation Transaction and additional entities that together completely represent the Operation Transaction. The main entity and its additional entities form the Mechanics Transaction Profile. The structure of the Entity-Relationship of the Mechanics Transaction Profile follows the Relational Normalization Data Modeling Technique.

2.9.4.2 The Structure of the Mechanics Transaction Associative Entities

A Mechanics Transaction Associative Entity could have Profile Entities the same way as a Mechanics Transaction Entity.

2.10 INTERLINKS' RESTRICTIONS ON APPARATUS, MACHINERY, & OPERATION

The Apparatus, Machinery, and Operation interlink with each other. Diagram 2.1 illustrates and Table 2.1 summarizes these Interlinks. This Section describes some of these Interlinks. Section 2.12 describes the interlinks of the incidences of the Apparatus, Machinery, and Operation. This section clarifies some restrictions on the Interlinks between the Apparatus, Machinery, & Operation.

49

2.10.1 The Interlinks of the Apparatus Elementary Activities to the Operation Sessions

Since the Apparatus Activities encompass the Enterprise internal and external directives, instructions, guidelines, techniques, etc. controlling and governing the Operation Sessions of the Enterprise (Ref. Section 2.2.2), very often an Operation Session interlinks to only one Apparatus Elementary Activity. There might be some business cases where different directives and instructions (therefore belonging to different incidences of an Apparatus Elementary Activity or different Apparatus Elementary Activities) are controlling an Operation Session.

Furthermore an Operation Session Incidence should not be modified unless there are errors (Ref. Section 2.4.1); therefore an Operation Session Incidence is generated once and could not be modified. The interlinks between the incidences of the Apparatus Elementary Activities and the incidences of the Operation Sessions are further examined in Section 2.12.1.

If there are Operation Session and Operation Session Detail, where the interlink between the Operation Session and the Operation Session Detail is One-to-Many, the Operation Session Incidence would be controlled by an Apparatus Elementary Activity and the Operation Session Detail Incidence would be controlled by the same Apparatus Elementary Activity thru the Operation Session or directly by another Apparatus Elementary Activity.

2.10.2 The Interlinks of the Machinery Elementary Procedures to the Operation Transactions

Since the Machinery Procedures encompass the Enterprise internal and external rules and regulations, guidelines, techniques, etc. governing the Operation Transactions of the Enterprise (Ref. Section 2.3), very often an Operation Transaction interlinks to only one Machinery Elementary Procedure. There might be some business cases where different rules and regulations (therefore belonging to different incidences of a Machinery Elementary Procedure or different Machinery Elementary Procedures) are governing an Operation Transaction. The interlinks between the incidences of the Elementary Procedures and the incidences of the Operation Transactions are further examined in Section 2.12.2.

If there are Operation Transaction and Operation Transaction Detail, where the interlink between the Operation Transaction and Operation Transaction Detail is One-to-Many, the Operation Transaction would be governed by Machinery Elementary Procedure(s) and the Operation Transaction Detail would be governed by the same and/or other Machinery Elementary Procedure(s) either thru the Operation Transaction and/or directly by the other Machinery Elementary Procedure(s).

2.10.3 The Interlinks of the Operation Sessions to the Operation Transactions

An Operation Session could generate and/or modify one or many Operation Transactions. Very often an Operation Transaction is generated by only one Operation Session; in this case the Operation Transaction interlinks to only one Operation Session. There might some business cases where different Operation Sessions (different incidences of an Operation Session or different Operation Session(s)) generate or modify an Operation Transaction. The interlinks

Dr. Eng. M. Naoulo

between the incidences of the Operation Sessions and the incidences of the Operation Transactions are further discussed in Section 2.12.3.

If there are Operation Transaction and Operation Transaction Detail, where the interlink between the Operation Transaction and Operation Transaction Detail is One-to-Many, the Operation Transaction Detail would not interlink to any Operation Sessions.

2.10.4 The Interlinks of the Apparatus Occurrence Events to the Operation Sessions

Since the Apparatus Occurrence Events trigger the Operation Sessions of the Enterprise (Ref. Section 2.4.1), very often an Operation Session interlinks to only one Occurrence Event. There might be some business cases where different Occurrence Events trigger an Operation Session. Furthermore an Operation Session Incidence should not be modified unless there are errors (Ref. Section 2.4.1); therefore an Operation Session Incidence is triggered once and could not be modified. The interlinks between the incidences of the Occurrence Events and the incidences of the Operation Sessions are further examined in Section 2.12.4.

If there are Operation Session and Operation Session Detail, where the interlink between the Operation Session and Operation Session Detail is One-to-Many, the Operation Session Detail would not interlink to any Occurrence Events.

2.11 INTERACTION OF THE MASTER DATA, MECHANISM & MECHANICS

The Interactions between the Master Data, Mechanism, and Mechanics represent/reflect/model in the Enterprise Engineering Model the Interlinks between the Apparatus, Machinery, and Operation. They are illustrated thru relationships in the Enterprise Engineering Model Entity-Relationship Diagram. Diagram 2.2 illustrates the Interactions of the Mechanics Sessions and Transactions with the Master Data and Mechanism which represent/reflect/model the Interlinks between the Operation Sessions and Transactions with the Apparatus and Machinery. Chapters 3, 4, 5, 12, 13 & 14 detail and discuss this subject.

The instantiation of the Incidences of the Apparatus, Machinery, Operation Sessions and Transactions is represented/reflected/modeled in the Enterprise Engineering Model by Instances of the Master Data, Mechanism Procedure, Mechanics Sessions and Transactions respectively. An Incidence of the Operation Session must have a beginning and end date/time. An Incidence of the Operation Transaction must have incident's timestamp(s).

2.12 INTERLINKS OF APPARATUS, MACHINERY, & OPERATION INCIDENCES

The two Theorems of Enterprise Information Architecture (Ref. Sections 2.6.1 & 2.6.3) provide a base for the interlinks between the Apparatus, Machinery, and Operation Incidences. An Operation Session Incidence or an Operation Transaction Incidence must interlink to at least one

Member of each Component of the Apparatus: therefore a Mechanics Session Instance or a Mechanics Transaction Instance must be related (directly or thru other entities) to at least one Instance of a Dimension of each Component of the Master Data.

2.12.1 The Interlinks between the Apparatus Elementary Activity Incidences & the Operation Session Incidences

An Operation Session is triggered by events that take place during the functioning of the Enterprise and are controlled by the rules and regulations stored in the Apparatus Activities.

> An Apparatus Elementary Activity could control one or many Operation Sessions.

> An Operation Session could be controlled by one or many Elementary Apparatus Activities.

> An Incidence of an Apparatus Elementary Activity could control one or many Operation Session Incidences either belonging to the same Operation Session or different Operation Sessions.

> An Operation Session Incidence is controlled by only one Apparatus Elementary Activity Incidence since the Operation Session Incidence is created once and cannot be modified unless there are errors (Ref. Section 2.4.1).

2.12.2 The Interlinks between the Machinery Elementary Procedure Incidences & the Operation Transaction Incidences

The Operation Transactions are controlled by the rules and regulations stored in the Machinery Procedures.

> A Machinery Elementary Procedure could regulate one or many Operation Transactions.

> An Operation Transaction could be regulated by one or many Machinery Elementary Procedures.

> A Machinery Elementary Procedure Incidence could regulate one or many Operation Transaction Incidences either belonging to the same Operation Transaction or different Operation Transactions.

> An Operation Transaction Incidence could be regulated by one or many Machinery Elementary Procedure Incidences either belonging to the same Machinery Elementary Procedure or different Machinery Elementary Procedures.

> Therefore there might be the need to interlink some Operation Transactions to many Machinery Elementary Procedures. Also there might be the need to have Many-to-Many interlinks between the Operation Transactions and the Machinery Elementary Procedures.

2.12.3 The Interlinks between the Operation Session Incidences & the Operation Transaction Incidences

The Operation Transactions are generated (created and/or modified and/or deleted) by the Operation Sessions.

> An Operation Session could generate and/or modify and/or delete one or many Operation Transactions.

> An Operation Transaction could be generated and/or modified and/or deleted by one or many Operation Sessions.

> An Incidence of an Operation Session could generate and/or modify and/or delete one or

Dr. Eng. M. Naoulo

many Operation Transaction Incidences either belonging to the same Operation Transaction or different Operation Transactions.

➤ An Operation Transaction Incidence could be generated and/or modified and/or deleted by one or many Operation Session Incidences either belonging to the same Operation Session or different Operation Sessions.

➤ An Operation Transaction is created once, could be modified many times, and could be deleted only once.

➤ Therefore there might the need to interlink some of the Operation Transactions to many Operation Sessions. Also there might be the need to have Many-to-Many interlinks between the Operation Transactions and the Operation Sessions.

2.12.4 The Interlinks between the Apparatus Occurrence Event Incidences & the Operation Session Incidences

An Apparatus Occurrence Event triggers Operation Sessions during the functioning of the Enterprise.

➤ An Apparatus Occurrence Event could trigger one or many Operation Sessions.

➤ An Operation Session could be triggered by one or many Apparatus Occurrence Events.

➤ An Incidence of an Apparatus Occurrence Event could trigger one or many Operation Session Incidences either belonging to the same Operation Session or different Operation Sessions.

➤ An Operation Session Incidence is triggered by only one Apparatus Occurrence Event Incidence since the Operation Session Incidence is created once and cannot be modified unless there are errors (Ref. Section 2.4.1).

2.13 INTERACTIONS OF MASTER DATA, MECHANISM, & MECHANICS INSTANCES

The Master Data, Mechanism, and Mechanics reflect in a Data Modeling milieu the Apparatus, Machinery, and Operation therefore the relations between the Master Data, Mechanism, and Mechanics reflect the interlinks between the Apparatus, Machinery, and Operation (Ref. Section 2.12).

2.13.1 The Interactions between the Elementary Activity Instances & the Mechanics Session Instances

From Section 2.12.1 it can be deduced:

➤ There might be relationships between an Elementary Activity Entity and many Mechanics Session Entities.

➤ There might be relationships between a Mechanics Session Entity and many Elementary Activity Entities.

➤ The relationship between an Elementary Activity Entity and a Mechanics Session Entity is One-to-Many.

➤ A Mechanics Session Instance must be related to only one Master Data Elementary Activity Instance.

Dr. Eng. M. Naoulo

2.13.2 The Interactions between the Mechanism Elementary Procedure Instances & the Mechanics Transaction Instances

From Section 2.12.2 it can be deduced:
  ➢ There might be relationships between a Mechanism Elementary Procedure Entity and many Mechanics Transaction Entities.
  ➢ There might be relationships between a Mechanics Transaction Entity and many Mechanism Elementary Procedure Entities.
  ➢ A Mechanism Elementary Procedure Instance could be related to one or many Mechanics Transaction Instances either belonging to the same Mechanics Transaction or different Mechanics Transactions.
  ➢ A Mechanics Transaction Instance could be related to one or many Mechanism Elementary Procedure Instances either belonging to the same Mechanism Elementary Procedure or different Mechanism Elementary Procedures.
  ➢ A Mechanics Transaction Instance must be related to at least one Mechanism Elementary Procedure Instance.
  ➢ The relationship between a Mechanism Elementary Procedure Entity and a Mechanics Transaction Entity could be Many-to-Many.

The decomposing of the Many-to-Many relationships between the Mechanism Elementary Procedures and Mechanics Transactions will be resolved as indicated in Section 13.9.

2.13.3 The Interactions between the Mechanics Session Instances & the Mechanics Transaction Instances

From Section 2.12.3 it can be deduced:
  ➢ There might be relationships between a Mechanics Session Entity and many Mechanics Transaction Entities.
  ➢ There might be relationships between a Mechanics Transaction Entity and many Mechanism Session Entities.
  ➢ A Mechanics Session Instance could be related to one or many Mechanics Transaction Instances either belonging to the same Mechanics Transaction or different Mechanics Transactions.
  ➢ A Mechanics Transaction Instance could be related to one or many Mechanics Session Instances either belonging to the same Mechanics Session or different Mechanics Sessions.
  ➢ A Mechanics Transaction Instance must be related to at least one Mechanics Session Instance.
  ➢ The relationship between a Mechanics Session Entity and a Mechanics Transaction Entity could be Many-to-Many.

The decomposing of the Many-to-Many relationships between the Mechanics Sessions and Mechanics Transactions will be resolved as indicated in Section 13.10.

Dr. Eng. M. Naoulo

2.13.4 The Interactions between the Occurrence Event Instances & the Mechanics Session Instances

From Section 2.12.4 it can be deduced:

- ➢ There might be relationships between an Occurrence Event Entity and many Mechanics Session Entities.
- ➢ There might be relationships between a Mechanics Session Entity and many Occurrence Event Entities.
- ➢ The relationship between an Occurrence Event Entity and a Mechanics Session Entity is One-to-Many.
- ➢ A Mechanics Session Instance must be related to only one Master Data Occurrence Event Instance.

2.14 THE ENTERPRISE DATA MODELS

The Enterprise Data Architecture encompasses many Data Models:
- ➢ The Data Models of the Legacy Systems
- ➢ The Data Models of the ODS and Central Data Repositories
- ➢ The Data Models of the Business and Enterprise Intelligence Data Marts
- ➢ The Data Models associated with the ETL, SOA, Staging Areas, Meta-Metadata, etc.

The Data Models of the Legacy Systems and the ODS reflect structures of data already established in the existing systems.

The Enterprise Engineering Model embodies the data structure of the Central Data Repositories (Ref. Section 2.8). The SAM O NAOULO Modeling Technique is to be used for the design of the Central Data Repositories and the Business and Enterprise Intelligence Data Marts. It could also be applied in the design of the ETL, SOA, and Staging Areas data models.

2.15 THE METHODOLOGY OF THE ENTERPRISE DATA FRAMEWORK

The Methodology of the Enterprise Data Framework covers the following major tasks:
1. Information Gathering covering the Enterprise Information Requirements.
2. Analysis and detail the Transactional Data and Business Intelligence Query and Reporting Requirements.
3. Analysis and detail the Enterprise Intelligence and Enterprise Engineering Query and Reporting Requirements.
4. Develop a Data and Information Strategy to respond to these Requirements.
5. Design the Overall Enterprise Data Architecture.
6. Develop the Implementation Plan of the Enterprise Data Framework.
7. Review, assessment, and evaluation of the Quality of the Legacy Systems Data.
8. Review, assessment, and evaluation of the Structure, Data Dictionary, and Metadata of the Legacy Systems.
9. Validate that all Business Intelligence, Enterprise Intelligence, and Enterprise

Engineering Query and Reporting Requirements could be supplied from the Legacy Systems.

10. Address missing metadata from the Legacy Systems.

11. Design the Enterprise Data Models covering the Central Data Repository, Business Intelligence and Enterprise Intelligence Data Marts. These models would follow the SAM O NAOULO Modeling Technique: using any other modeling technique would not provide comprehensive, integrated, and structured Enterprise Data Model nor comprehensive Enterprise Architecture.
    - Analysis and Design of the Apparatus and Master Data.
    - Analysis and Design of the Machinery and Mechanism Procedures.
    - Analysis and Design of the Operation, Mechanics Sessions and Transactions.
    - Analysis and Design all relationships between the Master Data, Mechanism Procedures, and Mechanics Sessions and Transactions in the Central Data Repository.

12. Conception of Consolidation and Integration Plan encompassing the data of the Legacy Systems into the Central Data Repository.

13. Design of a Data Quality Plan for the data of the Legacy Systems.

14. Design the Propagation and Extraction, Transformation, and Loading (ETL) Plan: Legacy Systems to Central Data Repository.

15. Construction of the Central Data Repository.

16. Implementation of the Data Quality Plan for the data of the Legacy Systems.

17. Implementation of the Propagation and ETL Plan: Legacy Systems to the Central Data Repository.

18. Implementation of the Consolidation and Integration Plan encompassing the data of the Legacy Systems into the Central Data Repository.

19. Design of the Feedback Propagation Plan (if needed): Central Data Repository to Legacy Systems.

20. Implementation of the Feedback Propagation Plan (if needed): Central Data Repository to Legacy Systems.

21. Detail design and implementation of the Business Intelligence Data Marts.

22. Detail design and implementation of the Enterprise Intelligence Data Marts.

23. Design of the Propagation, Aggregation, and Extraction, Transformation, and Loading (ETL) Plans: Central Data Repository to Business and Enterprise Intelligence Data Marts.

24. Implementation of the Propagation, Aggregation, and ETL Plans: Central Data Repository to Business and Enterprise Intelligence Data Marts.

25. Design of the Query and Reports from the Central Data Repository, Business and Enterprise Intelligence Data Marts.

26. Implementation of the Query and Reports from the Central Data Repository, Business and Enterprise Intelligence Data Marts.

The details of this methodology could be elaborated based on the above major tasks. These details could be formatted into a Project Management plan that includes detailed tasks, resources, deliverables, cost, time, etc. These detailed Tasks, Resources, Guidelines, and Deliverables would not be covered in this book in order to concentrate on MDM and the Enterprise Engineering techniques.

3.   SAM O NAOULO Modeling Technique

The Modeling Technique used in the design of the Enterprise Engineering Model involving the Master Data, Mechanism, and Mechanics is the **SAM O NAOULO Modeling Technique**. The following table illustrates the Implementation Methods, Techniques, and Data Model Diagram's Shapes of the three Data Architecture modeling approaches: Information Engineering, Data Warehousing, and Enterprise Engineering:

Data Architecture Modeling Approach	Information Engineering	Data Warehousing	Enterprise Engineering
Implementation Method	On-Line Transactional Processing (OLTP)	On-Line Analytical Processing (OLAP)	On-Line Mechanical Processing (OLMP)
Supported Data	Transactional Data	Business Intelligence Data	Enterprise Intelligence Data
Data Modeling Technique	Relational Normalization Data Modeling Technique	Multidimensional Data Modeling Technique	**SAM O NAOULO** Modeling Technique
Data Model Diagram (Entity-Relationship Diagram)'s Shape	3rd Normal Form (3NF) Diagram (the higher Normal Forms are not frequently used)	Star and/or Snow Flake Schema Diagram	Lily Flower Diagram

Table 3.1: Data Architecture Modeling Approaches' Implementation Methods, Supported Data, Data Modeling Techniques, & Diagram Shapes

Enterprise Engineering is carried out starting with the analysis of the System of Apparatus, Machinery, and Operation. SAM O NAOULO Modeling Technique involves the design of the Master Data, Mechanism, and Mechanics illustrating the Apparatus, Machinery, and Operation.
It is used for the On-Line Mechanical Processing (OLMP). Table 2.2 presents the Enterprise Constituents and their Interlinks and how they are represented/reflected/modeled in the Enterprise Engineering Model. It is important to note that SAM O NAOULO Modeling Technique incorporates, as part of its features, the Relational Normalization Data Modeling Technique advocated by Dr. Codd [2] and Dr. Date [3] for the design of the Central Data Repository. As in Information Engineering the normalization of the models will proceed usually to the 3rd Normal Form. It is important sometimes to further validate these entities and their relationships thru higher Normal Forms: Boyce-Codd Normal Form, Fourth Normal Form, Fifth Normal Form, etc. to handle complex cases.

SAM O NAOULO Modeling Technique incorporates also the Multidimensional Data Modeling

Technique advocated by Bill Inmon [9] and detailed by Ralph Kimball [13] for the design of the Enterprise Engineering Data Marts.

This chapter details the **SAM O NAOULO** Modeling Technique. The rules described in this chapter are directing principles. There might be some exceptional cases that might need to bend some of these rules. If such cases occur, very deep analysis must be conducted before implementing any exception.

3.1   THE INTERACTIONS WITHIN THE CONSTITUENT PROFILES

The Master Data Dimension Profile, the Mechanism Procedure Profile, the Mechanics Session Profile, and the Mechanics Transaction Profile hold all detail data about the Apparatus Member information (Ref. Section 2.8.1), the Machinery Procedure information (Ref. Section 2.8.2), the Operation Session information (Ref. Section 2.8.3.1), and the Operation Transaction information (Ref. Section 2.8.3.2) respectively. The Associative Entities Profile holds all detail data about the Associative Entities information (Ref. Sections 2.9.1.2, 2.9.2.2, 2.9.3.2, & 2.9.4.2).

The data within a profile is structured thru an Entity-Relationship Diagram incorporating the relationships between the entities using the Relational Normalization Data Modeling technique. Within a Profile the relationships are One-to-One or One-to-Many. No Many-to-Many relationships within a Profile.

3.2   THE RELATIONSHIPS BETWEEN ENTITIES OF THE MASTER DATA, MECHANISM, & MECHANICS

In the **SAM O NAOULO** models illustrating the System of Apparatus, Machinery, and Operation, the entities interact with each other thru relationships. These interactions are summarized in the following two tables. The techniques to handle these interactions are detailed in Chapters 2, 3, 4, and 5. Appendix A details the Interlinks of the System of Apparatus, Machinery, & Operation, Appendix B provides the Resolution of Relationships between the Entities, and Appendix C describes the Enterprise Engineering Model's Associative Entities.

Table 3.2 summarizes the One-to-One, One-to-Many, Many-to-Many, and recursive relationships:
  ➢ Within the Master Data,
  ➢ Within the Mechanism,
  ➢ Within the Mechanics' Transactions, and
  ➢ Within the Mechanics' Sessions.
It also provides references to the Sections detailing and analyzing these interactions.

INTERACTIONS	One-to-One	One-to-Many	Many-to-Many

Dr. Eng. M. Naoulo

Within Master Data (Dimension or Associative) Profile	OK, Ref. Sections 3.1 & 13.1.1	OK, Ref. Sections 3.1 & 13.1.6	Not Valid, Ref. Sections 3.1 & 13.1.11
Within a Master Data Component and across Master Data Profiles	Not Common, Ref. Sections 12.1.1 & 13.1.2	OK, Ref. Sections 12.1.1, & 13.1.7	Decomposed, Ref. Sections 12.1.1 & 13.1.12
	Note for Activities Ref. Section 12.1.2	Note for Activities Ref. Section 12.1.2	Note for Activities Ref. Section 12.1.2
Across Master Data Components or involving Master Data Associative Entities resulting from relationships across Master Data Components	Not Common, Ref. Sections 12.1.3 & 13.1.3	OK, Ref. Sections 12.1.3 & 13.1.8	Decomposed, Ref. Sections 12.1.3 & 13.1.13.
	Note for Activities Ref. Sections 12.1.4 & 13.1.4	Note for Activities Ref. Sections 12.1.4 & 13.1.9	Note for Activities Ref. Sections 12.1.4 & 13.1.14
	Note for Events Ref. Sections 12.1.5 & 13.1.5	Note for Events Ref. Sections 12.1.5 & 13.1.10	Note for Occurrence Events Ref. Sections 12.1.5 & 13.1.15
Recursive Relationships within Master Data Profile	Not Common, Ref. Sections 12.1.6 & 13.1.17	OK, Ref. Sections 12.1.6 & 13.1.18	Decomposed, Ref. Sections 12.1.6 & 13.1.19
			Note for Activities Ref. Sections 12.1.7 & 13.1.20
Within Mechanism Procedure Profile	OK, Ref. Sections 3.1 & 13.2.1	OK, Ref. Sections 3.1 & 13.2.3	Not Valid, Ref. Sections 3.1 & 13.2.4
Across Mechanism Procedure Profiles	Not Common, Ref. Sections 12.2.2 & 13.2.2	OK, Ref. Sections 12.2.2 & 13.2.3	Decomposed, Ref. Sections 12.2.2 & 13.2.5
Recursive Relationships within Mechanism Procedure Profile	Not Common, Ref. Sections 12.2.3 & 13.2.6	OK, Ref. Sections 12.2.3 & 13.2.7	Not Common, Ref. Sections 12.2.3 & 13.2.8
Within Mechanics Session Profile	OK, Ref. Sections 3.1 & 13.3.1	OK, Ref. Sections 3.1 & 13.3.3	Not Valid, Ref. Sections 3.1 & 13.3.4
Across Mechanics Session Profiles	Not Common, Ref. Sections 12.3.1 & 13.3.2	OK, Ref. Sections 12.3.1 & 13.3.3	Decomposed, Ref. Sections 12.3.1 & 13.3.5

Dr. Eng. M. Naoulo

Recursive Relationships within Mechanics Session Profile	Not Common, Ref. Sections 12.3.2 & 13.3.6	OK, Ref. Sections 12.3.2 & 13.3.7	Decomposed, Ref. Sections 12.3.2 & 13.3.8
Within Mechanics Transaction Profile	OK, Ref. Sections 3.1 & 13.4.1	OK, Ref. Sections 3.1 & 13.4.3	Not Valid, Ref. Sections 3.1 & 13.4.4
Across Mechanics Transaction Profiles	Not Common, Ref. Sections 12.4.1 & 13.4.2	OK, Ref. Sections 12.4.1 & 13.4.3	Decomposed, Ref. Sections 12.4.1 & 13.4.5
Recursive Relationships within Mechanics Transaction Profile	Not Common, Ref. Sections 12.4.2 & 13.4.6	OK, Ref. Sections 12.4.2 & 13.4.7	Decomposed, Ref. Sections 12.4.2 & 13.4.8

Table 3.2: Summary of Relationships within the Master Data, Mechanism, & Mechanics Sessions & Transactions

Table 3.3 summarizes the One-to-One, One-to-Many, Many-to-One, and Many-to-Many relationships:

➢ Between the Master Data and the Mechanism Procedures, Mechanics Sessions, and Mechanics Transactions,
➢ Between the Mechanism Procedures and the Mechanics Sessions and Transactions, and
➢ Between the Mechanics Sessions and Mechanics Transactions.

It also provides references to the sections detailing and analyzing these interactions.

From>> >>To	Master Data Entities	Mechanism Procedure Entities	Mechanics Session Entities	Mechanics Transaction Entities
Master Data Entities	Ref. Table 3.2	One-to-One: Not Common Ref. Sections 12.5.1 & 13.5.3 Exception for Activities Ref. Sections 12.5.5 & 13.5.2	One-to-One: Not Common Ref. Sections 12.6.1 & 13.6.2	One-to-One: Not Common Ref. Sections 12.7.1 & 13.7.4 Exception for Activities Ref. Sections 12.7.5 & 13.7.2 Exception for Occurrence Events Ref. Section 12.7.6 & 13.7.3
Master	Ref.	One-to-Many: OK	One-to-Many: OK	One-to-Many: OK

Dr. Eng. M. Naoulo

Data Entities	Table 3.2	Ref. Sections 12.5.2 & 13.5.4	Ref. Sections 12.6.2, & 13.6.3	Ref. Sections 12.7.2 & 13.7.5
		Exception for Activities Ref. Sections 12.5.5 & 13.5.2		Exception for Activities Ref. Sections 12.7.5 & 13.7.2
				Exception for Occurrence Events Ref. Section 12.7.6 & 13.7.3
Master Data Entities	Ref. Table 3.2	Many-to-One: Decomposed Ref. Sections 12.5.3 & 13.5.5	Many-to-One: Decomposed Ref. Sections 12.6.3 & 13.6.4	Many-to-One: Decomposed Ref. Sections 12.7.3 & 13.7.6
		Exception for Activities Ref. Sections 12.5.5 & 13.5.2		Exception for Activities Ref. Sections 12.7.5 & 13.7.2
		Exception for Occurrence Events Ref. Section 13.5.6		Exception for Occurrence Events Ref. Section 12.7.6 & 13.7.3
Master Data Entities	Ref. Table 3.2	Many-to-Many: Decomposed Ref. Sections 12.5.4 & 13.5.7	Many-to-Many: Decomposed Ref. Sections 12.6.4 & 13.6.5	Many-to-Many: Decomposed Ref. Sections 12.7.4 & 13.7.7
		Exception for Activities Ref. Sections 12.5.5 & 13.5.2		Exception for Activities Ref. Sections 12.7.5 & 13.7.2
		Exception for Occurrence Events Ref. Section 13.5.8		Exception for Occurrence Events Ref. Section 12.7.6 & 13.7.3
Mechanism Procedure Entities		Ref. Table 3.2	One-to-One: Not Valid Ref. Sections 12.8 & 13.8	One-to-One: Not Common Ref. Sections 12.9.1 & 13.9.2
Mechanism Procedure Entities		Ref. Table 3.2	One-to-Many: Not Valid Ref. Sections 12.8 & 13.8	One-to-Many: OK Ref. Sections 12.9.2 & 13.9.3
Mechanism Procedure Entities		Ref. Table 3.2	Many-to-One: Not Valid Ref. Sections 12.8 & 13.8	Many-to-One: Decomposed Ref. Sections 12.9.3 & 13.9.4

Mechanism Procedure Entities		Ref. Table 3.2	Many-to-Many: Not Valid Ref. Sections 12.8 & 13.8	Many-to-Many: Decomposed Ref. Sections 12.9.4 & 13.9.5
Mechanics Session Entities			Ref. Table 3.2	One-to-One: Not Common Ref. Sections 12.10.1 & 13.10.2
Mechanics Session Entities			Ref. Table 3.2	One-to-Many: OK Ref. Sections 12.10.2 & 13.10.3
Mechanics Session Entities			Ref. Table 3.2	Many-to-One: Decomposed Ref. Sections 12.10.3 & 13.10.4
Mechanics Session Entities			Ref. Table 3.2	Many-to-Many: Decomposed Ref. Sections 12.10.4 & 13.10.5
Mechanics Transaction Entities				Ref. Table 3.2

Table 3.3: Summary of Relationships between Entities of the Master Data, Mechanism, & Mechanics Sessions & Transactions

Table 3.4 summarizes the interactions between the instances of the Master Data, Mechanism Procedures, and Mechanics Sessions and Transactions and their restrictions. It provides references to the sections detailing and analyzing these interactions.

>> Between >>	Master Data (except Activities or Occurrence Events)	Master Data Activities	Master Data Occurrence Events	Mechanism Procedures	Mechanics Sessions	Mechanics Transactions
Master Data (except Activities or Occurrence Events)	Relationships OK Ref. Table 3.2	Relationships OK Ref. Table 3.2	Relationships OK Ref. Table 3.2	Relationships OK Ref. Table 3.3	Relationships OK Ref. Section 3.5.8	Relationships OK Ref. Table 3.3

Dr. Eng. M. Naoulo

Master Data Activities		Relationships OK Ref. Table 3.2	Relationships OK Ref. Table 3.2	No Relationships, Ref. Table 13.1 & 13.5.2	Relationships OK Ref. Sections 3.5.9	No Relationships, Ref. Section 3.6.5
Master Data Occurrence Events			Relationships OK Ref. Table 3.2	Relationships OK Restrictions Ref. Table 3.3	Relationships OK Ref. Section 3.5.10	No Relationships, Ref. Section 3.6.6
Mechanism Procedures				Relationships OK Ref. Table 3.2	No Relationships, Ref. Table 3.3	Relationships OK Ref. Sections 2.13.2
Mechanics Sessions					Relationships OK Ref. Table 3.2	Relationships OK Ref. Sections 2.13.3
Mechanics Transactions						Relationships OK Ref. Table 3.2

Table 3.4: The Restrictions of Instance Relationships between Entities of the Master Data, Mechanism, & Mechanics Sessions & Transactions

3.3   THE MASTER DATA'S MODELING TECHNIQUE

This section provides a high level approach and Best of Practice to the Technique to model the Master Data in an Enterprise Engineering milieu. This Technique is detailed in the next chapters and appendices.

The Master Data's Modeling Technique incorporates the rules enunciated in Sections 3.2 and 13.1. In addition this Technique includes the following:

1. The selection of the Master Data Dimension Entities would be based on the Apparatus Members identified and detailed in Step 6 of the Enterprise Engineering Methodology and its Guidelines (Sections 8.6 & 9.6).
2. At the logical level, each Apparatus Member is reflected in the Enterprise Engineering Model by a main Master Data Dimension Entity supported by additional Master Data Dimension Entities that encompass the attributes needed by this main Master Data Dimension. This main Master Data Dimension Entity and its additional related entities form the Master Data Dimension Profile.
3. One or many Mechanism Procedure Entities could be related to the Master Data Dimension and Associative Entities. The interrelation between the Mechanism Procedure Entities and the Master Data Entities is detailed in Section 13.5.
4. One or many Mechanics Session Entities could be related to the Master Data Dimension and Associative Entities. The interrelation between the Mechanics Session Entities and the Master Data Entities is detailed in Section 13.6.

Dr. Eng. M. Naoulo

5. One or many Mechanics Transaction Entities could be related to the Master Data Dimension and Associative Entities. The interrelation between the Mechanics Transaction Entities and the Master Data Entities is detailed in Section 13.7.

6. The logical design of the Master Data incorporates the Data Modeling rules of Relational Normalization Data Modeling technique developed by Dr. E. F. Codd [2] and C. Date [3].

7. At the physical design level, the entities of the Master Data Dimension Profiles could, in some cases, be collapsed into one or few tables for better processing performance (very often at the expenses of the normalization rules) .

8. Surrogate Keys (SK) or Business Keys could be used as Primary Keys (PK) of the main Master Data Dimension Entity and other Master Data Entities.

9. There might be relationships including Many-to-Many relationships between the entities of the Master Data that are either belonging to the same Master Data Component but different Master Data Dimensions, or different Master Data Components. Diagram 3.1 depicts, at a very high level, these interrelations. In Enterprise Engineering SAM O NAOULO Modeling Technique these relationships would be resolved during the analysis and design of the Master Data as detailed in Section 13.1.

10. The main Master Data Dimension Entities of the Occurrence component are the Events. An Event is an Occurrence Member. The Event Member could be modeled as one entity, one supertype entity with many subtypes, or many entities that from an Event Profile. The Event triggers one or many Mechanics Sessions. A Mechanics Session must be related to an Event Member. Diagram 10.1b provides an example of the design of the Occurrence component.

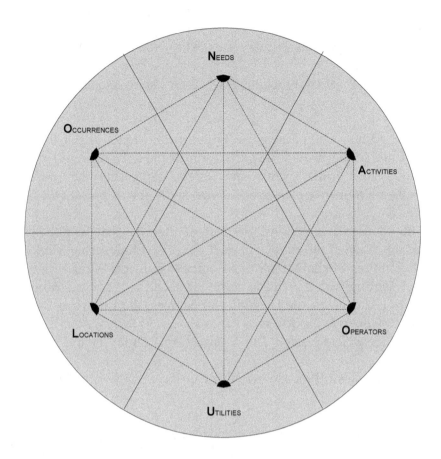

Diagram 3.1: The Apparatus/Master Data Components Interlinked

There are some directions for Best of Practice that would help in the design, illustration, and visualization of the entities and attributes of the Master Data:

1. The name of the Master Data entities and the attributes of these entities shall start with the letters: NED for Needs, ACT for Activities, OPR for Operators, UTL for Utilities, LOC for Locations, and OCC for Occurrences.
2. The use of the rainbow colors to illuminate the affiliation of the entities with the Master Data Components: Needs would be illuminated in magenta, Activities in dark blue, Operators in green, Utilities in yellow, Locations in orange, and Occurrences in red. The coloring of the entities provides visual help especially when the Enterprise Engineering Model becomes large and sophisticated. This also would help in the validation of Enterprise Engineering Model as elucidated in the next sections.
3. The order of the attributes of the Master Data Entities would be first those that are part of the PK followed by those that are FKs, then those that are not part of the PK or FKs. The order of attributes within the PK, the FKs, and outside the PK and FKs would be first the Foreign Keys related to the Master Data Dimensions: consecutively the Needs, Activities, Operators, Utilities, Locations, and Occurrences, then the attributes outside the FKs. The attributes pertinent to Master Data Components different from the Component of the Master Data Dimension under analysis are all FKs.
4. The name of the Elementary Activities (Ref. Section 2.2.2) would end with the word

Dr. Eng. M. Naoulo

CONTROL.
5. Use Surrogate Keys (SK) as Primary Keys (PK) for the main Master Data Dimension Entity.
6. Additional Best of Practice directions for Master Data Associative Entities are provided in Section 13.1.

After completing the design of the Enterprise Engineering Model as per the design techniques above, the shape of this Model would have the form of the Lily flower. This flower illustrates this shape brightly. The Corolla (petals and sepals) represents the Master Data and the Mechanism, while the reproductive elements: Stamen and Ovary represent the Mechanics.

Hereafter are some additional directions for Best of Practice that would help in the design, illustration, and visualization of the entities of the Enterprise Engineering Model:
1. Position the entities of the Master Data clockwise in the Model diagram as shown in Diagram 3.1 starting with the Needs at the top then the Activities 60 degrees clockwise, the Operators 120 degrees, the Utilities 180 degrees, the Locations 240 degrees, and the Occurrences 300 degrees clockwise.
2. Position the Mechanics Session and Transaction Entities in the Middle of the Model diagram.
3. Position the Mechanism Procedure Entities in the peripheries of the Model diagram as suitable.

Note: Best of Practice suggestions recommended here or elsewhere in the book are not mandatory to follow; however they enable better Design and Understanding of the Models and better Quality Assurances.

Dr. Eng. M. Naoulo

Figure 3.1: The Lily Flower: The Corolla represents the Master Data & the Mechanism while the reproductive elements represent the Mechanics

3.4   THE MECHANISM'S MODELING TECHNIQUE

This section provides a high level approach and Best of Practice to the Technique to model the Mechanism in an Enterprise Engineering milieu. This Technique is detailed in the next chapters and appendices.

The Mechanism's Modeling Technique incorporates the rules enunciated in Sections 3.2 & 13.2. In addition this Technique includes the following:

1. The selection of the Mechanism Entities would be based on the Machinery Procedures identified and detailed in Step 7 of the Enterprise Engineering Methodology and its Guidelines (Sections 8.7 & 9.7).
2. At the logical level, each Machinery Procedure is reflected in the Enterprise Engineering Model by a main Mechanism Procedure Entity supported by additional Mechanism

Dr. Eng. M. Naoulo

Procedure Entities that encompass the attributes needed by this main Mechanism Procedure. This main Mechanism Procedure Entity and its additional related entities form the Mechanism Procedure Profile.

3. The Mechanism Procedure Entities could not be related directly to the Mechanics Session Entities (Ref. Section 13.8).
4. One or many Mechanics Transaction Entities could be related to the Mechanism Procedure Entities. The interrelation between the Mechanics Transaction Entities and the Mechanism Procedure Entities is detailed in Section 13.9.
5. The logical design of the Mechanism Procedures incorporates the Data Modeling rules of Relational Normalization Data Modeling technique.
6. At the physical design level, the entities of the Mechanism Procedure Profiles could, in some cases, be collapsed into one or few tables for better processing performance (very often at the expenses of the normalization rules).
7. Surrogate Keys (SK) or Business Keys could be used as Primary Keys (PK) of the main Mechanism Procedure Entity and other Mechanism Procedure Entities.
8. There might be relationships including Many-to-Many relationships between the entities of the Mechanism. In SAM O NAOULO Modeling Technique these relationships would be resolved during the analysis and design of the Mechanism as detailed in Section 13.2.

There are some directions for Best of Practice that would help in the design, illustration, and visualization of the entities and attributes of the Mechanism:

1. The name of the Mechanism Entities and the attributes of these entities that are not FK to the Master Data shall start with the letter M.
2. The color of the Mechanism Procedure Entities would be dark pink.
3. The order of the attributes of the Mechanism Procedure Entities would first those that are part of the PK followed by those that are FKs, then those that are not part of the PK or FKs. The order of attributes within the PK, the FKs, and outside the PK and FKs would be first the Foreign Keys related to the Master Data: consecutively the Needs, Activities, Operators, Utilities, Locations, and Occurrences, followed by the Foreign Keys related to the Mechanism Procedure Entities, then the attributes outside the FKs. All the attributes outside the PKs and FKs are attributes of the Mechanism. The attributes pertinent to the Master Data are all FKs.
4. The name of the Elementary Procedures (Ref. Section 2.3) would end with the word **RULE**.
5. Use Surrogate Keys (SK) as Primary Keys (PK) of the main Mechanism Procedure Entity.
6. Additional Best of Practice directions for Mechanism Associative Entities are provided in Section 13.2.

3.5 THE MECHANICS SESSIONS' MODELING TECHNIQUE

This section provides a high level approach and Best of Practice to the Technique to model the Mechanics Sessions in an Enterprise Engineering milieu. This Technique is detailed in the next chapters and appendices.

Dr. Eng. M. Naoulo

The Mechanics Sessions' Modeling Technique incorporates the rules enunciated in Sections 3.2 & 13.3. In addition this Technique includes the following:

1. The selection of the Mechanics Session Entities would be based on the Operation Sessions identified and detailed in Step 8 of the Enterprise Engineering Methodology and its Guidelines (Sections 8.8 & 9.8).

2. At the logical level, each Operation Session is reflected in the Enterprise Engineering Model by a main Mechanics Session Entity supported by additional Mechanics Session Entities that encompass the attributes needed by this main Mechanics Session. This main Mechanics Session Entity and its additional related entities form the Mechanics Session Profile.

3. One or many Mechanics Transaction Entities could be related to the Mechanics Session Entities. The interrelation between the Mechanics Transaction Entities and the Mechanics Session Entities is detailed in Section 13.10.

4. The logical design of the Mechanics Sessions incorporates the Data Modeling rules of Relational Normalization Data Modeling technique.

5. The main Mechanics Session Entity could have many subtypes.

6. A Mechanics Session Entity could have Sub-sessions. The resolution of the links between the Session and sub-sessions will be performed during the analysis and design of Mechanics Sessions as detailed in Section 13.3.

7. A Mechanics Session Instance (an instance of a Mechanics Session Entity or an instance of a Supertype Mechanics Session Entity and its subtypes) reflects an Operation Session Incidence.

8. A Mechanics Session Instance must be related (directly or thru Associative Entities) to at least one instance of a Master Data Dimension in each Master Data Component. Therefore a Mechanics Session Instance must have at least one FK to each Component of the Master Data.

9. A Mechanics Session Instance must be related (directly or thru Master Data Associative Entities) to one and only one instance of a Master Data Elementary Activity Entity. Therefore a database stored procedure or other software restrictions must be developed to insure that between all FK attributes/columns in a Mechanics Session Instance related to the Master Data Elementary Activity Entities, only one attribute/column has values and all others are NULL.

10. A Mechanics Session Instance must be related (directly or thru Master Data Associative Entities) to one and only one instance of a Master Data Event Entity. Therefore a database stored procedure or other software restrictions must be developed to insure that between all FK attributes/columns in a Mechanics Session Instance related to the Master Data Event Entities, only one attribute/column has values and all others are NULL.

11. If a Mechanics Session Entity S1 is related One-to-One and Many-to-One to another Mechanics Session S2 (where the FK is located in the Mechanics Session Entity S1), S1 could, thru its FK to the Mechanics Session S2, relate to the Members of the Components of the Master Data.

12. There might be relationship including Many-to-Many relationships between the entities of the Mechanics Sessions. In SAM O NAOULO Modeling Technique these relationships would be resolved during the analysis and design of the Mechanics Sessions as detailed in Section 13.3.

13. The Mechanics Session Entity must include a Session Start Timestamp attribute and a Session End Timestamp attribute.

14. Sometimes the Mechanics Session Entity does not include any attributes beside the above two attributes and the FKs to the Master Data and other Mechanics Session Entities.

15. There would be no relationships between the Mechanics Session Entities and the Mechanism. Therefore No Mechanism Procedures FKs exist in the Mechanics Session Entities.

16. The non-Primary Key attributes of the Mechanics Session Entities that are not Foreign Keys (FK) to the Master Data Entities or the Mechanics Session Entities may include:
    - Numeric additive measures: money, etc.
    - Time related data: calendar figures, timestamps, etc.
    - Descriptive data.

17. The aggregation of the data of the Mechanics Session Entities for reporting analysis will be based on formulas:
    - Having as parameters the attributes of the Mechanics Session Entities that are not Foreign Keys (FK) to the Master Data Entities. These parameters might include the Session Start and End Timestamp attributes.
    - Grouped by the attributes of the Mechanics Session Entities that are Foreign Keys (FK) to the Master Data Entities.
    - The aggregation might be affected by the attributes of the Master Data Entities that are related directly to the Mechanics Session Entities thru the Foreign Keys in the Mechanics Session Entities.

There are some directions for Best of Practice that would help in the design, illustration and visualization of the entities and attributes of the Mechanics Sessions:

1. The name of the Mechanics Session Entities and the attributes of these entities that are not FK to the Master Data Entities shall start with the letters MS.

2. The color of the Mechanics Session Entities would be gray.

3. The order of the attributes of the Mechanics Session Entities would first those that are part of the PK followed by those that are FKs, then those that are not part of the PK or FKs. The order of attributes within the PK, the FKs, and outside the PK and FKs would be first the Foreign Keys related to the Master Data: consecutively the Needs, Activities, Operators, Utilities, Locations, and Occurrences, followed by the Foreign Keys related to the Mechanics Session Entities, then the attributes outside the FKs. All the attributes outside the PKs and FKs are attributes of the Mechanics Sessions. The attributes pertinent to the Master Data are all FKs. This would help in the validation of the Mechanics Session Entities as each Mechanics Session Entity (or the Session Entity and its subtypes) must include Foreign Key attributes to at least one Master Data Dimension of each Master Data Component therefore assuring that an Operation Session is related to at least one Member of each Apparatus Component.

4. The name of the Mechanics Session Entities (main entity and its sub-types) would end with the word **SESSION.**

5. Use Surrogate Keys (SK) as Primary Keys (PK) of the main Mechanics Session Entity.

6. Additional Best of Practice directions for Mechanics Session Associative Entities are provided in Section 13.3.

Dr. Eng. M. Naoulo

3.6 THE MECHANICS TRANSACTIONS' MODELING TECHNIQUE

This section provides a high level approach and Best of Practice to the Technique to model the Mechanics Transactions in an Enterprise Engineering milieu. This Technique is detailed in the next chapters and appendices.

The Mechanics Transactions' Modeling Technique incorporates the rules enunciated in Sections 3.2 & 13.4. In addition this Technique includes the following:

1. The selection of the Mechanics Transaction Entities would be based on the Operation Transactions identified and detailed in Step 9 of the Enterprise Engineering Methodology and its Guidelines (Sections 8.9 & 9.9).

2. At the logical level, each Operation Transaction is reflected in the Enterprise Engineering Model by a main Mechanics Transaction Entity supported by additional Mechanics Transaction Entities that encompass the attributes needed by this main Mechanics Transaction. This main Mechanics Transaction Entity and its additional related entities form the Mechanics Transaction Profile.

3. The logical design of the Mechanics Transaction model incorporates the Data Modeling rules of Relational Normalization Data Modeling technique.

4. A Mechanics Transaction Instance (an instance of a Mechanics Transaction Entity) reflects an Operation Transaction Incidence.

5. There would be no direct relationships between the Master Data Activity Entities and the Mechanics Transaction Entities. Any relationships between the Master Data Activity Entities and the Mechanics Transaction Entities must be thru the Mechanics Session Entities. This is because the Master Data Activity Entities control the Mechanics Session Entities and not the Mechanics Transaction Entities which are regulated by the Mechanism Procedure Entities. Therefore no Master Data Activity FKs exist in the Mechanics Transaction Entities.

6. There would be no direct relationships between the Master Data Occurrence Event Entities and the Mechanics Transaction Entities. Any relationships between the Master Data Occurrence Event Entities and the Mechanics Transaction Entities must be thru the Mechanics Session Entities. This is because the Master Data Occurrence Event Entities trigger the Mechanics Session Entities and not the Mechanics Transaction Entities which are regulated by the Mechanism Procedure Entities. Therefore no Master Data Occurrence Event FKs exist in the Mechanics Transaction Entities.

7. There might be relationships including Many-to-Many relationships between the entities of the Mechanics Transaction. In SAM O NAOULO Modeling Technique these relationships would be resolved during the analysis and design of Mechanics Transactions as detailed in Section 13.4.

8. The Mechanics Transaction Entity must include a Transaction Timestamp attribute that provide the time and date when this transaction occurred.

9. The non-Primary Key attributes of the Mechanics Transaction Entities that are not Foreign Keys (FK) to the Master Data Entities or the Mechanism Procedure Entities or the Mechanics Session Entities or the Mechanics Transaction Entities would include:
   - Numeric additive measures: money, etc.

- Time related data: calendar figures, timestamps, etc.
- Descriptive data.

10. The aggregation of the data of the Mechanics Transaction Entities for reporting analysis will be based on formulas:
    - Having as parameters the attributes of the Mechanics Transaction Entities that are not Foreign Keys (FK) to the Master Data Entities or the Mechanism Procedure Entities or the Mechanics Session Entities.
    - Grouped by the attributes of the Mechanics Transaction Entities that are Foreign Keys (FK) to the Master Data Entities either directly or thru the Foreign Keys of the related Mechanics Session Entities. In rare cases the grouping could occur thru the attributes of the Mechanics Transaction Entities that are Foreign Keys (FK) to the Mechanism Procedure Entities or the Mechanics Session Entities to satisfy certain business needs.
    - The aggregation might be affected by the attributes of the Master Data Entities that are related directly to the Mechanics Transaction Entities thru the Foreign Keys in the Mechanics Transaction Entities or that are related indirectly to the Mechanics Transaction Entities thru the Foreign Keys of the Mechanics Session Entities to which the Transaction Entities are related.

There are some directions for Best of Practice that would help in the design, illustration, and visualization of the entities and attributes of the Mechanics Transactions:

1. The name of the Mechanics Transactions Entities and the attributes of these entities that are not FK to the Master Data or the Mechanism Procedures or the Mechanics Sessions shall start with the letter X.
2. The color of the Mechanics Transaction Entities would be light pink.
3. The order of the attributes of the Mechanics Transaction Entities would be first those that are part of the PK followed by those that are FKs, then those that are not part of the PK or FKs. The order of attributes within the PK, the FKs, and outside the PK and FKs would be first the Foreign Keys related to the Master Data: consecutively the Needs, Activities, Operators, Utilities, Locations, and Occurrences, followed by the Foreign Keys related to the Mechanism Procedure Entities, then Foreign Keys related to the Mechanics Session Entities, then Foreign Keys related to the Mechanics Transaction Entities, and then the attributes outside the FKs. All the attributes outside the PKs and FKs are attributes of the Mechanics Transactions. The attributes pertinent to Master Data, Mechanism, and Mechanics Sessions are all FKs.
4. The name of the Mechanics Transaction Entities would end with the word **TRX**.
5. Use Surrogate Keys (SK) as Primary Keys (PK) for the main Mechanics Transaction Entity.
6. Additional Best of Practice directions for Mechanics Transaction Associative Entities are provided in Section 13.4.

3.7 THE ANALYSIS & RESOLUTION OF MODIFIABLE DATA INSTANCES

A Modifiable Data Instance is a Data Instance that can be modified or updated for business

Dr. Eng. M. Naoulo

needs. To capture the data associated with the creation and modification of the Data Instances three techniques are considered. The analysis of these techniques is derived from the slowly changing dimensions developed by Ralph Kimball [13, Pages 95-105] which is itself inherited from the generic approach for capturing historical data.

1. **<u>Overwriting the old Data</u>**. (Similar to the slowly changing dimension Type 1). The old data is superseded by the new data and only one record Instance is kept.

2. **<u>Add new Record for every Modification of the Data.</u>** (Similar to the slowly moving dimension Type 2). Any modification of the data would require the creation of a new record Instance to put the new data. The old record Instance would be kept in the database with slight change to indicate its expiration.

3. **<u>Add additional Attributes/Fields to the Record</u>**. (Similar to the slowly changing dimension Type 3). Additional attributes/fields are created in the record Instance to store the new data.

3.7.1 The Analysis & Resolution of Modifiable Master Data Dimensions

The techniques to be used for the resolution of modifiable Master Data Dimensions depend on the business requirements for each Component of the Master Data:

<u>Need, Operator, Utility, & Location Components</u>

Storing the modification of data pertinent to these Components depends on the business requirements and the Component Members. The same reasoning used in Data Warehousing to assess which technique to be used to address the Dimension Entities would apply here. A good analysis was provided by Ralph Kimball [13].

<u>Activity Component</u>

Similar reasoning to the discussion detailed for the Mechanics Transactions (Ref. Section 3.7.4) would be applied here. The complexity when dealing with the Interaction between the Master Data Activity Entities and the Mechanics Session Entities and the need for the full benefit of keeping the Master Data Activities' historical data for the Enterprise Engineering imply the use of the second technique: Add new Record for every Modification of the Data.

<u>Occurrence Component</u>

The Occurrence Component reflects the Time and its hierarchy and the Events.
  - ➤ For the Time and its hierarchy there is no historical data attached to it. In this case, a customized solution to add additional Attributes/Fields to the Record as needed would be appropriate. Also adding new tables to store additional Attributes/Fields as needed would be considered.
  - ➤ For the Events the same reasoning used for the Need, Operator, Utility, and Location Components would apply here.

Dr. Eng. M. Naoulo

3.7.2 The Analysis & Resolution of Modifiable Mechanism Procedures

The same reasoning detailed for the Master Data Activities (Ref. Section 3.7.1) would apply here. The complexity when dealing with the Interaction between the Mechanism Procedure Entities and the Mechanics Transaction Entities and the need for full benefit of keeping Mechanism Procedures historical data for the Enterprise Engineering imply the use of the second technique: Add new Record for every Modification of the Data.

3.7.3 The Analysis & Resolution of Modifiable Mechanics Sessions

The Operation Session Incidence is created once and would not be modified unless there is an error. Therefore the first technique: Overwriting the old Data is applied here. The second technique: Add new Record for every Modification of the Data might be applied if there is a business need to keep the errors' data.

3.7.4 The Analysis & Resolution of Modifiable Mechanics Transactions

The Operation Session Incidences generate Operation Transaction Incidences. The Operation Transaction Incidence is created once and could be modified many times. The Mechanics Transaction Instance represents/reflects/models the Operation Transaction Incidence. The three techniques indicated in Section 3.7 are evaluated hereafter to capture the data associated with the creation and modification of the Mechanics Transaction Instances.

1. **<u>Overwriting the old Data</u>**. The old data of the Transaction is superseded by the new data and only one Transaction Instance is kept. This technique is simple from the design point of view of the Transaction Entities however it implies complexity when dealing with the Interaction between the Mechanics Transaction Entities and the Mechanics Session Entities. It necessitates the creation of Many-to-Many relationships between these entities. Furthermore the transactional historical data related to all the Mechanics Sessions affecting the Mechanics Transaction (except the most recent data) are lost. If there is a need to keep this historical data, the attributes of the Transaction have to be moved to the Associative Entities resolving the above Many-to-Many relationships. Losing the historical data is not advantageous to the Enterprise Engineering System; also the above Associative Entities add additional complexity that could be prevented by choosing the second technique below. Therefore it is not advisable to use this technique.

2. **<u>Add new Transactions Record for every Modification of the Transactional Data.</u>** Any modification of the transactional data would require the creation of a new Mechanics Transaction Instance to put the new data. The record of the old Mechanics Transaction Instance would be kept in the database with slight change to indicate its expiration. This technique does not add additional complexity to the design and structure of the Transaction Entities/tables and does not require Many-to-Many relationships between the Mechanics Session Entities and the Mechanics Session Entities. This technique might require the addition of recursive relationships affecting the Mechanics Transaction Entities to capture the relationships between the associated instances within these entities. Also this technique implies that all historical data are kept in the Mechanics Transaction Profile Entities and therefore the size of these entities would increase if the business generates many transactional data modification.

This technique would provide the full benefit of storing Transactions' historical data for the Enterprise Engineering System of Apparatus, Machinery, and Operation as well as avoiding additional complexity to the design of the Enterprise Engineering Model. Therefore this technique is recommended and would be adopted in SAM O NAOULO Modeling Technique to store the Transactions' historical data. The modeling technique rules in this document reflect this technique.

A variation of this technique is to create a Many-to-Many relationship between the Mechanics Session Entity and the Mechanics Transaction Entity, resolve this Many-to-Many relationship thru an Associative Entity, and store all historical data in it. This solution is similar to the one adopted in the previous technique "Overwriting the old Data" to store historical data.

3. **Add additional Attributes/Fields to the Transactions Record**. The new data of the Transaction is stored in additional attributes/fields allocated to the Transaction Instance record. This technique adds additional complexity to the design and structure of the Transaction Entities/tables, and this complexity is comparable or more difficult than the complexity incurred in the first technique. This technique also requires Many-to-Many relationships between the Mechanics Transaction Entities and the Mechanics Session Entities. Therefore it is not advisable to use this technique unless in special cases.

3.8   CORRECTION OF GAPS OF INFORMATION ENGINEERING

The Data Modeling technique of the Information Engineering approach was established based on the Relational Data Modeling rules of Normal Forms: Six Normal Forms, Boyce-Codd Normal Form, and Domain/Key Normal Form developed by Dr. E. F. Codd [2], Dr. C. Date [3], and others. In practice the modeling progression stops usually at the 3rd Normal form: 3NF. This approach was popularized by Clive Finkelstein [6] and James Martin [4 & 5] in the 1980s and early 1990s and used in Data Architecture as the base for On-Line Transactional Processing (OLTP).

The Information Engineering approach suffers from many weaknesses:
1. No clear distinction between the Master Data and Transactional Data.
2. The link between the Process Modeling and Data Modeling is thru the CRUD Matrix. The CRUD Matrix is a powerful tool for directing the applications coding; however in Object Oriented Analysis, Design, and Programming, messages are used between Classes to request the CRUD on the Objects, and each Class is responsible for its own CRUD. The explosive expansion of the Internet and the languages associated with it that are based on the Object Oriented approach: Java, C++, etc., decreased the luster of the CRUD Matrix.
3. There is confusion and no clear distinction between Processes, Activities, and Procedures.
4. The Processes are not depicted by entities and attributes.
5. The Process Modeling is very weak in incorporating the rules associated with the Sessions and Transactions.
6. The Process Modeling interacts with the Data without distinction between Master Data

and Transactional Data.
7. No clear distinction between the roles of the Master Data.

The Enterprise Engineering curriculum based on the System of Apparatus and Machinery, and their Operation (**SAM O NAOULO**) and its Data Modeling Technique rectify the above gaps and enhance the design thoroughness:

1. In Enterprise Engineering there is a very clear distinction between the Master Data and Transactional Data.
2. In Enterprise Engineering there is a very clear distinction between the roles of Master Data: Needs, Activities, Operators, Utilities, Locations, and Occurrences. This distinction helps tremendously in the design and illustration of the Enterprise Engineering Model.
3. In Enterprise Engineering the Processes, Activities, and Procedures are depicted by entities and attributes and modeled thru Data Modeling Entity-Relationship Diagrams.
4. In Enterprise Engineering there is a very clear distinction between the Business Processes and Activities versus the Procedures. The Business Processes and their rules are depicted and implemented thru the Master data Activity Entities while Machinery Procedures and their rules are depicted and implemented thru the Mechanism Entities. The enterprise functioning information is implemented thru the Mechanics Session Entities and attributes and the enterprise transactional information is implemented thru the Mechanics Transaction Entities and attributes.
5. Enterprise Engineering provides the Interlink between the Business Processes and the Operational information and illustrates this Interlink in the Enterprise Engineering Model thru the relationships between the Master Data Activity Entities and the Mechanics Session Entities.
6. Enterprise Engineering provides the Interlink between the Machinery Procedures and the Transactional information and illustrates this Interlink in the Enterprise Engineering Model thru the relationships between the Mechanism Procedure Entities and the Mechanics Transaction Entities
7. In Enterprise Engineering the distinction between the Mechanism Procedures, Master Data Dimensions, and Mechanics Sessions and Transactions and the concept of entities profile is very suitable for Object Oriented Programming.
8. The decomposition of Many-to-One and Many-to-Many relationships between the constituents:
   - From the Master Data Dimensions (except Activities and Events) to the Mechanism Procedures
   - From the Master Data Dimensions to the Mechanics Sessions
   - From the Master Data Dimensions to the Mechanics Transactions
   - From the Mechanism Procedures to the Mechanics Transactions
   - From the Mechanics Sessions to the Mechanics Transactions
   and the absence of relationships between:
   - The Master Data Activities and the Mechanism Procedures, and between
   - The Mechanism Procedures and the Mechanics Sessions
   provide a very strong base for applying Object Oriented Programming as the structure of the databases becomes very suitable for Class Modeling.
7. Enterprise Engineering incorporates the business rules associated with the Sessions and

Transactions.

3.9   MODELING PARADIGM SHIFT

The Enterprise Engineering System of Apparatus, Machinery, and Operation **SAM O NAOULO** provides a comprehensive approach for analyzing the functioning of Enterprises. The SAM O NAOULO Modeling Technique conceived to support Enterprise Engineering is very powerful and is used for On-Line Mechanical Processing (OLMP).

The Enterprise Engineering Model reflects the Apparatus, Machinery, and Operation of the Enterprises. The Information Engineering Model reflects only part of the Apparatus and the Operation Transactions; it does not reflect the Operation Sessions (unless there is a specific need to analyze these sessions in the model). All data elements needed by the On-Line Transactional Processing (OLTP) would be included in the Enterprise Engineering. The Enterprise Engineering Model is superset (though using more integrated and sophisticated modeling technique) of the Information Engineering Model and therefore could be used for modeling of transactional info. On-Line Mechanical Processing would permit to achieve ample and thorough improvement and revitalization of the Enterprises (Ref. Part II).

SAM O NAOULO Modeling Technique provides thorough grouping and classification of the Master Data and a comprehensive approach to reflect the link of the Apparatus with Operation Sessions and Transactions. Therefore the Enterprise Engineering System of Apparatus, Machinery, and Operation SAM O NAOULO and its Modeling Technique would be excellent foundation for data modeling of the enterprise.

The Enterprise Engineering Models would be essential tools for improvement and revitalization of the operation and functioning of the Enterprises. They would contribute to conceive reliable Enterprise and Business Models.

3.10 SAM O NAOULO MODELING TECHNIQUE'S SUMMARY RULES

Following is the summary of the basic rules of SAM O NAOULO Modeling Technique (Ref. Tables 3.2 & 3.3):

Master Data

Rule 1: Within a Master Data Dimension or Associative Profile One-to-One and One-to-Many relationships could exist. No Many-to-Many relationships.

Rule 2: Within a Master Data Component and across Master Data Dimension Profiles One-to-Many and Many-to-Many relationships could exist. One-to-One relationships are Not Common. Specific restrictions involve the Master Data Activities. Many-to-Many relationships would be decomposed.

Rule 3: Across Master Data Components or involving Master Data Associative Entities resulting from relationships across Master Data Components One-to-Many and Many-to-Many relationships could exist. One-to-One relationships are Not Common. Specific restrictions involve the Master Data Activities and Occurrence Events. Many-to-Many relationships would be decomposed.

Rule 4: One-to-Many and Many-to-Many Recursive relationships could exist within the Master Data. One-to-One Recursive relationships are Not Common. Many-to-Many relationships would be decomposed. Many-to-Many Recursive relationships affecting the Master Data Activities are Not Common.

Mechanism Procedures

Rule 5: Within a Mechanism Procedure Profile One-to-One and One-to-Many relationships could exist. No Many-to-Many relationships.

Rule 6: Across Mechanism Procedure Profiles One-to-Many and Many-to-Many relationships could exist; One-to-One relationships are Not Common. Many-to-Many relationships would be decomposed.

Rule 7: One-to-Many Recursive relationships could exist

within the Mechanism. One-to-One and Many-to-Many Recursive relationships are Not Common.

Mechanics Sessions

Rule 8: Within a Mechanics Session Profile One-to-One and One-to-Many relationships could exist. No Many-to-Many relationships.

Rule 9: Across Mechanics Session Profiles One-to-Many and Many-to-Many relationships could exist. One-to-One relationships are Not Common. Many-to-Many relationships would be decomposed.

Rule 10: One-to-Many and Many-to-Many Recursive relationships could exist within the Mechanics Sessions. One-to-One Recursive relationships are Not Common. Many-to-Many relationships would be decomposed.

Mechanics Transactions

Rule 11: Within a Mechanics Transaction Profile One-to-One and One-to-Many relationships could exist. No Many-to-Many relationships.

Rule 12: Across Mechanics Transaction Profiles One-to-Many and Many-to-Many relationships could exist. One-to-One relationships are Not Common. Many-to-Many relationships would be decomposed.

Rule 13: One-to-Many and Many-to-Many Recursive relationships could exist within the Mechanics Transactions. One-to-One Recursive relationships are Not Common. Many-to-Many relationships would be decomposed.

From Master Data to Mechanism Procedures

Rule 14: No relationships between the Master Data Activity Entities and the Mechanism Procedure Entities.

Rule 15: One-to-One relationships are Not Common.

Rule 16: One-to-Many relationships are OK. Specific restrictions involve the Master Data Activities.

Rule 17: Many-to-One relationships would be decomposed.

Specific restrictions involve the Master Data Activities and Occurrence Events.

Rule 18: Many-to-Many relationships would be decomposed. Specific restrictions involve the Master Data Activities and Occurrence Events.

From Master Data to Mechanics Sessions

Rule 19: One-to-One relationships are Not Common.

Rule 20: One-to-Many relationships are OK.

Rule 21: Many-to-One relationships would be decomposed.

Rule 22: Many-to-Many relationships would be decomposed.

Rule 23: A Mechanics Session Instance is mandatory related to only one Master Data Elementary Activity Instance.

Rule 24: A Mechanics Session Instance is mandatory related to only one Master Data Occurrence Event Instance.

From Master Data to Mechanics Transactions

Rule 25: No relationships between the Master Data Activity Entities and the Mechanics Transaction Entities.

Rule 14: No relationships between the Master Data Occurrence Event Entities and the Mechanism Transaction Entities.

Rule 26: One-to-One relationships are Not Common.

Rule 27: One-to-Many relationships are OK. Specific restrictions involve the Master Data Activities and Occurrence Events.

Rule 28: Many-to-One relationships would be decomposed. Specific restrictions involve the Master Data Activities and Occurrence Events.

Rule 29: Many-to-Many relationships would be decomposed. Specific restrictions involve the Master Data Activities and Occurrence Events.

Between Mechanism Procedures & Mechanics Sessions

Rule 30: No relationships.

From Mechanism Procedures to Mechanics Transactions

Rule 31: One-to-One relationships are Not Common.

Dr. Eng. M. Naoulo

Rule 32: One-to-Many relationships are OK.

Rule 33: Many-to-One relationships would be decomposed.

Rule 34: Many-to-Many relationships would be decomposed.

Rule 35: A Mechanics Transaction Instance is mandatory related to at least one Mechanism Elementary Procedure Instance.

From Mechanics Sessions to Mechanics Transactions

Rule 36: One-to-One relationships are Not Common.

Rule 37: One-to-Many relationships are OK.

Rule 38: Many-to-One relationships would be decomposed.

Rule 39: Many-to-Many relationships would be decomposed.

Rule 40: A Mechanics Transaction Instance is mandatory related to at least one Mechanics Session Instance.

Dr. Eng. M. Naoulo

4.   Enterprise Intelligence

Enterprise Intelligence aims to analyze the performance of the enterprise thru historical, current, and predictive assessment of the enterprise's operation. It is based on analyzing, perceiving, evaluating, and mining enterprise Process Data such as time, effort, cost, revenues, and Customer Satisfaction aggregated by products, organization units, line of business, etc. to enhance decision making in order to better manage the enterprise and guide it in a competitive environment.

The Enterprise Engineering Model forms the basis for the devise and design of the Business and Enterprise Intelligence Data Marts. A Central Data Repository adopting the Enterprise Engineering Model would form the source of data that would be propagated to these Data Marts:

> **Business Intelligence Data Marts.** These Data Marts constitute the base for the classical Data Warehousing's Online Analytical Processing (OLAP) and provide query and reporting covering the historical aggregation of transactional features of the Enterprise. The transactional part of the Enterprise Engineering Model constitutes the base for Online Transactional Processing (OLTP) and would be the basis for the devise, design, and construction of the Business Intelligence Data Marts supporting the OLAP.

> **Enterprise Intelligence Data Marts.** These Data Marts constitute the base for the enterprise's improvement and revitalization and provide query and reporting covering the historical aggregation of sessions' features to illustrate the operation of the Enterprise. The functioning part of the Enterprise Engineering Model constitutes the base for Online Mechanical Processing (OLMP) and would be the basis for the devise, design, and construction of the Enterprise Intelligence Data Marts.

4.1   ENTERPRISE INTELLIGENCE DATA MARTS

The Enterprise Intelligence (EI) Data Marts do not deal with Transactional Data. Transactional Data is associated with OLTP and support the Business Intelligence analysis. Also EI Data Marts are different from Bill Inmon's Oper Marts which are defined as [11]:

"The Oper Mart is a subset of data derived from the operational data store used in tactical analysis and usually stored in multi-dimensional manner".

The EI Data Marts deal with Process Data. They are composed of Dimension and Fact Entities in a similar way to the BI Data Marts. The Fact Entities incorporate the process and session measures while the Dimension Entities incorporate the fact measures' aggregation levels and the description of these levels.

4.2   BUSINESS   INTELLIGENCE   VERSUS   ENTERPRISE INTELLIGENCE

Business Intelligence is dealing with the Mechanics Transaction Data, provides their analysis, and aims to evaluate the Operation of the enterprise thru historical and current assessment of this Transactional Data. Enterprise Intelligence is dealing with the Mechanics Process Data, provides

Dr. Eng. M. Naoulo

their analysis, and aims to evaluate the Operation of the enterprise thru historical and predictive assessment of this Process Data. Business Intelligence supports the Operation's transactional evaluation and assessment while Enterprise Intelligence supports Business Process Management, Business Process Improvement, and Business Process Re-engineering. Both Business and Enterprise Intelligence aim to support and enhance the decision making of the directors.

4.3 CONSTRUCTION OF THE TRANSACTIONAL PART OF THE ENTERPRISE ENGINEERING MODEL

The transactional part of the Enterprise Engineering Model does not include the Mechanics Sessions nor the Master Data component related the HOW (the Activities). The transactional part of the Enterprise Engineering Model consists of the Mechanics Transactions as described in Section 2.8.3.2. Appendix D presents the approaches to get the Transactional Data Model from the Enterprise Engineering Model.

4.3.1 Characterization of the Transactional Part of the Enterprise Engineering Model

The transactional part of the Enterprise Engineering Model holds all the characteristics of the Mechanics Transactions as detailed in Section 2.8.3.2.

4.3.2 Building the Transactional Part of the Enterprise Engineering Model

Building the transactional part of the Enterprise Engineering Model follows the SAM O NAOULO Modeling Technique detailed in Chapters 2, 3, 4, 5, 12, 13 & 14.

4.4 DESIGN OF THE BUSINESS INTELLIGENCE DATA MARTS FROM THE TRANSACTIONAL PART OF THE ENTERPRISE ENGINEERING MODEL

In the Enterprise Engineering Model many relationships between the Transactions and the Master Data are established thru the Mechanism Procedures and Mechanics Sessions. Removing the Mechanism Procedures and Mechanics Sessions from the Enterprise Engineering Model would necessitate establishing direct links between the Transactions and the Master Data to substitute those relationships.

The role of the components of the Master Data used in Enterprise Engineering is examined within the prospect of OLTP:

1. **Needs:** This component contributes mainly to define the objectives of the analysis of the enterprise's requests vis-à-vis financial, market, Customer Satisfaction, etc. The Needs will be part of the objectives of the design and construction of the Data Marts involving these requests but very often not expressed explicitly in this design.
2. **Activities**: This component is associated with Process Modeling and depicts the enterprise's Business Processes. The Activities control the Mechanics Sessions supporting the functioning of the enterprise and will not be part of the BI Data Marts.

Dr. Eng. M. Naoulo

3. **Operators:** This component is involved in most of the Data Marts.
4. **Utilities:** This component is involved in most of the Data Marts.
5. **Locations:** This component is involved in most of the Data Marts.
6. **Occurrences:** This component is involved in all the Data Marts. In fact the Time Dimension is a mandatory part of any OLTP Data Mart. However the Occurrence Events will very often not expressed explicitly in the design of the BI Data Marts.

4.4.1 The Structure of the BI Dimension Entities

The BI Dimension Entities include descriptive non-transactional data and non-process data. The Structure of the BI Dimension Entities follows two schemas (more details could be found in the Data Warehousing literature):

1. **Star Schema**: This schema is suitable if the hierarchy of the Dimension Entities is straight. Each Dimension's Entities would, at the physical level of the data model, structured in one table that includes all the features of a Dimension. De-normalization pertinent to repetitions of fields is acceptable. At the logical and physical levels the illustration of the Fact and the Dimension Entities reflects a Star shape.
2. **Snowflake Schema:** This schema is suitable for non-straight hierarchy of Dimension Entities: Example the Day-Time Dimension: the months and the weeks do not form straight hierarchy. This schema incorporates, at the logical and physical levels, all the features of a Dimension in many entities or many tables. De-normalization pertinent to repetitions of fields at the physical level is also acceptable. At the logical and physical levels the illustration of the Fact and the Dimension Entities reflects a Snowflake shape.

It is important to note that **Conformed Dimensions** (Dimensions related to many Fact tables) are very useful in the overall design of the Data Marts Architecture.

4.4.2 The Structure of the BI Fact Entities

The BI Fact Entities include transactional data and Foreign Keys. The Structure of the BI Fact Entities is based on a central Fact Entity(ies) surrounded by Dimension Entities. The relationships between the Dimension Entities and the Fact Entity(ies) are One-to-Many identifying relationships (if Surrogate Keys are used for the Fact tables these relationships would be non-identifying). More details could be found in the Data Warehousing literature.

4.4.3 Design of the BI Dimension Entities based on the Master Data Dimensions

At a high level, the Star Schema BI Dimension Entities' structure resembles the Master Data Dimensions' structure. To derive and customize the design of the Star Schema BI Dimension Entities from the design of the Master Data Dimension Entities the following rules are recommended:

➢ The Dimensions of the Master Data would participate to form directly the Dimensions of the BI Data Marts (very often One-to-One correlation between a Master Data Dimension and a BI Dimension exists).
➢ The entities of the Master Data Dimension Profile are collapsed to form one BI Dimension Entity using de-normalization.

Dr. Eng. M. Naoulo

➤ The entities of the hierarchies of the Master Data Dimensions would be collapsed to form one BI Dimension entity using de-normalization.

➤ Some attributes in the Master Data Dimensions might not be needed in the BI Dimensions.

➤ The attributes of the BI Dimensions would very often replicate (one-to-one or using some formulas) the attributes of the Master Data Dimensions.

The directions for Best of Practice that would help in the design, illustration, and visualization of the entities and attributes of the BI Dimension Entities are:

1. The name of the BI Dimension Entities and the attributes of these entities shall start with the letters **DIM** followed by the name of the Component of the corresponding Master Data: **NED** for Needs, **ACT** for Activities, **OPR** for Operators, **UTL** for Utilities, **LOC** for Locations, and **OCC** for Occurrences (Ref. Section 3.3)

2. The color of the BI Dimension Entities and the order of their attributes would follow the same Best of Practice adopted for the Master Data Entities (Ref. Section 3.3).

4.4.4 Design of the BI Dimension Entities based on the Master Data Associative Entities

The Master Data Associative Entities (Ref. Section 2.9.1.2) provide data pertinent to the association of the parents Master Data Entities involved in the Master Data Associative Entity. Three solutions to translate a Master Data Associative Entity to BI Dimension(s) are examined.

1. Build a Snowflake Schema BI Dimension. This will accommodate the structure of the BI Dimension Entities and the Master Data Associative Entity and its parents.

2. If there is no explicit need of the data pertinent to the association of the parents Master Data Entities involved in the Master Data Associative Entity, or this data is incorporated in the features (attributes) of the Fact Entity, use the parents of the Master Data Associative Entity as independent Dimensions and there is no need for the Snowflake BI Dimension.

3. If there is no explicit need for the descriptive data that is pertinent to a parent(s) of the Master Data Associative Entity, or this data is incorporated in the features (attributes) of the Fact Entity, do not incorporate these parent(s) as independent BI Dimension(s) and there is no need for the Snowflake BI Dimension.

4. If the number of rows of the Master Data Associative Entity is not huge, build a Star schema BI Dimension Entity with de-normalization to accommodate the repetition of attributes of the parents of the Master Data Associative Entity.

The choice between these four solutions depends on the requirements of the BI Query and Reporting.

At a high level, the Snowflake Schema BI Dimension Entities' structure resembles the Master Data Associative Entities' structure. To derive and customize the design of the Snowflake Schema BI Dimension Entities from the design of the Master Data Associative Entities the following rules are recommended:

➤ The Master Data Associative Entities would participate to form directly the Snowflake Schema BI Dimension Entities (very often One-to-One correlation between a Master Data Associative Entity and a Snowflake Schema BI Dimension Entity exists).

Dr. Eng. M. Naoulo

➤ The entities of the Master Data Associative Entities Profile are collapsed to form one Snowflake Schema BI Dimension Entity using de-normalization.

➤ The entities of the hierarchies of the Master Data Dimensions of the parents of the Master Data Associative Entities would be collapsed to form BI Dimension entities using de-normalization.

➤ Some attributes from the Master Data Associative Entities might not be needed in the Snowflake Schema BI Dimension Entities.

➤ The attributes of the Snowflake Schema BI Dimension Entities would very often replicate (one-to-one or using some formulas) the attributes of the Master Data Associative Entities.

The directions for Best of Practice that would help in the design, illustration, and visualization of the entities and attributes of the BI Dimension Entities based on Master Data Associative Entities:

1. The name of the BI Dimension Entities and the attributes of these entities shall be as in Section 4.4.3.

2. The name of the Snowflake Schema BI Dimension Entities corresponding to the Master Data Associative Entities resulting across the Master Data Components and the attributes of these entities shall start with the letters **DIM** followed by the letter **A**.

3. The color of the Snowflake Schema BI Dimension Entities corresponding to the Master Data Associative Entities would be medium blue as the Master Data Associative Entities resulting across the Master Data Components (Ref. Section 13.1).

4. The order of the attributes of the Snowflake Schema BI Dimension Entities corresponding to the Master Data Associative Entities would follow the same Best of Practice adopted for the Master Data entities (Ref. Section 3.3).

4.4.5 Design of the BI Fact Entities based on the Mechanics Transaction Entities

The BI Fact Entities are designed to respond to the BI Query and Reporting business needs. The Fact attributes of BI Fact Entities are deduced from the measure attributes of the Mechanics Transaction Entities. To derive and customize the design of the BI Fact Entities from the design of the Mechanics Transaction Entities the following rules are recommended:

➤ Many attributes from the Mechanics Transaction Entities might not be needed in the BI Fact Entities.

➤ The attributes of the BI Fact Entities reflect measure attributes of the Mechanics Transaction Entities or are the results of computation formulas involving these measure attributes.

➤ The aggregation grouping of the BI Fact Attributes defines the Dimensions of the BI Data Marts.

The Key of the BI Fact Entities is the concatenation of the Foreign Keys to the BI Dimension Entities (if Surrogate Keys are used, a unique Alternate Key is constructed from the concatenation of the Foreign Keys). The attributes of the BI Fact Entities are the counts, measures, aggregation of measures, etc. related to the attributes of the **SAM O NAOULO** Transactions. The selection of these measures depends on the requirements of the BI Query and

Dr. Eng. M. Naoulo

Reporting.

The directions for Best of Practice that would help in the design, illustration, and visualization of the entities and attributes of the BI Fact Entities:

1. The name of the BI Fact Entities and the attributes of these entities that are not FK to the BI Dimension Entities shall start with the letter **F**.
2. The color of the BI Fact Entities would be light green.
3. The order of the attributes of the BI Fact Entities would be first the PK followed by the FKs (if a Surrogate Key is not used, the concatenation of the FKs is the PK), then those that are not part of the PK or FKs. The order of attributes within the PK or the FKs would be first the Foreign Keys related to the BI Dimension Entities: consecutively the Needs, Activities, Operators, Utilities, Locations, and Occurrences. All the attributes outside the PK and FKs are attributes derived from the attributes of the Mechanics Transaction Entities. The attributes pertinent to the BI Dimension Entities are all FKs.

4.5 CONSTRUCTION OF THE FUNCTIONING PART OF THE ENTERPRISE ENGINEERING MODEL

The functioning part of the Enterprise Engineering Model holds the Process Data and does not include the Mechanics Transactions or the Mechanism Procedures. It consists of the Mechanics Sessions as described in Section 2.8.3.1 and its associated Master Data.

4.5.1 Characterization of the Functioning Part of the Enterprise Engineering Model

The functioning part of the Enterprise Engineering Model holds all the characteristics of the Mechanics Sessions as detailed in Section 2.8.3.1.

4.5.2 Building the Functioning Part of the Enterprise Engineering Model

Building the functioning part of the Enterprise Engineering Model follows the SAM O NAOULO Modeling Technique detailed in Chapters 2, 3, 4, 5, 12, 13 & 14.

4.6 DESIGN OF THE ENTERPRISE INTELLIGENCE DATA MARTS FROM THE FUNCTIONING PART OF THE ENTERPRISE ENGINEERING MODEL

The Enterprise Intelligence Data Marts would use the same Dimensional Technique used by the BI Data Marts. The EI Data Marts include all components of the Master Data.

4.6.1 The Structure of the EI Dimension Entities

The EI Dimension Entities include descriptive non-transactional and non-process data. The Structure of the EI Dimensional Entities is similar to the Structure of the BI Dimensional Entities and follows two schemas: Snowflake and Star schemas.

Here also **Conformed Dimensions** are very useful in the overall design of the EI Data Marts

Architecture. Using Conformed Dimensions across BI and EI Data Marts simultaneously would provide additional benefits.

4.6.2 The Structure of the EI Fact Entities

The EI Fact Entities include process data and Foreign Keys. The Structure of the EI Fact Entities is similar to the Structure of the BI Fact Entities (Ref. Section 4.4.2). It is based on a central Fact Entity(ies) surrounded by Dimension Entities.

4.6.3 Design of the EI Dimension Entities based on the Master Data Dimensions

The design of EI Dimension Entities based on Master Data Dimensions and the directions for Best of Practice are similar to the design of BI Dimension Entities based on the Master Data Dimensions and their directions for Best of Practice (Ref. Section 4.4.3). Diagram 10.9 provides an example of an EI Data Mart where the EI Dimension Entities are directly derived from the Master Data Dimension Entities.

4.6.4 Design of the EI Dimension Entities based on the Master Data Associative Entities

The design of EI Dimension Entities based on Master Data Associative Entities and the directions for Best of Practice are similar to the design of BI Dimension Entities based on Master Data Associative Entities and their directions for Best of Practice (Ref. Section 4.4.4). Diagram 10.10 provides an example of an EI Data Mart based on Master Data Dimension and Associative Entities.

4.6.5 Design of the EI Fact Entities based on the Mechanics Session Entities

The design of EI Fact Entities based on the Mechanics Session Entities and the directions for Best of Practice are similar to the design of BI Fact Entities based on the Mechanics Transaction Entities and their directions for Best of Practice (Ref. Section 4.4.5).

The Key of the EI Fact Entities is the concatenation of the keys of the EI Dimension Entities (if Surrogate Keys are used, a unique Alternate Key is constructed from the concatenation of these Keys). The attributes of the EI Fact Entities are the counts, measures, aggregation of measures, cost, etc. related to the attributes of the **SAM O NAOULO** Sessions. The selection of these measures depends on the requirements of the EI Query and Reporting.

4.7   SLICING & DICING OF BI & EI DATA MARTS

Since the BI and EI Data Marts are using the same Dimensions which are based on the Master Data Dimension and Associative Entities, it is very easy to slice and dice the data as per any Master Data Component and Master Data Hierarchy Level.

5. Enterprise Data Mapping: Legacy Systems, Central Data Repository, Data Marts

The Central Data Repository, based on the Enterprise Engineering Model, uses the SAM O NAOULO Modeling Technique. This chapter describes the mapping of the enterprise's data within the context of the Enterprise Engineering Model.

By adopting this model as a basis for the Central Data Repository design and BI and EI Data Marts design, the mapping is significantly simplified and streamlined. There are three steps of mapping:
  - From the Legacy Systems to the Central Data Repository.
  - From the Central Data Repository to the BI Data Marts.
  - From the Central Data Repository to the EI Data Marts.

5.1 MAPPING THE MASTER DATA FROM THE LEGACY SYSTEMS TO THE CENTRAL DATA REPOSITORY

The mapping of the Master Data from the Legacy Systems to the Central Data Repository could be developed in a similar way to the mapping from the Legacy Systems to the ODS (more details could be found in the Data Architecture literature). The ODS uses Relational 3NF Data Modeling technique (sometimes the Data Vault technique is used [19]) while the Central Data Repository uses the SAM O NAOULO Modeling Technique.

It is important to note that Data Integration, Consolidation, and Quality Assurance are very important tasks that need to be performed and accomplished during this step.

5.2 MAPPING THE TRANSACTIONAL DATA FROM THE LEGACY SYSTEMS TO THE CENTRAL DATA REPOSITORY

The mapping of the Transactional Data from the Legacy Systems to the Central Data Repository could be developed in a similar way to the mapping from the Legacy Systems to the ODS.

Additional complexities arise if similar transactions are handled by many Legacy Systems. The modeling of the Central Data Repository's Mechanics Transactions should support the consolidation of Legacy System Transactions and the integration and consolidation of their Master Data.

5.3 MAPPING THE PROCESS DATA FROM THE LEGACY SYSTEMS TO THE CENTRAL DATA REPOSITORY

Currently very few Legacy Systems incorporate the Process Data of the Enterprise. Furthermore these systems might not hold Process Data that is suitable for the EI Query and Reporting requirements. There would be the needs to develop systems and databases to capture Process

Dr. Eng. M. Naoulo

data and then map this data to the Sessions Data of the Central Data Repository. The mapping of this data could be developed in a similar way to the mapping of the Transactional Data from the Legacy Systems to the Central Data Repository (Ref. Section 5.2).

There are three approaches to accommodate the Process Data with the Source/Legacy Systems: Enhance the Legacy Systems to incorporate the Process data and to accommodate any new data requirements, or design and implementation of new Systems to accommodate the Mechanics Process Data and run them in parallel with the Legacy Systems, or design and implementation of new Source Systems to replace the Legacy Systems and accommodate the Mechanics Process Data.

5.3.1 Enhance the Legacy Systems to incorporate the Mechanics Process Data

The OLTP Legacy Systems (applications, programs, and databases) would be updated to accommodate **SAM O NAOULO** requirements. This undertaking is accomplished as hereafter:

 - ➤ The Legacy Systems data were gathered including their Database Schemas and the DDL.
 - ➤ The Legacy Systems Data Models were reversed-engineered from the DDL (if possible).
 - ➤ The Data Models and Databases were updated to accommodate capturing **SAM O NAOULO** data requirements.
 - ➤ The coding of the OLTP Legacy Systems was performed to accommodate capturing **SAM O NAOULO** data requirements.
 - ➤ The frequency of extraction from the Legacy Systems to the Central Data Repository would be set.
 - ➤ Data Profiling, Data Cleansing, Data Quality assessment, and Metadata design and generation would be added to assure the integrity and correctness of data on which the strategic decisions will be based.
 - ➤ After the design of the Apparatus, Machinery, Operation, and the Enterprise Engineering Model reflecting them, the transformation rules to load the data into the Enterprise Engineering Model would be developed. The ETL development would be accomplished using an ETL tool.

This approach is cumbersome and not recommended unless the number of Legacy Systems is small and/or these systems were developed recently, well documented, and most of the staff who worked on them are still working in the company.

5.3.2 Design and implementation of new Systems to accommodate the Mechanics Process Data

The new Systems should accommodate the Mechanics Process Data. This undertaking is accomplished as hereafter:

 - ➤ The **SAM O NAOULO** data requirements for the Mechanics Process Data should be gathered.
 - ➤ Data Models should be developed for the new Systems.
 - ➤ The coding of these source systems should be performed and the systems tested.
 - ➤ The frequency of extraction from the Legacy Systems and from the new source systems to the Central Data Repository would be set.
 - ➤ Data Profiling, Data Cleansing, Data Quality assessment, and Metadata design and

Dr. Eng. M. Naoulo

generation would be added to assure the integrity and correctness of data on which the strategic decisions will be based.

➢ Metadata Integration and Consolidation with the OLTP Legacy Systems should be performed.

➢ After the design of the Apparatus, Machinery, Operation, and the Enterprise Engineering Model reflecting them, the transformation rules to load the data into the Central Data Repository would be developed. The ETL development would be accomplished using an ETL tool.

➢ Data Integration and Consolidation with the OLTP Legacy Systems and the Central Data Repository should be performed

This approach is difficult to implement. It adds to the number of source systems from which data should be extracted, integrated, and consolidated. However it is the best solution if the number of Legacy Systems is high, not developed recently, not well documented, most of the staff who worked on them left the development area, and the number of the new systems to accommodate the Mechanics Process Data is low.

5.3.3 Design and implementation of new Source Systems to replace the Legacy Systems and accommodate the Mechanics Process Data

The new Source Systems should replace the Legacy Systems and accommodate the Mechanics Process Data. This undertaking is accomplished as hereafter:

➢ The **SAM O NAOULO** data requirements for the Mechanics Transactional and Process Data should be gathered.

➢ The Legacy Systems data were gathered including their Database Schemas and the DDL.

➢ The Legacy Systems Data Models were reversed-engineered from the DDL (if possible).

➢ Data Models should be developed for the new Source Systems.

➢ The coding of these Source Systems should be performed and the systems tested.

➢ The frequency of extraction from the new Source Systems to the Central Data Repository would be set.

➢ Data Profiling, Data Cleansing, Data Quality assessment, and Metadata design and generation would be added to assure the integrity and correctness of data on which the strategic decisions will be based.

➢ Metadata Integration and Consolidation between the Systems should be performed.

➢ After the design of the Apparatus, Machinery, Operation, and the Enterprise Engineering Model reflecting them, the transformation rules to load the data into the Central Data Repository would be developed. The ETL development would be accomplished using an ETL tool.

➢ Data Integration and Consolidation with the Central Data Repository should be performed.

➢ The old Legacy Systems should be phased out.

This approach implies the overhaul of the FR&TP systems. However it is lengthy. It is the best solution for the long run strategy. It is not difficult to implement if the number of Legacy Systems is not high and well documented.

Dr. Eng. M. Naoulo

5.4 MAPPING THE DATA OF THE CENTRAL DATA REPOSITORY TO THE BI DATA MARTS

The mapping of the Transactional Data of the Central Data Repository to the Business Intelligence Data Marts is simple and straightforward.

5.4.1 Mapping the Master Data to the BI Dimensional Data

Since the design and construction of the BI Dimension Entities (Sections 4.4.3 & 4.4.4) is based directly on the design and attributes of the Master Data Entities, the mapping from the Master Data in the Central Data Repository to the BI Dimensional Data is straightforward and very often it is One-to-One.

5.4.2 Mapping the Mechanics Transaction Data to the BI Facts Data

Since the design and construction of the BI Fact Entities (Section 4.4.5) is based directly on the design and attributes of the Mechanics Transaction Entities, the mapping from the Mechanics Transaction Data in the Central Data Repository to BI Facts Data is straightforward and very often it is One-to-One or simple aggregation.

5.5 MAPPING THE DATA OF THE CENTRAL DATA REPOSITORY TO THE EI DATA MARTS

The mapping of the Process Data of the Central Data Repository to the Enterprise Intelligence Data Marts is also simple and straightforward.

5.5.1 Mapping the Master Data to the EI Dimensional Data

It is similar to the mapping of the Master Data to the BI Dimensional Data. Since the design and construction of the EI Dimension Entities (Sections 4.6.3 & 4.6.4) is based directly on the design and attributes of the Master Data Entities, the mapping from the Master Data in the Central Data Repository to EI Dimensional Data is straightforward and very often it is One-to-One.

5.5.2 Mapping the Mechanics Session Data to the EI Facts Data

It is similar to the Mapping of the Mechanics Transaction Data to BI Facts Data. Since the design and construction of the EI Fact Entities (Section 4.6.5) is based directly on the design and attributes of the Mechanics Session Entities, the mapping from the Mechanics Session Data in the Central Data Repository to EI Facts Data is straightforward and very often it is One-to-One or simple aggregation.

6. Enterprise Data Architecture involving Master, Transactional, & Process Data Integration, Consolidation, Synchronization, & Consistency

Many articles and books tried to cover Master Data Integration and Consolidation [18, 20, 21, etc.]. Very few elaborated on the complexity and implementation difficulties of MDM. MDM is still a curriculum that needs enormous effort to mature. The research and publications covering the Integration and Consolidation of the Transactional Data are very limited. Also there is no research or studies covering the Integration and Consolidation of the Process Data.

This chapter presents and details the ODS architecture, the Central Data Repository architectures including Master, Transactional, and Process Data Integration and Consolidation, and the Enterprise Data Architectures involving them. It describes, besides the ODS architecture nineteen major architectures involving the Central Data Repository. These architectures are grouped as follows:

> ➤ Group 1 involves five architectures where the Central Data Repository includes only Master Data.
> ➤ Group 2 involves seven architectures where the Central Data Repository includes Master and Transactional Data.
> ➤ Group 3 involves seven architectures where the Central Data Repository includes Master, Transactional, and Process Data.

The seven architectures of Group 2 are comparable to the seven architectures of Group 3 however without the Process Data. There are also hybrid architectures involving combination of features from the above architectures.

Master, Transactional, and Process Data Integration and Consolidation comprise:

> ➤ Profiling, cleansing, proofing, and applying all Data Quality processes to the Master, Transactional, and Process Data residing in the Legacy Systems.
> ➤ Integration and consolidating this data.
> ➤ Design the structure of the Central Data Repository to store this data.
> ➤ Extraction, transformation, loading, and storing the data in the Central Data Repository.

The Enterprise Data Architecture involves Master, Transactional, and Process Data and comprises:

> ➤ Design the overall Enterprise Data Architecture including the Central Data Repositories and ODS.
> ➤ Design the Business Intelligence Data Marts responding to the BI Analytical requirements and needs.
> ➤ Design the Enterprise Intelligence Data Marts responding to the EI Analytical requirements and needs.
> ➤ Extraction, transformation, loading, and storing the data in the Data Marts.
> ➤ Design and development of query and reporting technical milieu to generate comprehensible results responding to the Analytical needs.

Dr. Eng. M. Naoulo

The Central Data Repository stores the integrated and consolidated Master Data and ultimately the Mechanism and Mechanics Transactional and Process Data. The Enterprise Data Architectures incorporate the ODS or the Central Data Repository which would be used – depending on the architecture – as:

- System of Reference for the Legacy Systems.
- Repository for Master Data query and reporting.
- System of Reference for the Business and Enterprise Intelligence Data Marts.
- System of Records for Master, Transactional, and Process Data representing the source for the Business and Enterprise Intelligence Data Marts.

Note: It is very important to emphasize that the feedback from the Central Data Repository to the Legacy Systems in the architectures that encompass such feedback involves only Master Data. No feedback of Transactional or Process Data. Any attempt to feedback Transactional or Process Data would complicate enormously the Enterprise Architecture and is Not Cost Effective.

Note: Adding Process Data to the Legacy Systems is very cumbersome and Not Cost Effective.

Note: Adopting an Enterprise Data Architecture that includes Integration and Consolidation of the Transactional and Process Data in the Central Data Repository would provide consistent OLMP Query and Reporting.

There is no clear and distinct definition across the IT literature for System of Reference and System of Records. The definitions adopted in this book are:

System of Reference:

"System of Reference includes complete data covering a certain Line of Business or a Constituent of the Enterprise or the whole Enterprise's Data. No direct Data Entry is affecting this system. All data updating this system is migrated and propagated from source systems. This system is accessed by other systems to retrieve data".

System of Records:

"System of Records includes complete data covering a certain Line of Business or a Constituent of the Enterprise or the whole Enterprise's Data. Direct Data Entry would be affecting this system. Part of the Data updating this system might be migrated and propagated from other systems. This system is accessed by other systems to retrieve data".

Note: Line of Business could be limited by Product, Geographic Area, Market, Time Period, etc.

Two major differences between the System of Reference and the System of Records:
- The System of Records supports data entered directly to it besides the data entered thru

other systems while all the data of the System of Reference is entered thru other systems then migrated and propagated to the System of Reference.

➢ Since data is entered directly to the System of Records, it is recommended that the data entered to other source system to be migrated and propagated in real-time or near real-time to this system. In the case of System of Reference the data entered to other source system could be migrated and propagated in batch. Therefore the data in the System of Records is mostly current while the data in the System of Reference loses its freshness quickly after the batch update and continue to be out-of-date till the next batch update.

The outline of this chapter includes:
➢ The ODS Architecture is described and evaluated in Section 6.1
➢ The ODS Architecture is compared to the Central Data Repository architectures in Section 6.2.
➢ The Master, Transactional, and Process Data Integration and Consolidation architectures are detailed in Section 6.3.
➢ The Enterprise Data Architecture involving the ODS is depicted in Section 6.4.
➢ The Enterprise Data Architectures involving the Central Data Repository are depicted in Section 6.5.
➢ The transition from the Enterprise Data Architecture involving the ODS to the Enterprise Data Architectures involving the Central Data Repository is depicted in Section 6.6.
➢ The paths for Enterprise Data Architectures upgrade are described in Section 6.7.
➢ The Integration, Consolidation, Synchronization, and Consistency of Enterprise Data within the Enterprise Data Framework are described in Section 6.8.
➢ Section 2.15 enumerated the major tasks of the Methodology to implement the Enterprise Data Framework and develop the Enterprise Data Architecture involving Master, Transactional, and Process Data Integration and Consolidation.

The Master, Transactional, and Process Data Administration and Stewardship tasks are elaborated in many books related to Data Quality and Data Governance. They include:
➢ **Data Quality:** Data Profiling, Data Cleansing, Data Proofing, Referential Integrity, Data Accuracy/Precision, Data Completeness, Data Reliability, Data Availability, Data Timelessness/freshness, Data consistency, and Data Uniqueness.
➢ **Data Governance**: Data Stewardship, Data Administration, Data Entry, ETL, Data Query and Reporting.
➢ **Data Propagation**
➢ **Data Feedback** from the Central Data Repository to the Legacy Systems
➢ **Data Synchronization.**
These topics would not be covered in this book and could be compiled from many publications in this area.

6.1   THE ODS ARCHITECTURE

The Operational Data Store (ODS) architecture was conceived before the concept of Master Data Management. It aims to integrate and consolidate the data of the Legacy Systems in one store. The ODS Architecture did not differentiate between Master Data and Transactional Data

Dr. Eng. M. Naoulo

(Process Data was not contemplated). The Data Entry points for all Master and Transactional Data are thru the Legacy Systems. The data extracted from the Legacy Systems would be processed, sometimes, in a staging area preceding the ODS thru data profiling, cleansing, proofing, and applying Data Quality tests and correction needed to assure the quality of data before storing it in the ODS. The Legacy Systems will update the ODS with Master and Transactional Data either real-time or near real-time or batch. In principle there is no feedback from the ODS to the Legacy Systems.

The ODS stores Master and Transactional Data and.is used as System of Reference for the Business Intelligence Data Marts. The ODS is sometimes used as System of Reference for the Legacy Systems. The Modeling Technique for the ODS is Relational 3NF Data Modeling technique. Diagram 6.1 represents the ODS Architecture.

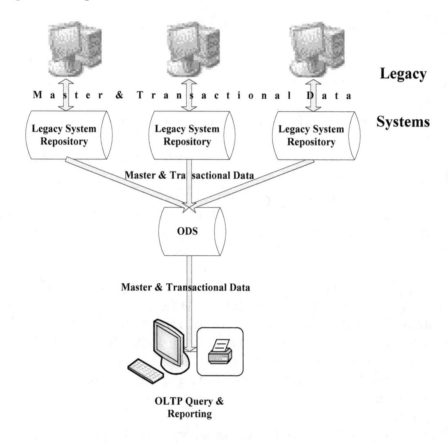

The ODS Architecture

Diagram 6.1: The ODS Architecture

Note: It will require a lot of effort and time to enhance the ODS to support Process Data. Very often this effort is not cost effective. It is recommended to conceive a Central Data Repository to support the Process Data.

Dr. Eng. M. Naoulo

6.2 DIFFERENCE BETWEEN THE CENTRAL DATA REPOSITORY & THE ODS ARCHITECTURES

The difference between the Central Data Repository and the Operational Data Store (ODS) architectures is:

➤ The ODS includes partial Integration and Consolidation of Master Data and these Integration and Consolidation do not follow any methodological approach. Also the design techniques are not coherent nor homogeneous nor consistent across the enterprises. Furthermore there is no Best of Practice to implement the Integration and Consolidation of Master Data in the ODS. The Central Data Repository outlined in this book includes Integration and Consolidation of Master Data and is supported by methodological approach and design techniques that are coherent and homogenous and could be applied across different enterprise architectures. These methodological approach and design techniques would be the base for Best of Practice.

➤ The design of the ODS conducts entangled Master Data and Transactional Data while the design of the Central Data Repository separates between the Master Data, Transactional Data, and Process Data although they are interacting with each other.

➤ The ODS is often not used as System of Reference for the Legacy Systems. It is used as the System of Reference for the Business Intelligence Data Marts. The Central Data Repository (depending on the architecture) is used as Repository for Master Data query and reporting, System of Reference for the Legacy Systems, System of Reference for the Business and Enterprise Intelligence Data Marts, and ultimately System of Records for Master, Transactional and Process Data.

➤ The ODS modeling technique is based on Relational 3NF Data Modeling technique. The Central Data Repository modeling technique follows sophisticated and elegant Master Data structuring and uses the SAM O NAOULO Modeling Technique.

➤ The ODS does not feedback its data to update the Legacy Systems, while in many Central Data Repository architectures the Central Data Repository feedbacks its data to update the Legacy Systems (the feedback from the Central Data Repository to update the Legacy Systems is not advisable as discussed in Section 6.3.18).

➤ Data Profiling, Data Cleansing, Data Proofing, and applying all Data Quality processes after extracting the data from the Legacy Systems and before loading it are required for both the ODS and the Central Data Repository.

➤ The ODS cannot be enhanced or expanded to include integrated and consolidated Master Data, Transactional Data, and Process Data without tremendous overhauling of the ODS structure. However it would be, if it exists already, a good reference for conceiving the Transaction Consolidation Repository architecture and other Transactional architectures.

6.3 MASTER, TRANSACTIONAL, & PROCESS DATA INTEGRATION & CONSOLIDATION ARCHITECTURES

There are several architectures for Master Data Integration and Consolidation. Dreibelbis & all [18] describe some of these architectures. Hereafter is the description of the major Enterprise Data Architectures involving not only the Master Data but also the Mechanism and Mechanics'

Data. Table 6.1 summarizes the ODS and the Central Data Repository architectures. Sections 6.4 & 6.5 detail the Enterprise Data Architectures based on these Data Integration and Consolidation architectures.

	Architecture	ODS/Central Data Repository	Master Data Entry	Transactions Data Entry	Process Data Entry	Feedback of Master Data to Legacy Systems	Architecture Diagram	Architecture Section	Enterprise Data Architecture Diagram	Enterprise Data Architecture Section	Status of the ODS/Central Data Repository vis-à-vis the Legacy Systems	Status of the ODS/Central Data Repository vis-à-vis the Data Marts
1	ODS	Includes all Master and Transactional Data. No distinction between Master Data and Transactional Data. No special techniques to analyze the Master Data	Legacy Systems	Legacy Systems	No Process Data	No	6.1	6.1	6.14	6.4	System of Reference	System of Reference
2	MDM Registry Repository	Includes Links to the Legacy Systems' Master Data. Might include some main attributes	Legacy Systems	Legacy Systems	Legacy Systems	No	6.2	6.3.1	6.15			
3	MDM Consolidation Repository	Includes all Master Data	Legacy Systems	Legacy Systems	Legacy Systems	No	6.3	6.3.2	6.16		MDM System of Reference	MDM System of Reference
4	MDM Consolidation Hub	Includes all Master Data	Legacy Systems	Legacy Systems	Legacy Systems	Yes	6.4	6.3.3	6.17	6.5.1	MDM System of Reference	MDM System of Reference
5	MDM Master Data Repository	Includes all Master Data	Legacy Systems & directly to Central Data Repository	Legacy Systems	Legacy Systems	No	6.5	6.3.4	6.18		MDM System of Records	MDM System of Records
6	MDM Master Data Hub	Includes all Master Data	Legacy Systems & directly to Central Data Repository	Legacy Systems	Legacy Systems	Yes	6.6	6.3.5	6.19		MDM System of Records	MDM System of Records
7	Transaction Consolidation Repository	Includes all Master & Transactional Data	Legacy Systems	Legacy Systems	No Process Data	No	Similar to 6.7 (No Process Data)	6.	Similar to 6.20 (No Process Data)	6.5.2	MDM & Transactional System of Reference	MDM & Transactional System of Reference

Dr. Eng. M. Naoulo

#												
8	Transaction Consolidation Hub	Includes all Master & Transactional Data	Legacy Systems	Legacy Systems	No Process Data	Yes	Similar to 6.8 (No Process Data)		Similar to 6.21 (No Process Data)		MDM & Transactional System of Reference	MDM & Transactional System of Reference
9	Transaction Repository Stage 1	Includes all Master & Transactional Data	Legacy Systems & directly to Central Data Repository	Legacy Systems	No Process Data	No	Similar to 6.9 (No Process Data)		Similar to 6.22 (No Process Data)		MDM System of Records, Transactional System of Reference	MDM System of Records, Transactional System of Reference
10	Transaction Hub Stage 1	Includes all Master & Transactional Data	Legacy Systems & directly to Central Data Repository	Legacy Systems	No Process Data	Yes	Similar to 6.10 (No Process Data)		Similar to 6.23 (No Process Data)		MDM System of Records, Transactional System of Reference	MDM System of Records, Transactional System of Reference
11	Transaction Repository Stage 2	Includes all Master & Transactional Data	Legacy Systems & directly to Central Data Repository	Legacy Systems & directly to Central Data Repository	No Process Data	No	Similar to 6.11 (No Process Data)		Similar to 6.24 (No Process Data)		MDM & Transactional System of Records	MDM & Transactional System of Records
12	Transaction Hub Stage 2	Includes all Master & Transactional Data	Legacy Systems & directly to Central Data Repository	Legacy Systems & directly to Central Data Repository	No Process Data	Yes	Similar to 6.12 (No Process Data)		Similar to 6.25 (No Process Data)		MDM & Transactional System of Records	MDM & Transactional System of Records
13	Transaction Hub Stage 3	Includes all Master & Transactional Data	Directly to Central Data Repository	Directly to Central Data Repository	No Process Data	No	Similar to 6.13 (No Process Data)		Similar to 6.26 (No Process Data)		No Legacy Systems	MDM & Transactional System of Records
14	Process Consolidation Repository	Includes all Master, Transactional & Process Data	Legacy Systems	Legacy Systems	Legacy Systems	No	6.7	6.3.6	6.20	6.5.3	MDM, Transactional, & Business Process System of Reference	MDM, Transactional, & Business Process System of Reference
15	Process Consolidation Hub	Includes all Master, Transactional & Process Data	Legacy Systems	Legacy Systems	Legacy Systems	Yes	6.8	6.3.7	6.21	6.5.3	MDM, Transactional, & Business Process System of Reference	MDM, Transactional, & Business Process System of Reference

Dr. Eng. M. Naoulo

16	Process Repository Stage 1	Includes all Master, Transactional & Process Data	Legacy Systems & directly to Central Data Repository	Legacy Systems	Legacy Systems	No		6.9	6.3.8	6.22		MDM System of Records, Transactional & Business Process System of Reference	MDM System of Records, Transactional & Business Process System of Reference
17	Process Hub Stage 1	Includes all Master, Transactional & Process Data	Legacy Systems & directly to Central Data Repository	Legacy Systems	Legacy Systems	Yes		6.10	6.3.9	6.23		MDM System of Records, Transactional & Business Process System of Reference	MDM System of Records, Transactional & Business Process System of Reference
18	Process Repository Stage 2	Includes all Master, Transactional & Process Data	Legacy Systems & directly to Central Data Repository	Legacy Systems & directly to Central Data Repository	Legacy Systems & directly to Central Data Repository	No		6.11	6.3.10	6.24		MDM, Transactional, & Business Process System of Records	MDM, Transactional, & Business Process System of Records
19	Process Hub Stage 2	Includes all Master, Transactional &Process Data	Legacy Systems & directly to Central Data Repository	Legacy Systems & directly to Central Data Repository	Legacy Systems & directly to Central Data Repository	Yes		6.12	6.3.11	6.25		MDM, Transactional, & Business Process System of Records	MDM, Transactional, & Business Process System of Records
20	Process Hub Stage 3	Includes all Master, Transactional &Process Data	Directly to Central Data Repository	Directly to Central Data Repository	Directly to Central Data Repository	No		6.13	6.3.12	6.26		No Legacy Systems	MDM, Transactional, & Business Process System of Records

Table 6.1: Summary of Master, Transactional, & Process Data Integration & Consolidation Architectures & ODS Architecture

The Modeling Technique for the Central Data Repository is **SAM O NAOULO Modeling Technique**. It is important to note that the entities in many of the Central Data Repositories (MDM Registry Repository, MDM Consolidation Repository, etc.) will include their own keys (Natural/Business or Surrogates) as well as they might include (the MDM Registry Repository must include) references to the Legacy Systems' records: name of the system, name of the entity, and Key attribute(s) of the record (at the physical level: name of the system, name of the table, and Key field(s) of the record). The ETL software and tools should support the mapping from the Legacy Systems to the Central Data Repository.

SAM O NAOULO Modeling Technique would be applied (without including the Process Data) in the Transaction Repositories and Hubs to design the Transactional Data. The architectures

Dr. Eng. M. Naoulo

involving Transaction Repositories and Hubs are similar to the architectures (Diagrams 6.7 to 6.13 & Diagrams 6.20 to 6.26) involving Process Repositories and Hubs but they do not carry Process Data. In the Transaction Repositories and Hubs the Sessions are not part of the Model and the Transactions would link directly to the Apparatus.

6.3.1 The MDM Registry Repository Architecture

The MDM Registry Repository holds only main data about the Master Data and links to the Legacy Systems for additional Master Data retrieval. The Legacy Systems will be the Data Entry point for all Master, Transactional, and Process Data. These systems will update the MDM Registry Repository with part of the Master Data either real-time or near real-time or batch. No Data Feedback from the MDM Registry Repository to the Legacy Systems and therefore no updating of the Legacy Systems resulting from the MDM Registry Repository.

Since the MDM Registry Repository does not include complete Master Data, it cannot be used alone as System of Reference for the next stages of Business and Enterprise Intelligence Data Marts. It needs the links to the Legacy Systems and their data. Data Federation is used to retrieve data from the Legacy Systems to perform Master Data query and reporting.

Diagram 6.2 represents the MDM Registry Repository Architecture.

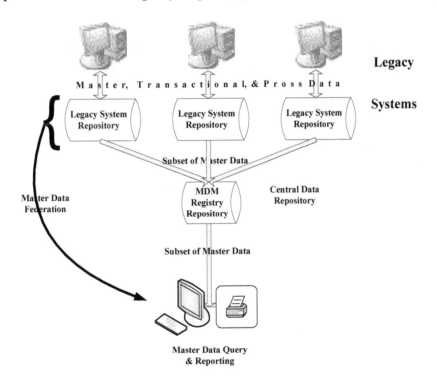

**The MDM Registry Repository
Architecture**

Diagram 6.2: The MDM Registry Repository Architecture

Dr. Eng. M. Naoulo

Advantages

The advantages of the MDM Registry Repository Architecture are:

- ➢ No code or data structure or GUI modifications to the Legacy Systems.
- ➢ No feedback from the MDM Registry Repository to the Legacy Systems. However there would be a need to add into the Legacy Systems, during MDM Registry Repository updates, the Key of the Master Data records of the MDM Registry Repository for fast MDM records retrieval by these Legacy Systems in order to access the other Legacy Systems data for query and reporting.
- ➢ No mandatory real-time Master Data update to the MDM Registry Repository.

Disadvantages

The disadvantages of the MDM Registry Repository Architecture are:

- ➢ If the MDM Registry Repository includes some attributes/fields/data elements besides the keys, the Master Data of the Legacy Systems would be out of sync between each other and with the Master Data of the MDM Registry Repository.
- ➢ If the MDM Registry Repository includes some attributes/fields/data elements besides the keys and if the update of the MDM Registry Repository is batch, the MDM Registry Repository will not include the latest updates needed by the Legacy Systems between the batch update periods, and therefore the up-to-date (freshness) validity and correctness of Master Data query and reporting from the MDM Registry Repository is short lived.
- ➢ The MDM Registry Repository could not be used alone as Master Data System of Reference for the Legacy Systems and for the Business and Enterprise Intelligence Data Marts; it needs additional data from the Legacy Systems. Even so, there might be discrepancies between the data of the different Legacy Systems that would affect the Query and reporting results.

The disadvantages of the MDM Registry Repository would surge if the MDM Registry Repository includes some attributes/fields/data elements besides the keys.

Implementation Difficulties

To satisfy the Master Data query and reporting, further data retrieval from the Legacy Systems is needed. This data retrieval is enabled thru the links incorporated in the MDM Registry Repository.

Operational Difficulties

The operational difficulties associated with the MDM Registry Repository Architecture result from:

- ➢ There is almost always the need to access the Legacy Systems for data retrieval.
- ➢ If the batch update period is long, there might be the need to access the latest updates occurring in other Legacy Systems. This necessitates login into these systems to retrieve the appropriate data.
- ➢ If the MDM Registry Repository includes some attributes/fields/data elements besides the keys, the Data Integration, Consolidation, Synchronization, and Consistency associated with the Data Propagation from the Legacy Systems to the MDM Registry Repository is strenuous.

Dr. Eng. M. Naoulo

6.3.2 The MDM Consolidation Repository Architecture

The MDM Consolidation Repository holds all the Master Data. The Legacy Systems will be the Data Entry point for all Master, Transactional, and Process Data. These systems will update the MDM Consolidation Repository with Master Data either real-time or near real-time or batch. No Data Feedback from the MDM Consolidation Repository to the Legacy Systems and therefore no updating of the Legacy Systems channeled from the MDM Consolidation Repository.

The MDM Consolidation Repository stores consolidated and integrated Master Data. It will be used as Master Data System of Reference for the Legacy Systems and for the Business and Enterprise Intelligence Data Marts. It can be used as an initial or intermediate step for the next stages of Enterprise Data Architectures (Ref. Section 6.7).

Diagram 6.3 represents the MDM Consolidation Repository Architecture.

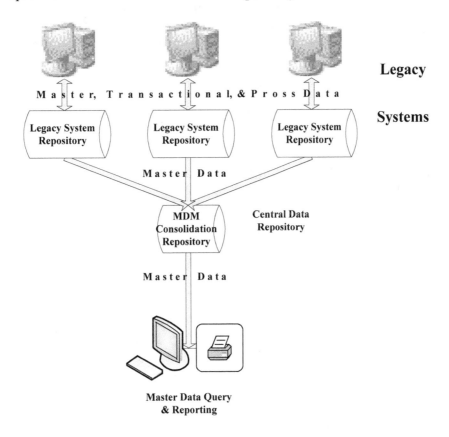

**The MDM Consolidation Repository
Architecture**

Diagram 6.3: The MDM Consolidation Repository Architecture

Dr. Eng. M. Naoulo

Advantages

The advantages of the MDM Consolidation Repository Architecture are:

- ➢ No code or data structure or GUI modifications to the Legacy Systems.
- ➢ No feedback from the MDM Consolidation Repository to the Legacy Systems. However there might be a need to add into the Legacy Systems, during the MDM Consolidation Repository updates, the Key of the Master Data records of the MDM Consolidation Repository for fast MDM records retrieval by the Legacy Systems.
- ➢ No mandatory real-time Master Data update to the MDM Consolidation Repository.
- ➢ The MDM Consolidation Repository includes integrated and consolidated Master Data.

Disadvantages

The disadvantages of the MDM Consolidation Repository Architecture are:

- ➢ Since there is no feedback from the MDM Consolidation Repository to the Legacy Systems the Master Data of the Legacy Systems are out of sync between each other and with the Master Data of the MDM Consolidation Repository.
- ➢ If the update of the MDM Consolidation Repository is batch, the MDM Consolidation Repository will not include the latest updates to the Legacy Systems between the batch update periods. The up-to-date (freshness), validity, and correctness of the Master Data in the MDM Consolidation Repository is short lived and its function as Master Data System of Reference for the Legacy Systems, for Master Data query and reporting, and for the Business and Enterprise Intelligence Data Marts is hindered.

Implementation Difficulties

The implementation of the MDM Consolidation Repository Architecture is among the simplest between all subsequent architectures. In fact all subsequent architectures would include all implementation tasks conducted by the MDM Consolidation Architecture. This does not alleviate the fact that the Legacy Systems data profiling, cleansing, proofing, and applying all Data Quality processes and the need for complete Data Governance for the Data Entry, ETL, and data reporting involves very complicated time and effort consuming tasks.

Operational Difficulties

The operational difficulties associated with the MDM Consolidation Repository Architecture result from:

- ➢ If the batch update period is long, there might be the need to access the latest updates occurring in other Legacy Systems. This necessitates login into these systems to retrieve the appropriate data.
- ➢ The Data Integration, Consolidation, Synchronization, and Consistency associated with the Data Propagation from the Legacy Systems to the MDM Consolidation Repository are strenuous.

6.3.3 The MDM Consolidation Hub Architecture

The MDM Consolidation Hub holds all the Master Data. The Legacy Systems will be the Data Entry point for all Master, Transactional, and Process Data. These systems will update the MDM Consolidation Hub with Master Data either real-time or near real-time or batch. The MDM Consolidation Hub will feedback its data to update the Legacy Systems either real-time or near

104

real-time or batch. The updates of the Legacy Systems will affect only the fields which their corresponding Central Data Repository fields have been modified. No alteration of the structure of the Legacy Systems databases would occur.

Here also the MDM Consolidation Hub stores consolidated and integrated Master Data. It will be used as Master Data System of Reference for the Legacy Systems and for the Business and Enterprise Intelligence Data Marts. It can be used as an initial or intermediate step for the next stages of Enterprise Data Architectures (Ref. Section 6.7).

Diagram 6.4 represents the MDM Consolidation Hub Architecture.

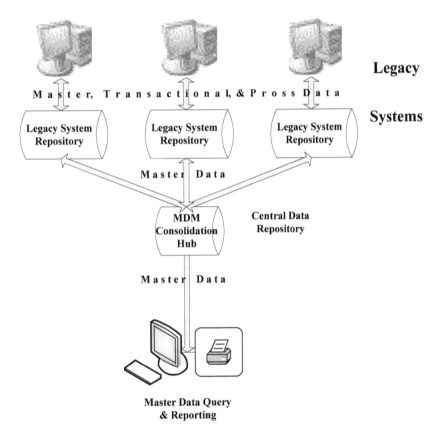

The MDM Consolidation Hub Architecture

Diagram 6.4: The MDM Consolidation Hub Architecture

Advantages
The advantages of the MDM Consolidation Hub Architecture are:
- ➤ No code or data structure or GUI modifications to the Legacy Systems.
- ➤ No mandatory real-time Master Data update to the MDM Consolidation Hub.
- ➤ The MDM Consolidation Hub includes integrated and consolidated Master Data.

Dr. Eng. M. Naoulo

Disadvantages

The disadvantages of the MDM Consolidation Hub Architecture are:

> ➤ If the update of the MDM Consolidation Repository is batch, the MDM Consolidation Repository will not include the latest updates to the Legacy Systems between the batch update periods. The up-to-date (freshness), validity, and correctness of the Master Data in the MDM Consolidation Repository is short lived and its function as Master Data System of Reference for the Legacy Systems, for Master Data query and reporting, and for the Business and Enterprise Intelligence Data Marts is hindered.

> ➤ If the feedback from the MDM Consolidation Hub to the Legacy Systems is batch, the Legacy Systems will not include the latest updates of other Legacy Systems occurring between the batch update periods, and therefore they will be are out of sync with the Central Data Repository and between each other.

Implementation Difficulties

> ➤ The Data Feedback from the MDM Consolidation Hub to the Legacy Systems adds another layer of implementation difficulties (in comparison to MDM Consolidation Repository).

> ➤ The Master Data Integration and Consolidation in the MDM Consolidation Hub necessitates Data Synchronization between the different Legacy Systems. If there are many Legacy Systems and the Master Data of these systems is modified frequently, this task would become very difficult.

Operational Difficulties

The operational difficulties associated with the MDM Consolidation Hub Architecture comprise those associated with the MDM Consolidation Repository Architecture. In addition:

> ➤ The Data Synchronization associated with the Data Feedback from the MDM Consolidation Hub to the Legacy Systems is arduous.

6.3.4 The MDM Master Data Repository Architecture

The MDM Master Data Repository holds all the Master Data. The Legacy Systems will be a Data Entry point for Master and all Transactional and Process Data. The Master Data could also be entered directly into the MDM Master Data Repository. The Legacy Systems will update the MDM Master Data Repository with Master Data either real-time or near real-time or batch. Since the Master Data could be entered directly into the MDM Master Data Repository and in order to avoid data discrepancies between the Legacy Systems and the MDM Master Data Repository, it is advisable that the Legacy Systems will update the MDM Master Data Repository with Master Data either real-time or near real-time. No Data Feedback from the MDM Master Data Repository to the Legacy Systems and therefore no updating of the Legacy Systems channeled from the MDM Master Data Repository.

The MDM Master Data Repository stores complete consolidated and integrated Master Data. It will be used as Master Data System of Records for the Legacy Systems and for the Business and Enterprise Intelligence Data Marts. It can be used as an initial or intermediate step for the next stages of Enterprise Data Architectures (Ref. Section 6.7).

Dr. Eng. M. Naoulo

Diagram 6.5 represents the MDM Master Data Repository Architecture.

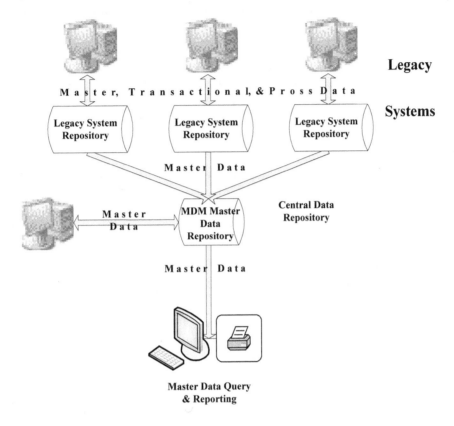

**The MDM Master Data Repository
Architecture**

Diagram 6.5: The MDM Master Data Repository Architecture

Advantages

The advantages of the MDM Master Data Repository Architecture are:
- ➤ No code or data structure or GUI modifications to the Legacy Systems.
- ➤ No feedback from the MDM Consolidation Repository to the Legacy Systems. However there might be a need to add into the Legacy Systems, during the MDM Consolidation Repository updates, the Key of the Master Data records of the MDM Consolidation Repository for fast MDM records retrieval by the Legacy Systems.
- ➤ The MDM Consolidation Repository includes integrated and consolidated Master Data.

Disadvantages

The disadvantages of the MDM Master Data Repository Architecture comprise the disadvantages of the MDM Consolidation Repository Architecture.

Dr. Eng. M. Naoulo

Implementation Difficulties

The implementation difficulties of the MDM Master Data Repository Architecture comprise those associated with the MDM Consolidation Repository Architecture. In addition there is the need:

> For additional time and effort to develop the software for direct Master Data entry into the Master Data Repository.

> To design and develop the Integration, Consolidation, Synchronization, and Consistency of the Master Data entered directly into the Master Data Repository with the Master Data coming from the Legacy Systems.

Operational Difficulties

The operational difficulties associated with the MDM Master Data Repository Architecture result from:

> The Data Integration, Consolidation, Synchronization, and Consistency associated with the Data Propagation from the Legacy Systems to the MDM Master Data Repository are strenuous.

> There is the need to integrate and consolidate the Master Data entered directly into the Master Data Repository with the Master Data coming from the Legacy Systems.

6.3.5 The MDM Master Data Hub Architecture

The MDM Master Data Hub Architecture is similar to the MDM Consolidation Hub Architecture. In addition the Master Data would also be entered directly into the MDM Master Data Hub. In order to avoid data discrepancies between the Legacy Systems and the MDM Master Data Repository, it is advisable that the Legacy Systems will update the MDM Master Data Repository with Master Data either real-time or near real-time.

The MDM Master Data Hub stores complete consolidated and integrated Master Data. It will be used as Master Data System of Records for the Legacy Systems and for the Business and Enterprise Intelligence Data Marts. It can be used as an intermediate step for the next stages of Enterprise Data Architectures (Ref. Section 6.7).

Diagram 6.6 represents the MDM Master Data Hub Architecture.

Dr. Eng. M. Naoulo

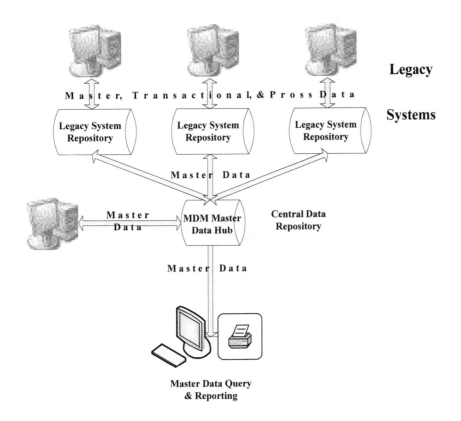

The MDM Master Data Hub
Architecture

Diagram 6.6: The MDM Master Data Hub Architecture

Advantages

The advantages of the MDM Master Data Hub Architecture are:
- No code or data structure or GUI modifications to the Legacy Systems.
- The MDM Master Data Hub includes integrated and consolidated Master Data.

Disadvantages

The disadvantages of the MDM Master Data Hub Architecture comprise the disadvantages of the MDM Consolidation Hub Architecture.

Implementation Difficulties

The implementation difficulties of the MDM Master Data Hub Architecture comprise the implementation difficulties of the MDM Consolidation Hub Architecture. In addition there is the need:
- For additional time and effort to develop the software for direct Master Data entry into the Master Data Hub.
- To design and develop the Integration, Consolidation, Synchronization, and Consistency of the Master Data entered directly into the Master Data Hub with the Master Data

Dr. Eng. M. Naoulo

coming from the Legacy Systems.

Operational Difficulties

The operational difficulties of the MDM Master Data Hub Architecture comprise the operational difficulties of the MDM Consolidation Hub Architecture. Furthermore the Integration, Consolidation, Synchronization, and Consistency of the Master Data entered directly into the Master Data Hub with the Master Data coming from the Legacy Systems add additional difficulties.

6.3.6 The Process Consolidation Repository Architecture

The Process Consolidation Repository holds all the Master, Transactional, and Process Data. The Legacy Systems will be a Data Entry point for all Data. These systems will update the Process Consolidation Repository with Master, Transactional, and Process Data either real-time or near real-time or batch. No Data Feedback from the Process Consolidation Repository to the Legacy Systems and therefore no updating of the Legacy Systems channeled from the Process Consolidation Repository.

The Process Consolidation Repository stores integrated and consolidated Master, Transactional, and Process Data and shall be used as System of Reference (as it would include copy of all Records) for the Legacy Systems and for the Business and Enterprise Intelligence Data Marts. It can be used as an intermediate step for the next stages of Enterprise Data Architectures (Ref. Section 6.7).

Diagram 6.7 represents the Process Consolidation Repository Architecture.

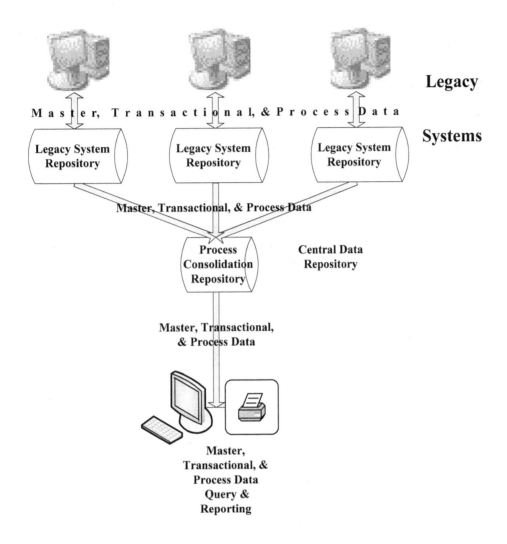

**The Process Consolidation Repository
Architecture**

Diagram 6.7: The Process Consolidation Repository Architecture

Advantages
The advantages of the Process Consolidation Repository Architecture comprise the advantages of the MDM Consolidation Repository Architecture applied to Master, Transactional, and Process Data.

Disadvantages
The disadvantages of the Process Consolidation Repository Architecture comprise the disadvantages of the MDM Consolidation Repository Architecture applied to Master, Transactional, and Process Data.

Implementation Difficulties

Dr. Eng. M. Naoulo

The Legacy Systems data profiling, cleansing, proofing and applying all Data Quality processes and the need for complete Data Governance for the Data Entry and ETL of Master, Transactional, and Process Data involve very complicated time and effort consuming tasks.

Operational Difficulties
The operational difficulties of the Process Consolidation Repository Architecture comprise the operational difficulties of the MDM Consolidation Repository Architecture applied to Master, Transactional, and Process Data.

6.3.7 The Process Consolidation Hub Architecture

The Process Consolidation Hub holds all the Master, Transactional, and Process Data. The Legacy Systems will be a Data Entry point for all Data. These systems will update the Process Consolidation Hub with Master, Transactional, and Process Data either real-time or near real-time or batch.

The Process Consolidation Hub will feedback its data to update the Legacy Systems either real-time or near real-time or batch. Two options are evaluated for the Process Consolidation Hub as well as for Process Hubs Stage 1 and 2 (also the same for Transaction Consolidation Hub and for Transaction Hubs Stage 1 and 2):

1. The Process Consolidation Hub will feedback only Master Data to update the Legacy Systems either real-time or near real-time or batch. The Transactional and Business Process Query and Reports processed from the Legacy Systems are restricted to the Data of each Legacy System and do not cross Legacy Systems. The Transactional and Business Process Query and Reports processed from the Process Consolidation Hub retrieve data stored in the Process Consolidation Hub that was propagated from all Legacy Systems. If the update of the Process Consolidation Hub or the Feedback from the Process Consolidation Hub to the Legacy Systems is batch, there would be discrepancies amid the Query and Reports generated from the Legacy Systems and those generated from the Process Consolidation Hub between the periods of the batch updates. The up-to-date (freshness), validity, and correctness of the Data in the Process. Consolidation Hub is short-lived and its function as Master Data System of Reference for the Legacy Systems, for Master Data query and reporting, and for the Business and Enterprise Intelligence Data Marts is hindered.

2. The Process Consolidation Hub will feedback Master, Transactional, and Process Data to update the Legacy Systems. This requires enormous effort for Data Integration, Consolidation, Propagation, Feedback, Synchronization, Governance, and Quality Assurance and might require the modification of the Legacy Systems. In order to alleviate this effort it is important to design the Business Functions as independently as possible within the Legacy Systems. This is very often not possible as the majority of the Legacy Systems were developed already and these systems were put into operation a long time ago, and to modify them is less effective than to aim to the Process Hub Stage 3 architecture. Therefore this option is not recommended and this book will adopt option 1 for the feedback to the Legacy Systems.

The Process Consolidation Hub stores consolidated and integrated Master, Transactional, and

Dr. Eng. M. Naoulo

Process Data. It will be used as Master, Transactional, and Business Process Data System of Reference (as it would include copy of all the Operational Records) for the Legacy Systems and for the Business and Enterprise Intelligence Data Marts. It can be used as an intermediate step for the next stages of Enterprise Data Architectures (Ref. Section 6.7).

Diagram 6.8 represents the Process Consolidation Hub Architecture. The notations associated with the double arrows between the Central Data Repository and the Legacy Systems specify that the update of the Central Data Repository by the Legacy Systems involves Master, Transactional, and Process Data while the update of the Legacy Systems by the Central Data Repository involves only Master Data. Similar notations were adopted in Diagrams 6.10, 6.12, 6.13, 6.21, 6.23, 6.25, & 6.26.

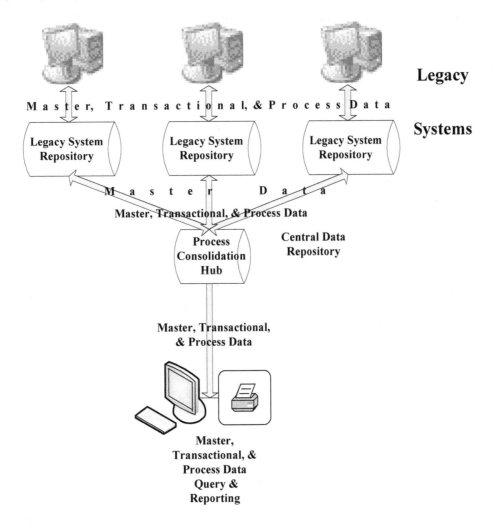

**The Process Consolidation Hub
Architecture**

Diagram 6.8: The Process Consolidation Hub Architecture

Dr. Eng. M. Naoulo

Advantages
The advantages of the Process Consolidation Hub Architecture comprise the advantages of the MDM Consolidation Hub Architecture applied to Master, Transactional, and Process Data. The Process Consolidation Hub includes integrated and consolidated Master, Transactional, and Process Data.

Disadvantages
The disadvantages of the Process Consolidation Hub Architecture comprise the disadvantages of the MDM Consolidation Hub Architecture applied to Master, Transactional, and Process Data.

Implementation Difficulties
The implementation difficulties of the Process Consolidation Hub Architecture comprise the implementation difficulties of the MDM Consolidation Hub Architecture applied to Master, Transactional, and Process Data. Furthermore the additional efforts to integrate, consolidate, and establish the database structure in the Process Consolidation Hub for Transactional and Process Data are arduous.

Operational Difficulties
The operational difficulties of the Process Consolidation Hub Architecture comprise the operational difficulties of the MDM Consolidation Repository Architecture applied to Master, Transactional, and Process Data, and the operational difficulties of the Data Feedback and Data Synchronization.

6.3.8 The Process Repository Stage 1 Architecture
The Process Repository Stage 1 holds all the Master, Transactional, and Process Data. The Legacy Systems will be a Data Entry point for Master, and all Transactional, and Process Data. The Master Data could also be entered directly into the Process Repository Stage 1. The Legacy Systems will update the Process Repository Stage 1 with Master, Transactional, and Process Data either real-time or near real-time or batch. Since the Master Data could be entered directly into the Process Repository Stage 1 and in order to avoid data discrepancies between the Legacy Systems and the Process Repository Stage 1, it is advisable that the Legacy Systems will update the Process Repository Stage 1 with Master Data either real-time or near real-time. No Data Feedback from the Process Repository Stage 1 to the Legacy Systems and therefore no updating of the Legacy Systems channeled from the Process Repository Stage 1.

The Process Repository Stage 1 stores complete consolidated and integrated Master, Transactional, and Process Data. It will be used as Master Data System of Records and Transactional and Business Process Data System of Reference (as it would include copy of all the Operational Records: Transactional and Business Process) for the Legacy Systems and for the Business and Enterprise Intelligence Data Marts. It can be used as an intermediate step for the next stages of Enterprise Data Architectures (Ref. Section 6.7).

Diagram 6.9 represents the Process Repository Stage 1 Architecture.

Dr. Eng. M. Naoulo

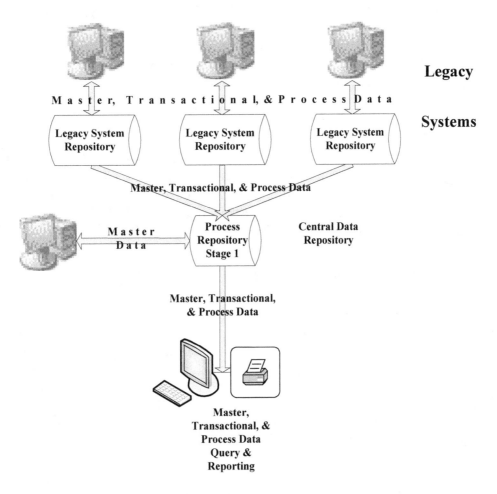

The Process Repository Stage 1
Architecture

Diagram 6.9: The Process Repository Stage 1 Architecture

Advantages
The advantages of the Process Repository Stage 1 Architecture comprise the advantages of the MDM Master Data Repository Architecture applied to Master, Transactional, and Process Data. The Process Repository Stage 1 includes integrated and consolidated Master, Transactional, and Process Data.

Disadvantages
The disadvantages of the Process Repository Stage 1 Architecture comprise the disadvantages of the MDM Master Data Repository Architecture applied to Master, Transactional, and Process Data.

Implementation Difficulties
The implementation difficulties of the Process Repository Stage 1 Architecture comprise the

Dr. Eng. M. Naoulo

implementation difficulties of the MDM Master Data Repository applied to Master, Transactional, and Process Data and the implementation difficulties of the Process Consolidation Repository architectures. Furthermore there is the need to design and develop the Integration, Consolidation, Synchronization, and Consistency of the Master Data entered directly into the Process Repository Stage 1 with the Master Data coming from the Legacy Systems.

Operational Difficulties

The operational difficulties of the Process Repository Stage 1 Architecture comprise the operational difficulties of the Process Consolidation Repository applied to Master, Transactional, and Process Data and the implementation difficulties of the Process Consolidation Repository architectures. Furthermore there is the need to design and develop the Integration, Consolidation, Synchronization, and Consistency of the Master Data entered directly into the Process Repository Stage 1 with the Master Data coming from the Legacy Systems.

6.3.9 The Process Hub Stage 1 Architecture

The Process Hub Stage 1 holds all the Master, Transactional, and Process Data. The Legacy Systems will be a Data Entry point for Master Data and all Transactional and Process Data. The Master Data could also be entered directly into the Process Hub Stage 1. The Legacy Systems will update the Process Hub Stage 1 with Master, Transactional, and Process Data either real-time or near real-time or batch. Since the Master Data could be entered directly into the Process Hub Stage 1 and in order to avoid data discrepancies between the Legacy Systems and the Process Hub Stage 1, it is advisable that the Legacy Systems will update the Process Hub Stage 1 with Master Data either real-time or near real-time. The Process Hub Stage 1 will feedback its Master Data (Ref. discussion in Section 6.3.7) to update the Legacy Systems either real-time or near real-time or batch.

The Process Hub Stage 1 stores complete consolidated and integrated Master, Transactional, and Process Data. It will be used as Master Data System of Records and Transactional and Business Process Data System of Reference (as it would include copy of all the Operational Records: Transactional and Business Process) for the Legacy Systems and for the Business and Enterprise Intelligence Data Marts. It can be used as an intermediate step for the next stages of Enterprise Data Architectures (Ref. Section 6.7).

Diagram 6.10 represents the Process Hub Stage 1 Architecture.

Dr. Eng. M. Naoulo

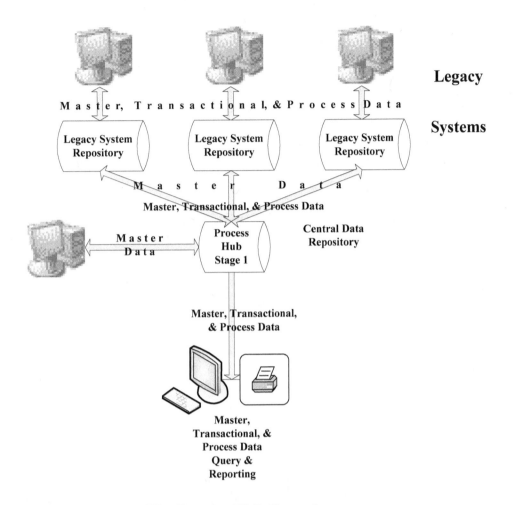

**The Process Hub Stage 1
Architecture**

Diagram 6.10: The Process Hub Stage 1 Architecture

Advantages
The advantages of the Process Hub Stage 1 Architecture comprise the advantages of the Process Consolidation Hub Architecture.

Disadvantages
The disadvantages of the Process Hub Stage 1 Architecture comprise the disadvantages of the Process Consolidation Hub Architecture.

Implementation Difficulties
The disadvantages of the Process Hub Stage 1 Architecture comprise the implementation difficulties of the Process Consolidation Hub Architecture. In addition there is the need:
- For additional time and effort to develop the software for direct Master Data entry into the Process Hub Stage 1.
- To design and develop the Integration, Consolidation, Synchronization, and Consistency

117

of the Master Data entered directly into the Process Hub Stage 1 with the Master Data coming from the Legacy Systems.

Operational Difficulties

The operational difficulties of the Process Hub Stage 1 Architecture comprise the operational difficulties of the Process Consolidation Hub Architecture. Furthermore the Integration, Consolidation, Synchronization, and Consistency of the Master Data entered directly into the Process Hub Stage 1 with the Master Data coming from the Legacy Systems add additional difficulties.

6.3.10 The Process Repository Stage 2 Architecture

The Process Repository Stage 2 holds all the Master, Transactional, and Process Data. The Legacy Systems will be a Data Entry point for Master, Transactional, and Process Data. The Master, Transactional, and Process Data could also be entered directly into the Process Repository Stage 2. The Legacy Systems will update the Process Repository Stage 2 with Master, Transactional, and Process Data either real-time or near real-time or batch. Since the Master, Transactional, and Process Data could be entered directly into the Process Repository Stage 2 and in order to avoid data discrepancies between the Legacy Systems and the Process Repository Stage 2, it is advisable that the Legacy Systems will update the Process Repository Stage 2 with Master, Transactional, and Process Data either real-time or near real-time. No Data Feedback from the Process Repository Stage 2 to the Legacy Systems and therefore no updating of the Legacy Systems channeled from the Process Repository Stage 2.

The Process Repository Stage 2 stores complete consolidated and integrated Master, Transactional, and Process Data. It will be used as Master, Transactional, and Business Process Data System of Records (as it would include copy of all the Operational Records: Transactional and Business Process) for the Legacy Systems and for the Business and Enterprise Intelligence Data Marts. It can be used as an intermediate step for the next stage of Enterprise Data Architectures (Ref. Section 6.7).

Diagram 6.11 represents the Process Repository Stage 2 Architecture.

Dr. Eng. M. Naoulo

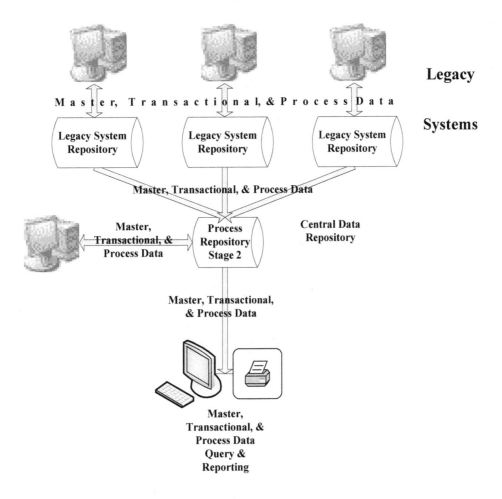

Legacy

M a s t e r, T r a n s a c t i o n a l, & P r o c e s s D a t a

Systems

Legacy System Repository

Legacy System Repository

Legacy System Repository

Master, Transactional, & Process Data

Master, Transactional, & Process Data

Process Repository Stage 2

Central Data Repository

Master, Transactional, & Process Data

Master, Transactional, & Process Data Query & Reporting

The Process Repository Stage 2 Architecture

Diagram 6.11: The Process Repository Stage 2 Architecture

Advantages
The advantages of the Process Repository Stage 2 Architecture comprise the advantages of the Process Repository Stage 1 Architecture applied to Master, Transactional, and Process Data.

Disadvantages
The disadvantages of the Process Repository Stage 2 Architecture comprise the disadvantages of the Process Repository Stage 1 Architecture applied to Master, Transactional, and Process Data.

Implementation Difficulties
The implementation difficulties of the Process Repository Stage 2 Architecture comprise the implementation difficulties of the Process Repository Stage 1 Architecture applied to Master, Transactional, and Process Data. Furthermore there is the need to design and develop the Integration, Consolidation, Synchronization, and Consistency of the Transactional and Process Data entered directly into the Process Repository Stage 2 with the Transactional and Process

Dr. Eng. M. Naoulo

Data coming from the Legacy Systems.

Operational Difficulties

The operational difficulties of the Process Repository Stage 2 Architecture comprise the operational difficulties of the Process Repository Stage 1 Architecture applied to Master, Transactional, and Process Data. Furthermore there is the need to design and develop the Integration, Consolidation, Synchronization, and Consistency of the Transactional and Process Data entered directly into the Process Repository Stage 2 with the Transactional and Process Data coming from the Legacy Systems.

6.3.11 The Process Hub Stage 2 Architecture

The Process Hub Stage 2 holds all the Master, Transactional, and Process Data. The Legacy Systems will be a Data Entry point for Master, Transactional, and Process Data. The Master, Transactional, and Process Data could also be entered directly into the Process Hub Stage 2. The Legacy Systems will update the Process Hub Stage 2 with Master, Transactional, and Process Data either real-time or near real-time or batch. Since the Master, Transactional, and Process Data could be entered directly into the Process Hub Stage 2 and in order to avoid data discrepancies between the Legacy Systems and the Process Hub Stage 2, it is advisable that the Legacy Systems will update the Process Hub Stage 2 with Master, Transactional, and Process Data either real-time or near real-time. The Process Hub will feedback its data (Ref. discussion in Section 6.3.7) to update the Legacy Systems either real-time or near real-time or batch.

The Process Hub Stage 2 stores complete consolidated and integrated Master, Transactional, and Process Data. It will be used as Master, Transactional, and Business Process Data System of Records ((as it would include copy of all the Operational Records: Transactional and Business Process) for the Legacy Systems and for the Business and Enterprise Intelligence Data Marts. It can be used as an intermediate step for the Process Hub Stage 3 Architecture (Ref. Section 6.7).

Diagram 6.12 represents the Process Hub Stage 2 Architecture.

Dr. Eng. M. Naoulo

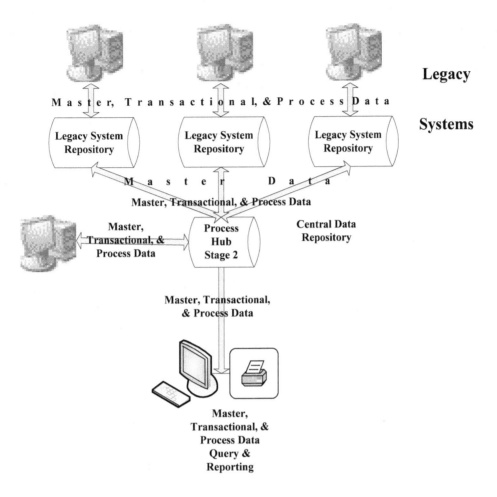

Legacy

Systems

**The Process Hub Stage 2
Architecture**

Diagram 6.12: The Process Hub Stage 2 Architecture

Advantages

The advantages of the Process Hub Stage 2 Architecture comprise the advantages of the Process Hub Stage 1 Architecture. In addition it allows the Mechanism, and Mechanics Data to be entered directly into the Process Hub.

Disadvantages

The disadvantages of the Process Hub Stage 2 Architecture comprise the disadvantages of the Process Hub Stage 1 Architecture.

Implementation Difficulties

The implementation difficulties associated with the Process Hub Stage 2 Architecture comprise the implementation difficulties of the Process Hub Stage 1 Architecture. Furthermore this architecture necessitates additional time and effort to be operational as there is a need to develop the software to allow the direct Transactional and Process Data entry into the Process Hub Stage

Dr. Eng. M. Naoulo

2. Also there is the need to design and develop the Integration, Consolidation, Synchronization, and Consistency of the Transactional and Process Data entered directly into the Process Repository Stage 2 with the Transactional and Process Data coming from the Legacy Systems. This architecture is the most difficult to be implemented.

Operational Difficulties

The operational difficulties associated with the Process Hub Stage 2 Architecture comprise the operational difficulties of the Process Hub Stage 1 Architecture applied to Master, Transactional, and Process Data.

6.3.12 The Process Hub Stage 3 Architecture

At this stage the Legacy Systems are phased out and all Data Entry for Master, Transactional, and Process Data will be carried out to update directly the Process Hub Stage 3. There is no more need for Data Integration, Consolidation, Propagation, Feedback or Synchronization as the Legacy Systems are phased out.

The Process Hub Stage 3 stores complete consolidated and integrated Master, Transactional, and Process Data. It will be used as Master, Transactional, and Business Process Data System of Records for the Business and Enterprise Intelligence Data Marts.

Diagram 6.13 represents the Process Hub Stage 3 Architecture.

Note: The implementation and operation of the Transaction Hub Stage 3 or the Process Hub Stage 3 architectures are feasible because of the enormous technical progress in Data Storage and Data Communication which enables fast Data Entry, Communication, Storage, and Reporting from and to the different Data Entry/Query/Retrieval/Reporting/Storage points around the globe. The phasing out of the Legacy Systems and replacing them with systems that directly update the Central Data Repository is challenging and would require a lot of efforts as many of the Legacy Systems would be very old and there are no documentation supporting their functionality and coding.

Dr. Eng. M. Naoulo

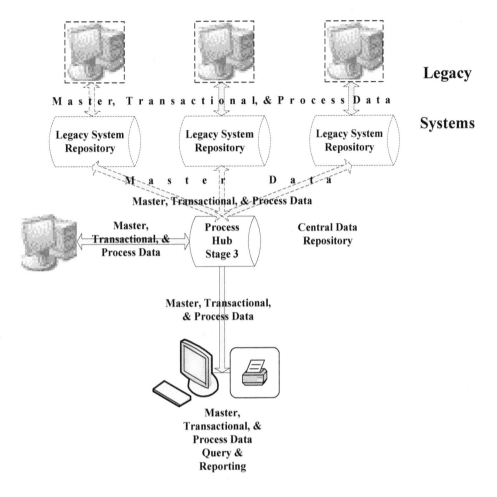

**The Process Hub Stage 3
Architecture**

Diagram 6.13: The Process Hub Stage 3 Architecture

Advantages

This architecture has tremendous advantages as it has a single Central Data Repository supporting all Data and there is no more need for data Integration, Consolidation, Propagation, Feedback, and Synchronization between different systems.

Disadvantages

This architecture necessitates additional time and effort to be operational in order to phase out the Legacy Systems and to train the Operational staff to use the new software.

Implementation Difficulties

The implementation difficulties are both technical difficulties related to data storage, data access, data communication, data partitioning and tuning, application design and development, and human participation difficulties as there is the need to phase out the old Legacy Systems and to train the Operational staff to use the new software.

Dr. Eng. M. Naoulo

Operational Difficulties
This architecture is the simplest to operate. Technical difficulties related to data storage, data access, data partitioning and tuning, data communication, etc. would arise as all the databases are stored in one "logical" area.

6.3.13 The Architectures of the Central Data Repositories
To analyze the Data Propagation thru the Architectures involving of the Central Data Repositories these Architectures are classified into four categories:

1. The Registry Architecture. It includes the MDM Registry Repository.

2. The Architectures of the Central Repositories. They do not comprise Feedback to the Legacy Systems. They include:
   - MDM Consolidation Repository
   - MDM Master Data Repository
   - Transaction Consolidation Repository
   - Transaction Repository Stage 1
   - Transaction Repository Stage 2
   - Process Consolidation Repository
   - Process Repository Stage 1
   - Process Repository Stage 2

3. The Architectures of the Central Hubs. They comprise Feedback to the Legacy Systems. The Hubs include:
   - MDM Consolidation Hub
   - MDM Master Data Hub
   - Transaction Consolidation Hub
   - Transaction Hub Stage 1
   - Transaction Hub Stage 2
   - Process Consolidation Hub
   - Process Hub Stage 1
   - Process Hub Stage 2

4. The Architectures of the Transaction and Process Hubs Stage 3.

6.3.14 The Data Propagation in the Registry Repository Architecture
The MDM Registry Repository is detailed in Section 6.3.1.

The Data Propagation from the Legacy Systems to the MDM Registry Repository is either real-time or near real-time or batch. However it is very often batch and on daily basis: the period between the updates is 24 hours. A record is created in the MDM Registry Repository for every new record of Master Data created in the Legacy Systems. This MDM Registry Repository record would contain a Surrogate Key, Link to the record of the Legacy System where the Master Data is created, and very few attributes if any (as needed by the business) of the Legacy

Dr. Eng. M. Naoulo

Systems Master Data record. If the MDM Registry Repository contains some Master Data attributes, the data to fill these attributes is propagated from the Legacy Systems.

No Data Feedback from the MDM Registry Repository to the Legacy Systems and therefore no propagation of data in this direction. Sometimes a Link to the record of the Master Data of the MDM Registry Repository is added to the Legacy Systems for fast retrieval, thru the links that are stored the MDM Registry Repository to the Legacy Systems, of the most current values of the Master Data attributes.

6.3.15 The Data Propagation in the Repositories Architecture not comprising Feedback to the Legacy Systems

The Data Propagation from the Legacy Systems to the Central Repository
The Legacy Systems will update the Central Repository either real-time or near real-time or batch.

The Data Propagation from the Central Repository to the Legacy Systems
No feedback from the Central Repository to the Legacy Systems unless there is a need to add into the Legacy Systems, during the Central Repository updates, the Key of the Master Data records of the Central Repository for fast Master Data records retrieval by the Legacy Systems.

6.3.16 The Data Propagation in the Hubs Architecture comprising Feedback to the Legacy Systems

The Data Propagation from the Legacy Systems to the Central Hub
The Legacy Systems will update the Central Hub either real-time or near real-time or batch.

The Data Propagation from the Central Hub to the Legacy Systems
Only the Master Data is fed back from the Central Hubs to the Legacy Systems. The Central Hub will feedback its data to update the Legacy Systems either real-time or near real-time or batch.

6.3.17 The Data Propagation in the Transaction & Process Hubs Stage 3

Since the Legacy Systems are phased out there is no data propagation to the Legacy Systems and no feedback from and the Legacy Systems. All data is entered directly into the Central Data Repository.

6.3.18 Effort, Performance, & Cost Comparison to develop the Architectures of the Central Data Repositories

> The effort to develop the Registry Repository is much less than the effort to develop the Central Repositories or the Central Hubs. The operational performance of the Registry Repository is very often beneath the performance of the Central Repositories or the Central Hubs.
> The Enterprise Data Architectures of the Central Repositories (not involving feedback to the Legacy Systems) are more cost effective and require less time to develop than the architectures of the Central Hubs. The Enterprise Data Architectures involving feedback

Dr. Eng. M. Naoulo

include updates to the databases of the Legacy Systems and sometimes there is the need to overhaul these databases and the Legacy Systems' applications. The retrieval of data from the Central Data Repository by the Legacy Systems, very often, is much faster than the feedback, needs less implementation effort, and comprises fewer difficulties. Also the feedback would require additional Synchronization between the Legacy Systems and between them and the Central Data Repository.

6.3.19 Real Life Scenarios

In large enterprises there might be Master, Transactional, and Process Data Integration and Consolidation architectures that are hybrid and might incorporate one or two or more different features of the above analyzed architectures. In this case the solution should be investigated, assessed, and evaluated to confirm its compliance to address the needs of the enterprise.

6.4 THE ENTERPRISE DATA ARCHITECTURE INVOLVING THE ODS

The current Data Architecture of enterprises were mostly developed based on the ODS as an essential repository for the integration of the Legacy Systems data and as a stage between the Legacy Systems and Data Marts. Diagram 6.14 represents the Enterprise Data Architecture involving the ODS. The Master Data in the ODS do not follow comprehensive modeling design and techniques, therefore the Integration and Consolidation of this data could not be easily verified.

Since the ODS does not carry Process Data, the Enterprise Intelligence Data Marts cannot retrieve data from it, and there is the need to retrieve this data from the Legacy Systems repositories (if they support such data or being modified to contain it) or from specific Process Data repositories thru Data Federation. Using Data Federation is complicated and has many issues and difficulties with data Integration, Consolidation, and Freshness. Enhancing the ODS to support Process Data requires a lot of effort and time and definitely is not cost effective.

Advantages
If the ODS is already in place, and if the scope of the Data Warehouse is very limited and requires no integration of Transactional Data, and if no Enterprise Engineering is required, and if the OLTP Query and Reporting from the BI Data Marts do not require embracing several Legacy Systems this architecture is fast to implement.

Disadvantages
If the scope of the Data Warehouse necessitates the Integration, Consolidation, Synchronization, and Consistency of Transactional Data, or if there is a need for Enterprise Engineering, or if the OLTP Query and Reporting from the BI Data Marts do require embracing several Legacy Systems this architecture, the ODS architecture is not appropriate and there is a need to build an Enterprise Data Architecture involving Transaction or Process Repositories or Hubs (Group 2 or 3). Furthermore the ODS Architecture is not suitable for enhancement as it is built without a comprehensive Data Architecture Technique, therefore any effort built on it is susceptible in the future to be pure waste as the transition to move to an Enterprise Data Architecture involving

Dr. Eng. M. Naoulo

Transaction or Process Repositories or Hubs would require the phase out of the ODS Architecture.

Implementation Difficulties

Since the Enterprise Data Architecture involving the ODS is based on ODS already in place, The implementation difficulties are encountered in the ETL of data extracted from the ODS to the BI Data Marts because the mapping is not straightforward as in the case of Central Data Repositories or Hubs using the SAM O NAOULO Modeling Technique.

Operational Difficulties

Since the ODS does not carry Process Data, the Enterprise Intelligence Data Marts cannot retrieve data from it, and there is the need to retrieve this data from the Operational Systems' Databases that include Process Data thru Data Federation. Using Data Federation is complicated, has many issues and difficulties with data Integration, Consolidation, and Freshness.

Dr. Eng. M. Naoulo

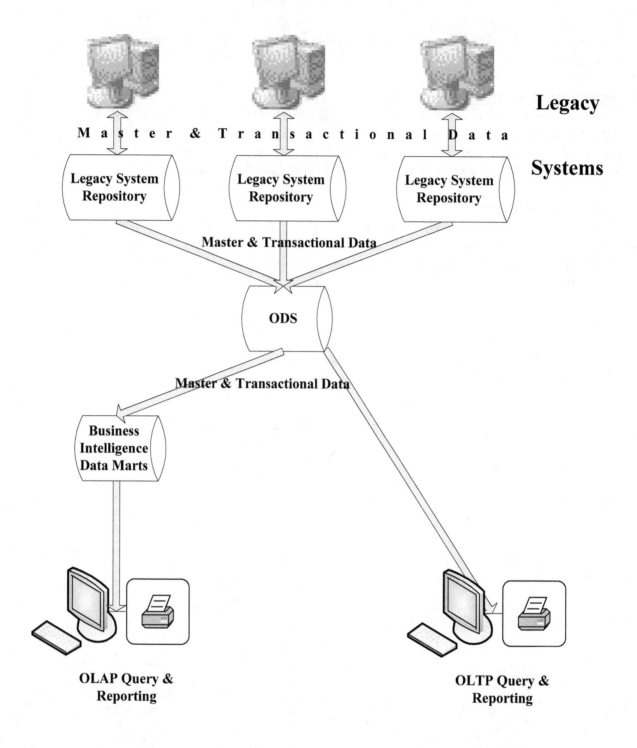

The Enterprise Architecture involving the ODS

Diagram 6.14: The Enterprise Data Architecture involving the ODS

Dr. Eng. M. Naoulo

6.5   THE ENTERPRISE DATA ARCHITECTURE INVOLVING THE CENTRAL DATA REPOSITORY

The Enterprise Data Architecture involving the Central Data Repository is based on the architectures detailed in Section 6.3 that would comprise Master, Transactional, and Process Data Integration, Consolidation, Synchronization, and Consistency.

6.5.1 The Enterprise Data Architectures involving the MDM Repositories/Hubs

Diagrams 6.15 to 6.19 represent the five Enterprise Data Architectures of Group 1 involving the MDM Repositories and Hubs:
> The MDM Registry Repository: Diagram 6.15.
> The MDM Consolidation Repository: Diagram 6.16.
> The MDM Consolidation Hub: Diagram 6.17.
> The MDM Master Data Repository: Diagram 6.18.
> The MDM Master Data Hub: Diagram 6.19.

The five architectures of Group 1 do not carry Transactional or Process Data in the Central Data Repository. Therefore the Central Data Repository can provide only Master Data Query and Reporting. OLTP Query and Reporting embracing a specific Legacy System is carried out from this Legacy System. OLTP Query and Reporting embracing several Legacy Systems is very difficult and not recommended within these architectures. If OLTP Query and Reporting embracing several Legacy Systems is needed, Group 2 or 3 architectures would be the answer. Furthermore the data required for OLAP and OLMP Query and Reporting is propagated from the Legacy Systems to the Business and Enterprise Intelligence Data Marts thru Data Federation.

Advantages
If the scope of the Data Warehouse and/or Enterprise Engineering is very limited and requires no integration of Transactional or Process Data, and if the OLTP or OLMP Query and Reporting from the BI and EI Data Marts do not require embracing several Legacy Systems these architectures are fast to implement.

Disadvantages
If the scope of the Data Warehouse and/or Enterprise Engineering necessitates the Integration, Consolidation, Synchronization, and Consistency of Transactional and/or Process Data coming from different Legacy Systems, these architectures would not be appropriate and there is a need to upgrade to Transaction or Process Repository or Hub architectures (Group 2 or 3).

Implementation Difficulties
The implementation difficulties are encountered in the ETL of data extracted from the Central Data Repository and in the Data Federation of the Transactional and/or Process Data extracted from the Legacy Systems to the Business and Enterprise Intelligence Data Marts. Additional difficulties occur in the development and implementation effort to synchronize these data.

Dr. Eng. M. Naoulo

Operational Difficulties

Since the MDM Repositories/Hubs do not carry Transactional and Process Data, the Business and Enterprise Intelligence Data Marts cannot retrieve data from it, and there is the need to retrieve this data from the Legacy Systems Repositories thru Data Federation. Using Data Federation is complicated, has many issues and difficulties with data Integration, Consolidation, and Freshness.

The operational difficulties arise also from the need to perform Data profiling, Data Cleansing, Data Proofing, and Referential Integrity during Data Federation of the Transactional and/or Process Data from the Legacy Systems to the Business and Enterprise Intelligence Data Marts.

Dr. Eng. M. Naoulo

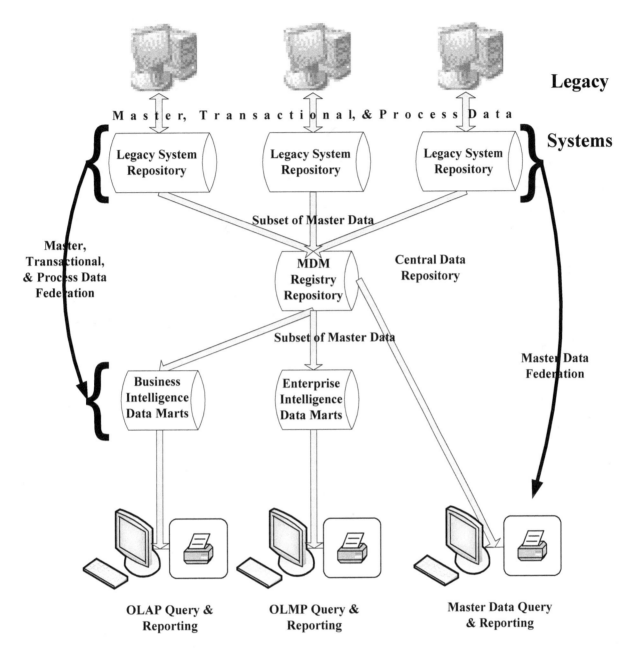

**The Enterprise Architecture involving the
MDM Registry Repository**

Diagram 6.15: The Enterprise Data Architecture involving the MDM Registry Repository

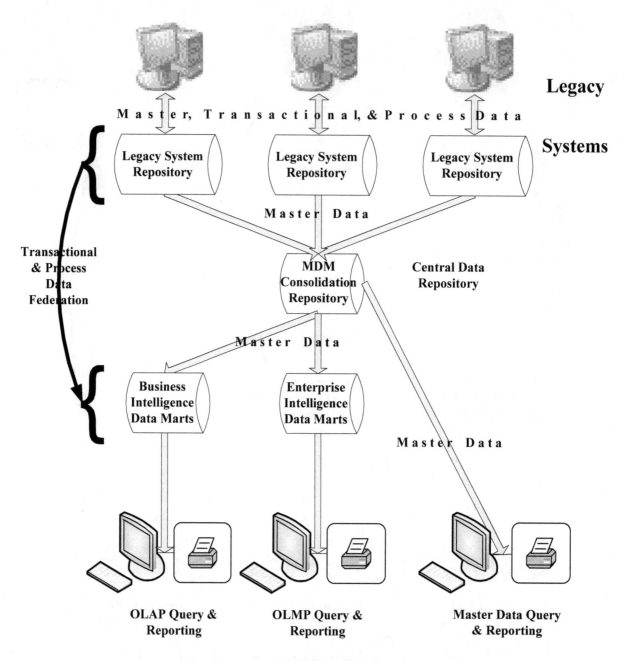

The Enterprise Architecture involving the
MDM Consolidation Repository

Diagram 6.16: The Enterprise Data Architecture using the MDM Consolidation Repository

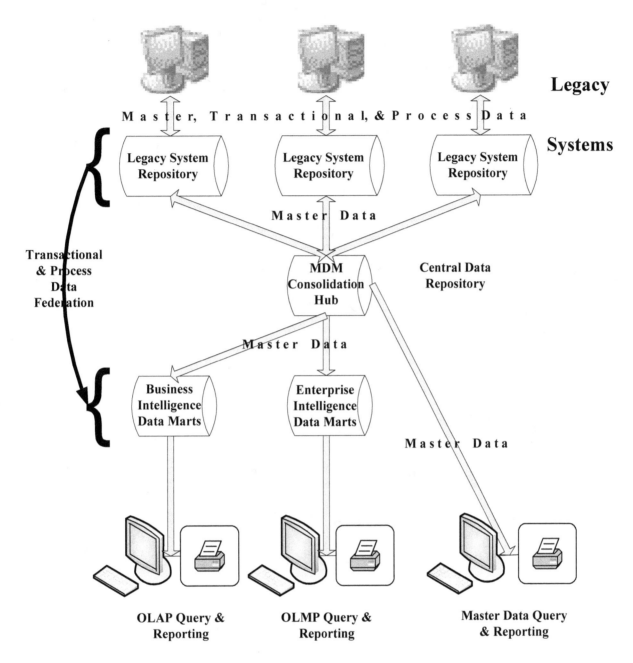

Legacy Systems

M a s t e r, T r a n s a c t i o n a l, & P r o c e s s D a t a

Legacy System Repository

Legacy System Repository

Legacy System Repository

M a s t e r   D a t a

Transactional & Process Data Federation

MDM Consolidation Hub

Central Data Repository

M a s t e r   D a t a

Business Intelligence Data Marts

Enterprise Intelligence Data Marts

M a s t e r   D a t a

OLAP Query & Reporting

OLMP Query & Reporting

Master Data Query & Reporting

**The Enterprise Architecture involving the
MDM Consolidation Hub**

Diagram 6.17: The Enterprise Data Architecture involving the MDM Consolidation Hub

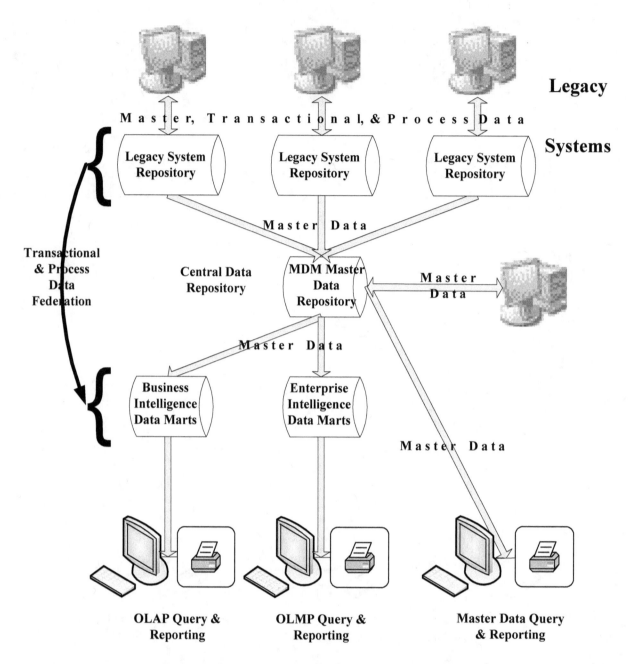

The Enterprise Architecture involving the MDM Master Data Repository

Diagram 6.18: The Enterprise Data Architecture involving the MDM Master Data Repository

Dr. Eng. M. Naoulo

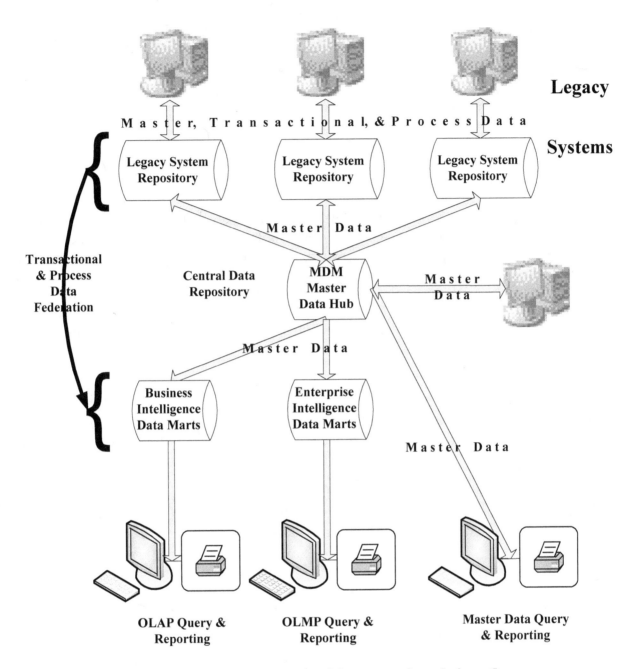

**The Enterprise Architecture involving the
MDM Master Data Hub**

Diagram 6.19: The Enterprise Data Architecture involving the MDM Master Data Hub

6.5.2 The Enterprise Data Architectures involving the Transaction Repositories/Hubs

The seven Enterprise Data Architectures involving Group 2 Transaction Repositories and Hubs are:

- ➢ The Transaction Consolidation Repository.
- ➢ The Transaction Consolidation Hub.
- ➢ The Transaction Repository Stage 1.
- ➢ The Transaction Hub Stage 1.
- ➢ The Transaction Repository Stage 2.
- ➢ The Transaction Hub Stage 2.
- ➢ The Transaction Hub Stage 3.

If the strategy of the enterprise does not incorporate Business Process Improvement and/or Revitalization then the Process Data, OLMP Query and Reporting, Enterprise Intelligence, and Enterprise Engineering are not needed. The diagrams representing these architectures are similar to those representing Group 3 (Ref. Section 6.5.3) except that the architectures of Group 2 do not carry Process Data. The Enterprise Data Architectures involving Group 2 Transaction Repositories and Hubs can provide, thru their Transaction Repositories and Hubs and Business Intelligence Data Marts and Cubes, Master Data, OLTP, and OLAP Query and Reporting. They cannot provide OLMP Query and Reporting.

The Enterprise Data Architectures involving Group 2 Transaction Repositories and Hubs require the Integration, Consolidation, Synchronization, and Consistency of the Transactional Data in the Transaction Repositories and Hubs. Retrieving this data from the Transaction Repositories and Hubs for further intelligence analysis has tremendous advantages over retrieving this data from the Legacy Systems. The Integration, Consolidation, Synchronization, and Consistency of the Transactional Data require enormous analysis, design, implementation, and operational effort to store, integrate, consolidate, synchronize, and keep up-to-date the Transactional Data in the Transaction Repositories and Hubs and these tasks are executed during the periods between batch updates of the Transaction Repositories and Hubs.

Advantages

The advantages of these architectures are:

- ➢ They support all Master Data, OLTP, and OLAP Query and Reporting, and Business Intelligence.
- ➢ They could be an intermediate step toward complete, integrated, and consolidated Enterprise Data Architectures supporting Master, Transactional, and Process Data (Section 6.5.3).
- ➢ Since the Transaction Repositories and Hubs are System of Reference or System of Records, there is no need to retrieve Master and Transactional Data from the Legacy Systems for the next stages of Business Intelligence Data Marts.

Disadvantages

These architectures do not support Business Process Improvement and/or Revitalization, Process Data, OLMP Query and Reporting, or Enterprise Intelligence. Adding the data and software to support them necessitates additional coding and some restructuring of the databases.

Dr. Eng. M. Naoulo

Implementation Difficulties

The implementation difficulties arise from:

> ➢ Design and implementation of the Transaction Repositories and Hubs containing both Master and Transactional Data.
> ➢ ETL design and implementation of Master and Transactional Data from the Legacy Systems to the Transaction Repositories and Hubs.
> ➢ ETL design and implementation of Master and Transactional Data from the Transaction Repositories and Hubs to the Data Marts.
> ➢ Development and implementation effort to synchronize the data between the Legacy Systems and the Transaction Repositories and Hubs.

Operational Difficulties

The Operational Difficulties arise from the need to perform Data profiling, Data Cleansing, Data Proofing, and Referential Integrity before and/or during the ETL from the Legacy Systems to the Transaction Repositories and Hubs.

6.5.3 The Enterprise Data Architectures involving the Process Repositories/Hubs

The seven Enterprise Data Architectures involving Group 3 Process Repositories and Hubs are:

> ➢ The Process Consolidation Repository: Diagram 6.20.
> ➢ The Process Consolidation Hub: Diagram 6.21.
> ➢ The Process Repository Stage 1: Diagram 6.22.
> ➢ The Process Hub Stage 1: Diagram 6.23.
> ➢ The Process Repository Stage 2: Diagram 6.24.
> ➢ The Process Hub Stage 2: Diagram 6.25.
> ➢ The Process Hub Stage 3: Diagram 6.26

The diagrams representing these architectures are hereafter. The Enterprise Data Architectures involving Group 3 Process Repositories and Hubs can provide, thru their Process Repositories and Hubs and Business and Enterprise Intelligence Data Marts and Cubes, Master Data, OLTP, OLAP, and OLMP Query and Reporting.

Similar remark as in Section 6.5.2 related to the Integration, Consolidation, Synchronization, and Consistency would be applied to the Transactional and Process Data.

Advantages

The advantages of these architectures are:

> ➢ They support all Master, OLTP, OLAP, and OLMP Query and Reporting, and Business and Enterprise Intelligence.
> ➢ Since the Process Repositories and Hubs are System of Reference or System of Records, there is no need to retrieve Master, Transactional, or Process Data from the Legacy Systems for the next stages of Business and Enterprise Intelligence Data Marts.

Disadvantages

Dr. Eng. M. Naoulo

The implementation of these architectures covering all lines of business of and enterprise would be costly and might take long time. They could be implemented in stages and/or iterations based on prioritization, easiness, budget, business and infrastructure needs, and resources availability.

Implementation Difficulties

> The implementation difficulties of these architectures comprise the implementation difficulties of the architectures involving Transaction Repositories and Hubs applied to Master, Transactional, and Process Data.

> The design and implementation of these architectures require excellent Enterprise and Data Architects and Engineers.

Operational Difficulties

The operational difficulties of these architectures comprise the operational difficulties of the architectures involving Transaction Repositories and Hubs applied to Master, Transactional, and Process Data.

Dr. Eng. M. Naoulo

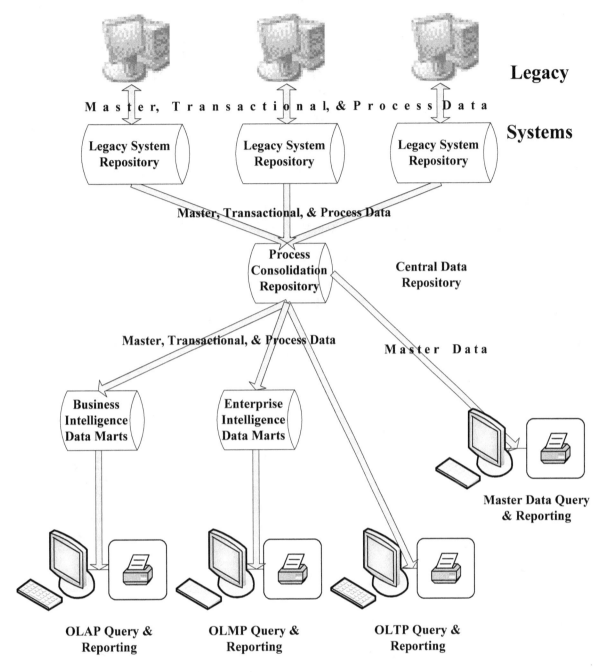

**The Enterprise Architecture involving the
Process Consolidation Repository**

*Diagram 6.20: The Enterprise Data Architecture involving the Process Consolidation
Repository*

Master, Transactional, & Process Data Management & Enterprise Engineering

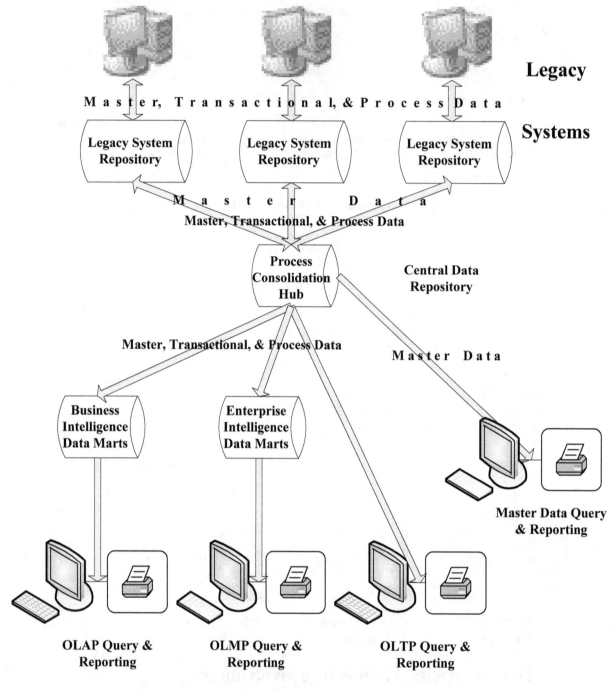

The Enterprise Architecture involving the Process Consolidation Hub

Diagram 6.21: The Enterprise Data Architecture involving the Process Consolidation Hub

Dr. Eng. M. Naoulo

Master, Transactional, & Process Data Management & Enterprise Engineering

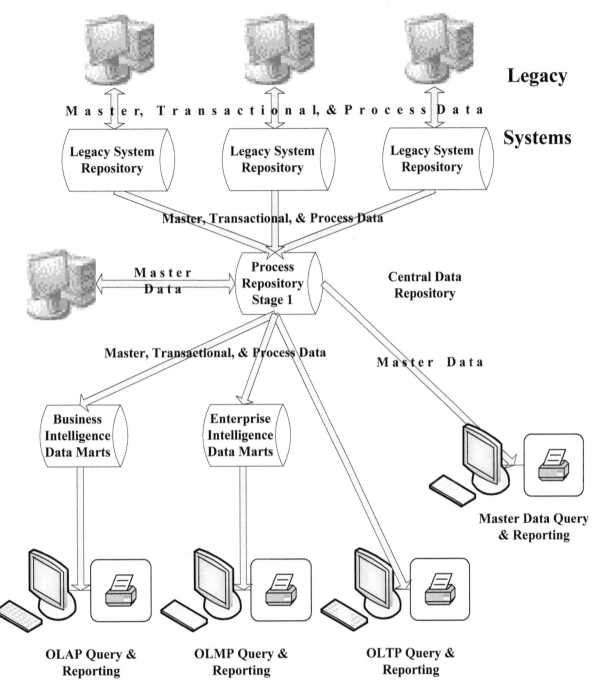

The Enterprise Architecture involving the
Process Repository Stage 1

Diagram 6.22: The Enterprise Data Architecture involving the Process Repository Stage 1

Dr. Eng. M. Naoulo

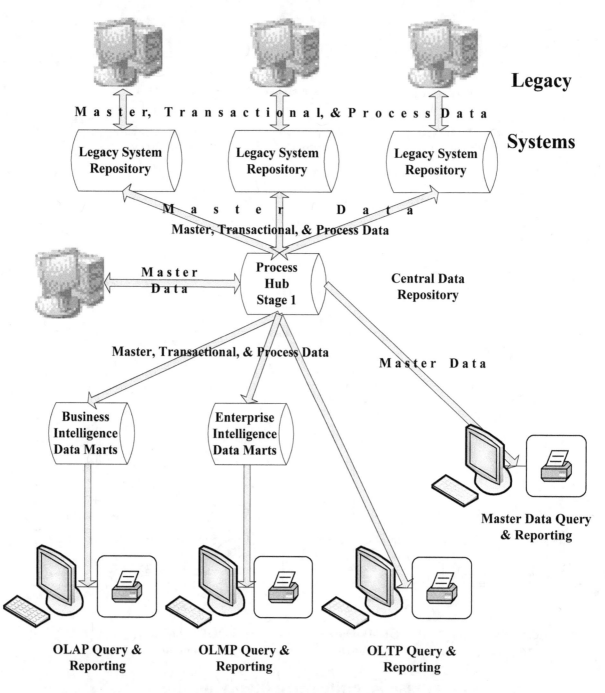

**The Enterprise Architecture involving the
Process Hub Stage 1**

Diagram 6.23: The Enterprise Data Architecture involving the Process Hub Stage 1

Dr. Eng. M. Naoulo

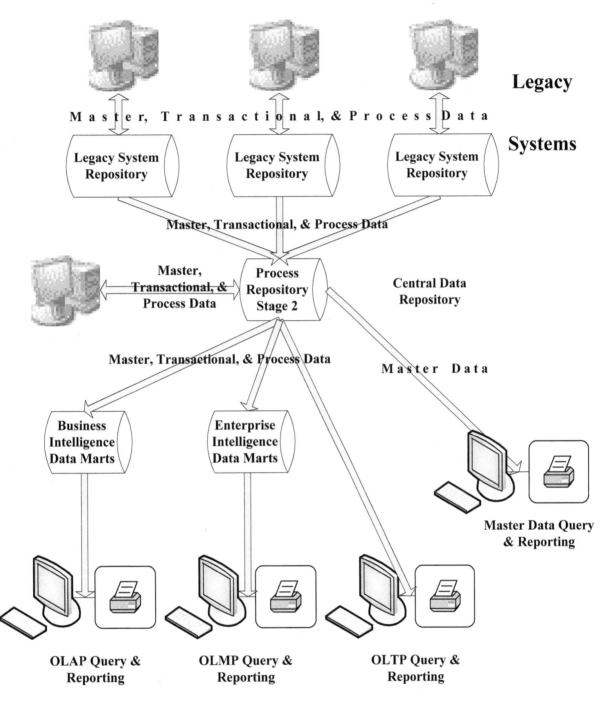

The Enterprise Architecture involving the
Process Repository Stage 2

Diagram 6.24: The Enterprise Data Architecture involving the Process Repository Stage 2

Dr. Eng. M. Naoulo

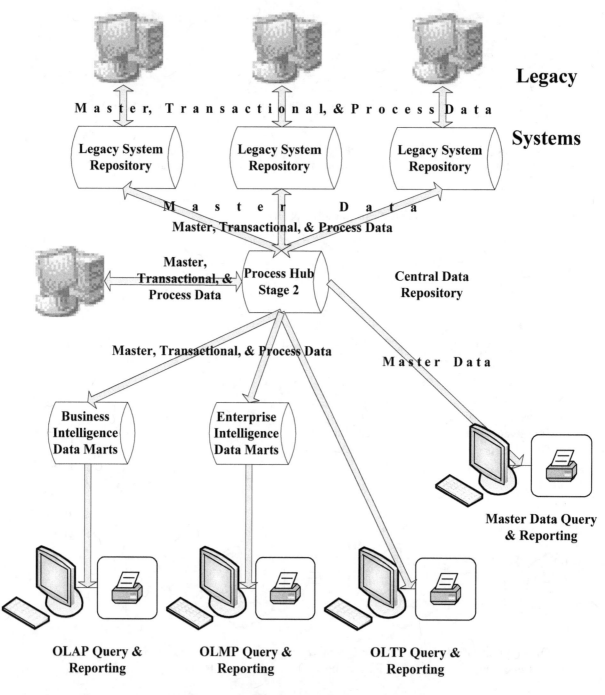

**The Enterprise Architecture involving the
Process Hub Stage 2**

Diagram 6.25: The Enterprise Data Architecture involving the Process Hub Stage 2

Dr. Eng. M. Naoulo

Master, Transactional, & Process Data Management
& Enterprise Engineering

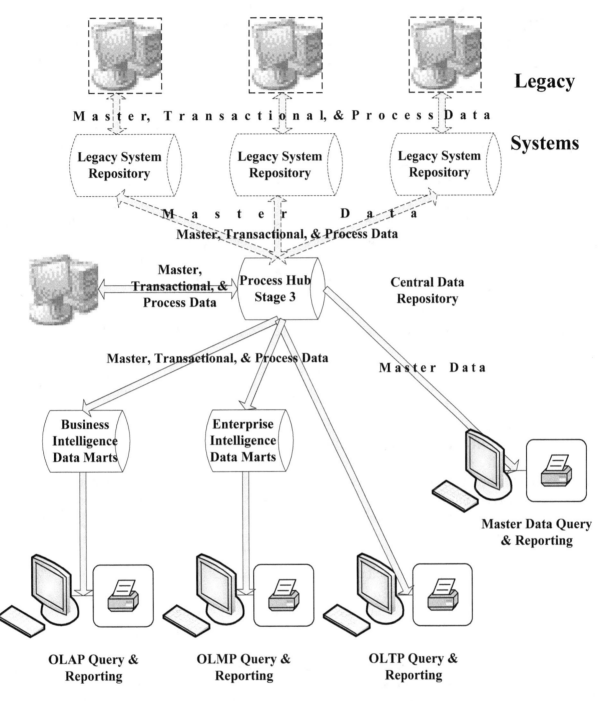

The Enterprise Architecture involving the
Process Hub Stage 3

Diagram 6.26: The Enterprise Data Architecture involving the Process Hub Stage 3

145

Dr. Eng. M. Naoulo

6.6 TRANSITION FROM THE ENTERPRISE DATA ARCHITECTURE INVOLVING THE ODS TO THE ENTERPRISE DATA ARCHITECTURES INVOLVING THE CENTRAL DATA REPOSITORY

Section 6.2 highlighted the differences between the Central Data Repository and the ODS architectures. Section 6.4 indicated the unsuitability and shortcomings of the ODS architecture to support the data requirements of enterprises. It is recommended to build a solid Enterprise Data Architecture and transit from the ODS to a Central Data Repository that uses the Enterprise engineering Model and its comprehensive SAM O NAOULO Modeling Technique. This Enterprise Data Architecture shall support the operation of the enterprise, provide the BI and EI Query and Reporting, and easily sustain the future expansions and data requirements.

This section shall describe and assess the transition from the Enterprise Data Architecture involving the ODS to the Enterprise Data Architectures involving the Central Data Repository comprising Master, Transactional, and Process Data. Section 6.7 details the roadmaps across the different Enterprise Data Architectures involving the Central Data Repository.

Three Transition approaches are assessed. In all these approaches the ODS would be very useful (if it was analyzed and modeled correctly) as a reference to understand the business and as a starting point/launching pad for this exercise.

6.6.1 Transition based on enhancing the ODS

The first impulsive approach for the transition from the Enterprise Data Architecture involving the ODS to the Enterprise Data Architectures involving the Central Data Repository is to aim to enhance and overhaul the ODS to add the Master, Transactional, and Process Data and implement their Integration. This approach incorporates insurmountable tasks due to the need to build a new Data Architecture that follows the SAM O NAOULO Modeling Technique on top of an old, inconsistent, and incomplete data structure. To follow the modeling technique used for the ODS would be absurd. Nevertheless the steps to accomplish this transition are:

1. Design and implementation of new Systems or enhance the Legacy Systems to incorporate the Mechanics Session Data and to accommodate any new data requirements (Ref. Sections 5.3.1, 5.3.2, & 5.3.3).
2. Overhaul the ODS System to incorporate the new structures for Master Data, Mechanism, and Mechanics Sessions and Transactions.
3. Analysis, Design, and Implementation of Data Mapping, Integration, Consolidation, Propagation, Feedback, Synchronization, Governance, and Quality Assurance from the Legacy Systems to the overhauled ODS architecture.
4. Overhaul the Business Intelligence Data Marts (if any) to incorporate the new structures for Master Data and Mechanics Transactions.
5. Design and build the Enterprise Intelligence Data Marts to incorporate the Business Process Sessions data.

Dr. Eng. M. Naoulo

This approach is cumbersome and not recommended even if the objective is to incorporate the new Master and Transactional Data without the Mechanics Sessions and Process Data.

6.6.2 Transition based on new Central Data Repository involving only Master & Transactional Data

This approach is based on the design and implementation of new Enterprise Data Architecture profiting from the knowledge acquired from the Enterprise Data Architecture involving the ODS. The steps to accomplish this are:

1. Enhance the Legacy Systems to accommodate any new data requirements.
2. Design and implementation of the Central Data Repository.
3. Analysis, Design, and Implementation of Data Mapping, Integration, Consolidation, Propagation, Feedback, Synchronization, Governance, and Quality Assurance from the Legacy Systems to the new Central Data Repository.
4. Overhaul the Business Intelligence Data Marts (if any) to incorporate the new structures for Master Data and Mechanics Transactions.

The two architectures (the old Enterprise Data Architecture involving the ODS and the new Enterprise Data Architecture involving the Central Data Repository) will run in parallel, then the ODS and its related BI Data Marts are phased out. The transition will occur gradually (one or several Legacy Systems at a time depending on the need for interlinks between the systems). It is advisable:

1. That the new Enterprise Data Architectures would aim to involve first the Transaction Consolidation Repository.
2. To apply the Modeling Techniques of SAM O NAOULO for the design of the Transactional Data in the Central Data Repository even if the Process Data is not incorporated. This can be accomplished by using the Sessions without any measures as key links between the Mechanics Transactions and the Master Data.

If this approach necessitates major redevelopment of the Legacy Systems, then this is a huge task requiring a lot of effort, resources, and time. In this case it is advisable to assess the implementation of the Enterprise Data Architecture based on the Transaction Hub Stage 3.

6.6.3 Transition based on new Central Data Repository involving Master, Transactional, & Process Data

This approach is similar to the approach described in Section 6.6.2 alongside incorporating Master and Mechanics Sessions and Transactions Data. The steps to accomplish this are:

1. Design and implementation of new systems and/or enhance the Legacy Systems to incorporate the Mechanics Session Data.
2. Design and implementation of the Central Data Repository.
3. Analysis, Design, and Implementation of Data Mapping, Integration, Consolidation, Propagation, Feedback, Synchronization, Governance and Quality Assurance from the Legacy Systems and the new systems to the new Central Data Repository.
4. Overhaul the Business Intelligence Data Marts 9if any) to incorporate the new structures for Master Data and Mechanics Transactions.
5. Design and build the Enterprise Intelligence Data Marts to incorporate the Business

Dr. Eng. M. Naoulo

Process Sessions Data.

Similar to Section 6.6.2, the two architectures will run in parallel then the ODS and its related BI Data Marts are phased out. It is advisable:

1. That the new Enterprise Data Architectures would aim to involve first the Process Consolidation Repository.
2. To implementing full Integrated and Consolidated Master, Transactional, and Process Data in the Central Data Repository following the Modeling Techniques of SAM O NAOULO and their Best of Practice.

Again, if this approach necessitates major redevelopment of the Legacy Systems, then this is a huge task requiring a lot of effort, resources, and time. In this case it is advisable to assess the implementation of the Enterprise Data Architecture based on the Process Hub Stage 3.

6.7 ROADMAPS ACROSS THE DIFFERENT ENTERPRISE DATA ARCHITECTURES INVOLVING THE CENTRAL DATA REPOSITORY

The path from the current architectures of the enterprises to more advanced architectures is lengthy, costly, and requires a lot of effort. Very often it is recommended to go thru intermediate architectures, assure its solidity and benefit from its advantages before embarking into more sophisticated architectures.

The roadmaps across the different Enterprise Data Architectures involving the Central Data Repository would include many transition steps involving intermediate architectures. Within each transition step, Data Mapping, Integration, Consolidation, Propagation, Feedback, Synchronization, Governance, and Quality Assurance are implemented as needed.

6.7.1 Transition within Group 1
The transitions within Group 1 could be implemented as follows:

1. MDM Registry Repository > MDM Consolidation Repository: By designing and adding all Master Data into the Central Data Repository. The links to the Legacy Systems Master Data could be kept or removed.
2. MDM Consolidation Repository > MDM Consolidation Hub: By adding Feedback from the Central Data Repository to the Legacy Systems.
3. MDM Consolidation Repository > MDM Master Data Repository: By adding direct Master Data entry into the Central Data Repository.
4. MDM Consolidation Hub > MDM Master Data Hub: By adding direct Master Data entry into the Central Data Repository.
5. MDM Master Data Repository > MDM Master Data Hub: By adding Feedback from the Central Data Repository to the Legacy Systems.

6.7.2 Transition within Group 2
The transitions within Group 2 could be implemented as follows:

Dr. Eng. M. Naoulo

1. Transaction Consolidation Repository > Transaction Consolidation Hub: By adding Feedback from the Central Data Repository to the Legacy Systems.
2. Transaction Consolidation Repository > Transaction Repository Stage 1: By adding direct Master Data entry into the Central Data Repository.
3. Transaction Consolidation Hub > Transaction Hub Stage 1: By adding direct Master Data entry into the Central Data Repository.
4. Transaction Repository Stage 1 > Transaction Hub Stage 1: By adding Feedback from the Central Data Repository to the Legacy Systems.
5. Transaction Repository Stage 1 > Transaction Repository Stage 2: By adding direct Transactional Data entry into the Central Data Repository.
6. Transaction Hub Stage 1 > Transaction Hub Stage 2: By adding direct Transactional Data entry into the Central Data Repository.
7. Transaction Repository Stage 2 > Transaction Hub Stage 2: By adding Feedback from the Central Data Repository to the Legacy Systems.
8. Transaction Hub Stage 2 > Transaction Hub Stage 3: By phasing out all Legacy Systems and establish all data entry directly into the Central Data Repository.

6.7.3 Transition within Group 3
Similar to the Transition within Group 2, but applied to both Transactional and Process Data.

6.7.4 Transition from Group 1 to Group 2
The transitions from Group 1 to Group 2 could be implemented by including all Transactional Data into the Central Data Repository as follows:
1. MDM Consolidation Repository > Transaction Consolidation Repository.
2. MDM Consolidation Hub > Transaction Consolidation Hub.
3. MDM Master Data Repository > Transaction Repository Stage 1.
4. MDM Master Data Hub > Transaction Hub Stage 1.

To accomplish this there is the need to add the structure of the Transactional Data into the Central Data Repository and use this Repository as System of Reference or System of Records for the Business Intelligence Data Marts.

6.7.5 Transition from Group 1 to Group 3
Similar to the Transition from Group 1 to Group 2, however it is applied to both Transactional and Process Data.

6.7.6 Transition from Group 2 to Group 3
It is produced by adding the Process Data to the architectures:
1. Transaction Consolidation Repository > Process Consolidation Repository.
2. Transaction Consolidation Hub > Process Consolidation Hub.
3. Transaction Repository Stage 1 > Process Repository Stage 1.
4. Transaction Hub Stage 1 > Process Hub Stage 1.
5. Transaction Repository Stage 2 > Process Repository Stage 2.
6. Transaction Hub Stage 2 > Process Hub Stage 2.
7. Transaction Repository Stage 3 > Process Repository Stage 3.

Dr. Eng. M. Naoulo

6.7.7 Guidelines for the Transition Roadmaps

The roadmap to implement the Enterprise Data Architecture involving Master Data could follow many paths. It is recommended:

1. To follow the Transition steps indicated above.
2. To implement the roadmap one Transition step at a time unless there are not many Legacy Systems involved and these Legacy Systems are not complicated and do not interfere with each other a lot.
3. If the ODS is in place, to transit to the Transaction Consolidation Repository.
4. Very often the Transaction Consolidation Repository and the Process Consolidation Repository provides very good ROI for the enterprises.

The enterprise should decide on the best roadmap that suits its requirements, budget, technical milieu and environment, future plans, and capability: resources, knowhow, and adaptability. The following paths are the most practical roadmaps:

➤ MDM Registry Repository > MDM Consolidation Repository > MDM Consolidation Hub > MDM Master Data Hub > Transaction/Process Hub Stage 1 > Transaction/Process Hub Stage 2 > Transaction/Process Hub Stage 3.
➤ MDM Registry Repository > MDM Consolidation Repository > MDM Master Data Repository > MDM Master Data Hub > Transaction/Process Hub Stage 1 > Transaction/Process Hub Stage 2 > Transaction/Process Hub Stage 3.

Or by skipping the MDM Registry Repository:

➤ MDM Consolidation Repository > MDM Consolidation Hub > MDM Master Data Hub > Transaction/Process Hub Stage 1 > Transaction/Process Hub Stage 2 > Transaction/Process Hub Stage 3.
➤ MDM Consolidation Repository > MDM Master Data Repository > MDM Master Data Hub > Transaction/Process Hub Stage 1 > Transaction/Process Hub Stage 2 > Transaction/Process Hub Stage 3.

One of the most cost effective roadmaps that provide the best Return-On-Investment (ROI) would be by skipping the feedback to the Legacy Systems altogether:

➤ MDM Consolidation Repository > MDM Master Data Repository > Transaction/Process Repository Stage 1 > Transaction/Process Repository Stage 2 > Transaction/Process Hub Stage 3.

It is recommended to establish the strategy and roadmap for Master Data Integration and Consolidation Architecture and the path to implement the Enterprise Data Architecture involving Master, Transactional, and Process Data during the first phases of the MDM, Enterprise Architecture, and Enterprise Engineering exercises.

Table 6.2 provides a summary of Transition Roadmaps between the Enterprise Data Architectures of Group 1, Group 3, and from Group 1 to Group 3. The Transition Roadmaps between the Enterprise Data Architectures of Group 2 and from Group 2 to Group 3 are similar to the outlined Transition Roadmaps.

Dr. Eng. M. Naoulo

	ODS	MDM Registry Repository	MDM Consolidation Repository	MDM Consolidation Hub	MDM Master Data Repository	MDM Master Data Hub	Process Consolidation Repository	Process Consolidation Hub	Process Repository Stage 1	Process Hub Stage 1	Process Repository Stage 2	Process Hub Stage 2	Process Hub Stage 3
ODS	===												
MDM Registry Repository		===	Designing and adding all Master Data into the Central Data Repository										
MDM Consolidation Repository			===	Adding Feedback from the Central Data Repository to the Legacy Systems	Adding direct Master Data entry into the Central Data Repository		Adding the Transactional & Process Data into the Central Data Repository						
MDM Consolidation Hub				===		Adding direct Master Data entry into the Central Data Repository		Adding the Transactional & Process Data into the Central Data Repository					
MDM Master Data Repository					===	Adding Feedback from the Central Data Repository to the Legacy Systems			Adding the Transactional & Process Data into the Central Data Repository				
MDM Master Data Hub						===				Adding the Transactional & Process Data into the Central Data Repository			

Dr. Eng. M. Naoulo

Process Consolidation Repository							===	Adding Feedback from the Central Data Repository to the Legacy Systems	Adding direct Master Data entry into the Central Data Repository				
Process Consolidation Hub								===	Adding direct Master Data entry into the Central Data Repository				
Process Repository Stage 1								===	Adding Feedback from the Central Data Repository to the Legacy Systems	Adding direct Transactional & Process Data entry into the Central Data Repository			
Process Hub Stage 1									===		Adding direct Transactional & Process Data entry into the Central Data Repository		
Process Repository Stage 2											===	Adding Feedback from the Central Data Repository to the Legacy Systems	
Process Hub Stage 2												===	Phasing out all Legacy Systems and establish all data entry directly into the Central Data Repository

Dr. Eng. M. Naoulo

Proce ss Hub Stage 3												===

Table 6.2: Summary of Transition Roadmaps between the different Enterprise Data Architectures

6.8 ENTERPRISE DATA INTEGRATION, CONSOLIDATION, SYNCHRONIZATION, & CONSISTENCY

The Integration and Consolidation of Master, Transactional, and Process Data either in the repositories or in the hubs, and the Synchronization and Consistency of this data between the different databases (Legacy System, ODS, and Central Data Repository databases, Business and Enterprise Intelligence Data Marts) require tremendous effort. The detailed analysis and design of this data was elaborated in Chapters 2, 3, 4, 5, 12, 13, & 14 following SAM O NAOULO Modeling Technique. The Enterprise Engineering System of Apparatus, Machinery, and Operation (**SAM O NAOULO**) would simplify the Integration, Consolidation, Synchronization, and Consistency of the Master, Transactional, and Process Data and facilitate the support for the Dimensions of the Data Marts.

Diagram 6.27 depicts the propagation of data from the Central Data Repository to the Business and Enterprise Intelligence Data Marts.

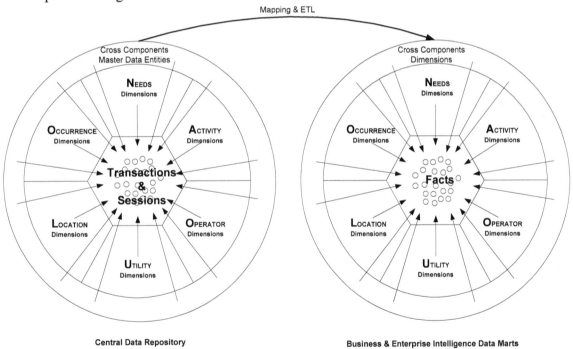

Diagram 6.27: The Propagation of Data from the Central Data Repository to the Business & Enterprise Intelligence Data Marts

Currently, in the majority of enterprises, the repository of the integrated OLTP data is the ODS. If the target of the Enterprise Data Architecture is only the Business Intelligence Data Marts, then using the ODS instead of the Central Data Repository does not provide comprehensive Master Data Management although it might provide some quick Return-On-Investment (ROI) if the ODS is already built correctly. However the use of the Central Data Repository is more effective and comprehensive, and very useful if there are many Business Intelligence Data Marts. Also the Central Data Repository is very adequate for future expansions with additional Operational Systems or Data Marts. Furthermore the need for Enterprise Intelligence Data Marts would definitely command the use of the Central Data Repository.

The Integration and Consolidation of the databases of the Legacy Systems require dealing with the features of the metadata and data structure: fields name, description, type, size, enumerated values, upper and lower limits, referential integrity, etc. The tasks to accomplish this require the involvement of Data Analysts, Business Staff, and Data Modelers. The Synchronization and Consistency of data require dealing with the content of the data fields. Data Governance, Data Stewardship, Data Quality, and ETL are very important to perform this endeavor. The tasks to accomplish this require the involvement of Data Stewards, Business Staff, and ETL architects and developers.

6.8.1 The Integration & Consolidation of Master Data

The Apparatus and its Master Data analysis and design ensue the appropriate grouping of the Master Data. The Integration and Consolidation of all Master Data governing OLTP, ALAP, and OLMP in one area would assure many features of Master Data Management (MDM) and their advantages advocated by IT experts and software tools suppliers. This Integration would endorse that all changes to the Master Data by any Legacy System would be reflected or transmitted to the Central Data Repository: One Truth or Single Version of Truth or Single Source of Truth. Also it shall ensure that the mapping and propagation of Master Data to the BI and EI is simple and straightforward. Then, depending on the adopted enterprise architecture, the data could be propagated back to the Legacy Systems.

The Integration and Consolidation of all the Master Data provide enormous advantage for the integration of the Enterprise's Information Systems. These Integration and Consolidation alleviate tremendously the problems encountered in Master Data Management, Customer Data Integration (CDI), Product Data Integration (PDI), Data Mapping, Propagation and Synchronization. Business and Enterprise Intelligence Data Marts can retrieve, from the Central Data Repository, exactly the same Master Data which is designed according to **SAM O NAOULO** Modeling Technique (Ref. Sections 5.4.1 & 5.5.1).

The following directions govern the Integration and Consolidation of Master Data in the MDM Repositories and Hubs:
  ➤ **MDM Registry Repository** (Ref. Section 6.3.1): The MDM Registry Repository does not contain all Master Data. It contains only some data and the keys to the Legacy Systems for additional Master Data retrieval. Therefore the Integration and Consolidation of Master Data are minimal and do not require extensive effort. The Integration and Consolidation are mandatory when the Master Data residing in the MDM Registry

Repository is updated in any Legacy System and when records handling Master Data in the Legacy Systems are created or deleted.

➢ **MDM Consolidation Repository** (Ref. Section 6.3.2): The Consolidation Repository does contain all Master Data with no feedback from the Consolidation Repository into the Legacy Systems and no direct Master Data entry into the Consolidation Repository. The Integration and Consolidation of Master Data in the MDM Consolidation Repository do require extensive effort.

➢ **MDM Consolidation HUB** (Ref. Section 6.3.3): The MDM Consolidation Hub does contain all Master Data with Master Data feedback from the MDM Consolidation Hub into the Legacy Systems, but no direct Master Data entry into the MDM Consolidation Hub. The Integration and Consolidation of Master Data in the MDM Consolidation Hub do require similar effort to the MDM Consolidation Repository.

➢ **MDM Master Data Repository** (Ref. Section 6.3.4): The MDM Master Data Repository does contain all Master Data with direct Master Data entry into the MDM Master Data Repository, but no feedback from the MDM Master Data Repository into the Legacy Systems. Therefore the Integration and Consolidation of Master Data in the MDM Master Data Repository do require additional effort – compared to the MDM Consolidation Repository – to accommodate the direct Master Data entry into the MDM Master Data Repository.

➢ **MDM Master Data Hub** (Ref. Section 6.3.5): The MDM Master Data Hub does contain all Master Data with direct Master Data entry into the MDM Master Data Hub and Master Data feedback from the MDM Master Data Hub into the Legacy Systems. The Integration and Consolidation of Master Data in the MDM Master Data Hub do require similar effort to the MDM Master Data Repository.

The directions governing the Integration and Consolidation of Master Data in the Transaction Repositories and Hubs and Process Repositories and Hubs are similar to the above directions.

It is important to note that:

➢ The design of the Master Data in the Central Data Repository based on the grouping approach used in **SAM O NAOULO** Modeling Technique and the Dimension and Associative Entities Profile details would be the base to construct the Master Data, BI, and EI Dimensions.

➢ Repetition and de-normalization are accepted in the Data Marts as per the Multidimensional Technique.

➢ The ETL to load the Dimensions of the Enterprise Intelligence Data Marts is similar to the ETL to load the Dimensions of the Business Intelligence Data Marts.

➢ The BI and EI Dimensions are formed by using:

- Master Data Dimensions.
- Master Data Associative Entities within a Master Data Component but across Master Data Dimension Profiles.
- Master Data Associative Entities across Master Data Components.
- Master Data Associative Entities resulting from Master Data recursive relationships. The recursive relationships of Master Data Entities would imply that some attributes of the Master Data Entities be put in the BI and EI Data Marts' Dimensions many

Dr. Eng. M. Naoulo

> times as needed. These attributes reflect in the BI and EI Dimensions the recursive hierarchies.
> ➤ Master Data Dimension and Associative Entities could be grouped as needed to form the BI and EI Dimensions.
> ➤ The attributes of the Master Data Dimension and Associative Entities would be part of the BI and EI Dimensions as needed.

In the ideal world of Master Data all Master Data would reside in only one Central Data Repository serving all applications including the Legacy Systems and Business and Enterprise Intelligence. This will help eliminating the Integration and Consolidation of Master Data in the Central Data Repository, eliminating the Synchronization and Consistency of Master Data between the different Legacy Systems, eliminating the Data Mapping and Propagation of Master Data from the Legacy Systems to the Central Data Repository, Feedback of Master Data from the Central Data Repository to the Legacy Systems, and assuring the Consistency of Master Data for the whole enterprise. This will also reduce significantly the mapping and ETL from the Central Data Repository to the Business and Enterprise Intelligence Data Marts. The Mechanics Sessions and Transactions in the Legacy Systems will link thru Foreign Keys to the Central Repository Master Data.

6.8.2 The Integration & Consolidation of Transactional Data

The Transactional Data analysis and design ensue the appropriate links between the Transactions to the Master Data, the Mechanism, and the Mechanics sessions. In the ideal world the Legacy Systems are independent and covering different Lines of Business; however in the real world a Line of Business could be covered by many Legacy Systems and a Legacy System could cover many Lines of Business. It is very important to assess the benefits of Integration & Consolidation of Transactional Data and establish the roadmap to implement it before embarking into such endeavor.

The directions governing the Integration and Consolidation of Transactional Data are similar to the directions indicated in Section 6.8.3, but without the Process Data. These directions would be applied to the Transaction Repositories and Hubs in a similar way to their application to the Process Repositories and Hubs.

The Transactional Data of the Legacy Systems could be integrated and consolidated in the Central Data Repository to provide consistent OLTP Query and Reporting and form the base for Data Mapping, ETL, and Data Propagation to the Business Intelligence Data Marts for OLAP Analysis, Query, and Reporting. This Integration and Consolidation will also reduce significantly the Data Synchronization of Transactional Data between the different Legacy Systems and the feedback from the Central Data repository to the Legacy Systems.

6.8.3 The Integration & Consolidation of Process Data

The Process Data's analysis and design ensue the appropriate links between the Mechanics Sessions to the Master Data. Currently, in the majority of enterprises, the Legacy Systems do not support Process Data. In the ideal world the systems carrying Process Data should be independent and covering different Lines of Business.

Dr. Eng. M. Naoulo

The following directions govern the Integration and Consolidation of Process Data in the Process Repositories and Hubs:

> **Process Consolidation Repository** (Ref. Section 6.3.6): The Process Consolidation Repository does contain all Master, Transactional, and Process Data with no feedback from the Process Consolidation Repository into the Legacy Systems and no direct Data entry into the Process Consolidation Repository. The Integration and Consolidation of Process Data do require extensive effort.

> **Process Consolidation Hub** (Ref. Section 6.3.7): The Process Consolidation Hub does contain all Master, Transactional, and Process Data with Master Data feedback from the Process Consolidation Hub into the Legacy Systems, but no direct Master, Transactional, and Process Data entry into the Process Consolidation Hub. The Integration and Consolidation of Process Data in the Process Consolidation Hub do require similar effort to the Process Consolidation Repository.

> **Process Repository Stage 1**: (Ref. Section 6.3.8): The Process Repository Stage 1 does contain all Master, Transactional, and Process Data with direct Master Data entry into the Process Repository Stage 1, but no feedback from the Process Repository Stage 1 into the Legacy Systems. Therefore the Integration and Consolidation of Master, Transactional, and Process Data in the Process Repository Stage 1 do require additional effort – compared to the Process Consolidation Repository – to accommodate the direct Master Data entry into the Process Repository Stage 1.

> **Process Hub Stage 1** (Ref. Section 6.3.9): The Process Hub Stage 1 does contain all Master, Transactional, and Process Data with direct Master Data entry into the Process Hub Stage 1 and Master Data feedback from the Process Hub Stage 1 into the Legacy Systems. Therefore the Integration and Consolidation of Master Data do require similar effort to the Process Repository Stage 1.

> **Process Repository Stage 2** (Ref. Section 6.3.10): The Process Repository Stage 2 does contain all Master, Transactional, and Process Data with direct Master, Transactional, and Process Data entry into the Process Repository Stage 2, but no feedback from the Process Repository Stage 2 into the Legacy Systems. Therefore the Integration and Consolidation of Master, Transactional, and Process Data in the Process Repository Stage 2 do require– compared to the Process Repository Stage 1– additional enormous effort to accommodate the direct Transactional and Process Data entry into the Process Repository Stage 2.

> **Process Hub Stage 2** (Ref. Section 6.3.11): The Process Hub Stage 2 does contain all Master, Transactional, and Process Data with direct Master, Transactional, and Process Data entry into the Process Hub Stage 2 and Master Data feedback from the Process Hub Stage 2 into the Legacy Systems. Therefore the Integration and Consolidation of Master, Transactional, and Process Data do require similar effort to the Process Repository Stage 2.

> **Process Hub Stage 3** (Ref. Section 6.3.12): The Process Hub Stage 3 does contain all Master, Transactional, and Process Data with direct Master, Transactional, and Process Data entry into the Process Hub Stage 3 and temporary feedback from the Process Hub Stage 3 into the Legacy Systems as they are phasing out. Therefore the Integration and Consolidation of Master, Transactional, and Process Data – compared to other

architectures – would be reduced tremendously.

6.8.4 The Synchronization & Consistency of Master Data between the Legacy Systems & the Central Data Repository

The design of the Legacy Systems in many enterprises would include often extreme variety of structures: 3NF, flat files, VSAM, etc. The ODS uses Relational 3NF Data Modeling technique. The design of the Central Data Repository as per the above outlined Enterprise Data Architectures (Ref. Section 6.5) would follow the **SAM O NAOULO** Modeling Technique. The Synchronization and Consistency of the Master Data between the Legacy Systems and the Central Data Repository are based on the following steps:

➢ The Central Data Repository Master Data fields are assessed to select their source fields from the Legacy Systems.

➢ Mapping and transformation rules are established to load the Master Data from the Legacy Systems into the Central Data Repository and for feedback from the Central Data Repository to the Legacy Systems.

➢ ETL implementation must assure the synchronization and Consistency of the data of the Central Data Repository's Master Data Dimension and Associative Entities with the Legacy Systems.

If the propagation of Master Data from the Legacy Systems to the Central Data Repository and/or the feedback from the Central Data Repository to the Legacy Systems is batch, there would be discrepancies and out-of-Sync between the data of these systems during the periods between batch updates.

Note: The approach and techniques for the development and implementation of Mapping, Transformation, Propagation, and ETL of Master Data could be found in the IT literature.

6.8.5 The Synchronization & Consistency of Transactional Data between the Legacy Systems & the Central Data Repository

In the Enterprise Data Architectures Group 2 & 3, the integrated and consolidated Transactional Data is residing in the Central Data Repository. The Synchronization and Consistency of the Transactional Data between the Legacy Systems and the Central Data Repository are based on the following steps:

➢ The Central Data Repository Transactional Data fields are assessed to select their source fields from the Legacy Systems.

➢ Mapping and transformation rules are established to load the Transactional Data from the Legacy Systems to the Central Data Repository.

➢ ETL implementation must assure the Synchronization and Consistency of the Central Data Repository's Transactional Data with the Legacy Systems.

If the propagation of Master and Transactional Data from the Legacy Systems to the Central Data Repository and/or the feedback of Master Data from the Central Data Repository to the Legacy Systems are batch, there would be discrepancies and out-of-Sync between the data of these systems during the periods between batch updates.

Note: The approach and techniques for the development and implementation of Mapping, Transformation, Propagation, and ETL of Transactional Data could be found in the IT literature.

6.8.6 The Synchronization & Consistency of Process Data between the Legacy Systems & the Central Data Repository

In the Enterprise Data Architectures Group 3, the integrated and consolidated Process Data is residing in the Central Data Repository. The Synchronization and Consistency of the Process Data between the Legacy Systems and the Central Data Repository are based on the following steps:

> ➢ The Central Data Repository Process Data fields are assessed to select their source fields from the Legacy and/or Operational Systems.
> ➢ Mapping and transformation rules are established to load the Process Data from the Legacy and/or Operational Systems to the Central Data Repository.
> ➢ ETL implementation must assure the synchronization and Consistency of the Central Data Repository's Process Data with the Legacy and/or Operational Systems.

If the propagation of Master, Transactional, and Process Data from the Legacy Systems to the Central Data Repository and/or the feedback of Master Data from the Central Data Repository to the Legacy Systems are batch, there would be discrepancies and out-of-Sync between the data of these systems during the periods between batch updates.

Note: The approach and techniques for the development and implementation of Mapping, Transformation, Propagation, and ETL of Process Data is similar to the approach and techniques used for Transactional Data.

6.8.7 The Consistency of Master Data between the Central Data Repository & the Business Intelligence Data Marts

The repository of OLAP data is the Business Intelligence Data Marts. Their design uses Multidimensional (Star and Snowflake schemas) Modeling Technique where the Master Data is stored in the Dimension tables and Transactional Data in the Fact tables. Business Intelligence Data Marts would acquire the Master Data from the Central Data Repository (in the case of Master Data Registry Repository architecture there is a need to acquire the Master Data also from the Legacy Systems via Data Federation). The Consistency of the Master Data between the Central Data Repository/Legacy Systems and the Business Intelligence Data Marts are based on the following steps:

> ➢ OLAP Query and Reporting needs are analyzed to design the structure of the Business Intelligence Data Marts Dimensions.
> ➢ The Business Intelligence Data Marts Dimension fields are assessed to select their source fields from the Central Data Repository (in the case of Master Data Registry Repository architecture there is a need to select the source fields also from the Legacy Systems and retrieve data from them).
> ➢ Mapping and transformation rules are established to load the Master Data from the Central Data Repository/Legacy Systems into the Business Intelligence Data Marts Dimension tables.

Dr. Eng. M. Naoulo

> ETL implementation must assure the Consistency of the data of the Central Data Repository/Legacy Systems' Master Data Dimension and Associative Entities with the Business Intelligence Data Marts Dimensions Data.

6.8.8 The Consistency of Transactional Data between the Central Data Repository & the Business Intelligence Data Marts

In the Enterprise Data Architectures using Transaction Repositories and Hubs and Process Repositories and Hubs the integrated and consolidated Transactional data is residing in the Central Data Repository and designed according to the **SAM O NAOULO** Modeling Technique. In the Business Intelligence Data Marts the Transactional Data is stored in the Fact tables. Business Intelligence Data Marts would acquire the Transactional Data from the Central Data Repository (in the case of Group 1 architectures there is a need to acquire the Transactional Data also from the Legacy Systems via Data Federation). The Consistency of the Transactional Data between the Central Data Repository/Legacy Systems and the Business Intelligence Data Marts are based on the following steps:

> OLAP Query and Reporting needs are analyzed to design the structure of the Business Intelligence Data Marts Fact tables.
> The Business Intelligence Data Marts Fact fields are assessed to select their source fields from the Central Data Repository (in the case of Group 1 architectures there is a need to select the source fields from the Legacy Systems and retrieve data from them).
> Mapping and transformation rules are established to load the Transactional Data from the Central Data Repository/Legacy Systems fields into the Business Intelligence Data Marts Fact tables.
> ETL implementation must assure the Consistency of the Central Data Repository/Legacy Systems Transactional Data with the Business Intelligence Data Marts Facts Data.

6.8.9 The Consistency of Master Data between the Central Data Repository & the Enterprise Intelligence Data Marts

The analysis and assurance of the Consistency of the Master Data between the Central Data Repository and the Enterprise Intelligence Data Marts is similar to the analysis and assurance of the Consistency of the Master Data between the Central Data Repository and the Business Intelligence Data Marts (Ref. Section 6.8.7).

6.8.10 The Consistency of Process Data between the Central Data Repository & the Enterprise Intelligence Data Marts

The analysis and assurance of the Consistency of the Process Data between the Central Data Repository and the Enterprise Intelligence Data Marts is similar to the analysis and assurance of the Consistency of the Transactional Data between the Central Data Repository and the Business Intelligence Data Marts (Ref. Section 6.8.8).

6.8.11 The Consistency of Master Data between the Business Intelligence Data Marts & the Enterprise Intelligence Data Marts

Since the Business Intelligence Data Marts and the Enterprise Intelligence Data Marts retrieve the Master Data from the same sources: the Central Data Repository/Legacy Systems, the consistency of the Master Data between the Business Intelligence Data Marts and the Enterprise Intelligence Data Marts is assured (unless there are time gaps between loading data into the Business Intelligence Data Marts versus loading data into the Enterprise Intelligence Data Marts).

Very often it is useful to use Master Data Conformed Dimensions supporting concurrently both the Business Intelligence Data Marts and the Enterprise Intelligence Data Marts.

PART II – Enterprise Engineering

This part of the book establishes the principles and fundamentals of Enterprise Engineering and Reengineering. It encompasses:

➤ The Enterprise Engineering Framework and aspects of Enterprise Engineering.
➤ The Enterprise Engineering Methodology.
➤ The Enterprise Engineering Guidelines and Deliverables.
➤ Two Case Studies illustrating the Enterprise Engineering Framework and applying the Methodology, Guidelines, Deliverables, and Techniques. These Case Studies were developed to show the optimization of FR&TP Operation for fictitious airline companies. The data pertinent to the functioning of these companies are made up for the Case Studies.

Dr. Eng. M. Naoulo

7. The Enterprise Engineering Framework

All type of Enterprises: Business Enterprises, Government Agencies, Organizations, International Conglomerates, Corporations, etc. are designated in this book by the word "Enterprise". They should have a Vision and a Mission. The Vision is an ideal and the Mission is a real objective/goal/target/aim that this Enterprise thrives to reach. The Mission stimulates the high level roadmap that the Enterprise must develop in order to reach the Vision. To survive and prosper in the route to accomplish its Mission and to reach its Vision, an Enterprise has to comply with the market needs in an ever-changing environment. This is difficult without the help of a solid and reliable operational analysis system.

All Enterprises aspire to survive and prosper. To achieve this, these Enterprises have to reach and accomplish the following objectives:
  ➤ Satisfy Customers' needs: availability and quality of products, Customer Support, etc.
  ➤ Satisfy the Enterprise's needs: financial, market foot print, etc.
  ➤ Execute the Enterprise's activities effectively and efficiently.
  ➤ Improve and ameliorate the Enterprise's processes.
  ➤ Validate and continuously enhance the Enterprise's business model.
  ➤ Continue to function and flourish in an ever-changing environment.

These objectives are difficult to attain specially with the global economic challenges. Very often these objectives are elusive for many Enterprises. One of the reasons for this shortcoming is the lack of reliable and effective operation measuring system to assess the Enterprise's functioning and addresses its imperfection. Currently, the decisions of the management to fulfill these objectives are based on insufficient and disconnected data and the management relies very often on gut-feeling.

The essence and goal of the Enterprise Engineering Framework are to institute the base for Enterprise Engineering.

7.1 DEFINITION OF ENGINEERING

The American Engineers' Council for Professional Development [1], also known as ECPD, (later ABET), defines Engineering as:

> "The creative application of scientific principles to design or develop structures, machines, apparatus, or manufacturing processes, or works utilizing them singly or in combination; or to construct or operate the same with full cognizance of their design; or to forecast their behavior under specific operating conditions; all as respects an intended function, economics of operation and safety to life and property."

The Webster Dictionary [22] defines Engineering as:

> "The application of mathematical and scientific principles to practical ends, as the design, construction, and operation of economical and efficient structures, equipment, and

Dr. Eng. M. Naoulo

systems."

Encyclopedia Britannica [22] defines Engineering as:

"Professional art of applying science to the optimum conversion of the resources of nature to the uses of humankind."

7.2   ESSENCE & DEFINITION OF ENTERPRISE ENGINEERING

The essence of Enterprise Engineering is to transform the design and processing of the Enterprise's Operation from specific manager(s)'s business operation approach tailored very often to these manager(s)'s capabilities and strength into an Engineering Curriculum.

The Enterprise Engineering curriculum encompasses the establishment of an enterprise blueprint depicting and illustrating the infrastructure of the current and future functioning of the enterprise. This blueprint should be designed as a **model incorporating all the measures affected by the functioning of the enterprise.** These measures must include the cost and operative time of the processes as well as the input, output, and interrelations between the processes and the objectives of the enterprise.

Inspired by the Engineering definition elaborated by the American Engineers' Council for Professional Development, Enterprise Engineering is defined as:

"The meticulous application of IT modeling principles to design and develop an Enterprise Engineering Framework and its Enterprise Engineering Model, reflecting the structures, apparatus, processes, machinery procedures, and operation, and their interlinks, and to proceed the current Model with full cognizance of its design; or to forecast their behavior under specific operating conditions; in order to assess and improve the performance of these enterprises."

Enterprise Engineering involves a comprehensive Enterprise Intelligence System to measure the functioning of enterprises. It enables the improvement and revitalization of enterprises' operation. It aims to reduce the operation cost of enterprises while improving their business model, processing performance, market presence, return on investment, financial profit, and image perception in an ever changing environment.

Enterprise Engineering will be used to assess the current performance of the enterprises' operation, to conceive and assess new operational ideas, and to support and verify the future implementation of changes to the business model and its operation. This is very important considering the fact that the world is already deep in globalization and that any edge an enterprise can master over its competition can contribute to the survival and prosperity of this enterprise.

Dr. Eng. M. Naoulo

7.3 OBJECTIVES OF ENTERPRISE ENGINEERING

The objective of enterprises is to achieve Business Expansion, Performance Improvement, Market Extension and Growth, Financial Profit, and Enterprise Adaptability and Flexibility.

The Enterprise Engineering curriculum aims to support and assure the following objectives of Business Management:
- ➢ Evaluating the Enterprises Functions, Processes, Activities, and Procedures
- ➢ Establishing a blueprint Model for the Enterprise Operation.
- ➢ Assessing the Enterprises' performance
- ➢ Improving and revitalizing the existing Enterprise's Functions and/or design of Processes and Activities for new Enterprise's Functions.
- ➢ Establishing a base to provide the Enterprise Engineers with the means to assure the Enterprises' Objectives.

This is achieved thru:
- ➢ Analysis and Design the Enterprise Engineering Model for the current enterprise's operation. The Enterprise Engineering Model must correctly reflect the Enterprise's functioning in order to use it successfully.
- ➢ Explore the Enterprise Engineering Model to assess the performance of the current Enterprise functioning.
- ➢ Ameliorate, enhance, and improve the Enterprise functioning in order to execute the Enterprise activities efficiently and effectively.
- ➢ Revitalize the Enterprise functioning to drastically enhance the operation of the enterprise and its Business Model.
- ➢ Satisfy the Enterprise's needs: financial, customer needs and satisfaction, market position and foot print, products coverage, etc.
- ➢ Engineering the Enterprise to adopt, adapt, and accommodate new objectives.
- ➢ Establish a framework to continuously enhancing the Enterprise's Business and Engineering Models in an ever-changing environment.

7.4 CONTEXT OF ENTERPRISE ENGINEERING

Everything in the world changes: Customers, Services, Products, Tools, Equipment, Environment, Competitors, Markets, Needs, Government Laws, etc. hence the Global Enterprise Engineering is a continuous activity.

The **Enterprise Engineering Curriculum** details a comprehensive approach for analyzing the functioning of enterprises and includes Framework, Methodology, Guidelines, Deliverables, and Modeling Techniques which provide the enterprises with the instruments to empower them to improve their performance and contribute to accomplish their objectives. The purpose of this curriculum is to bestow the edifice to enable the management of enterprises' operation to be based on an engineering framework. This curriculum permits and supports the improvement and revitalization of the Enterprises' operation and performance.

Dr. Eng. M. Naoulo

The Enterprise Engineering Curriculum comprises a comprehensive Enterprise Intelligence module for analyzing the functioning of the Enterprises that illustrates and measures the operation of Enterprises. In the global Corporate Information Factory (CIF) DW2.0 established by Bill Inmon [10], Bill Inmon mentioned the usage and structure of the Operational Marts (Ref. Section 4.1); however he did not elaborate on this subject.

The **Enterprise Engineering Framework** incorporates the System of Apparatus and Machinery (**SAM**) and their Operation (**O**) (Ref. Section 2.5). This system will drive the conception, design, and building of the Enterprise Engineering Model which represents accurately, correctly, and completely the functioning of the Enterprise and its operation.

The **Enterprise Engineering Model** represents the operational aspects of the Enterprises and their relations to the Enterprise's needs. It provides a blueprint of the functioning of Enterprises: current and proposed/future enterprise's operative. It provides a clear and concise technical infrastructure reflecting and illustrating the Enterprises' functioning and representing and measuring their operations. This Model encompasses the Master Data, Mechanism, and Mechanics which reflect in an IT Data Architecture milieu the Apparatus, Machinery, and Operation of Enterprises. The processing of this model reflects the execution of the Enterprise Engineering System of Apparatus, Machinery, and Operation (SAM O NAOULO) and underlines the strengths, weaknesses, efficiency, and performance of the Enterprise's operation.

Based on this Enterprise Engineering Model the Improvement and Revitalization of Enterprises could be conceived, assessed, designed, analyzed, and be ready for implementation.

SAM O NAOULO Modeling Technique elucidates the interlinks of the Operation with the Machinery and the Apparatus.

The **Technical Foundation of Enterprise Engineering** is:
> ➢ The Enterprise Engineering Framework
> ➢ The design approach covering the System of Apparatus, Machinery, and Operation: **SAM O NAOULO** (Ref. Chapter 2).
> ➢ SAM O NAOULO Modeling Technique (Ref. Chapter 3).
> ➢ Enterprise Intelligence (Ref. Chapter 4).
> ➢ Enterprise Data Mapping (Ref. Chapter 5).
> ➢ Enterprise Data Architecture involving Master, Transactional, and Process Data Integration, Consolidation, Synchronization, & Consistency (Ref. Chapter 6).
> ➢ Enterprise Engineering Methodology (Ref. Chapter 8).
> ➢ Enterprise Engineering Guidelines and Deliverables (Ref. Chapter 9).

The Enterprise Engineering Model differs from the Business Model. The Business Model is described by Mark W. Johnson [24] as:

"A business model defines the way the company delivers value to a set of customers at a profit."

Dr. Eng. M. Naoulo

The Business Model involves various aspects of the business, including its purpose, offerings, strategies, infrastructure, organizational structures, trading practices, and operational processes and policies.

Enterprise Engineering includes not only Processes but also Operation, Procedures, and the Apparatus in concordance with the Engineering's definition scope of the American Engineers' Council for Professional Development.

7.5 INNOVATIONS & STRENGTH OF THE ENTERPRISE ENGINEERING FRAMEWORK

The Enterprise Engineering Framework is a major innovation in Enterprise Management and Information Technology. Its importance and advantages corroborates also in Business Management and Administration as indicated earlier in the Abstract.

1. The Enterprise Engineering Framework is very powerful and provides (besides the technique) comprehensive methodology, guidelines, deliverables and guidance that are drastically lacking in the Information Engineering approach.

2. SAM O NAOULO Modeling Technique handles the Data Modeling of the On-Line Mechanical Processing (**OLMP**), the On-Line Transactional Processing (**OLTP**), and supports the design and implementation of the On-Line Analytical Processing (**OLAP**).

3. The Enterprise Engineering Model supports an elaborated approach to classify the Master Data and an integrated and consolidated Master Data Management (Ref. Section 2.2). This Master Data classification provides the basis for the interaction with the Transactional and Process Data and contributes tremendously to the design and mapping to the Business and Enterprise Intelligence Data Marts. (Ref. Chapter 5).

4. The Enterprise Engineering Model provides an elaborated and comprehensive approach to link the Master Data with Mechanics Sessions and Transactions. In Information Engineering the link between the Master Data and the Transactions is chaotic and does not follow any rules or approaches except applying the 3rd NF of the Relational Normalization Data Modeling Technique.

5. The Enterprise Engineering Model is a superset of the Transactional Data Model. The Enterprise Engineering Model covers beside the Transactional Data Model, the Mechanism Procedures supporting the rules governing the Mechanics Transactions, the Activities supporting the rules controlling the Mechanics Sessions, the Events that trigger the Mechanics Sessions, and the Mechanics Sessions reflecting the Operation of the functioning of the Enterprise.

6. The Master Data Activities incorporates the Information Engineering Process Model.

7. A complete, comprehensive, consolidated, and integrated representation of the

Dr. Eng. M. Naoulo

Information Engineering Transactional Data Model and On-Line Transactional Processing (OLTP) that covers the Operation Transactions and their Master Data that is needed by the Operation Transactions used in OLTP could be derived easily from the Enterprise Engineering Model (Ref. Appendix D).

8. The Enterprise Engineering Model rectifies many gaps not covered in Information Engineering including how to address the link between the Process Modeling and Data Modeling (Ref. Section 3.8). In the Enterprise Engineering Model the Business Processes are implemented thru the Master Data Activity Entities. The link between the Process Model and the OLTP Data Model is implemented thru the interrelation of the Master Data Activity Entities with other Master Data Entities and the Mechanics. The link between the Mechanism Procedures and the OLTP Data Model is implemented thru the interrelation of the Mechanism Procedure Entities with Master Data Entities and the Mechanics Transactions.

9. The Enterprise Engineering Model provides a comprehensive basis for Metadata Management. Its consolidated Master Data design helps integrating the Master Data of different systems and simplifies Metadata Management.

7.6   APPROACH OF ENTERPRISE ENGINEERING

The approach for developing and implementing Enterprise Engineering encompasses the following major undertakings:

> Gather, identify, and define the Business Requirements.
> Develop the Implementation Master and Detailed Plans.
> Develop the Milieu: Hardware, Basic Software, Resources, etc.
> Develop the Standards.
> Involve the Stakeholders.
> Assign the Resources.
> Develop the Overall Data Architecture (Ref. Chapter 6).
> Follow a Methodology (Ref. Chapter 8).
> Define, follow, and implement the Techniques (Ref. Chapters 2, 3, 4, 5, 12, 13 & 14).
> Follow the Guidelines (Ref. Chapter 9).
> Identify the Deliverables (Ref. Chapter 9).
> Implement the Master and Detailed Plans.
> Process the new Engineering Model.
> Produce and validate the Deliverables.
> Get approval and execution green light from top management.
> Assess execution results.

The documentation covering some of the above undertakings could be found in the IT literature of System Development Life Cycle (SDLC) and are not detailed in this book.

7.7   THE SCOPE OF ENTERPRISE ENGINEERING

Enterprise Engineering aims to enhance the performance of the Enterprise. The scope of Enterprise Engineering might cover part or the whole enterprise. If the scope of Enterprise Engineering covers limited objectives, the Business Functions supporting these objectives are considered. In this case the Enterprise Engineering Model would include subsets of the Master Data, Mechanism, and Mechanics reflecting the subsets of the Apparatus, Machinery, and Operation that support these Business Functions. Data pertinent to the OLTP could be included in the scope of the Business Functions if needed.

The analysis and design of the Enterprise Engineering Model and its data elements, and the analysis, design, and processing of the Enterprise Intelligence Data Marts would provide many clues to help in the improvement and revitalization of the Enterprises. The analysis of the information pertinent to OLTP requirements for Transactional Applications and Business Intelligence Data Marts might be needed. Enterprise Engineering drill down, statistics, and implementing Enterprise Engineering with a small scope that is tailored to particular subsets of the Business Functions would also help the Enterprise Engineering.

Dr. Eng. M. Naoulo

8.   The Enterprise Engineering Methodology

Enterprise Engineering aims to bolster the efficacy, effectiveness, and efficiency of the Enterprise, reduce cost, and improve Customer Satisfaction. The scope of the Enterprise Engineering project could cover the whole Enterprise business operation or be limited to a part of this operation. The extent of the Enterprise Engineering exercise could be evaluated thru the analysis of the span of the Enterprise's System of Apparatus, Machinery, and Operation (**SAM O NAOULO**) to provide the boundaries of the business operation of the specific subject(s) under investigation. The Enterprise Engineering exercise incorporates the design and implementation of improvements and/or revitalization of the scoped area to boost its effectiveness and efficiency.

The Enterprise Engineering Model supporting this exercise includes the Master Data, the Mechanism, and Mechanics representing respectively the Apparatus, the Machinery, and the Operation, and their Interaction. It bestows a clear and concise vision on how the Enterprise operates and it provides the means to improve its operation.

The **SAM O NAOULO** Methodology's steps are:
1. Identification of the Business Objectives of the project.
2. Identification of the scope of the Enterprise Engineering exercise: the Business Functions of the Enterprise that will be analyzed and optimized to reach these objectives.
3. Identification of the Enterprise Engineering Optimization Goals and translating these goals into numeric figures. These figures reflect the Objectives' KPIs, Metrics, etc. or directly derived from them.
4. Identification of the extent of areas, topics, disciplines and infrastructure to be exploited and implemented in the analysis and design to carry out the exercise of Enterprise Engineering in order to reach these objectives.
5. Identification and gathering the portrayal details and other information related to the Business Functions identified in Step 2.
6. Selection and assortment of the Current Apparatus information needed by these Business Functions.
7. Delineation and evaluation of the Current Machinery Procedures that govern the business transactions.
8. Identification, information gathering, and evaluation of the Current Operation Sessions that are used by the Business Functions identified in Step 2.
9. Information gathering and evaluation of the Current Operation Transactions that are ruled by the Machinery Procedures identified in Step 7.
10. Design the Current Enterprise Engineering Model that incorporates the current Master Data, Mechanism, Mechanics, and the Interaction between them reflecting respectively the current Apparatus, Machinery, Operation, and the Interlink between them.
11. Processing the current Enterprise Mechanics and generation and interpretation of results.
12. Conceivability and conceptualization of the Enterprise's operation improvements.
13. Envisagement and conception of the Enterprise's operation revitalization.
14. Analysis of the appropriate target Apparatus, Machinery, Operation, and design the Enterprise Engineering Model that incorporates the target Master Data, Mechanism,

Mechanics, and the Interaction between them. This model would be used to engineer and improve the business in order to attain the enunciated objectives identified in Step 1.

15. Processing the target Mechanics and generation and interpretation of results.
16. Evaluation of the target model and the business operation decisions behind it and elaborate the appropriate strategic decisions for the future operation of the Enterprise that fulfill the objectives identified in Step 1.
17. Implementing the operational decisions indicated in the previous step.
18. Design of the Global Enterprise Engineering Model (if the scope covers the whole Enterprise).
19. Implementation of the Global Enterprise Engineering Design (if the scope covers the whole Enterprise).
20. Defining the Resources handling the Enterprise Engineering assignment and detailing their roles and responsibilities.

Although it is always tempting to go and improve the whole Enterprise and get the entire Enterprise Engineering Model, it is recommended to follow an iterative approach to carry out the engineering of the subsets of the Enterprise. Each iteration would include additional subset(s) and/or increase the scope of the subsets of the Enterprise Engineering Model under analysis.

The first iteration would include one or some (but not many) business function(s). This is very important in order to keep the scope manageable, building the infrastructure and know-how for the endeavor, and getting quick results exhibiting the Return-On-Investment (ROI). After studying these function(s), analyzing them, designing the Enterprise Engineering Model, and generating the results, the next iteration would start.

It is not always necessary to wait to complete the exercise related to an iteration before starting the next one (sometimes the iterations could overlap slightly). It is always advisable, even if the staff working on this assignment has strong experience in the development and implementation of Enterprise Engineering, to start with a pilot project including the construction of the exercise infrastructure and the establishment of the Enterprise Engineering building blocks (Ref. Chapter 2), then based on the experience learned from it, to continue with the analysis of the Apparatus, Machinery, and the Operation for one or many other iterations.

8.1   THE BUSINESS OBJECTIVES' IDENTIFICATION

The First Step of the Methodology is to identify the Business Objectives of the exercise. These objectives must be defined by the Top Management and Business Staff and made clear to the Enterprise Engineers. The objectives could be as substantial as incorporating a new line of business or streamlining the manufacturing or retail processes, or as minor as the optimization related to a specific point of business operation: example optimizing the additional cost an airline would charge its customers to cover part of the airline's staff cost for performing Flight Reservation and/or Ticket Purchasing (FR&TP) resulting from the customers' contact with the airline's staff by telephone or personally at the airline's offices on top of the cost of the ticket; no charges are added if the customers perform these tasks themselves on the Internet (Ref. the Cases Study).

Notes:

1. During this step it is very important to review and assess the Business Model of the Enterprise if it exists. If there is no Business Model it is important to capture the main information about it that would affect the Enterprise Engineering endeavor.

2. Not all the information captured in this step is related to the objectives. However it is very important to capture any information related to the whole exercise that are available to the Enterprise Engineers and might help in the analysis and design of the solution.

8.2   THE BUSINESS FUNCTIONS SCOPE'S IDENTIFICATION

The Second Step is to identify the scope of the Business Functions that would be involved in the Enterprise Engineering exercise to attain the Business Objectives identified in Step 1 and enclose the scope within boundaries. These Business Functions must be identified by the Business Staff and discussed with the Enterprise Engineers. The scope could be large and encompass all the Business Functions of the Enterprise or could be restricted to encompass one or few business processes. This step is critical as the whole exercise would focus within the scope's boundaries.

8.3   THE ENTERPRISE ENGINEERING OPTIMIZATION GOALS' IDENTIFICATION

The Third Step is to identify the Enterprise Engineering Optimization Goals which indicate the targets for the development/improvement/expansion of the Enterprise Function Areas. These goals must be identified, enunciated, and be available to the Enterprise Engineers. It is recommended that these goals are or could be translated into numeric figures. This step is very important. It is often advisable to announce realistic goals for Business Improvement, and pseudo-realistic goals for Business Revitalization while providing the Enterprise Engineers with free hand to invigorate the Enterprise while thinking out-of-box.

To measure these goals, KPIs and/or business Metrics should be used. The Enterprise Engineering exercise aims to set up and improve the efficiency and efficacy of the Enterprise to attain these figures. The ensuing Enterprise Engineering Model that implements the target Apparatus, Machinery, and Operation would provide the potentially attainable KPI and business Metrics.

8.4   THE ENTERPRISE ENGINEERING EXERCISE'S EXTENT IDENTIFICATION

The Fourth Step is to identify the extent of the Enterprise Engineering that would be embraced in the Enterprise Engineering exercise to attain the Enterprise Engineering Optimization Goals identified in Step 3. This extent must be defined by the Enterprise Engineers and discussed with the Business Staff. The extent identification includes four topics:

> ➤ Optimization areas within the Business Functions identified in Step 2.
> ➤ Optimization topics that would be addressed: KPIs and/or business Metrics, Best of

Dr. Eng. M. Naoulo

Practice, etc.
➤ Optimization disciplines. They could be numerous: Out-Of-Box Thinking, Mathematical Operation Research, Statistics, Business Intelligence, etc. or could be restricted to one discipline.
➤ Optimization technical infrastructure: technical approach, techniques, methods, tools, means, formulas, etc.

8.5 THE BUSINESS FUNCTIONS' PORTRAYAL

The Fifth Step is to describe in details the Business Functions identified in Step 2. These Business Functions must be defined by the Business Staff and detailed into Processes and Elementary Activities and discussed with the Enterprise Engineers. The results are delineated and evaluated from the point of view of the Business Objectives enunciated in Step 1. Again it is important to note that at least one Apparatus Elementary Activity must be identified for each Business Function.

8.6 THE CURRENT APPARATUS' IDENTIFICATION & ASSORTMENT

The Sixth Step is to detail the current Apparatus involved in the Business Functions identified in Step 2 including the Processes and Elementary Activities identified in Step 5, and assort them according to the six Components identified in Section 2.2. It is important to note that at least one Member must be identified in each Component.

8.7 THE CURRENT MACHINERY'S DELINEATION & EVALUATION

The Seventh Step is to detail the Machinery Procedures governing the current Transactions generated by the Apparatus Elementary Activities identified and described in Step 5.

8.8 THE CURRENT OPERATION SESSIONS' IDENTIFICATION, INFORMATION GATHERING, & EVALUATION

The Business Operation Sessions of the Enterprise involve the enactment of the functioning of the Business Processes and their Elementary Activities. The Operation Sessions encompass the Process Data pertinent to the Business Functions. The Eighth Step is to identify, gather, and detail the Operation Sessions that support the Business Functions identified in Step 2 and detailed in Step 5. It is important to note:
➤ At least one Operation Session must be identified for each Apparatus Elementary Activity.
➤ The Operation Sessions are evaluated and assessed from the point of view of the Business Objectives enunciated in Step 1.
➤ The Apparatus Elementary Activities identified within the Scope (Step 5) would control these Operation Sessions.
➤ The Apparatus Members identified within the Scope (Step 6) would participate in these

Dr. Eng. M. Naoulo

Operation Sessions.

The evaluation of the current Enterprise Operation is carried out thru the analysis of the current Operation Sessions that are related to the Business Function(s) and their Processes under investigation. The data of the Operation Sessions form the base for Enterprise Intelligence Data Marts, OLMP, and Enterprise Engineering.

8.9 THE CURRENT OPERATION TRANSACTIONS' IDENTIFICATION, INFORMATION GATHERING, & EVALUATION

The Operation Transactions encompass the transactional data pertinent to the Business Functions identified in Step 2 and detailed in Step 5. The Ninth Step is to detail the Operation Transactions generated by the Business Functions and governed by the Machinery Procedures identified, described, and detailed in Step 7. It is important to note:
  ➢ At least one Operation Transaction must be identified for each Machinery Elementary Procedure.
  ➢ The Operation Transactions are evaluated and assessed from the point of view of the Business Objectives enunciated in Step 1.
  ➢ The Operation Sessions identified within the Scope (Step 8) would generate these Operation Transactions.
  ➢ The Machinery Procedures identified within the Scope (Step 7) would regulate these Operation Transactions.
  ➢ The Apparatus Members identified within the Scope (Step 6) would participate in these Operation Transactions.

The data of the Operation Transactions form the base for Business Intelligence Data Marts and OLAP. It is important to note that Steps 6, 7, 8 and 9 are very interlinked and could be performed as a package and correlate with each other to get the complete picture of the assignment.

8.10 THE CURRENT ENTERPRISE ENGINEERING MODEL & EI DATA MARTS' DESIGN

The Master Data, Mechanism, and Mechanics portraying respectively the current Apparatus, Machinery, and Operation are illustrated thru an Enterprise Engineering Model comprising a Data Entity-Relationship Diagram and manifesting the current functioning of the enterprise. It is important to note that:
  ➢ The current Apparatus Members are reflected thru the entities of the Master Data Dimensions and some of the Many-to-Many interlinks between the Apparatus Members are reflected thru the Master Data Associative Entities.
  ➢ The current Machinery Procedures are reflected thru the Mechanism Procedures.
  ➢ The current Operation Sessions are reflected thru the Mechanics Sessions.
  ➢ The current Operation Transactions are reflected thru the Mechanics Transactions.

Dr. Eng. M. Naoulo

This step includes also the design of EI Data Marts. The techniques to be used for Enterprise Engineering Modeling are detailed in Chapters 2, 3, 4, 5, 12, 13 & 14.

8.11 THE CURRENT MECHANICS PROCESSING & RESULTS' GENERATION & INTERPRETATION

The processing of the Mechanics of the Current Enterprise Engineering Model developed in Step 10 reveals the current functioning of the Enterprise. The Mechanics' results captured from this processing represent the current Operation. The interpretation of these results provides a clear idea how the current Enterprise functions and its current performance.

8.12 THE ENTERPRISE'S IMPROVEMENT

The conceivability and conceptualization of the Enterprise's Operation Improvement is realized thru the analysis of the processing and the optimization of the **SAM O NAOULO** Enterprise Engineering Model representing the business functions. The Apparatus under analysis represents the parts and ingredients of the Enterprise affecting and/or affected by the Business Function(s). The Machinery regulates the Transactions of the Enterprise. The Operation represents the functioning of the Business Function(s) and Processes. Processing and optimizing the Enterprise Engineering Model provides the basis for the Business Function(s) Improvement.

The Twelfth Step would include creative thinking. Creative thinking is always in demand to achieve the Business Objectives enunciated in Step 1. This creative thinking spread from high level as the redefinition of a business function usefulness down to detail level as the redesign and optimization of certain processes and elementary activities. This Step is based on the results of the previous steps and guided by the Best of Practice, and the experience, expertise, technological skills, business skills, and knowledge of the participants in the Enterprise Engineering exercise.

8.13 THE ENTERPRISE'S REVITALIZATION

The envisagement and conception of the Enterprise's Operation Revitalization is realized thru the redesign of the **SAM O NAOULO** Enterprise Engineering Model representing the business functions.

The Thirteenth Step involves substantial creative thinking that is at a more drastic level than the previous step. It is effective thru revisiting and putting in question the role of Component Members of the Apparatus, assessment of a Business Function's usefulness, and revisiting and considering new ways to implement the Operation. The out-of-box thinking is very much in demand here.

8.14 THE TARGET APPARATUS, MACHINERY, OPERATION, ENTERPRISE ENGINEERING MODEL, & EI DATA MARTS' DESIGN

The ideas, Best of Practice, new processes, etc. fleshed out in the previous two steps are incorporated into the design of the Target Apparatus, Machinery, Operation, their Enterprise Engineering Model, and the target EI Data Marts. It is important to note that these new Apparatus, Machinery, Operation and Model should aim to satisfy the Business Objectives identified in Step 1. The technique to be used in the design of the Target Enterprise Engineering Model and EI Data Marts is the same technique used in the design of the current Enterprise Engineering Model.

Note: Very often the design of many target EI Data Marts is similar to the design of their corresponding current EI Data Marts

8.15 THE TARGET MECHANICS PROCESSING & RESULTS' GENERATION & INTERPRETATION

The processing of the Target Enterprise Engineering Model provides the anticipated functioning of the Enterprise. The Mechanics' results captured from this processing represent the Operation designed in Steps 12, 13 and 14. The interpretation of the Mechanics' results reflects how the target Enterprise would function and its expected performance.

It is important to note that Steps 12, 13, 14 and 15 could be repeated many times in order to achieve the Operation that would provide the Enterprise functioning with best results.

8.16 THE ENTERPRISE ENGINEERING STRATEGIC OPERATION DECISIONS

The Sixteenth step of the exercise involves taking strategic decisions based on the interpretation of the results of the previous step. The Enterprise Executive and Directors evaluate the results presented to them by the Enterprise Engineers and direct the Enterprise Operation executives to implement the appropriate improvements and revitalization.

These decisions would affect the Operation of the Enterprise, its Business Model, its market footprint, the career of many employees, and the finance of the Enterprise including budgets, Profit and Loss, equity value, etc.

8.17 THE TARGET ENTERPRISE ENGINEERING IMPLEMENTATION

The Seventeenth step of the exercise is the last step in an iteration of the Enterprise Engineering exercise and involves:
   ➢ Developing detailed Plans to implement the decisions approved in Step 16.
   ➢ Implement these Plans.

Dr. Eng. M. Naoulo

It is important to note that this step would involve huge Human Resources participation, new staff, training and/or reallocation of current staff, new equipment or materiel, etc. Very often the implementation is not without roadblocks, staff resistance, business environment change, etc.

8.18 THE GLOBAL ENTERPRISE ENGINEERING MODEL'S DESIGN

The complete exercise covering all the business of the Enterprise addresses the Master Data of all the Apparatus of the Enterprise and assesses and redesigns the complete Mechanism and Mechanics reflecting the Machinery of this Enterprise and its Operation. The Global Enterprise Engineering Model based on this methodology represents the whole enterprise. The processing of the Global Enterprise Model reflects the functioning of the Global Enterprise.

8.19 THE GLOBAL ENTERPRISE ENGINEERING

The Global Enterprise Engineering would support high-level strategic objectives. To implement the new strategies the Global Enterprise Engineering is executed involving two facets:
1. Global Enterprise Improvement: It is carried out thru the conceivability and conceptualization of improvements to the whole Enterprise's Operation. The Apparatus delineated in the Global Enterprise Engineering Model represents all the parts and ingredients of the Enterprise. The Machinery and Operation delineated in the Global Enterprise Engineering Model represents the complete functioning of the Enterprise's Processing. Optimizing the Global Enterprise Engineering Model provides the basis for the Global Enterprise Improvement.
2. Global Enterprise Revitalization: It is carried out thru envisagement, conception, and redesign of the whole Enterprise's operation. It involves revisiting and putting in question every Component and Members of the Apparatus and especially the Needs, and revisiting and considering new ways to implement the Machinery and Operation. It spread from top strategic levels as the redefinition of the whole Enterprise raison-d'être and strategy to detail levels as the reassignment of a task to the customer or outsourcing it. The creative thinking and out-of-box thinking are essential in this area.

8.20 THE RESOURCES HANDLING THE ENTERPRISE ENGINEERING ASSIGNMENT

A new Organization Unit should handle the Data Architecture and Enterprise Engineering. Diagram 8.1 represents a typical Organization Structure of this Unit. The Chief Enterprise Architecture & Engineering Officer (CEAEO) and the EE Business, Enterprise Data Architecture, and EE Technical Directors must be assigned fulltime to this Unit. This Organization Unit would be responsible for the Data Architecture, Data Modeling, Data Warehousing, Business Intelligence, Enterprise Intelligence as well as Enterprise Engineering.

The Enterprise Architecture & Engineering Unit would be composed of three teams: Business, Data Architecture, and EE Technical teams.
1. The **Enterprise Engineering Business Team** must be very familiar with the business

functions in the scope and in business functional analysis. This team would be formed from business staff that got training in IT, BI, EI, and Enterprise Engineering and assigned fulltime to the Enterprise Architecture & Engineering Unit, and additional business staff from the business functions under investigation who are assigned temporarily/part time to this Unit. This team will be responsible for the business analysis of the Apparatus, Machinery, and Operation Sessions and Transactions and for the Business and Enterprise Intelligence query and reporting requirements.

2. The **Enterprise Data Architecture Team** is composed of Data Architects and Data Modelers who are certified in Enterprise Data Architecture and the three Data Modeling techniques:
   - Relational Normalization Data Modeling Technique
   - Multidimensional Data Modeling Technique
   - **SAM O NAOULO** Modeling Technique.

   They are assigned fulltime to the Enterprise Architecture & Engineering Unit. They will handle the architectural and modeling design of the Master Data, Mechanism, and Mechanics Sessions and Transactions. This team is also responsible for the design of Business and Enterprise Data Marts responding to the BI and EI query and reporting requirements.

3. The **Enterprise Engineering Technical Team** is composed of Enterprise Engineers who are certified or have degrees in Enterprise Engineering. They are assigned fulltime to the Enterprise Architecture & Engineering Unit. The Certification and Degree in Enterprise Engineering must include advanced education covering all aspects of Data Architecture, Data Warehousing, Data Modeling, Data Governance, Business and Enterprise Intelligence, Business Process Reengineering, Statistics, and Operation Research. The Enterprise Engineers must be very knowledgeable in Enterprise Engineering Best of Practice, Techniques, and Tools.

Whereas the Enterprise Architecture & Engineering Unit aims to engineer the Enterprise and improve its Operation, its role goes beyond the expertise and dominion of the IT Unit therefore it is recommended that this Unit reports directly to the Chief Executive Officer (CEO) or to the Chief Operation Officer (COO) and not to the Chief Information Officer (CIO).

There would be close working relation between the Enterprise Architecture & Engineering Unit and both the Business Function Units and the IT Organization. The Business Function Units would help in gathering the business information, in the analysis of the operation of their Units, and in the assessment of the Enterprise Engineering results. The IT Organization would help in implementing the Enterprise Engineering Model in the IT milieu and in carrying out the Extraction, Transformation and Loading (ETL) of the data between the different databases and systems.

Dr. Eng. M. Naoulo

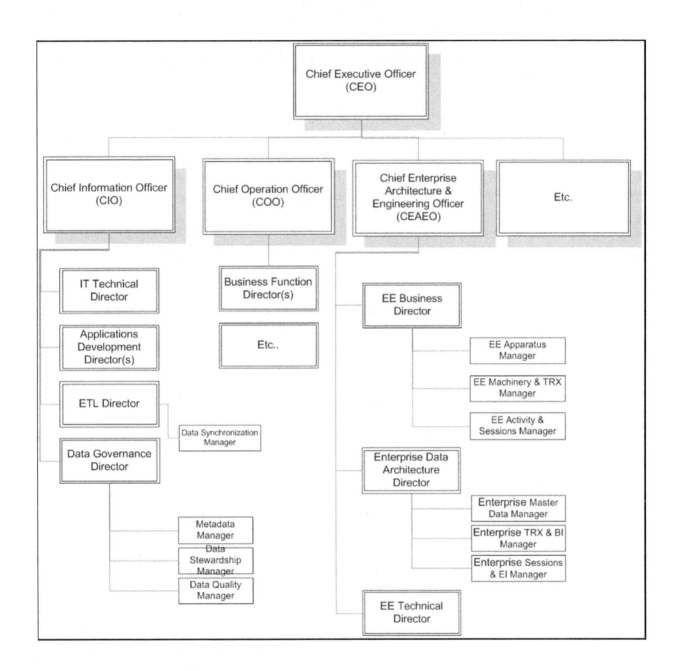

Diagram 8.1: The Enterprise Architecture & Engineering Organization Structure

9. The Enterprise Engineering Guidelines & Deliverables

The Guidelines of Enterprise Engineering provide the Enterprise Engineers with the mandatory and optional directions to how-to-perform their tasks to execute the 20 steps of the Enterprise Engineering Methodology outlined in Chapter 8. These Guidelines draw on practices from many disciplines: Information Engineering, Data Warehousing, Business Strategy, Out-Of-Box Thinking, Operation Research, Statistics, etc. This chapter indicates also the deliverables to be produced from the Enterprise Engineering Methodology steps.

It is important to note that the deliverables of each step of the Methodology might include miscellaneous info related to the Enterprise Engineering exercise which would be classified as per the other steps of the Methodology.

9.1 THE BUSINESS OBJECTIVES IDENTIFICATION'S GUIDELINES

The Guidelines to identify the Enterprise Engineering Business Objectives and their Deliverables include:
  - ➢ Info gathering from the Top Management related to the Business Model.
  - ➢ Requirements gathering from the Operation Director(s)/Staff for info needed to help them with strategic decisions.
  - ➢ Gathering clear Business Objectives for the engineering exercise.
  - ➢ If possible gathering information related to the target Machinery and Operation's cost of functioning.

The deliverables of this step could be gathered in MS Office formats. They include:
  - ➢ Enterprise Engineering Business Objectives.

9.2 THE BUSINESS FUNCTIONS SCOPE IDENTIFICATION'S GUIDELINES

Scoping the Business Functions is to define the area of the Business Functions exercise and enclosing it within boundaries. The deliverables should indicate the processes, activities, and procedures within the scope of the exercise and any limitations to them. The Enterprise Engineers would receive this documentation from the Business Staff, validate them, and capture the name and position of the Business Staff owners of these functions.

The deliverables of this step could be gathered in MS Office formats. They include:
  - ➢ The Business Functions within the scope of the exercise. The info gathered should include at a high level the answers to the six questions indicated in Section 2.2:
    - ▪ Name, description, and objectives of these Business Functions.
    - ▪ How these Business Functions are working.
    - ▪ Who is involved in these Business Functions.
    - ▪ What equipment, materiel, material, tools, software, and systems are involved in

Dr. Eng. M. Naoulo

in these Business Functions.
- Where these Business Functions are performed.
- When these Business Functions are running.
➢ List of the Use Cases that are identified in scope.

Also at a high level:
- The description of the Sessions that implement these Business Functions.
- The description of the Transactions generated by these Business Functions with main input and output data.

9.3 THE ENTERPRISE ENGINEERING OPTIMIZATION GOALS IDENTIFICATION'S GUIDELINES

Identifying the Enterprise Engineering Optimization Goals is a very important step in Enterprise Engineering. The goals provide the targets for the Enterprise Engineers toward which they aim their study and optimization. The Enterprise Engineers should receive these Optimization Goals from the Business Staff, evaluate them, cross validate them with the Best of Practice and re-discuss them with the Business Staff before espouse them into the Enterprise Engineering exercise. The Enterprise Engineers should also capture and assess the contribution of all Key Performance Indicators (KPIs), Best of Practice figures, and Metrics related to the goals for the Business Functions identified in Step 2. At the end of this step clear and measurable goals must be identified and agreed upon by the Business Staff and the Enterprise Engineers.

The deliverables of this step could be gathered in MS Office formats. They include:
➢ Identification, assessment, and evaluation of the Optimization Goals.
➢ Cross validation of the Optimization Goals with the Best of Practice.
➢ List of KPIs, Best of Practice figures, and Metrics that contribute to the Optimization Goals.
➢ Approved list of measurable goals that would be the target for the Enterprise Engineering exercise with their description and rationalization.

9.4 THE ENTERPRISE ENGINEERING EXERCISE EXTENT IDENTIFICATION'S GUIDELINES

Delineating the extent of the exercise is to identify and describe the optimization areas, topics, disciplines, and technical infrastructure to be used and implemented to carry out the exercise.

The deliverables of this step could be gathered in MS Office formats. They include:
➢ The areas of optimization, their prioritization, cost factors involved with each area, the options related to each area, etc.
➢ The topics of optimization: which KPIs and/or business Metrics should be addressed, should Best of Practice be used, which Enterprise should be emulated, options to be considered, etc.
➢ The disciplines used for optimization: Information Engineering, Business Strategy, Business Intelligence, Out-Of-Box Thinking, Operation Research, Statistics, etc. within

Dr. Eng. M. Naoulo

the scope of the exercise. Also the justification to use these disciplines and any limitations to be considered. The Enterprise Engineers should assess these disciplines, validate their potential for the exercise, and discuss them with the Business Staff and report the outcome of these discussions.
- ➢ The technical infrastructure to be used: technical approach, tools, means, formulas, databases, software, etc. What tools should be acquired from outside the enterprise and what tools should be developed in-house.

9.5 THE BUSINESS FUNCTIONS PORTRAYAL'S GUIDELINES

The information to be gathered in this step involves two types:
- ➢ The information pertinent to the operations defining the Business Functions identified in Step 2. The recommended approach to get this information would be the Process Modeling as developed by Clive Finkelstein [6] and James Martin [4 & 5] or the Use Cases of the Object Oriented Analysis approach developed by Ivar Jacobson [7 & 8]. The Use Cases should also include the information related to the current size of operations. It is recommended to use the Use Cases and profit from the full extent of their details.
- ➢ The information related to the source systems from where the data would be extracted. This information could be obtained from the DDL, Database Schema, Metadata, ETL tools, Copybooks, and Data Models. It is recommended to get, if possible, definition of tables and fields, frequency of extraction needed for the Enterprise Engineering exercise, data profiling, cleansing and integration information, the transformation rules to load the data, and other metadata info. This information will contribute into the design of the Enterprise Engineering Model reflecting the Apparatus, Machinery, and Operation,

The Use Cases information needed for the OLMP would include many of the data needed for OLTP. If the Use Cases describing the OLTP were developed and available, it is better to add to them the requirements needed by OLMP and further complete the **SAM O NAOULO** requirements with some additional Uses Cases if needed. If the Use Cases describing the OLTP were not yet developed, it is recommended to develop the OLMP Use Cases including the OLTP requirements as many of the attributes needed by the OLTP requirements would be needed by OLMP. It is also feasible in some special cases to develop Use Cases for OLMP requirements and overlook the OLTP requirements.

The deliverables of this step could be gathered in MS Office formats, Data and Process Models using Modeling tools formats: CA Erwin, Sybase Power Designer, IBM InfoSphere Data Architect, and other modeling tools, and ETL tools formats. They include:
- ➢ The Business Functions within the scope of the exercise. The info gathered should include at a detail level the answers to the six questions indicated in Section 2.2 (Ref. Section 9.2). Also the info gathered should include at a detail level:
  - ▪ The description of the Sessions that implement these Business Functions.
  - ▪ The description of the Transactions generated by these Business Functions with main input and output data.
  - ▪ The figures related to the operation details (cost, performance, impact on market, etc.).

Dr. Eng. M. Naoulo

- The information related to the current size of operations.
- All the info details pertinent to the complete Use Cases.

➤ Detail metadata of the information related to the source systems: definition of tables and fields, type, size, enumerated values, and domain of fields, data models if they exist if not reverse engineering of the databases structure, frequency of extraction needed for the Enterprise Engineering exercise, etc.

9.6   THE   CURRENT   APPARATUS   IDENTIFICATION   & ASSORTMENT'S GUIDELINES

The Apparatus Identification and Assortment would be based on the information gathered in the Use Cases in Step 5 and further discussions with the Business staff and the IT staff responsible of the source systems. The Apparatus Assortment should pursue the following rules:

1. Each Apparatus Component consists of Members: Customer, Airplane, Flight, etc.
2. The selection of the Apparatus Members would satisfy the requirements to attain the Enterprise Business Objectives identified in Step 1, the Business Functions identified in Step 2, and the Enterprise Engineering's extent identified in Step 4.
3. An Apparatus Member follows the rules enunciated in Sections 2.2 & 12.1.

The deliverables of this step could be gathered in MS Office formats and Data Models. They include:

➤ Description of the entities and attributes reflecting the Apparatus including type, size, enumerated values, and domain of attributes, relationships between entities and their cardinality and optionality details, referential integrity, etc.

➤ The Data Models representing the Apparatus and following the SAM O NAOULO Modeling Technique and its Best of Practice.

9.7   THE CURRENT MACHINERY DELINEATION & EVALUATION'S GUIDELINES

The Machinery Delineation and Evaluation would be based on the information gathered in the Use Cases in Step 5 and further discussions with the Business staff and the IT staff responsible of the source systems. They should pursue the following rules:

1. The selection and description of the Machinery Procedures would regulate the Operation Transactions generated by the Business Functions identified in Step 2. Starting from the information gathered in the Use Cases in Step 5, a comprehensive analysis is needed to detail the Machinery Procedures.
2. A Machinery Procedure follows the rules enunciated in Sections 2.3 & 12.2.
3. Each Machinery Elementary Procedure rules and regulates Operation Transaction(s): Ticket Purchasing, Flight Reservation, Bank Account Deposit, Cash Withdrawal, etc.

The deliverables of this step could be gathered in MS Office formats and Data Models. They include:

➤ Description of the entities and attributes reflecting the Machinery including type, size, enumerated values, and domain of attributes, relationships between entities and their

Dr. Eng. M. Naoulo

cardinality and optionality details, referential integrity, etc.
> The Data Models representing the Machinery and following the SAM O NAOULO Modeling Technique and its Best of Practice.

9.8 THE CURRENT OPERATION SESSIONS IDENTIFICATION, INFORMATION GATHERING & EVALUATION'S GUIDELINES

The Operation Sessions' Identification and Evaluation would be based on the information gathered in the Use Cases in Step 5 and further discussions with the Business staff and the IT staff responsible of the source systems. They should pursue the following rules:

1. Each Elementary Activity controls Operation Session(s).
2. The selection and description of the Operation Sessions would follow the Business Functions identified in Step 2, the Enterprise Engineering's extent identified in Step 4, and the assessment of the Activities identified in Step 6. Starting from the information gathered in the Use Cases in Step 5, a comprehensive analysis is needed to detail the Operation Sessions.
3. An Operation Session follows the rules enunciated in Sections 2.4.1 & 12.3.
4. An Operation Session Incidence is controlled by only one Apparatus Elementary Activity Incidence.
5. An Operation Session Incidence is triggered by only one Occurrence Event Incidence.
6. An Operation Session could generate one or many Operation Transactions.

The deliverables of this step could be gathered in MS Office formats and Data Models. They include:

> Description of the entities and attributes reflecting the Operation Sessions including type, size, enumerated values, and domain of attributes, relationships between entities and their cardinality and optionality details, referential integrity, etc.
> The Data Models representing the Operation Sessions and following the SAM O NAOULO Modeling Technique and its Best of Practice.

9.9 THE CURRENT OPERATION TRANSACTIONS IDENTIFICATION, INFORMATION GATHERING, & EVALUATION'S GUIDELINES

The Operation Transactions' Identification and Evaluation would be based on the information gathered in the Use Cases in Step 5 and further discussions with the Business staff and the IT staff responsible of the source systems. They should pursue the following rules:

1. Each Elementary Procedure rules and regulates one or many Operation Transaction(s).
2. The selection of the Operation Transactions would follow the Business Functions identified in Step 2, the Enterprise Engineering's extent identified in Step 4, and the implementation of the Operation Sessions identified in Step 8. Starting from the information gathered in the Use Cases in Step 5, comprehensive analysis is needed to detail the Operation Transactions.
3. An Operation Transaction follows the rules enunciated in Sections 2.4.2 & 12.4.

Dr. Eng. M. Naoulo

The deliverables of this step could be gathered in MS Office formats and Data Models. They include:

> ➢ Description of the entities and attributes reflecting the Operation Transactions including type, size, enumerated values, and domain of attributes, relationships between entities and their cardinality and optionality details, referential integrity, etc.
> ➢ The Data Models representing the Operation Transactions and following the SAM O NAOULO Modeling Technique and its Best of Practice.

9.10 THE CURRENT ENTERPRISE ENGINEERING MODEL & EI DATA MARTS DESIGN'S GUIDELINES

The Enterprise Engineering Model comprises the Master Data, the Mechanism, and the Mechanics reflecting respectively the Apparatus, the Machinery, and the Operation of the Business Functions identified in Step 2 as detailed in Steps 5, 6, 7, 8 and 9. The design of the Mechanics would capture the Mechanics Sessions and Transactions reflecting the Operation of the functioning of the Enterprise. The Guidelines to implement the Current Enterprise Engineering Model Design are:

1. The Master Data's Model Design Technique is elaborated in Sections 3.3, & 13.1.
2. The Mechanism's Model Design Technique is elaborated in Sections 3.4 & 13.2.
3. The Mechanics Sessions' Model Design Technique is elaborated in Sections 3.5 & 13.3.
4. The Mechanics Transactions' Model Design Technique is elaborated in Sections 3.6 & 13.4.
5. The Interaction of the Master Data with the Mechanism's Technique is elaborated in Section 13.5.
6. The Interaction of the Master Data with the Mechanics Sessions' Technique is elaborated in Section 13.6.
7. The Interaction of the Master Data with the Mechanics Transactions' Technique is elaborated in Section 13.7.
8. No Interlink between the Machinery and the Operation's Sessions as detailed in Section 13.8.
9. The Interaction of the Mechanism with the Mechanics Transactions' Technique is elaborated in Section 13.9.
10. The Interaction of the Mechanics Sessions with the Mechanics Transactions' Technique is elaborated in Section 13.10.
11. The analysis of modifiable Data Instances would employ the Technique elaborated in Section 3.7.
12. The EI Data Marts Design Technique is elaborated in Sections 4.6, 4.6.1, 4.6.2, 4.6.3, 4.6.4, and 4.6.5.

The deliverables of this step could be gathered in MS Office formats and Data Models. They include:

> ➢ The complete and integrated current Enterprise Engineering Model covering the interactions between the Master Data, the Mechanism, and the Mechanics Sessions and Transactions.

Dr. Eng. M. Naoulo

> ➤ The complete and integrated current EI Data Marts.
> ➤ The Data Dictionary pertinent to the current Enterprise Engineering Model and EI Data Marts.

The design of the Master Data, the Mechanism, and the Mechanics Sessions and Transactions reflecting respectively the Apparatus, the Machinery, and the Operation would imply the Enterprise Engineering Model to have the form of the Lily flower depicted hereafter:

Figure 9.1: The Lily Flower: The Pictorial Representation of a simple System of Apparatus, Machinery, & Operation (SAM O NAOULO)

Dr. Eng. M. Naoulo

Figure 9.2: The Water Lily Flower: The Pictorial Representation [28] of an intricate System of Apparatus, Machinery, & Operation (SAM O NAOULO)

9.11 THE CURRENT MECHANICS PROCESSING & RESULTS GENERATION & INTERPRETATION'S GUIDELINES

The following points related to the steps of the methodology should be considered and completed before and during the processing and generation of the results of the current mechanics, and before the interpretation of these results:

1. The Business Objectives enunciated in Step 1 and the Enterprise Engineering Optimization Goals identified in Step 3 must be clear and could be translated into numeric figures.
2. The information pertinent to the Apparatus, Machinery, and Operation Sessions and Transactions, identified in Steps 6, 7, 8 and 9 which are based on the Business Functions depicted in Step 2 and detailed in Step 5 must be gathered.
3. The formulas that bestow the numeric figures requested by the Enterprise Engineering Optimization Goals (Key Performance Indicators, Best of Practice figures, Metrics, and Measures) should be established, developed, and formulated based on the attributes/fields of the current Enterprise Engineering Model.
4. The period of running the Current Enterprise Engineering Model must be defined.
5. All data needed from the Legacy Systems by the Current Enterprise Engineering Model for the analysis period must be loaded into the Central Data Repository using ETL tools

Dr. Eng. M. Naoulo

like Ab Initio, DataStage, Informatica, etc.

6. The generation of reports from the Enterprise Engineering Model accommodating the above formulas would, preferably, be executed by using reporting tools like Business Objects, MicroStrategy, etc. Developing programs for this task is not cost-effective unless the programs are very simple.

7. The results produced by these reports reflect the current efficiency and efficacy of the Business Functions under study and their corresponding operations.

The interpretation of the current mechanics operation results is ensued from the analysis of these reports, taking into consideration the factors and assumptions that contributed to the design of the current System of Apparatus, Machinery, and Operation and the Enterprise Engineering Model, and the elaboration of the underlying formulas.

The deliverables of this step could be gathered in MS Office, ETL, and reporting tools formats. They include:

> The reports generated from the Current Enterprise Engineering Model that reflect the current mechanics operation results.
> The interpretation of these reports.

9.12 THE ENTERPRISE IMPROVEMENT' GUIDELINES

The Enterprise Improvement includes many levels from slight tuning of a process into overhaul of the whole Enterprise Function(s), their processes, and the procedures supporting them. Many management articles, books, and research were conducted and published in this area. The Enterprise Engineer should be familiar with the topics of this area and their techniques which include Process Improvement, Process Innovation, Total Improvement Management, etc.

The results of the Enterprise Improvement would imply new Use Cases or modification to the current Use Cases to describe the new Business Operations. These Use Cases are developed in a similar way as those in Step 5.

As part of this step the Operation Sessions and Transactions should be assessed and evaluated:

The Operation Sessions
If an Operation Session is not used by any Business Function, it could be eliminated altogether. The Transactions generated by it could also be eliminated as long as there is no other Operation Sessions that generate them.

The Operation Transactions
If an Operation Transaction is not generated by any Operation Session, it could be eliminated altogether.

The deliverables of this step could be gathered in MS Office formats and Data Models. They include:

> The suggestions and recommendations for the Enterprise Improvement with the

Dr. Eng. M. Naoulo

assessment and evaluation of their effectiveness and impact on the enterprise functioning.

9.13 THE ENTERPRISE REVITALIZATION'S GUIDELINES

The Enterprise Revitalization's Guideline includes many levels from revisiting the functioning of a process to put in question the need for many Enterprise Function(s), their processes, and the procedures supporting them. This revitalization might induce drastic changes on the functioning of the Enterprise. Here also many management articles, books, and research were conducted and published in this area. Many Reengineering ideas elaborated by Dr. Michael Hammer [26], Thomas H. Davenport [14], H. James Harrington [15 & 16] and others provide good references. The Enterprise Engineer should be familiar with these topics and their techniques which include Re-Engineering the Enterprise, Business Process Re-engineering, out-of-box thinking, etc.

Michael Hammer and Steven A. Stanton [25] defined Reengineering as:

"The fundamental rethinking and radical design of business processes to bring about dramatic improvement in performance."

The results of the Enterprise Revitalization would imply also new Use Cases or modification to the current Use Cases to describe the new Business Operations to implement the Enterprise Revitalization and Reengineering. These Use Cases are developed in a similar way as those in Step 5

The deliverables of this step could be gathered in MS Office formats and Data Models. They include:
 ➢ The suggestions and recommendations for the Enterprise Revitalization with the assessment and evaluation of their effectiveness and impact on the enterprise functioning.

9.14 THE TARGET APPARATUS, MACHINERY, & OPERATION, ENTERPRISE ENGINEERING MODEL, & EI DATA MARTS DESIGN'S GUIDELINES

The target Apparatus, Machinery, and Operation evaluation and Enterprise Engineering Model Design's Guidelines follow the same Guidelines used for the current Apparatus, Machinery, and Operation evaluation and Enterprise Engineering Model Design as depicted in Steps 5, 6, 7, 8, 9, and 10. These Guidelines would be applied to the target Business Functions and operations resulting from the Enterprise Improvement and Revitalization performed in Steps 12 and 13.

It is important to note that developing pilot projects is very useful here. These projects could be implemented for critical or specific Business Function(s). These Business Function(s) should be chosen to provide enterprise-wide visibility, good representation of the Enterprise business, and quick Return-On-Investment (ROI). They could be considered as a base to extrapolate the target Enterprise Engineering implementation to the whole Enterprise.

The deliverables of this step could be gathered in MS Office formats and Data Models. They

include:
  ➢ The complete and integrated Target Enterprise Engineering Model covering the interactions between the Master Data, the Mechanism, and the Mechanics Sessions and Transactions.
  ➢ The complete and integrated target EI Data Marts.
  ➢ The Data Dictionary pertinent to the target Enterprise Engineering Model.

9.15 THE TARGET MECHANICS PROCESSING & RESULTS GENERATION & INTERPRETATION'S GUIDELINES

After designing the Apparatus, Machinery, Operation, and Enterprise Engineering Model for the target Enterprise Business Function(s), the results from the processing of this Model could be generated in a similar way to the results generated from the processing of the Current Enterprise Engineering Model (Step 11). It is important to note that:

1. The formulas to bestow the numeric figures requested by the Enterprise Engineering Optimization Goals (Key Performance Indicators, Best of Practice figures, Metrics, and Measures) should be established based on the attributes/fields of the Target Enterprise Engineering Model. There might be slight or big change from the formulas of the Current Enterprise Engineering Model depending on the extension of the change applied in Steps 12 and 13.

2. There is a need to create test sample data to process the Target Enterprise Engineering Model. This data would originate from the Current Enterprise Engineering Model plus some modification/improvisation/anticipation to accommodate the changes implied from Steps 12 and 13.

3. The period of running the Target Enterprise Engineering Model must be defined. The timeframe would be in the future; hence the data coming from the Current Enterprise Engineering Model should reflect this point. Example: if the data is sensible to the population strata, demographics trends must be accommodated.

4. The results produced by these reports would provide the target efficiency and efficacy of the Business Functions under study and their corresponding operations.

The interpretation of the target mechanics operation results is ensued from the analysis of these reports taking into consideration the improvement and changes introduced in Steps 12 and 13, the factors and assumptions that contributed to the design of the target System of Apparatus, Machinery, and Operation and the Enterprise Engineering Model, and the elaboration of the underlying formulas. If the results do not provide the targeted Enterprise Engineering Optimization Goals enunciated in Step 3 then the Steps 12 and 13 should be revisited and Step 14 reconstructed. Then the processing and results generation and interpretation should be redone to get new results satisfying the Enterprise functioning with best optimization.

The deliverables of this step could be gathered in MS Office, ETL, and reporting tools formats. They include:
  ➢ The reports generated from the Target Enterprise Engineering Model that reflect the target mechanics operation results.
  ➢ The interpretation of these reports.

Dr. Eng. M. Naoulo

9.16 THE ENTERPRISE ENGINEERING STRATEGIC OPERATION DECISIONS' GUIDELINES

Since this step involves making decisions that would affect directly the Business Functions involved in the Enterprise Engineering exercise and implicitly the whole Enterprise, it is very important that the results obtained from the steps 11 and 15 would be carefully assessed and evaluated. The Enterprise Engineers have a critical assignment to present these results in an objective, comprehensive, clear, concise, comprehensible, and reliable manner to the Business Staff and Top Management. Also the presentation must include decision options with advantages and disadvantages of each option.

After the decisions of Top Management and Business Directors, the Enterprise Engineers in collaboration with the Business Functions and Operation Directors must establish comprehensive high level Project Management and Change Management Plans to implement these decisions.

The deliverables of this step could be gathered in MS Office and MS Project formats. They include:
  ➤ The decisions of Top Management and Business Directors.
  ➤ High level Project Management and Change Management Plans to implement these decisions. They include including tasks, resources, timeframes, iterations, deployment plans, cost, necessary training, etc.

9.17 THE TARGET ENTERPRISE ENGINEERING IMPLEMENTATION'S GUIDELINES

After the decision of the Enterprise Executive and Directors, the Enterprise Engineers in collaboration with the Business Functions and Operation Directors must elaborate and detail comprehensive Project Management, Change Management, Implementation, and Operation Plans. These Plans are presented to the Enterprise Executive and Directors for approval. Once approved the implementation would start. Of course during the implementation, many ideas, features, aspects, etc. would be discovered and assessed. These ideas might alter and would improve the Plans and the target Enterprise Engineering Model.

The deliverables of this step could be gathered in MS Office including MS Project formats. They include:
  ➤ Detailed and comprehensive Project Management, Change Management, Implementation, and Operation Plans to implement the strategic decisions. They include tasks, resources (current and additional), timeframes, iterations, deployment plans, cost, budget, task dependencies, necessary training for operation staff, milestones, etc.

9.18 THE GLOBAL ENTERPRISE ENGINEERING MODEL DESIGN'S GUIDELINES

Dr. Eng. M. Naoulo

The Global Enterprise Engineering Model would be extensive and sophisticated. It reflects the total Apparatus, Machinery, and Operation of the Enterprise. In order to handle such large model the following guidelines might be helpful:

Conformed Apparatus Members & Conformed Master Data Dimensions

Apparatus Members and their Interlinks could participate in the optimization of several Business Functions and their corresponding operations. Some of these Business Functions might require additional and/or different attributes of the Apparatus Members/Interlinks than other Business Functions. It is Best of Practice to consolidate these Apparatus Members/Interlinks and include in them the attributes needed by all the Business Functions. These Apparatus Members/Interlinks are called Conformed Apparatus Members/Interlinks and are implemented in the Enterprise Engineering Model thru Conformed Master Data Dimensions. Subsets of these Conformed Master Data Dimensions could be applied into each Business Function(s) Entity-Relationship Diagram as needed. This sub-setting could be implemented using Views. This Conformed concept is very important in reducing discrepancies between the Master Data Dimensions data across the Business Functions. The implementation's final structure would be coordinated between the Enterprise Engineers and the IT Organization.

It is important to note that the Conformed Master Data Dimensions could be applied in the Central Data Repository, Business Intelligence Data Marts, and Enterprise Intelligence Data Marts. Using Conformed Dimensions across BI and EI Data Marts simultaneously would provide additional benefits (Ref. Section 4.6.1). However trying to use Conformed Dimensions across the Central Data Repository, EI, and BI Data Marts simultaneously is difficult and not advisable as the Central Data Repository follows the Relational 3NF Data Modeling technique while the Data Marts follow the Multidimensional technique.

9.19   THE GLOBAL ENTERPRISE ENGINEERING'S GUIDELINES

The Global Enterprise Engineering Guidelines address the two aspects of the Global Enterprise Engineering:

1. **Global Enterprise Improvement**: It follows the same Guidelines described in Step 12 applied at the whole Enterprise level. They are addressing the improvement of all the Business Functions and the optimization of the processing of the Enterprise Engineering Model for the whole Enterprise.
2. **Global Enterprise Revitalization**: It follows the same Guidelines described in Step 13 applied at the whole Enterprise level. They are addressing the revitalization and drastic change of all the Business Functions and the reevaluation of the processing of the Enterprise Engineering Model for the whole Enterprise.

It is always important to note that the improvement and revitalization of the whole Enterprise at the strategic level would have more impact on the Enterprise and would imply more organizational changes than dealing with few Business Functions.

Dr. Eng. M. Naoulo

9.20 THE RESOURCES HANDLING THE ENTERPRISE ENGINEERING ASSIGNMENT'S GUIDELINES

The teams conducting the Enterprise Engineering exercise should follow the Organization Structure indicated in Section 8.20. Table 9.1 represents the Responsible, Accountable, Consulted, and Informed role (RACI chart) of the Enterprise Engineering staff performing the Enterprise Engineering steps.

#		Chief Executive Officer (CEO)	Chief Information Officer (CIO)	IT Technical Director & Staff	Applications Development Director(s) & Staff	ETL Director & Staff	Data Governance Director & Staff	Chief Operation Officer (COO)	Business Function Directors & Staff	Chief Enterprise Architecture & Engineering Officer (CEAEO)	EE Business Director	EE Apparatus Manager & Staff	EE Machinery & TRX Manager & Staff	EE Activity & Sessions Manager & Staff	Enterprise Data Architecture Director	Enterprise Master Data Manager & Staff	Enterprise TRX & BI Manager & Staff	Enterprise Sessions & EI Manager & Staff	EE Technical Director
1	Business Objectives' Identification	C	I					RA	R	I									
2	Business Functions Scope's Identification	C	I					R	RA	I	C	C	C	C	I				
3	Enterprise Engineering Optimization Goals' Identification	RA	I					R	R	I	I	I	I	I	I				
4	Enterprise Engineering Exercise's Extent Identification	I	I	I	I	I	I	C	C	RA	R	R	R	R	R	C	C	C	R
5	Business Functions' Portrayal		I					R	RA	I	I	I	I	I	I	I	I	I	I
6	Current Apparatus' Identification & Assortment		C		I			R	C	R	C	RA	C	I	R	C	C	C	C
7	Current Machinery's Delineation & Evaluation		C		I			R	C	R	C	C	RA	I	C	R	C	C	C
8	Current Operation Sessions' Identification, Information Gathering, & Evaluation		C		I			R	C	R	C	C	C	RA	I	C	C	R	C
9	Current Operation Transactions' Information Gathering, & Evaluation		C		I			R	C	R	C	C	C	RA	I	C	R	C	C
10	Current Enterprise Engineering Model & EI Data Marts' Design		C	I	C	C	C	I	C	C	C	C	C	C	RA	R	R	R	C
11	Current Mechanics Processing & Results' Generation & Interpretation	I	C		C			I	C	C	C	C	C	C	R	R	R	R	RA
12	Enterprise's Improvement	I	C		C			I	R	R	RA	R	R	R		C	C	C	C

Dr. Eng. M. Naoulo

#	Task																		
13	Enterprise Revitalization	I	C		C			I	R	R	R A	R	R	R		C	C	C	C
14	Target Apparatus, Machinery, Operation, Enterprise Engineering Model, & EI Data Marts' Design		C	I	C	C	C	I	C	C	C	C	C	C	R A	R	R	R	C
15	Target Mechanics Processing & Results' Generation & Interpretation	I	C		C			I	C	C	C	C	C	C	R	R	R	R	R A
16	Enterprise Engineering Strategic Operation Decisions	R A	C	C	C	C	C	R	R	R	R	C	C	C	C	C	C	C	R
17	Target Enterprise Engineering Implementation	C	R	R	R	R	R	RA	R	R	R	R	R	R	R	R	R	R	R

R = Responsible
A = Accountable (there can only be one of these per line item in the RACI chart)
C = Consulted
I = Informed

Table 9.1: The Responsibility, Accountability, Consultation, & Informed role of the Enterprise Engineering staff performing the Enterprise Engineering Steps

Dr. Eng. M. Naoulo

10. Case Study 1: ABC Airline's FR&TP

The Enterprise Engineering Case Studies 1 and 2 pursue the strategic assessment and optimization of the extra charges ABC Airline would impose on the customers to cover part of ABC Airline's staff cost for performing Flight Reservation and/or Ticket Purchasing (FR&TP) as the result from the customers' contact of ABC Airline's staff by telephone or personally at ABC Airline's offices on top of the cost of the ticket; no charges are added if the customers perform these tasks themselves on the Internet. The FR and TP functions are part of the same operation unit of ABC Airline and are handled by the same Airline Staff.

This Case Study aims to provide the director(s) of ABC Airline's FR&TP Operation with information to help them in the following strategic decisions:

1. Should ABC Airline impose extra charge(s) on the customers for the Flight Reservation and Ticket Purchasing by telephone or personally coming to ABC Airline's office versus using the Internet? If yes what are the optimum amount(s) to be charged and the rules regulating these charges?
2. Should the charges be the same or different?
   - For Flight Reservation by telephone,
   - For Flight Reservation at ABC Airline's office,
   - For Ticket Purchasing by telephone,
   - For Ticket Purchasing at ABC Airline's office.
3. How to combine and apply the charges and what are the rules regulating these charges and their combination? E.g. would the applied charge be the maximum charge (resulting from either telephone calls or from contacts at ABC Airline's office) or would it be the total of all charges?

The Enterprise Engineering exercise would help the directors to validate and justify their decisions to implement the extra charges and adding or combining these charges. The analysis would be realized thru the engineering of ABC Airline's FR&TP Operation using the Enterprise Engineering System of Apparatus, Machinery, and Operation (**SAM O NAOULO**).

It is important to note that the Improvement and especially the Revitalization of the enterprise might imply taking different strategy for the Business Functions under investigation and might render obsolete many efficacy and effectiveness questions.

Note: In real life some of the information captured in a step might be part of information needed by other steps. Example: while executing the Business Functions Scope's Identification (Step 2), information details pertinent to the Business Functions' Portrayal (Step 5), Current Apparatus' Identification and Assortment (Step 6), and/or Current Machinery's Delineation and Evaluation (Step 7) might be captured. It is important to document all captured information. In this Case Study, these circumstances were included to reflect the real life situations.

10.1 ABC AIRLINE'S BUSINESS OBJECTIVES IDENTIFICATION

The First Step of the Methodology is to identify the Business Objectives of the exercise. The tasks to identify these objectives embrace gathering the objectives requirement from the Operation Director(s)/Staff responsible for the FR&TP.

The Step's Result

The first task is to identify and assess the Business Model of the enterprise; but there was no documented Business Model (not surprising). Nevertheless the Enterprise Engineers were able to find out that the main guiding strategy of the Enterprise is to **support high class and business customers and provide them with high class services**.

The Business Objectives of this Case Study embrace providing the director(s) of ABC Airline's FR&TP Operation with solid information to help them with the following strategic decisions:

1. Should ABC Airline charge the customer anything at all to cover part of ABC Airline's staff cost for performing Flight Reservation and/or Ticket Purchasing (FR&TP) resulting from the customers' contact of ABC Airline's staff by telephone or personally at ABC Airline's offices on top of the price that ABC Airline would charge the customer for performing these activities thru the Internet?
2. Should ABC Airline eliminates altogether FR&TP by telephone and/or at ABC Airline's offices and keeps these activities only thru the Internet?

ABC Airline currently applies an extra charge of $20.00 per ticket for purchasing the tickets by phone or at ABC Airline's office and there are no additional charges for doing the Flights Reservation neither by phone nor at ABC Airline's office. This extra charge would be applied on top of the price of the ticket when purchased. In other words the extra charge is implemented depending on the Ticket Purchasing method and not the Flight Reservation method.

One of the directors suggested, based on some gut-feeling, that ABC Airline should implement an extra charge of $10.00 per ticket for FR&TP by phone, and an extra charge of $20.00 per ticket for FR&TP at ABC Airline's office.

Another director suggested giving incentives to the customer for FR&TP thru the Internet: example Frequent Flyers points. The values of the Frequent Flyer points are to be calculated on the basis that 100 points are equivalent to one Dollar.

Currently this Airline Company, like many other airlines, allows Flight Reservation to Customers without the requirements to purchase the tickets. In some cases purchasing the ticket is mandatory with the Flight Reservation.

The following points are considered:

➤ To optimize the Enterprise effectiveness, the extra charges of the tickets would address and compensate the additional cost of ABC Airline's Agents.
➤ Eliminating completely the FR&TP thru the Telephone and Office agents is an option that would be contemplated by the top management. Appropriate business and cost

Dr. Eng. M. Naoulo

evaluation should be assessed to support this option.

➤ The case of initiating the Flight Reservation or follow up on the Flight Reservation thru Telephone and/or Office agents then purchasing the ticket thru the internet would imply extra charges to the ticket price.

➤ There is a need to decide on the extra charges: are they fixed or they depend on the number of contacts, and/or the time spent by ABC Airline's Agents to accommodate the FR&TP, and/or other factors. The optimization based on the number of contacts or the time spent by the agents and type and location of agents needs to be addressed, analyzed and justified.

Deliverables

The FR&TP Directors indicated that the Business Objectives from this exercise are the validation of the operation data and figures (current and target) to support or dispute the suggested ideas, and, if possible, to determine the optimum amounts of extra charges. If new ideas were explored during the exercise which improve the operation better than these suggested ideas, the new ideas would be considered. Also the Directors indicated that they are interested to explore any additional engineering of ABC Airline's FR&TP Operations that would improve the Business Functions and reduce cost.

The CEO, in correlation with the Marketing Department, stressed the issue of Customer Satisfaction and required that Customer Satisfaction surveys should be conducted to assess the changes and their impact on the customers and on ABC Airline's business.

10.2 ABC AIRLINE'S BUSINESS FUNCTIONS SCOPE IDENTIFICATION

The Second Step is to identify the scope of the Business Functions that would be involved in the Enterprise Engineering exercise to attain the Business Objectives identified in Step 1. In this Case Study these Business Functions include the two areas of FR&TP Operation: Flight Reservation and Ticket Purchasing.

The scope of this Case Study covers analyzing the data including time and cost pertinent to the elementary activities of the functions of FR&TP Operation.

The Step's Result

The following boundaries were identified for this Case Study:

➤ FR&TP Operations are performed by the Customer thru the Internet, initiated by the Customer calling ABC Airline by telephone, or instigated by the Customer going personally to ABC Airline's office.

➤ All traveling trip types: One way, return flight, or many legs flights would be captured.

➤ ABC Airline's Staff's working time during the contact with the Customer and after session work would be captured.

➤ ABC Airline's Staff's cost and staff's location cost would be captured. These costs differ by location and type of staff serving the customer either on the phone or personally. The cost could be obtained from the FR&TP Directors and/or from Activity Based Costing

(ABC) analysis' information if available.

> It is acceptable to consider the cost of performing FR&TP thru the internet as negligible as the FR&TP staff has also to access the internet for FR&TP.

> Any emails, faxes or letters sent by mail related to the FR&TP Operations are out of scope because they are not that common, require more analysis, and their percentage of the overall FR&TP contacts cost is small.

> The FR&TP Office Staff are located in USA and Canada while the FR&TP Telephone Staff are located in USA, Canada and India.

In order not to complicate this exercise and to focus on the Enterprise Engineering aspect, the purchasing methods of the tickets: Cash, Credit Cards, Checks, Frequent Flyers points, Vouchers, Special Discounts, Corporate Discounts, etc. are not addressed in this Case Study.

The main Apparatus' attribute that specifies a Flight Reservation is the Reservation Confirmation Number (RCN). The contact types between the Customers and ABC Airline's office or Telephone staff or the ABC Airline's FR&TP site on the Internet could be classified into three categories as related to the RCN. For the scoping of this exercise, and in order not to complicate it, the scope boundaries were addressed as follows:

> All contacts that are not related to RCN(s). I.e.: inquiries not related or not ending with RCN(s), attempts to book flights but not ending with RCN(s), etc. are out of scope. Of course all contacts of the Customer with the Telephone Agent(s) and/or Office Agent(s) impact the cost, and it is necessary to capture the information related to these contacts in a comprehensive study.

> All contacts that are related or pertinent or ending in more than one RCN are out of scope. This includes the initial contact to establish the reservations and any other contacts related to them: modifying the reservations (number of passengers, names, itinerary, etc.), attempt to modify the reservation but no changes to the reservations, seats allocation, purchasing the ticket(s), canceling reservation(s), etc.

> All contacts with the customers that are related or ending in only one RCN are in scope.

Since a very large number of contacts between the Customers and ABC Airline's office or Telephone staff or the ABC Airline's FR&TP Internet site are related to one RCN, the scope limitation still gives good perspective on the FR&TP operation of ABC Airline. Of course a complete and comprehensive Enterprise Engineering study of the Business Functions of FR&TP must include all these three categories.

Some design points might be considered in a complete study but are out of scope in this exercise:

> In the case of contacts that are not related to RCN(s), the information discussed and/or captured during these contacts: flights, number of passengers, itinerary, etc. are usually not complete, therefore it might not be important to store them in the database; however the information captured during these contacts that affect the overall operation cost and time: start and end of contacts, Agents Code etc. must be captured and stored.

> In the case of contacts that are related to many RCNs, all information captured during these contacts including those related to the RCNs and those that affect the operation cost and time: start and end of contacts, Agents Code etc. must be captured and stored. It

Dr. Eng. M. Naoulo

might be important to assess and determine the correlation, distribution and/or allocation of the operation cost and time among the RCNs.

Other points that need to be evaluated in a complete study:
- ➤ The extra charges to the Customer for doing the reservation and/or purchasing the tickets by telephone might differ from the extra charges to the Customer for doing the reservation and/or purchasing the tickets personally at ABC Airline's office.
- ➤ If the Flight Reservation was handled many times thru the internet, telephone and/or at ABC Airline's office, the cost of all contacts would be aggregated.

It was pointed out to the Enterprise Engineers that Customer Satisfaction Survey's sessions should be conducted. A Customer Satisfaction Survey's session could be related to one or many FR&TP sessions. An FR&TP session could impact one or many Customer Satisfaction Survey's sessions. For the scoping of this exercise the Customer Satisfaction Survey's sessions would be related to only one RCN.

The following table illustrates the scope of this exercise:

UC #	Use Case Name	Pre-Condition	Post-Condition	In/Out of Scope	UC Combination
1	Flight Reservation	No RCN	1 RCN	In Scope	
2	Flight Reservation	No RCN	Many RCNs	Out of Scope	
3	Flight Inquiry	No RCN		Out of Scope	
4	Flight Inquiry	1 RCN		In Scope	
5	Flight Inquiry	Many RCNs		Out of Scope	
6	Flight Modification	1 RCN	Same RCN & same Itinerary	In Scope	
7	Flight Modification	1 RCN	Same RCN but different Itinerary	In Scope	
8	Flight Modification	1 RCN	Different RCN	Out of Scope	
9	Flight Modification	1 RCN	Many RCNs	Out of Scope	
10	Flight Modification	Many RCNs	1 RCN	Out of Scope	
11	Flight Modification	Many RCNs	Same RCNs & same Itinerary	Out of Scope	
12	Flight Modification	Many RCNs	Same RCNs but different Itinerary(ies)	Out of Scope	
13	Flight Modification	Many RCNs	Different RCNs	Out of Scope	
14	Flight Cancellation	1 RCN	1 RCN cancelled	In Scope	
15	Flight Cancellation	Many RCNs	One or Many RCNs is/are cancelled	Out of Scope	
16	Ticket Purchasing	1 RCN	Same RCN + Its Ticket(s)	In Scope	
17	Ticket Purchasing	Many RCNs	Same RCNs + Their Tickets	Out of Scope	

Dr. Eng. M. Naoulo

18	Ticket Refund	1 RCN & Ticket(s)	1 RCN cancelled & Ticket(s) refunded	In Scope	
19	Ticket Refund	Many RCNs & Tickets	One or Many RCNs cancelled & One or many Ticket(s) refunded	Out of Scope	
20	Flight Reservation & Ticket Purchasing	No RCN	1 RCN + Its Ticket(s)	In Scope	UC # 1 & 16
21	Flight Reservation & Ticket Purchasing	No RCN	Many RCNs + Their Ticket(s)	Out of Scope	UC # 2 & 17
22	Flight Modification & Ticket Purchasing	1 RCN	Same RCN + Its Ticket(s)	In Scope	UC # 6 or 7 & 16
23	Flight Modification & Ticket Purchasing	1 RCN	Different RCN + Its Ticket(s)	Out of Scope	UC # 8 & 16
24	Flight Modification & Ticket Purchasing	1 RCN	Many RCNs + Their Ticket(s)	Out of Scope	UC # 9 & 17
25	Flight Modification & Ticket Purchasing	Many RCNs	1 RCN + Its Ticket(s)	Out of Scope	UC # 10 & 16
26	Flight Modification & Ticket Purchasing	Many RCNs	Same or Different RCNs + Their Ticket(s)	Out of Scope	UC # 11, 12 or 13 & 17
27	Flight Cancellation & Ticket Refund	1 RCN & Ticket(s)	1 RCN cancelled & Ticket(s) refund	In Scope	UC # 14 & 18
28	Flight Cancellation & Ticket Refund	Many RCNs & Tickets	One or Many RCNs cancelled & One or Many Ticket(s) refund	Out of Scope	UC # 15 & 19
29	Any combination of Flight Inquiry/Reservation/Modification/Cancellation & Ticket Purchasing/Refund including only one RCN	No RCN or 1 RCN	1 RCN (New or Same)	In Scope	Combination of above UC
30	Any combination of Flight Inquiry/Reservation/Modification/Cancellation & Ticket Purchasing/Refund including only one RCN	1 RCN	No RCN or 1 RCN (Same)	In Scope	Combination of above UC
30	Any combination of Flight Inquiry/Reservation/Modification/Cancellation & Ticket Purchasing/Refund including different RCNs	No RCN or 1 RCN	Different RCN	Out of Scope	Combination of above UC
31	Any combination of Flight Inquiry/Reservation/Modification/Cancellation & Ticket Purchasing/Refund including many RCNs	0, 1 or many RCNs	0,1 or many RCNs (not 1 same RCN)	Out of Scope	Combination of above UC
32	Customer Satisfaction Survey	No RCN	No RCN	Out of Scope	
33	Customer Satisfaction Survey	1 RCN	Same RCN	In Scope	
34	Customer Satisfaction Survey	Many RCNs	Many RCNs	Out of Scope	

Table 10.1a: Scope of the Case Study

Dr. Eng. M. Naoulo

Deliverables

The Business Functions within the scope of the exercise are: FR&TP and Customer Satisfaction Survey related to FR&TP.

	FR&TP	Customer Satisfaction Survey related to FR&TP
Name, description, and objectives of this Business Function	This Business Function includes the activities of FR&TP of ABC Airline and controls their Sessions. Its objectives are to assure that FR&TP Sessions follow the rules and regulations established by ABC Airline related to FR&TP	This Business Function includes the activities of Customer Satisfaction Surveys related to FR&TP of ABC Airline and controls their Sessions. Its objectives are to assure that Customer Satisfaction Survey Sessions related to FR&TP of ABC Airline follow the rules and regulations established by ABC Airline related to these surveys
How this Business Function works	➢ The Customer would supply and discuss with the FR&TP Office Staff during the Customers' visit to ABC Airline's Office the info related to FR&TP ➢ The Customer would supply and discuss with the FR&TP Telephone Staff during the Customers' telephone conversation with them the info related to FR&TP ➢ The Customer would supply the FR&TP software applications thru the Internet the info related to FR&TP	➢ The Customer would supply, the Customer Satisfaction Survey software applications related to FR&TP, thru the Internet, with the survey info requested ➢ The Customer would supply the Telephone call with the survey info requested
Who is involved in this Business Function	➢ The Customer ➢ FR&TP Office Staff for Customers' visit to ABC Airline's Office ➢ FR&TP Telephone Staff for Customers calling by phone ABC Airline	➢ The Customer ➢ FR&TP Office Staff or Telephone Staff
What equipment, materiel, material, tools, software, and systems are involved in this Business Function	➢ Computers and Network, the Internet, the FR&TP software applications	➢ Computers and Network, the Internet, the Customer Satisfaction Survey software applications related to FR&TP

Dr. Eng. M. Naoulo

Where this Business Function is performed	➢ FR&TP Office for Customers' visit ➢ FR&TP Office or Telephone Staff home for Customers calling ABC Airline by phone	➢ The Customer's location
When this Business Function is running	FR&TP could be initiated by a Customer's visit to ABC Airline's Office, a Customer calling by phone ABC Airline, or by a Customer handling FR&TP thru the Internet	Customer Satisfaction Survey related to FR&TP could be initiated by a: ➢ Customer handling the Survey thru the Internet ➢ By an automatic ABC Airline telephone call ➢ By a FR&TP Office Staff or Telephone Staff requesting the Customer to participate in a Survey related to FR&TP

Table 10.2: The Business Functions within the scope

The following Use Cases are identified in scope (Ref. Table 10.1a):

Use Cases	Pre-Condition	Post Condition
Flight Reservation	No RCN	1 RCN
Flight Inquiry	1 RCN	
Flight Modification	1 RCN	Same RCN (Same or different Itinerary)
Flight Cancellation	1 RCN	1 RCN cancelled
Ticket Purchasing	1 RCN	Same RCN + Its Ticket(s)
Ticket Refund	1 RCN & Ticket(s)	1 RCN cancelled & Ticket(s) refunded
Customer Satisfaction Survey	1 RCN	

Table 10.1b: Scope of the Use Cases

The following Sessions would implement these Business Functions:
- ➢ FR&TP: **MS FR&TP SESSION:** This Session implements the activities of the FR&TP. FR&TP could be initiated by a Customer's visit to ABC Airline's Office, a Customer calling by phone ABC Airline, or by a Customer handling FR&TP thru the Internet. **MS FR&TP SESSION** might have three subtypes to support these scenarios.
- ➢ Customer Satisfaction Survey related to FR&TP: **MS FR&TP CUSTOMER SATISFACTION SURVEY SESSION:** This Session implements the activities of the Customer Satisfaction Surveys related to FR&TP. Customer Satisfaction Survey related

to FR&TP could be initiated by a Customer responding by phone to ABC Airline's Survey request without the involvement of ABC Airline's staff capturing the survey (Ref. Section 10.5.1), or by a Customer handling the FR&TP Survey thru the Internet.

The following Transactions would be generated by these Business Functions:

- FR&TP: **X PASSENGER RESERVATION TRX:** This Transaction records the reservation details for Passenger(s). It might be composed of a main entity and a detail entity supporting the data of each Passenger. Its input data include Passenger info, Flight info, and Reservation Leg Class. Its output data include Leg Price, Seat Code, and Transaction's Timestamps.
- FR&TP: **X CUSTOMER PAYMENT TRX:** This Transaction records the payment details for Passenger(s). Its input data include Passenger(s) info, Flight info, and payment details. Its output data include payment acceptance and Timestamps.
- Customer Satisfaction Survey related to FR&TP: **X FR&TP CUSTOMER SATISFACTION SURVEY TRX:** This Transaction records the Customer Satisfaction Survey details related to FR&TP. Its input data include Passenger(s) info and Flight info. Its output data include the survey results and Timestamps.

10.3 ABC AIRLINE'S ENTERPRISE ENGINEERING OPTIMIZATION GOAL IDENTIFICATION

The Third Step is to identify the Enterprise Engineering Optimization Goals that specify the targets for the development/improvement/expansion of the Enterprise Operation Function Areas: ABC's Airline FR&TP.

The Step's Result

In order to streamline more efficient and comprehensive operation reporting, the following info is needed:

- Details related to Telephone Agents' services: Number of telephone calls per 15 min time intervals, Number of unanswered telephone calls per 15 min time intervals, duration of calls, reason for calls, answering staff's location, answering staff's level, etc.
- Details related to Office Agents' services: Number of Office Agents contacts with customers per 15 min time intervals, duration of customers' visit, reason for customers' visit, office location, answering staff's level, etc.

Deliverables

The following goals were identified by the FR&TP Directors:

- Decrease the overall cost of the FR&TP Operations by 25%. This goal could be attained thru the Enterprise Engineering improvement and revitalization as the efficiency and efficacy of the current FR&TP Operations were not addressed before at ABC Airline. It is difficult to get info related to the Best of Practice as the competitors try to restrict this info as confidential.
- Increase the Customer Satisfaction related to the FR&TP Operations by 50%. This goal needs substantial Enterprise Engineering out-of-box thinking as the competition in the market is targeting aggressively this goal. Furthermore it is difficult to get info related to

Dr. Eng. M. Naoulo

the Best of Practice as many competitors inflate these figures deliberately to use them as advertising points.

> The List of KPIs and Metrics that contribute to the Optimization Goals are:
>   - Individual Staff Cost per Month
>   - Individual Staff Cost per Sec
>   - Number of RCNs handled per Staff per Month
>   - Business Offices Cost per Sec
>   - Business Offices Cost per Staff per Sec
>   - Cost/RCN
> In order to reach the goal of "Decrease the overall cost of the FR&TP Operations by 25%", the targeted goal for the exercise was set to 40%. This would allow driving the Enterprise Engineers toward advanced goals and allow room for maneuver.
> In order to reach the goal of "Increase the Customer Satisfaction related to the FR&TP Operations by 50%", the targeted goal for the exercise was set to 75%. The Marketing Department inspired, advocated, and encouraged this leaning.

Note: In order to keep this exercise within practical size, only few of these goals are addressed.

10.4 ABC AIRLINE'S ENTERPRISE ENGINEERING EXERCISE EXTENT IDENTIFICATION

The fourth Step is to identify the extent of the Enterprise Engineering exercise.

The Step's Result

The Enterprise Engineering's extent identified for this exercise encompasses and indicates:

> The FR&TP conducted using the telephone, or going personally to ABC Airline's office would require, on top of the Hardware and software, the involvement of ABC Airline's Agents. The optimization would address only the cost of the Telephone and Office agents and the cost of their offices.
> The processing of the current and target FR&TP Enterprise Engineering Models will be the base for assessing the results of the Enterprise Engineering exercise.
> The computers and networking Hardware and Software to support the FR&TP using the Internet should be available to customers 24/7. The customers would access the same databases as ABC Airline's staff (with slight difference related to some specific security and business rules).

Deliverables

> The areas of optimization include FR&TP across all ABC Airline. However the analysis would cover only a subset related to reservations treating only one RCN as indicated in Step 2. The cost factors are indicated in Step 3.
> The List of KPIs and Metrics are indicated in Step 3.
> The Enterprise Engineering exercise would rely heavily for optimization on the Out-Of-Box Thinking.
> The software to be used for the exercise, besides the databases and the programming languages used at ABC Airline, include MS Office, ERD Tool: E.g. CA Erwin, ETL Tool:

Dr. Eng. M. Naoulo

E.g. Informatica, Reporting Tool: E.g. Business Objects and MicroStrategy.

10.5 ABC AIRLINE'S BUSINESS FUNCTIONS PORTRAYAL

The Fifth Step of the Methodology is to identify and gather the information pertinent to:
- ➤ The operations related to the Business Functions identified in Step 2. The technique used is the Use Cases introduced by Ivar Jacobson [7 & 8] as part of the Object Oriented Analysis. These Use Cases should be complete and include at a detail level the answers to the six questions indicated in Section 2.2. Also they should include at a detail level:
  - ▪ The description of the Sessions that implement these Business Functions.
  - ▪ The description of the Transactions generated by these Business Functions with main input and output data.
  - ▪ Detailed numeric figures from the Operation Directors related to the current size, performance, impact on market, etc. of the FR&TP Operation implemented thru the telephone or at ABC Airline's office.
- ➤ Detailed numeric figures from the Operation Directors related to the current cost of the FR&TP Operation implemented thru the telephone or at ABC Airline's office (Staff cost, Location cost, and other costs).
- ➤ Detailed metadata info related to the Legacy/Operational Systems from where the data is going to be extracted (Ref. Section 9.3).

As mentioned at the beginning of this chapter, it is possible during this step to ask questions and get some feedback pertinent to the estimated size and cost of operations related to a preliminary conceived target design (if any). This information should be reevaluated during Steps 12 to 15.

10.5.1 The Use Cases describing the OLTP & OLMP

The Step's Result

ABC Airline indicated some Business Rules:
1. Different itineraries for different passengers would necessitate different RCN(s), while passengers traveling as a group with the same itinerary could have one RCN.
2. Any addition to the number of passengers or changing the itinerary to some (and not all) passengers for an existing Reservation implies generation of new RCN(s).
3. As mentioned in Section 10.2, Customer Satisfaction Survey's sessions could be related to one or many FR&TP sessions and an FR&TP session could impact one or many Customer Satisfaction Survey's sessions.

Deliverables

The Use Cases were detailed into their lowest level of granularity: Flight Reservation, Flight Inquiry, Flight Modification, Flight Cancellation, Ticket Purchasing, Ticket Refund, and Customer Satisfaction Survey (Table 10.1b). Any combination of Flight Inquiry/Reservation/Modification/Cancellation & Ticket Purchasing/Refund could be sustained by a combination of the above Use Cases. The Use Cases cover the following activities:
- ➤ **FR&TP Flight Inquiry/Reservation/Modification/Cancellation & Ticket Purchasing/Refund.** They handle the scenarios of Customers calling the Telephone

Agents or personally speaking with the Office Agents at ABC Airline's office to handle FR&TP tasks. FR&TP Use Cases using the Internet would also be evaluated to assess the overall FR&TP Function info.

- ➤ **FR&TP Customer Satisfaction.** The Customer Satisfaction surveys are conducted thru the Telephone or the Internet without involving ABC Airline's staff. The Customer Satisfaction surveys thru the Telephone Agents are not cost effective and they were eliminated by previous decisions.

The information needed for OLTP covers the following (not all Airline companies capture all these info and many Airline companies capture much more):

- ➤ Information related to the contact of the Customer with the Telephone Agent(s) or Office Agent(s). The info captured would include:
    - Type of contact: Telephone or ABC Airline's office. Emails, faxes or letters sent by mail are out of scope as indicated in Section 10.2.
    - Result of the contact: Inquiry with comments, Initial reservation (number of passengers, names, itinerary, etc.), modification info, seats allocation, purchasing the ticket(s), canceling a reservation, etc.
    - All transactional info related to the Contact.
- ➤ Additional info handled by the agents during the after-contact work.

The information needed for OLMP within the scope of this exercise cover the following:

- ➤ Info related to the Start and End Timestamps of the contact of the Customer with the Telephone Agent(s) or Office Agent(s). The information captured would include info about the Agents involved in the contacts with their Codes and Start and End Timestamps for each Agent involvement. Info related to contacts aiming to modify the reservation but no changes occurred to the reservation were also included.
- ➤ Info related to the Start and End Timestamps for all after-contact work that the agents perform pertinent to the contact.

More information might be needed for more detailed analysis.

The Use Cases should detail the business functions including the info pertinent to OLTP and OLMP. In this exercise since ABC Airline did not have in their system development documentation the Use Cases describing the OLTP, the Use Cases were developed for the exercise. These Use Cases would incorporate the information needed by both the OLTP and OLMP requirements. They would cover the basic and alternate courses of action.

These Use Cases are:

- ➤ FR001: New Flight Reservation thru FR&TP's Telephone and/or Office Agents
- ➤ FR002: New Flight Reservation thru the Internet
- ➤ FI001: Flight Inquiry thru FR&TP's Telephone and/or Office Agents
- ➤ FI002: Flight Inquiry thru the Internet
- ➤ FM001: Flight Modification thru FR&TP's Telephone and/or Office Agents
- ➤ FM002: Flight Modification thru the Internet
- ➤ FC001: Flight Cancellation thru FR&TP's Telephone and/or Office Agents
- ➤ FC002: Flight Cancellation thru the Internet

Dr. Eng. M. Naoulo

- ➤ TP001: Ticket Purchasing thru FR&TP's Telephone and/or Office Agents
- ➤ TP002: Ticket Purchasing thru the Internet
- ➤ TR001: Ticket Refund thru FR&TP's Telephone and/or Office Agents
- ➤ TR002: Ticket Refund thru the Internet
- ➤ CSS01: Customer Satisfaction Survey thru the Internet (software interaction).

These Use Cases are not detailed here in order to keep the exercise concise.

10.5.2 The Information related to the FR&TP Operation Cost

It was indicated by the FR&TP Directors that they have no detailed info about the cost of their FR&TP Operation per stratum: type of reservation, RCN, origin of reservation etc. However they know globally – and sometimes in detail – the cost per Business Location and per Airline Agent.

Personnel, Payroll & Process Data

The current FR&TP Human Resources, Payroll, and Operation Cost data were gathered from the Business HR and Operation departments. Table 10.8 illustrates these figures:

- ➤ Current Office Staff working in the USA and Canada during dayshift is 455, their cost is $2,500,000 per month, and number of RCN handled per month is 900,000. The Business Offices Cost per Month is $300,000.
- ➤ Current Office Staff working in the USA and Canada during nightshift is 168, their cost is $1,100,000 per month, and number of RCN handled per month is 340,000. The Business Offices Cost per Month is $300,000.
- ➤ Current Telephone Staff working in the USA and Canada during dayshift is 688, their cost is $2,140,000 per month, and number of RCN handled per month is 1,600,000. The Business Offices Cost per Month is $350,000.
- ➤ Current Telephone Staff working in the USA and Canada during nightshift is 95, their cost is $330,000 per month, and number of RCN handled per month is 190,000. The Business Offices Cost per Month is $100,000.
- ➤ Current Telephone Staff working in India during dayshift is 212, their cost is $132,000 per month, and number of RCN handled per month is 190,000. The Business Offices Cost per Month is $50,000.
- ➤ Current Telephone Staff working in India during nightshift is 314, their cost is $250,000 per month, and number of RCN handled per month is 280,000. The Business Offices Cost per Month is $50,000.
- ➤ All staff working in India is Telephone Staff.
- ➤ The total FR&TP Staff operation cost per Month is $6,452,000.
- ➤ The total FR&TP Business Offices Cost per Month is $1,150,000
- ➤ The FR&TP Cost per Month is 6,452,000 + 1,150,000 = $7,602,000 per month.
- ➤ The total number of RCNs handled per month by the FR&TP staff is 3,500,000.
- ➤ The same RCN could be handled by many Office and Telephone staff and this staff could belong to different regions and time period. Even the customers using the Internet could handle these RCN: create, assign seats, etc. The FR&TP Operation could not provide more details about how many RCNs were created by each Staff group or by the Internet; however they indicated that the overall total number of RCNs created each month is 2,900,000 (the Number of RCNs handled per Month by

the Staff is 3,500,000 due to some RCNs are handled many times).

➢ The income from the currently imposed extra fees for Flight Reservation and/or Ticket Purchasing thru Telephone or Office Agents is: $3,450,000 per month.

➢ The ratio of RCNs ending up with Ticket Purchase to the total number of RCNs is around 0.38.

10.5.3 The Information related to the Legacy Systems

The number of OLTP Legacy Systems covering FR&TP is small and these systems were developed recently and most of the staff who worked on them is still working in ABC Airline. After discussions with the Directors and IT staff it was decided to enhance these systems to accommodate **SAM O NAOULO** requirements. The applications, programs, and databases were updated. The tasks to accomplish this are (Ref Section 5.3.1):

➢ The Legacy Systems data from which **SAM O NAOULO** data would be extracted were gathered including their Database Schemas and the DDL.

➢ The Legacy Systems Data Models were reversed-engineered from the DDL (if possible). Unfortunately ABC Airline did not have any definition of tables and fields or any metadata information. Also ABC Airline did not perform any data cleansing on its data.

➢ The Data Models and Databases were updated to accommodate capturing **SAM O NAOULO** data requirements.

➢ The coding of the OLTP Legacy Systems was performed to accommodate capturing **SAM O NAOULO** data requirements.

➢ The frequency of extraction from the Legacy Systems to the Central Data Repository was set on daily basis.

➢ Data Profiling, Data Cleansing, Data Quality assessment, and Metadata design and generation were added to the exercise to assure the integrity and correctness of data on which the strategic decisions will be based.

➢ After the design of the Apparatus, Machinery, Operation, and the Enterprise Engineering Model reflecting them, the transformation rules to load the data into the Central Data Repository were developed. The ETL development was accomplished using an ETL tool.

10.6 ABC AIRLINE'S CURRENT APPARATUS IDENTIFICATION & ASSORTMENT

The Sixth Step is to identify and assort the Apparatus Members. This is accomplished thru identifying and detailing the Apparatus Master Data Entities involved in the Engineering process and assorting them according to the **NAOULO** six Components identified in Section 2.2. It is important to note that at least one Member must be identified in each Component.

The Step's Result

The Apparatus Members involved in this Enterprise Engineering exercise and covering the Needs, Activities, Operators, Utilities, Locations, and Occurrences are:

➢ **Needs**: Financial Revenue, Flight Revenue, Enterprise Operation Cost, FR&TP Operation Cost, and Customer Satisfaction.

➢ **Activities**: Flight Management, Flight Admin, FR&TP Control, and FR&TP Customer Satisfaction Survey (CSS) Gathering Control.

Dr. Eng. M. Naoulo

> **O**perators: Customer, FR&TP Staff (Telephone Agent and Office Agent), and Passenger. Since a Customer could be a Passenger and vice-versa and a FR&TP Staff could be a Customer or a Passenger, a supertype entity: **OPR PARTY** is created. It has as subtypes **OPR CUSTOMER**, **OPR PASSENGER**, and **OPR FR&TP STAFF.**
> Utilities: Airplane Model, Airplane, Flight, Flight Seat, RCN, and Ticket.
> Locations: Business Office, Telephone Number, Internet Address, Airport, and State.
> Occurrences: Date, FR&TP Event, FR&TP CSS Event, and FR&TP Cost Time Interval.

Deliverables

The hierarchies, lowest levels of granularity on which aggregation could be conducted, and aggregation possibilities (in addition to the aggregation on the lowest level of granularity) of the Apparatus Members and their Interlinks (reflected in the Enterprise Engineering Model by the Master Data Dimension and Associative Entities and their attributes) are presented in Table 10.3 (Ref. Diagram 10.1a). These hierarchies, lowest levels of granularity, and aggregation possibilities of the Master Data Entities and attributes could be straight forward translated into hierarchies, lowest levels of granularity, and aggregation possibilities of the Dimensions of BI and EI Data Marts.

Master Data Entities	Hierarchy	Lowest Level of Granularity in the Master Data Dimension and Associative Entities on which Aggregation could be conducted	Aggregation Possibilities of Master Data Attributes (In addition to the Aggregations on the lowest Level of Granularity)
NED ENTERPRISE OPERATION COST		> **NED Enterprise Operation Cost ID**	
NED FR&TP OPERATION COST	> **NED ENTERPRISE OPERATION COST**	> **NED FR&TP Operation Cost ID**	> **NED Enterprise Operation Cost ID** > Hierarchy of **NED ENTERPRISE OPERATION COST** for **NED Enterprise Operation Cost ID**
NED CUSTOMER SATISFACTION		> **NED Customer Satisfaction ID**	
NED FINANCIAL REVENUE		> **NED Financial Revenue ID**	

Dr. Eng. M. Naoulo

NED FLIGHT REVENUE	➢ NED FINANCIAL REVENUE	➢ NED Flight Revenue ID	➢ NED Financial Revenue ID ➢ Hierarchy of **NED FINANCIAL REVENUE** for **NED Financial Revenue ID**
ACT FLIGHT MANAGEMENT		➢ ACT Flight Management ID	
ACT FLIGHT ADMIN	➢ ACT FLIGHT MANAGEMENT	➢ ACT Flight Admin ID	➢ ACT Flight Management ID ➢ Hierarchy of **ACT FLIGHT MANAGEMENT** for ACT Flight Management ID
ACT FR&TPCONTROL	➢ ACT FLIGHT ADMIN	➢ ACT FR&TP Control ID	➢ ACT Flight Admin ID ➢ Hierarchy of **ACT FLIGHT ADMIN** for **ACT** Flight Admin ID
ACT FR&TP CSS GATHERING CONTROL	➢ ACT FLIGHT ADMIN	➢ ACT FR&TP CSS Gathering Control ID	➢ ACT Flight Admin ID ➢ Hierarchy of **ACT FLIGHT ADMIN** for **ACT** Flight Admin ID
OPR PARTY		➢ Party ID	
OPR PASSENGER		➢ OPR Passenger Party ID (Role-name of **OPR Party ID**) as **OPR PASSENGER** Entity is subtype of **OPR PARTY**	➢ OPR Passenger Medallion Level

Dr. Eng. M. Naoulo

OPR FR&TP STAFF	Staff Hierarchy is not part of the scope of this exercise	➤ **OPR FR&TP Staff Party ID** (Role-name of **OPR Party ID**) as **OPR FR&TP STAFF** Entity is subtype of **OPR PARTY**	➤ Strata of **OPR FR&TP Dayshift Staff Cost per Sec** ➤ Strata of **OPR FR&TP Nightshift Staff Cost per Sec** ➤ **OPR FR&TP Staff Sex** ➤ Date Hierarchies of **OPR FR&TP Staff Date of Birth** ➤ **OPR FR&TP Staff Education Level** ➤ **OPR FR&TP Staff Traveling Experience Level** ➤ Date Hierarchies of **OPR FR&TP Staff Date of Assignment** ➤ **OPR FR&TP Staff Position**
OPR CUSTOMER		➤ **OPR Customer Party ID** (Role-name of **OPR Party ID**) as **OPR CUSTOMER** Entity is subtype of **OPR PARTY**	
UTL RCN		➤ **UTL RCN ID**	➤ **UTL Reservation Itinerary Type** ➤ **UTL Reservation Status** ➤ **UTL Ticket Class IND** ➤ Date & Time Hierarchies of **UTL Reservation Hold TS** ➤ **UTL Number of Passengers** ➤ Strata of **UTL Anticipated Ticket Price**
UTL TICKET	➤ **UTL RCN**	➤ **UTL Ticket Number**	➤ **UTL RCN ID** ➤ Hierarchy of **UTL RCN** for **UTL RCN ID** ➤ Strata of **UTL Ticket Price** ➤ Strata of **UTL Ticket Extra Charge**
UTL AIRPLANE MODEL		➤ **UTL Airplane Model ID**	

Dr. Eng. M. Naoulo

UTL AIRPLANE	➢ UTL AIRPLANE MODEL	➢ UTL Airplane ID	➢ UTL Airplane Model ID ➢ Hierarchy of UTL AIRPLANE MODEL for UTL Airplane Model ID ➢ Strata of UTL Airplane In the Air Cost per Sec
UTL FLIGHT	➢ UTL AIRPLANE	➢ UTL Flight Number + UTL Flight Scheduled Start TS	➢ UTL Flight Number ➢ Date & Time Hierarchies of UTL Flight Scheduled Start TS ➢ UTL Scheduled Airplane ID ➢ Hierarchy of UTL AIRPLANE for UTL Scheduled Airplane ID ➢ UTL Actual Airplane ID ➢ Hierarchy of UTL AIRPLANE for UTL Actual Airplane ID ➢ Date & Time Hierarchies of UTL Flight Scheduled End TS
UTL FLIGHT SEAT	➢ UTL FLIGHT	➢ UTL Flight Number + UTL Flight Scheduled Start TS + UTL Seat CD	➢ UTL Flight Number ➢ Hierarchy of UTL FLIGHT for UTL Flight Number ➢ UTL Flight Scheduled Start TS ➢ Hierarchy of UTL FLIGHT for UTL Flight Scheduled Start TS ➢ UTL Seat CD ➢ UTL Seat Status

Dr. Eng. M. Naoulo

LOC BUSINESS OFFICE	Business Office Hierarchy is not part of the scope of this exercise	➤ **LOC Business Office ID**	➤ Strata of **LOC Business Office Cost per FR&TP Dayshift Office Staff per Sec** ➤ Strata of **LOC Business Office Cost per FR&TP Nightshift Office Staff per Sec** ➤ Strata of **LOC Business Office Cost per FR&TP Dayshift Telephone Staff per Sec** ➤ Strata of **LOC Business Office Cost per FR&TP Nightshift Telephone Staff per Sec** ➤ **LOC Business Office Zipcode** ➤ **LOC Business Office City** ➤ **LOC Business Office State** ➤ **LOC Business Office Country**
LOC TELEPHONE NUMBER	➤ **OPR PARTY**	➤ **LOC Telephone Number ID**	➤ **OPR PARTY ID** ➤ Hierarchy of **OPR PARTY** for **OPR PARTY ID** ➤ LOC Telephone Number Area Code (digits 1-3 of USA and Canada Telephone Number): from **LOC Telephone Number ID** ➤ LOC Telephone Number Country Code: from **LOC Telephone Number ID**
LOC INTERNET ADDRESS	➤ **OPR PARTY**	➤ **LOC Internet Address ID**	➤ **OPR PARTY ID** ➤ Hierarchy of **OPR PARTY** for **OPR PARTY ID** ➤ **LOC Internet Address Value**
LOC AIRPORT		➤ **LOC Airport CD**	
LOC STATE		➤ **LOC State CD**	
OCC DATE		➤ **OCC DT**	➤ Date Hierarchies of **OCC DATE** for **OCC DT**

OCC FR&TP EVENT	➢ OCC DATE	➢ OCC FR&TP Event ID	➢ OCC DT ➢ Date Hierarchies of **OCC DATE** for **OCC DT**
OCC FR&TP CSS EVENT	➢ OCC DATE	➢ OCC FR&TP CSS Event ID	➢ OCC DT ➢ Date Hierarchies of **OCC DATE** for **OCC DT**
OCC FR&TP COST TIME INTERVAL	➢ OCC DATE	➢ OCC DT + OCC FR&TP Cost Time Interval ID	➢ OCC DT ➢ Date Hierarchies of **OCC DATE** for **OCC DT** ➢ OCC FR&TP Cost Time Interval ID
A CUSTOMER DRIVING LICENSE STATE	➢ OPR PARTY ➢ LOC STATE ➢ OCC DATE	➢ OPR Party ID + LOC Customer Driving License Issuer State CD + OCC Customer Driving License Expiration DT	➢ **OPR Party ID** ➢ Hierarchy of **OPR PARTY** for **OPR PARTY ID** ➢ **LOC Customer Driving License Issuer State CD** ➢ Hierarchy of **LOC STATE** for **LOC Customer Driving License Issuer State CD** ➢ **OCC Customer Driving License Expiration DT** ➢ Date Hierarchies of **OCC DATE** for **OCC Customer Driving License Expiration DT**
A FR&TP OFFICE STAFF	➢ OPR FR&TP STAFF ➢ LOC BUSINESS OFFICE	➢ OPR FR&TP Office Staff Party ID + LOC Business Office ID	➢ **OPR FR&TP Office Staff Party ID** ➢ Hierarchy of **OPR FR&TP STAFF** for **OPR FR&TP Office Staff Party ID** ➢ **LOC Business Office ID** ➢ Hierarchy of **LOC BUSINESS OFFICE** for **LOC Business Office ID**

Dr. Eng. M. Naoulo

A FR&TP OFFICE STAFF COST	➢ A FR&TP OFFICE STAFF ➢ OCC FR&TP COST TIME INTERVAL	➢ OPR FR&TP Office Staff Party ID + LOC Business Office ID + OCC DT + OCC FR&TP Cost Time Interval ID	➢ OPR FR&TP Office Staff Party ID ➢ Hierarchy of OPR FR&TP OFFICE STAFF for OPR FR&TP Office Staff Party ID ➢ LOC Business Office ID ➢ Hierarchy of OPR FR&TP OFFICE STAFF for LOC Business Office ID ➢ OPR FR&TP Office Staff Party ID+ LOC Business Office ID ➢ Hierarchy of A FR&TP OFFICE STAFF for OPR FR&TP Office Staff Party ID + LOC Business Office ID ➢ OCC DT ➢ Date Hierarchies of OCC FR&TP COST TIME INTERVAL for OCC DT ➢ OCC FR&TP Cost Time Interval ID ➢ OCC DT + OCC FR&TP Cost Time Interval ID ➢ Hierarchy of OCC FR&TP COST TIME INTERVAL for OCC DT + OCC FR&TP Cost Time Interval ID ➢ Strata of A FR&TP Office Staff Cost per Sec

| A FR&TP TELEPHONE STAFF COST | ➤ OPR FR&TP STAFF
➤ LOC BUSINESS OFFICE
➤ LOC TELEPHONE NUMBER
➤ OCC FR&TP COST TIME INTERVAL | ➤ OPR FR&TP Telephone Staff Party ID + LOC Business Office ID + LOC Telephone Number ID + OCC DT + OCC FR&TP Cost Time Interval ID | ➤ OPR FR&TP Telephone Staff Party ID
➤ Hierarchy of OPR FR&TP STAFF for OPR FR&TP Telephone Staff Party ID
➤ LOC Business Office ID
➤ Hierarchy of LOC BUSINESS OFFICE for LOC Business Office ID
➤ LOC Telephone Number ID
➤ Hierarchy of LOC TELEPHONE NUMBER for LOC Telephone Number ID
➤ OCC DT
➤ Date Hierarchies of OCC FR&TP COST TIME INTERVAL for OCC DT
➤ OCC FR&TP Cost Time Interval ID
➤ OCC DT + OCC FR&TP Cost Time Interval ID
➤ Hierarchy of OCC FR&TP COST TIME INTERVAL for OCC DT + OCC FR&TP Cost Time Interval ID
➤ Strata of A FR&TP Telephone Staff Cost per Sec |

Table 10.3: The Hierarchies, Lowest Levels of Granularity, & Aggregation Possibility of Master Data Dimension and Associative Entity Attributes

The Case Study exercise analysis might not need all the aggregations expressed in Tables 10.3. It is important to note that a comprehensive Enterprise Engineering study would encompass many more Master Data Dimension and Associative Entities and attributes including data related to demographics, cost, descriptive data, contact data, traveling agencies, etc. The design of the Apparatus and its representation by the Master Data would be affected by the business requirements: E.g. there might be the need for education details of the Operational Staff.

Note: To ensure the clarity of the models, abbreviations were used to the minimum, although this implied very long attribute names at the logical model level. The abbreviations used comprise: CSS for Customer Satisfaction Survey, DT for Date, CD for Code, IND for

Dr. Eng. M. Naoulo

Indicator, Desc for Description, etc. Every enterprise should have Abbreviation Standard(s) that would be applied in Data Modeling, Database Schema, Coding, etc. The Abbreviation Standards are not included in this exercise in order to keep it concise.

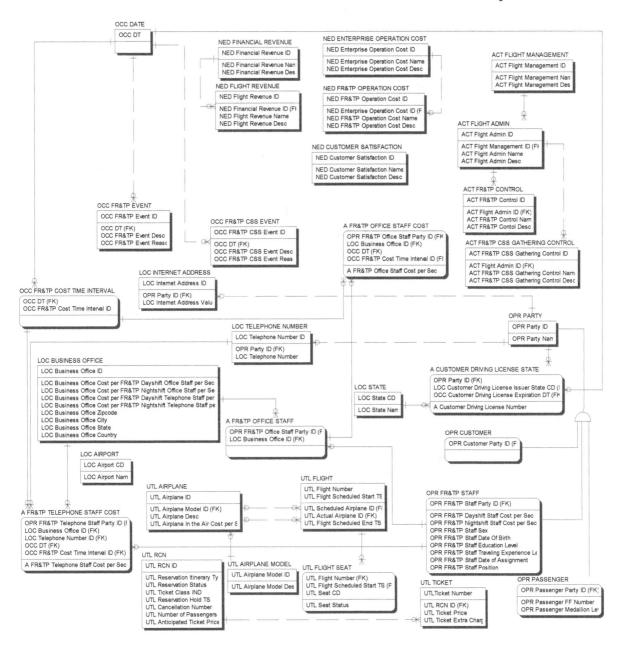

Diagram 10.1a: The Master Data Dimension & Associative Entities involved in the Current FR&TP Function

Diagram 10.1a illustrates the Master Data satisfying the business requirements of the Current FR&TP Function. A supertype entity **PARTY** was created to store the common attributes and relationships for the subtype entities **CUSTOMER**, **FR&TP STAFF**, and **PASSENGER**. It can

Dr. Eng. M. Naoulo

accommodate:
- ➢ Multiple Telephone Numbers for a **PARTY**.
- ➢ Multiple Internet Addresses for a **PARTY**.
- ➢ Multiple Driving Licenses for a **PARTY** that might be issued by the same or different States (to accommodate historical info).

In this Case study, the info pertinent to the Occurrence Events: **OCC FR&TP EVENT** and **OCC FR&TP CSS EVENT** that trigger the **MS FR&TP SESSION**s and **MS FR&TP CSS SESSION**s might not be known completely. It is better to compile as much info as possible as this info would be useful for marketing analytics: Business Events, Family Events, Vacations, etc. Also in this Case Study it is not necessary to know the Timestamp of the Event, just the Date. Diagram 10.1b illustrates this.

In the example illustrated in Diagram 14.2b, the info pertinent to the Occurrence Events: **OCC CLASS GIVING EVENT** and **OCC CLASS ATTENDANCE EVENT** that trigger the **MS CLASS GIVING SESSION**s and **MS STUDENT ATTENDANCE SESSION**s should be known completely. In this example it is necessary to know the Timestamps of the Event.

Note 1: It is also possible to combine Time Interval Entities if they have the same granularity. A design of conformed Time Interval Entity(ies) that support the lowest level granularity for many Time Interval analytics might provide also a possible solution.

Note 2: Metadata info including description of the entities and attributes reflecting the Apparatus, type, size, enumerated values, and domain of attributes, relationships between entities and their cardinality and optionality details, referential integrity, etc. are not detailed here in order to keep the exercise concise. Many of the type and size of attributes in the models are made-up.

Note 3: The security and encryption of data was not included in this exercise to keep the exercise concise.

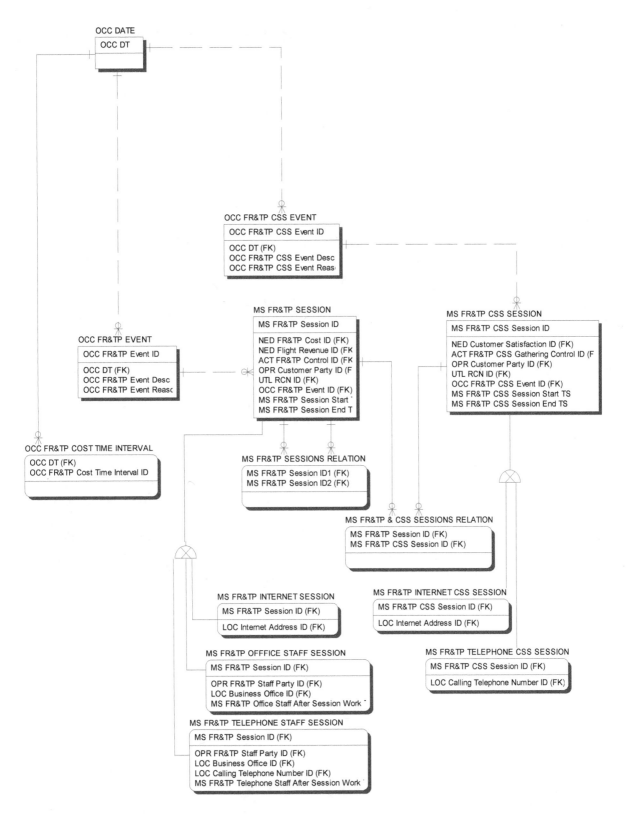

Diagram 10.1b: The Occurrence Members involved in the Current FR&TP Function

Dr. Eng. M. Naoulo

10.7 ABC AIRLINE'S CURRENT MACHINERY DELINEATION & EVALUATION

The Seventh Step involves the design of the Machinery's Procedures which indicate the rules and regulations governing the Business Transactions. This is accomplished thru identifying and detailing the Mechanism's Entities as gathered from the Use Cases.

The Step's Result: FR&TP Flight Reservation
The main Mechanism Entity regulating the Flight Reservation is **M FLIGHT RESERVATION RULE**. It has subtypes for **M NEW RESERVATION RULE, M RESERVATION MODIFICATION RULE, M RESERVATION CANCELLATION RULE**, and **M RESERVATION INQUIRY RULE**. Another entity regulates the Flight Reservation Detail: **M FLIGHT RESERVATION DETAIL RULE**.

The Step's Result: FR&TP Customer Satisfaction Survey
The Mechanism Entity regulating the Customer Satisfaction Survey is **M FR&TP CSS RULE**.

The Step's Result: FR&TP Ticket Purchasing
The Mechanism Entity regulating the Ticket Purchasing is **M TICKET PURCHASING RULE**. This Mechanism Entity regulates, among other rules, the type of Credit Card accepted for purchasing the tickets.

Deliverables

As in the case of Apparatus, Metadata info reflecting the Mechanism is not detailed here in order to keep the exercise concise. Many of the type and size of attributes in the models are made-up.

Diagram 10.2 represents the Mechanism involved in the Current FR&TP Function. It is important to note that a comprehensive Enterprise Engineering study would include many more Mechanism Procedure Entities and attributes regulating the FR&TP Transactions.

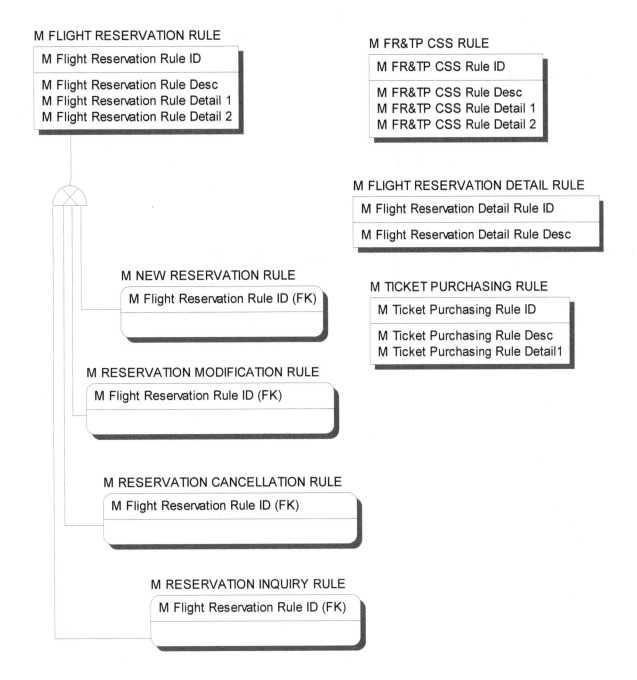

Diagram 10.2: The Mechanism Procedures involved in the Current FR&TP Function

10.8 ABC AIRLINE'S CURRENT OPERATION SESSION IDENTIFICATION, INFORMATION GATHERING, & EVALUATION

The Eighth Step involves the Identification, Information Gathering, and Evaluation of the Operation Sessions supporting the Enterprise Engineering exercise. The aggregations expressed in Tables 10.3, 10.4, and 10.5 would form the base for Business Intelligence Data Marts.

Dr. Eng. M. Naoulo

The Step's Result: FR&TP Session

The Activity guiding this Operation is: **ACT FR&TP CONTROL**. The Mechanics for FR&TP involves the Session instances implementing this activity to reflect the Customer contact with Telephone or Office Agents, or thru the Internet. Three Mechanics Session Entities are needed to manifest them. These session entities have many common attributes and relationships, therefore a supertype Mechanics Session Entity: **MS FR&TP SESSION** is created with 3 subtype session entities: **MS FR&TP TELEPHONE STAFF SESSION, MS FR&TP OFFICE STAFF SESSION**, and **MS FR&TP INTERNET SESSION**. The Primary Key of **MS FR&TP SESSION** is a Surrogate Key and it is inherited by the 3 subtype entities.

The Step's Result: Recursive Relationship: FR&TP Session to Itself

An FR&TP Session could be related to many FR&TP Sessions therefore a Many-to-Many recursive convoluted relationship is associated with the entity **MS FR&TP SESSION**. This Many-to-Many relationship is resolved thru a Mechanics Session Associative Entity **MS FR&TP SESSIONS RELATION**. The business requirements should be addressed to assess the data attributes related to this entity.

It is important to note:
- There must be Interlinks between an Operation Session and a Member of each Apparatus Component. So **MS FR&TP SESSION** and each of its subtypes should have between them relationships to at least one Master Data Dimension or a Master Data Associative Entity related to Dimensions of each Master Data Component.
- The non-Primary Key attributes of the Mechanics Session Entities that are not Foreign Keys (FK) to the Master Data Entities must include the start and end time of the **MS FR&TP SESSION.**
- After-Session Staff Work Time duration is needed for Cost evaluation.

Formulas were developed to capture the cost of FR&TP and incorporate the FR&TP Office Staff cost, the FR&TP Telephone Staff cost and the Locations cost. These formulas are detailed in Section 10.10.

Deliverables

The aggregation possibilities from the Mechanics Sessions could be performed based on:
- Master Data presented thru the Foreign Keys in the Mechanics Sessions. These aggregations are detailed in Table 10.3 for the exercise.
- The measures in the Mechanics Sessions. These measures and aggregation possibilities are presented in Table 10.4 (Ref. Diagram 10.3).

These measures and aggregation possibilities could be straight forward translated into measures and aggregation possibilities of the EI Data Marts. The reporting requirements of many enterprises might not need all these aggregations.

Dr. Eng. M. Naoulo

Mechanics Session	Measures	Aggregation Possibility from Mechanics Sessions
MS FR&TP SESSION	➤ **MS FR&TP Session Start TS** ➤ **MS FR&TP Session End TS**	➤ Date & Time Hierarchies of **MS FR&TP Session Start TS** ➤ Date & Time Hierarchies of **MS FR&TP Session End TS** ➤ Intervals of MS FR&TP Session Duration: **MS FR&TP Session End TS - MS FR&TP Session Start TS** ➤ Thru any combination of the Mechanics Session's Measures and the Master Data Foreign Keys including Labor and Facility Time and Cost, and the hierarchies of the Master Data Entities to whom the Foreign Keys are related
MS FR&TP OFFICE STAFF SESSION	➤ **MS FR&TP Office Staff After Session Work Time**	➤ Intervals of **MS FR&TP Office Staff After Session Work Time** ➤ Thru any combination of the Mechanics Session's (Supertype and Subtype) Measures and the Master Data Foreign Keys including Labor and Facility Time and Cost, and the hierarchies of the Master Data Entities to whom the Foreign Keys are related
MS FR&TP TELEPHONE STAFF SESSION	➤ **MS FR&TP Telephone Staff After Session Work Time**	➤ Intervals of **MS FR&TP Telephone Staff After Session Work Time** ➤ Thru any combination of the Mechanics Session's (Supertype and Subtype) Measures and the Master Data Foreign Keys including Labor and Facility Time and Cost, and the hierarchies of the Master Data Entities to whom the Foreign Keys are related

Dr. Eng. M. Naoulo

MS FR&TP INTERNET SESSION		➤ Thru any combination of the Mechanics Session's (Supertype and Subtype) Measures and the Master Data Foreign Keys including Labor and Facility Time and Cost, and the hierarchies of the Master Data Entities to whom the Foreign Keys are related
MS FR&TP SESSIONS RELATION		➤ **MS FR&TP Session ID1** ➤ Hierarchy **of MS FR&TP SESSION** for **MS FR&TP Session ID1** ➤ **MS FR&TP Session ID2** ➤ Hierarchy **of MS FR&TP SESSION** for **MS FR&TP Session ID2** ➤ **MS FR&TP Session ID1 + MS FR&TP Session ID2** ➤ Hierarchy of **MS FR&TP SESSION** for **MS FR&TP Session ID1 + MS FR&TP Session ID2**

Table 10.4: The Measures & Aggregation Possibility of FR&TP Mechanics Sessions

The Step's Result: FR&TP Customer Satisfaction Survey Session

The Activity guiding this Operation is: **ACT FR&TP CSS GATHERING CONTROL**. The Mechanics for Customer Satisfaction Survey involves the Session instances implementing this activity to reflect the Customer Satisfaction feedback. The Customer Satisfaction Survey would occur only thru the Telephone or the Internet without involving ABC Airline's staff (Ref. Section 10.5.1). No Customer Satisfaction Surveys are captured by the Agents either on the phone or in the office. Two Mechanics Session Entities are needed to manifest them. These session entities have many common attributes and relationships, therefore a supertype Mechanics Session Entity: **MS FR&TP CSS SESSION** is created with 2 subtype session entities: **MS FR&TP TELEPHONE CSS SESSION** and **MS FR&TP INTERNET CSS SESSION**. The Primary Key of **MS FR&TP CSS SESSION** is a Surrogate Key and it is inherited by the 2 subtype entities.

The Step's Result: Associative Relationship: FR&TP Session to FR&TP Customer Satisfaction Survey Session

ABC Airline's directors indicated that a Customer Satisfaction Survey Session most of the time is related to one FR&TP Session and a FR&TP Session has most of the time zero or one Customer Satisfaction Survey Session. However sometimes it occurs that a Customer Satisfaction Survey Session is related to many FR&TP Sessions and a FR&TP Session has sometimes many Customer Satisfaction Survey Sessions; therefore the relationship between the

Dr. Eng. M. Naoulo

entities **MS FR&TP SESSION** and **MS FR&TP CSS SESSION** is Many-to-Many. This Many-to-Many relationship is resolved thru a Mechanics Session Associative Entity **MS FR&TP & CSS SESSIONS RELATION**.

Deliverables

Here also the aggregation possibilities from the Mechanics Sessions could be performed based on:

➢ Master Data presented thru the Foreign Keys in the Mechanics Sessions. These aggregations are detailed in Table 10.3 for the exercise.
➢ The measures in the Mechanics Sessions. These measures and aggregation possibilities are presented in Table 10.5 (Ref. Diagram 10.3).

These measures and aggregation possibilities could be straight forward translated into measures and aggregation possibilities of the EI Data Marts. The reporting requirements of many enterprises might not need all these aggregations.

Mechanics Session	Measures	Aggregation Possibility from Mechanics Sessions
MS FR&TP CSS SESSION	➢ **MS FR&TP CSS Session Start TS** ➢ **MS FR&TP CSS Session End TS**	➢ Date & Time Hierarchies of **MS FR&TP CSS Session Start TS** ➢ Date & Time Hierarchies of **MS FR&TP CSS Session End TS** ➢ Intervals of MS FR&TP **CSS Session Duration: MS FR&TP CSS Session End TS - MS FR&TP CSS Session Start TS** ➢ Thru any combination of the Mechanics Session's Measures and the Master Data Foreign Keys, and the hierarchies of the Master Data Entities to whom the Foreign Keys are related
MS FR&TP TELEPHONE CSS SESSION		➢ Thru any combination of the Mechanics Session's Measures and the Master Data Foreign Keys, and the hierarchies of the Master Data Entities to whom the Foreign Keys are related
MS FR&TP INTERNET CSS SESSION		➢ Thru any combination of the Mechanics Session's Measures and the Master Data Foreign Keys, and the hierarchies of the Master Data Entities to whom the Foreign Keys are related

Dr. Eng. M. Naoulo

MS FR&TP & CSS SESSIONS RELATION		➢ MS FR&TP Session ID ➢ Hierarchy of MS FR&TP SESSION for MS FR&TP Session ID ➢ MS FR&TP CSS Session ID ➢ Hierarchy of MS FR&TP CSS SESSION for MS FR&TP CSS Session ID

Table 10.5: The Measures & Aggregation Possibility of FR&TP Customer Satisfaction Survey Mechanics Sessions

Note: A Survey Session could be related to one, many or no RCN. The scope of this exercise involves Survey Sessions that are related to only one RCN (Ref. Table 10.1b).

Deliverables

As in the case of Apparatus, Metadata info reflecting the Operation Sessions is not detailed here in order to keep the exercise concise. Many of the type and size of attributes in the models are made-up.

Diagram 10.3 represents the Mechanics Sessions involved in the Current FR&TP Function. It is important to note that a comprehensive Enterprise Engineering study would include many more Mechanics' Session Entities and attributes: call details, comment attributes to the **MS FR&TP OFFICE STAFF SESSION** and **MS FR&TP TELEPHONE STAFF SESSION** to capture any FR&TP Office or Telephone Staff comments about the session, etc.

Dr. Eng. M. Naoulo

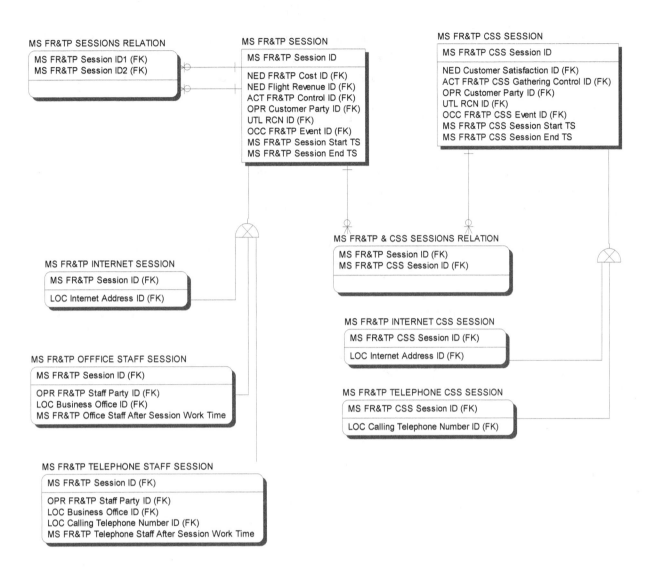

Diagram 10.3: The Mechanics Sessions involved in the Current FR&TP Function

10.9 ABC AIRLINE'S CURRENT OPERATION TRANSACTIONS IDENTIFICATION, INFORMATION GATHERING, & EVALUATION

The Ninth Step involves the Identification, Information Gathering, and Evaluation of the Operation Transactions supporting the Enterprise Engineering exercise. The aggregations expressed in Tables 10.3, 10.6, and 10.7 would form the base for Business Intelligence Data Marts.

The Step's Result: FR&TP Operation Transactions
Three transaction entities support the FR&TP Operation: **X PASSENGER RESERVATION TRX** that captures the data pertinent to the Reservations, **X CUSTOMER PAYMENT TRX** that captures the data pertinent to the Customer Payments, and **X PASSENGER**

Dr. Eng. M. Naoulo

RESERVATION DETAIL TRX that captures the data pertinent to the Passenger Reservation Transaction details. The last entity includes the attributes: **X Passenger Reservation Leg Class, X Passenger Reservation Leg Price**, and **X Passenger Reservation Seat CD**.

The Step's Result: Recursive Relationship: Passenger Reservation TRX to Itself

A Passenger Reservation Transaction could be related to many Passenger Reservation Transactions therefore a Many-to-Many recursive convoluted relationship is associated with the entity **X PASSENGER RESERVATION TRX**. This Many-to-Many relationship is resolved thru an Associative Entity **X PASSENGER RESERVATION TRX RELATION**. The business requirements should be addressed to assess the data attributes related to this entity.

The Step's Result: Recursive Relationship: Customer Payment TRX to Itself

A Customer Payment Transaction could be related to many Customer Payment Transactions therefore a Many-to-Many recursive convoluted relationship is associated with the entity **X CUSTOMER PAYMENT TRX**. This Many-to-Many relationship is resolved thru an Associative Entity **X CUSTOMER PAYMENT TRX RELATION**. The business requirements should be addressed to assess the data attributes related to this entity.

The Step's Result: Associative Relationship: Customer Payment TRX to Passenger Reservation TRX

ABC Airline's directors indicated that a Customer Payment Transaction most of the time is related to only one Passenger Reservation Transaction and a Passenger Reservation Transaction has most of the time zero or one Customer Payment Transaction. However a Passenger Reservation Transaction might have many Customer Payment Transactions (the case of paying by eVoucher and a Credit Card or splitting the payment between many Credit Cards), and a Customer Payment Transaction could be related to many Passenger Reservation Transactions (although many other airlines prefer to have a separate payment for each Reservation Transaction). Thus the analysis indicates that the relationship between Passenger Reservation Transaction and Customer Payment Transaction is Many-to-Many.

Since one Customer Payment Transaction could be related to many Passenger Reservation Transactions and one Passenger Reservation Transaction could be related to many Customer Payment Transactions, the relationship between the entities **X PASSENGER RESERVATION TRX** and **X CUSTOMER PAYMENT TRX** is Many-to-Many. This Many-to-Many relationship is resolved thru a Mechanics Transaction Associative Entity **X RESERVATION PAYMENT TRX RELATION** which provides the Customer Payment Transactions link to the Passenger Reservation Transactions.

Deliverables

The aggregation possibilities from the Mechanics Transactions could be performed based on:
- Master Data presented thru the Foreign Keys in the Mechanics Sessions. These aggregations are detailed in Table 10.3 for the exercise.
- The measures in the Mechanics Transactions. These measures and aggregation possibilities are presented in Table 10.6 (Ref. Diagram 10.4).

Dr. Eng. M. Naoulo

These measures and aggregation possibilities could be straight forward translated into measures and aggregation possibilities of the BI Data Marts. The reporting requirements of many enterprises might not need all these aggregations.

Mechanics Transaction	Measures	Aggregation Possibility from the Mechanics Transactions
X PASSENGER RESERVATION TRX	➤ **X Passenger Reservation TRX TS**	➤ Date & Time Hierarchies of **X Passenger Reservation TRX TS** ➤ Thru any combination of the Mechanics Transaction's Measures, the Master Data, Mechanism, and Mechanics Sessions Foreign Keys, and the hierarchies of the Master Data, Mechanism, and Mechanics Sessions Entities to whom the Foreign Keys are related
X PASSENGER RESERVATION DETAIL TRX	➤ **X Passenger Reservation Detail TRX TS** ➤ **X Passenger Reservation Leg Class** ➤ **X Passenger Reservation Leg Price** ➤ **X Passenger Reservation Seat CD**	➤ Date & Time Hierarchies of **X Passenger Reservation Detail TRX TS** ➤ **X Passenger Reservation Leg Class** ➤ Intervals of **X Passenger Reservation Leg Price** ➤ **X Passenger Reservation Seat CD** ➤ Thru any combination of the Mechanics Transaction's Measures, the Master Data, Mechanism, and Mechanics Sessions Foreign Keys, and the hierarchies of the Master Data, Mechanism, and Mechanics Sessions Entities to whom the Foreign Keys are related

X PASSENGER RESERVATION TRX RELATION		➢ **X Passenger Reservation TRX ID1** ➢ Hierarchy **of X PASSENGER RESERVATION TRX for X Passenger Reservation TRX ID1** ➢ **X Passenger Reservation TRX ID2** ➢ Hierarchy **of X PASSENGER RESERVATION TRX for X Passenger Reservation TRX ID2** ➢ **X Passenger Reservation TRX ID1 + X Passenger Reservation TRX ID2** ➢ Hierarchy **of X PASSENGER RESERVATION TRX for X Passenger Reservation TRX ID1 + X Passenger Reservation TRX ID2**
X CUSTOMER PAYMENT TRX	➢ **X Customer Payment TRX TS** ➢ **X Payment Type** (Cash, Credit Card, etc.) ➢ **X Credit/Debit Card Type** (Debit or Credit) ➢ **X Credit/Debit Card Issuer** (Visa, Amex, etc.) ➢ **X Credit/Debit Card Number** ➢ **X Card Billing City** ➢ **X Card Billing State/Province** (the link of this field with the entity **LOC STATE** was omitted for simplicity) ➢ **X Card Billing Zipcode** ➢ **X Card Billing Country** ➢ **X Card Billing Telephone Number** (the link of this field with the entity **LOC TELEPHONE NUMBER** was omitted for simplicity) ➢ **X Check Financial Institution Name** ➢ **X Payment Amount**	➢ Date & Time Hierarchies of **X Customer Payment TRX TS** ➢ **X Payment Type** ➢ **X Credit/Debit Card Type** ➢ **X Credit/Debit Card Issuer** ➢ **X Credit/Debit Card Number** ➢ **X Card Billing City** ➢ **X Card Billing State/Province** ➢ **X Card Billing Zipcode** ➢ **X Card Billing Country** ➢ **X Card Billing Telephone Number** ➢ **X Check Financial Institution Name** ➢ Intervals of **X Payment Amount** ➢ Thru any combination of the Mechanics Transaction's Measures, the Master Data, Mechanism, and Mechanics Sessions Foreign Keys, and the hierarchies of the Master Data, Mechanism, and Mechanics Sessions Entities to whom the Foreign Keys are related

Dr. Eng. M. Naoulo

X CUSTOMER PAYMENT TRX RELATION		➤ X Customer Payment TRX ID1 ➤ Hierarchy **of X CUSTOMER PAYMENT TRX** for **X Customer Payment TRX ID1** ➤ **X Customer Payment TRX ID2** ➤ Hierarchy **of X CUSTOMER PAYMENT TRX** for **X Customer Payment TRX ID2** ➤ **X Customer Payment TRX ID1 + X Customer Payment TRX ID2** ➤ Hierarchy **of X CUSTOMER PAYMENT TRX** for **X Customer Payment TRX ID1 + X Customer Payment TRX ID2**
X RESERVATION PAYMENT TRX RELATION		➤ **X Passenger Reservation TRX ID** ➤ Hierarchy of **X PASSENGER RESERVATION TRX** for **X Passenger Reservation TRX ID** ➤ **X Customer Payment TRX ID** ➤ Hierarchy of **X CUSTOMER PAYMENT TRX** for **X Customer Payment TRX ID**

Table 10.6: The Measures & Aggregation Possibility from FR&TP Mechanics Transactions

The Step's Result: FR&TP Customer Satisfaction Survey Transaction

One transaction entity is supporting the FR&TP Customer Satisfaction Survey: **X FR&TP CSS TRX**. It captures the data pertinent to the Customer Satisfaction Survey: the customer response to the Survey questions.

Dr. Eng. M. Naoulo

Deliverables

Mechanics Transaction	Measures	Aggregation Possibility from the Mechanics Transactions
MS FR&TP CSS TRX	➤ **X FR&TP CSST TS** ➤ **X FR&TP CSST Responsiveness Quality** ➤ **X FR&TP CSST Responsiveness Speed** ➤ **X FR&TP CSST Staff Knowledge** ➤ **X FR&TP CSST Staff Professionalism** ➤ **X FR&TP CSST Staff Friendliness** ➤ **X FR&TP CSST Results Correctness** ➤ **X FR&TP CSST Overall Customer Satisfaction**	➤ Date & Time Hierarchies of **X FR&TP CSST TS** ➤ **X FR&TP CSST Responsiveness Quality** ➤ **X FR&TP CSST Responsiveness Speed** ➤ **X FR&TP CSST Staff Knowledge** ➤ **X FR&TP CSST Staff Professionalism** ➤ **X FR&TP CSST Staff Friendliness** ➤ **X FR&TP CSST Results Correctness** ➤ **X FR&TP CSST Overall Customer Satisfaction** ➤ Thru any combination of the Mechanics Transaction's Measures, the Master Data, Mechanism, and Mechanics Sessions Foreign Keys, and the hierarchies of the Master Data, Mechanism, and Mechanics Sessions Entities to whom the Foreign Keys are related

Table 10.7: The Measures & Aggregation Possibility from FR&TP Customer Satisfaction Survey Mechanics Transactions

It is important to note:
  ➤ CSST is abbreviation for Customer Satisfaction Survey Transaction
  ➤ The attributes capturing the result of the surveys (**X FR&TP CSST Responsiveness Quality, X FR&TP CSST Responsiveness Speed, X FR&TP CSST Staff Knowledge, X FR&TP CSST Staff Professionalism, X FR&TP CSST Staff Friendliness, X FR&TP CSST Results Correctness, and X FR&TP CSST Overall Customer Satisfaction**) were numeric (values 1 to 10).

Deliverables

As in the case of Apparatus, Metadata info reflecting the Operation Transactions is not detailed here in order to keep the exercise concise. Many of the type and size of attributes in the models are made-up.

Diagram 10.4 represents the Mechanics Transactions involved in the Current FR&TP Function. It is important to note that a comprehensive Enterprise Engineering study would include many more Mechanics' Transaction Entities and Attributes.

Dr. Eng. M. Naoulo

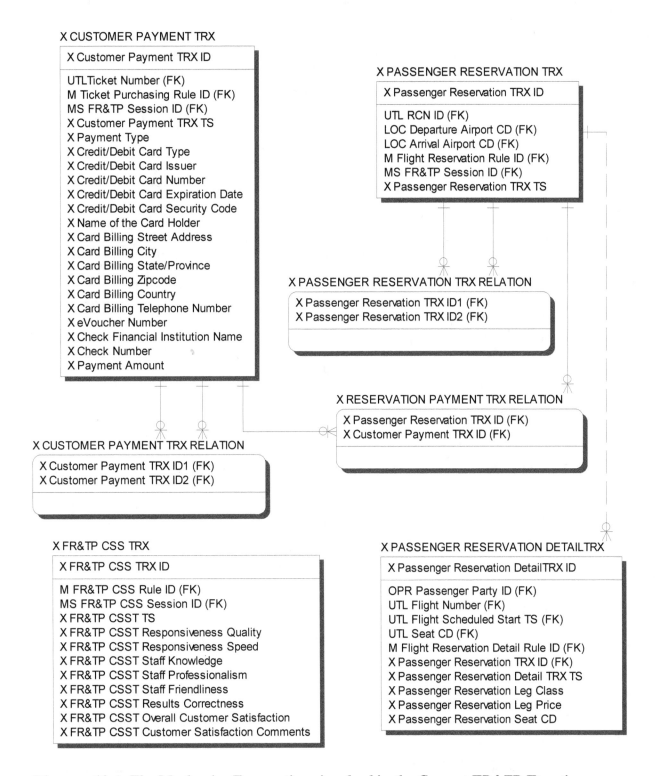

Diagram 10.4: The Mechanics Transactions involved in the Current FR&TP Function

Diagram 10.5 represents the Mechanics Sessions and Transactions involved in the Current FR&TP Function.

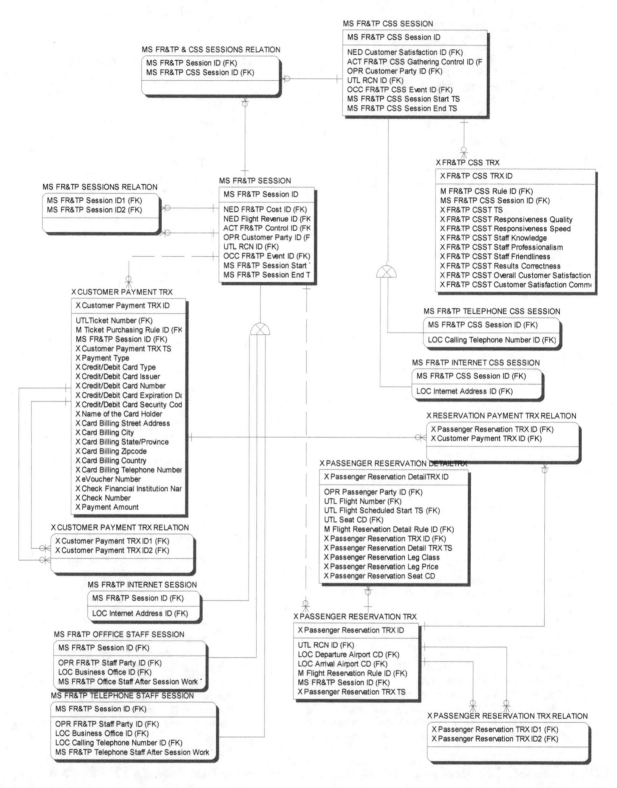

Diagram 10.5: The Mechanics Sessions & Transactions involved in the Current FR&TP Function

Dr. Eng. M. Naoulo

10.10 ABC AIRLINE'S CURRENT ENTERPRISE ENGINEERING MODEL & EI DATA MARTS DESIGN

The Step's Result:

Enterprise Engineering Model
Enterprise Engineering Model Granularity
The Human Resources and Payroll Unit provided the following information:
 ➤ Geographic info: Business Offices and their addresses in USA, Canada, and India.
 ➤ Airport Codes.
 ➤ Staff type: Office Staff, Telephone Staff.
 ➤ Detailed Cost of Staff and Business Offices (including Dayshift and Nightshift) in each country for each Staff type and each Time Interval.

The Enterprise Engineering Model incorporated this information and allocated it into the following levels of granularity:
 ➤ Geographic level: Business Office, Zipcode, City, State, and Country.
 ➤ Office Staff and Telephone Staff: The individual FR&TP Staff Cost per Second and the Offices Cost per Office and Telephone Staff per Second for Dayshift and Nightshift were received and/or deducted from the Human Resources, Payroll, and operational cost data.
 ➤ Time intervals could be at any level of detail down to 15 minutes intervals.

Furthermore additional Location Component's data and their granularity are introduced in the Model: Telephone Number and Telephone Country Code.

Deliverables
The Enterprise Engineering Model supporting the Current Apparatus and Machinery is shown in Diagrams 10.6, 10.7, and 10.8:
 ➤ Diagram 10.6 represents the Enterprise Engineering Model reflecting the current FR&TP Function.
 ➤ Diagram 10.7 represents the Enterprise Engineering Model reflecting the current Customer Survey function.
 ➤ Diagram 10.8 represents the Enterprise Engineering Model reflecting the current FR&TP Function and its related Customer Survey function and Cost.
Diagrams 10.9 and 10.10 represent EI Data Marts:
 ➤ Diagram 10.9 represents an EI Data Mart with Dimension Entities based on Master Data Dimensions and Fact Entities supporting the exercise analysis.
 ➤ Diagram 10.10 represents an EI Data Mart with Dimension Entities based on Master Data Dimension and Associative Entities and Fact Entities supporting the ABC Airline's Cost of Fleet Operation in Airports (not part of this exercise).

In real life the Enterprise Engineering Model would be much more complex and sophisticated. A comprehensive Enterprise Engineering study would include many more Master Data, Mechanism, and Mechanics Session and Transaction Entities and attributes. This model represents the minimum entities and attributes to illustrate the Case Study.

235

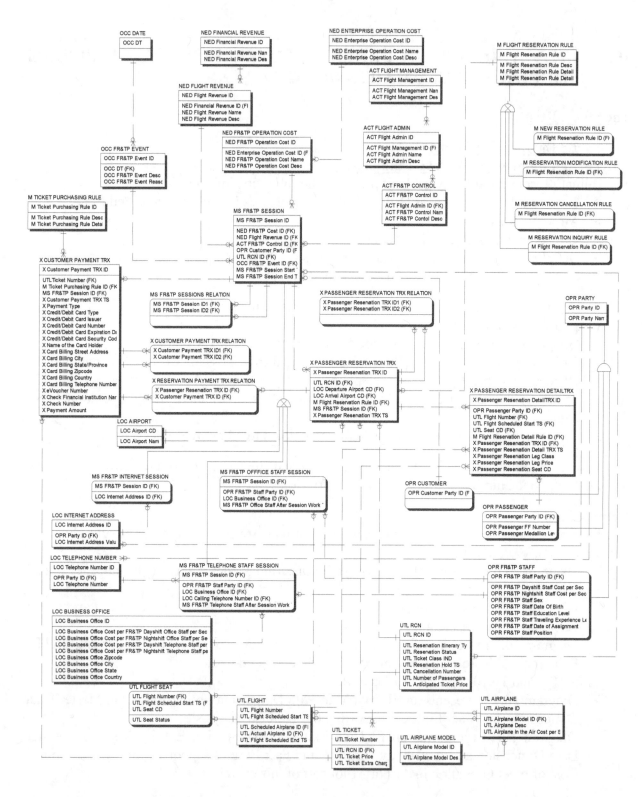

Diagram 10.6: A Concise Enterprise Engineering Model reflecting the Current FR&TP Function

Diagram 10.7 represents the Customer Survey function related to the FR&TP Function.

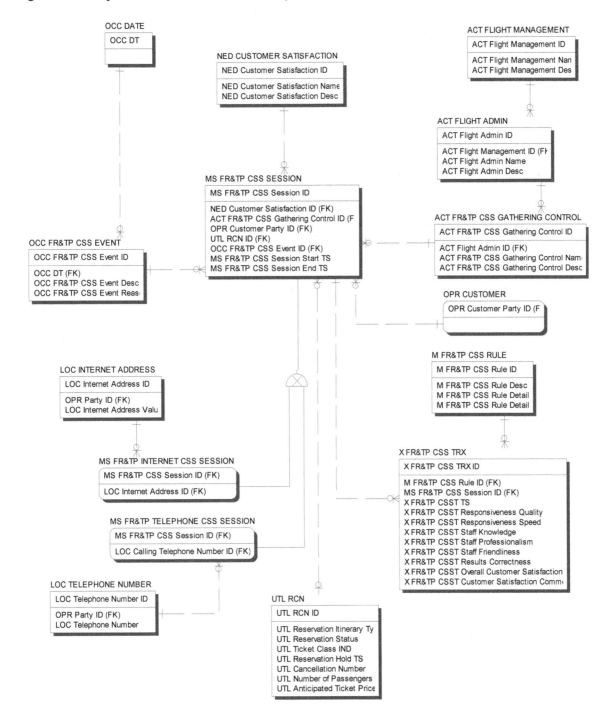

Diagram 10.7: A Concise Enterprise Engineering Model reflecting the Customer Survey Function

Diagram 10.8 represents the current FR&TP Function, its related Customer Survey and Cost.

Dr. Eng. M. Naoulo

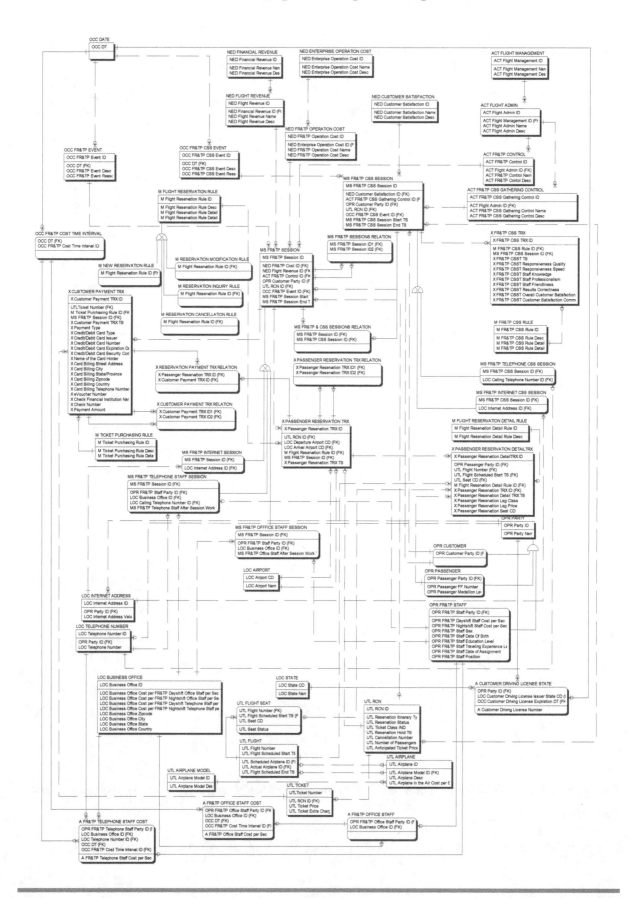

Dr. Eng. M. Naoulo

Diagram 10.8: A Concise Enterprise Engineering Model reflecting the Current FR&TP Function & related Customer Survey Function

Formulas:

Based on the Enterprise Engineering Model many operational formulas could be elaborated. The links in the model between the Mechanics and Master Data Entities is assured thru the FK-PK relationships.

Examples: The formulas to calculate the FR&TP Office and Telephone Staff cost for the sessions occurring during the Dayshift are (Ref. Diagram 10.8):

FR&TP Office Staff Cost = $\sum$ ((**MS FR&TP Session End TS - MS FR&TP Session Start TS + MS FR&TP Office Staff After Session Work Time) * (OPR FR&TP Dayshift Staff Cost Per Second + LOC Business Office Cost per FR&TP Dayshift Office Staff Per Sec)).**

FR&TP Telephone Staff Cost = $\sum$ ((**MS FR&TP Session End TS - MS FR&TP Session Start TS + MS FR&TP Telephone Staff After Session Work Time) * (OPR FR&TP Dayshift Staff Cost Per Second + LOC Business Office Cost per FR&TP Dayshift Telephone Staff Per Sec)).**

The symbol $\sum$ is a mathematical notation for Sum. During nightshift the cost could be calculated using similar formulas. The cost of a staff does not change if this staff is working on the phone or in an office responding directly to the customer requests but it could change if this staff is working dayshift or nightshift. Also the cost could be assessed in more details, if needed, per the features of the Master Data: Location, etc.

These formulas would be the base for aggregation into the EI Data Marts. Also old approaches (not recommended anymore with the advance of Data Marts design and modeling) could be used by translating these formulas into SQL after developing the Physical Model and the Database Schema (or using MS Excel after storing the query results in Excel).

Current EI Data Marts

An EI Data Mart with Dimension Entities based on Master Data Dimensions is presented in Diagram 10.9. It contains four Dimensions and two Fact Entities. This Data Mart provides aggregation of the FR&TP Telephone Staff Cost per:
  - ➢ FR&TP Staff Party ID
  - ➢ Business Office ID
  - ➢ Called ABC Airline Telephone Number ID (ABC Airline assigns specific Telephone Numbers for specific tasks)
  - ➢ Date
  - ➢ FR&TP Cost Time Interval ID.

E.g. ABC Airline assigns a telephone number to certain customer services or type of customers: Elite Customers, etc., and staff the responders to theses telephone numbers with staff having different qualifications and cost. It also provides aggregation the FR&TP Office Staff Cost per:
  - ➢ FR&TP Staff ID

239

Dr. Eng. M. Naoulo

> ➤ Business Office ID
> ➤ Date
> ➤ FR&TP Cost Time Interval ID.

The EI Data Mart Dimension Entities are:
> ➤ OPR FR&TP Staff Dimension: **DIM OPR FR&TP STAFF** Entity and its supertype **DIM OPR PARTY** Entity. At the physical level – after de-normalization – the attribute **DIM OPR Party Name** from **DIM OPR PARTY** Entity would be incorporated in the **DIM OPR FR&TP STAFF** Dimension table.
> ➤ LOC Business Office Dimension: **DIM LOC BUSINESS OFFICE**.
> ➤ LOC Telephone Number Dimension: **DIM LOC TELEPHONE NUMBER**.
> ➤ OCC Time Dimension: **DIM OCC FR&TP COST TIME INTERVAL** Entity and **DIM OCC DATE** Entity.

It is important to note that the hierarchies, lowest levels of granularity, and aggregation possibilities of the Dimensions of EI Data Marts (as well as BI Data Marts) are similar to those indicated in Table 10.3 for the Master Data Entities of the Enterprise Engineering Model.

The Fact Entities are:
> ➤ FR&TP Telephone Staff Cost Fact: **F FR&TP TELEPHONE STAFF COST**. It includes two measures: **F FR&TP Telephone Staff Cost** and **F FR&TP Office Cost,** This Fact Entity has as Primary Key a Surrogate Key: **F FR&TP Telephone Staff Cost SK**. It has also a unique Alternate Key: the concatenation of the Foreign Keys: **DIM OPR FR&TP Staff Party ID + DIM LOC Business Office ID + DIM LOC Telephone Number ID + DIM OCC DT + DIM OCC FR&TP Cost Time Interval ID**.
> ➤ FR&TP Office Staff Cost Fact: **F FR&TP OFFICE STAFF COST**. It includes two measures: **F FR&TP Office Staff Cost** and **F FR&TP Office Cost**. This Fact Entity has as Primary Key a Surrogate Key: **F FR&TP Office Staff Cost SK**. It has also a unique Alternate Key: the concatenation of the Foreign Keys: **DIM OPR FR&TP Staff Party ID + DIM LOC Business Office ID + DIM OCC DT + DIM OCC FR&TP Cost Time Interval ID**.

If there is no need for cost aggregation by the ABC Airline Telephone Numbers, the two Facts Entities could be merged together.

An EI Data Mart example with Dimension Entities based on Master Data Dimension and Associative Entities is presented in Diagram 10.10. It is a snowflake model. It contains three Dimension Entities, one Snowflake Schema Entity, and one Fact Entity. This Data Mart provides aggregation of the operational cost of airplanes while sitting at airports per:
> ➤ Airplane ID
> ➤ Airport Code
> ➤ Date
> ➤ Airport Operation Cost Time Interval ID.

The EI Data Mart Dimension Entities are:

Dr. Eng. M. Naoulo

> UTL Airplane Dimension: **DIM UTL AIRPLANE** and **DIM UTL AIRPLANE MODEL**. At the physical level – after de-normalization – the attribute **DIM UTL Airplane Model Desc** from **DIM UTL AIRPLANE MODEL** Entity would be incorporated in the **DIM UTL AIRPLANE** Dimension table.
> LOC Airport Dimension: **DIM LOC AIRPORT**.
> OCC Time Dimension: **DIM OCC AIRPORT OPERATION COST TIME INTERVAL** Entity and **DIM OCC DATE** Entity.

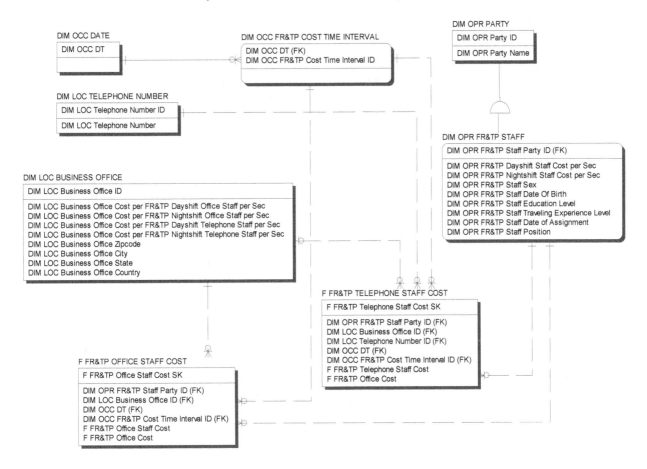

Diagram 10.9: EI Data Mart with Dimension Entities based on Master Data Dimensions

The EI Data Mart Snowflake Schema Entity is:
> Flight Operation in Airport Cost Entity: **DIM A FLIGHT OPERATION IN AIRPORT COST**. It is an Associative Entity between the two dimensions: **DIM LOC AIRPORT** and **DIM UTL AIRPLANE**.

The Fact Entity is:
> Airport Operation Cost Fact: **F AIRPORT OPERATION COST**. It includes one measure: **F Airport Operation Cost**. This Fact Entity has as Primary Key a Surrogate Key: **F Airport Oper Cost SK**. It has also a unique Alternate Key: the concatenation of the Foreign Keys: **DIM UTL Airplane ID** + **DIM LOC Airport CD** + **DIM OCC DT** + **DIM OCC Airport Operation Cost Time Interval ID**.

Dr. Eng. M. Naoulo

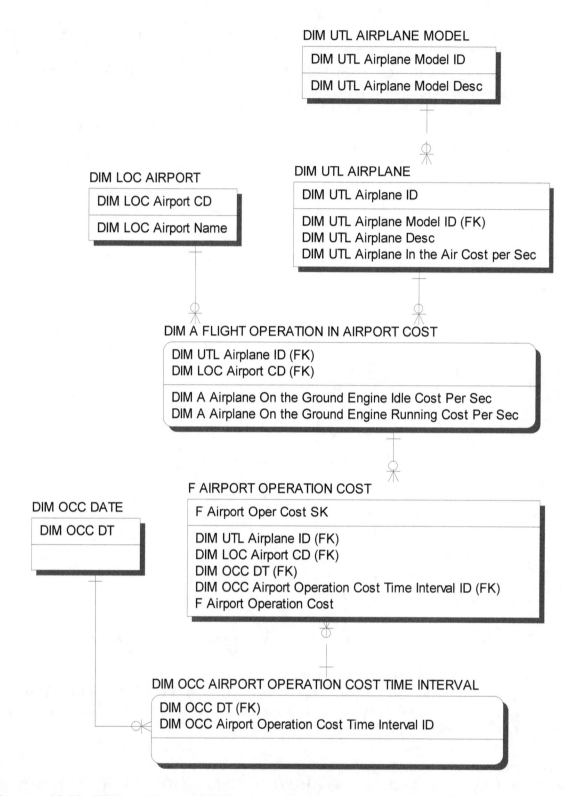

Diagram 10.10: EI Data Mart with Dimension Entities based on Master Data Dimensions &
Associative Entities

Dr. Eng. M. Naoulo

10.11 ABC AIRLINE'S CURRENT MECHANICS PROCESSING & RESULTS GENERATION & INTERPRETATION

The Eleventh Step involves the generation and interpretation of the results of the current Operation. The figures indicated here are three months average figures.

Deliverables

From the data gathered in Steps 3 & 5 the following table (Table 10.8) is compiled and the following measures were deducted for each staff group:

- Individual Staff Cost per Month
- Individual Staff Cost per Second (based on 20 working days per month, 8 hours per day, and 3600 seconds per hour)
- Number of RCN handled per Staff per Month
- Business Offices Cost per Second
- Business Offices Cost per Staff per Sec
- Cost per RCN.

It is important to notice that the performance ratio (based on the number of RCN handled per Staff per Month) of FR&TP Telephone Staff located in the USA/Canada is 2325.58/896.23=2.595 more than the FR&TP Telephone Staff located in India for the dayshift and 2000/891.72=2.243 for the nightshift. This is attributed to the higher experience and knowledge of the staff in the USA and Canada and their better communication skills.

Also it was indicated that relocating Telephone Staff to work from home will reduce their cost and drastically decrease the cost of Business Offices of this staff.

	Staff Number	Staff Cost per Month (including Overhead)	Individual Staff Cost per Month	Individual Staff Cost per Sec	Number of RCNs handled per Month by the Staff	Number of RCNs handled per Staff per Month	Business Offices Cost per Month	Business Offices Cost per Sec	Business Offices Cost per Staff per Sec	Cost/RCN
Office Staff working in the USA & Canada during dayshift	455	$2,500,000.00	$5,494.51	$0.009539	900,000	1978.02	$300,000.00	$0.520833	$0.001145	$3.111111
Office Staff working in the USA & Canada during nightshift	168	$1,100,000.00	$6,547.62	$0.011367	340,000	2023.81	$300,000.00	$0.520833	$0.003100	$4.117647
Telephone Staff working in the USA & Canada during dayshift	688	$2,140,000.00	$3,110.47	$0.005400	1,600,000	2325.58	$350,000.00	$0.607639	$0.000883	$1.556250
Telephone Staff working in the USA & Canada during nightshift	95	$330,000.00	$3,473.68	$0.006031	190,000	2000.00	$100,000.00	$0.173611	$0.001827	$2.263158
Telephone Staff working in India during dayshift	212	$132,000.00	$622.64	$0.001081	190,000	896.23	$50,000.00	$0.086806	$0.000409	$0.957895
Telephone Staff working in India during nightshift	314	$250,000.00	$796.18	$0.001382	280,000	891.72	$50,000.00	$0.086806	$0.000276	$1.071429
TOTAL	1,932	$6,452,000.00			3,500,000		$1,150,000.00			

Dr. Eng. M. Naoulo

Table 10.8: Current FR&TP Cost

The Step's Result
Based on the data received from the Legacy Systems, Human Resources, Payroll, and Operational Cost and introduced into the Enterprise Engineering Model, the following results were obtained from the processing of this model:

➤ For the dayshift staff the number of Customer Telephone calls per RCN received by the FR&TP Telephone Staff who are located in India is 1.78 times the number of Customer Telephone calls per RCN received by the FR&TP Telephone Staff who are located in the USA/Canada, and the average duration of these calls is higher by 1.48. They are 1.68 and 1.32 respectively for the nightshift staff. This is in correlation with the results obtained from the Operational Cost data above (2325.58/896.23=2.595 compared to 1.78*1.48 = 2.6344 for the dayshift and 2000/891.72=2.243 compared to 1.68*1.32 = 2.2176 for the nightshift).

➤ The performance of the staff (in every staff group) varies during the work period: It follows the same performance curve encountered in the manufacturing process.

➤ The number of Customer Telephone calls drops significantly after 11:00 PM Pacific Daylight Time (PDT) and rebounds after 8:00 AM Eastern Daylight Time (EDT).

➤ The learning curve of the staff in the USA and Canada (measured by months) to reach the accredited performance level for the FR&TP Operation is around 1 Month while the learning curve of the staff in India is 2.5 Months (because the Indian staff need additional training in the North American culture, ethics, and improve their English accent).

➤ The ratio of results obtained from the Customer Satisfaction Survey related to the FR&TP Telephone Staff in the USA and Canada to the results obtained from the Customer Satisfaction Survey related to the FR&TP Telephone Staff in India provide high figures: Responsiveness Quality (2.33), Responsiveness Speed (1.64), FR&TP Staff Knowledge (1.52), FR&TP Staff Professionalism (1.45), FR&TP Staff Friendliness (1.23), Results Correctness (1.44), and Overall Customer Satisfaction (2.66).

➤ A more detailed analysis of the results provided an additional hint: For international travels the number of Customer Telephone calls per RCN received by the Canadian FR&TP Telephone Staff is lower by 32% and the duration of these calls is lower by 25% compared the figures related to the USA FR&TP Telephone Staff. Comparing the figures for international travels between the Indian FR&TP Telephone Staff to the USA FR&TP Telephone Staff, the USA results are slightly better than those of India results. This divergence is attributed to the fact that Canadian and Indian staff is better educated in the World Geography than their USA counterparts.

Deliverables: The Step's Result interpretation
The examination of the Step's Result above provides two important points that affect drastically the operation of FR&TP:

1. The cost of FR&TP Telephone Operation is much in favor of outsourcing this function to India:
   - Telephone Staff Dayshift cost per RCN for USA and Canada: $1.556 versus $0.958 for India (May be the cost's comparison is more appropriate between USA

and Canada Dayshift and India Nightshift as there is around 12 hours' time zone difference between the two countries (it is 10.5 hours for EST, 11.5 hours for CST and 13.5 hours for PST)).

- Telephone Staff Nightshift cost per RCN for USA and Canada: $2.263 versus $1.071 for India.

2. The Customer Satisfaction is much in favor of keeping all FR&TP Operation in the USA and Canada.

To alleviate cost, outsourcing to India would be a quick solution however the Customer Satisfaction would be hit by such resolution. An optimization of the FR&TP Operation thru better allocation and distribution of the FR&TP Telephone operation is compulsory but needs more innovation, analysis, and assessment.

10.12 ABC AIRLINE'S ENTERPRISE IMPROVEMENT

The Twelfth Step involves the improvement of the FR&TP Operation based on the data gathered in Section 10.11.

Deliverables
The following improvement points were suggested:
- ➢ Since the cost of FR&TP Operation per RCN using the Office Staff is very high vis-à-vis the cost using the Telephone Staff, it was suggested to reduce the FR&TP Office Staff by 75% thru eliminating all office locations supporting FR&TP except at the airports and further assessing the reduction of the FR&TP airports staff.
- ➢ The comparison between the cost of FR&TP Telephone Staff per RCN in the USA/Canada and the corresponding cost in India indicates that cost reduction would be achieved by relocating all FR&TP Telephone support to India. However the Marketing Department was adamant in blocking this resolution as the Customer Satisfaction would take a hit.
- ➢ In order to satisfy both the FR&TP Operation's Cost Reduction and the Marketing Department's Customer Satisfaction level a compromise solution was considered:
  - There would be a differentiation in allocating the FR&TP Telephone staff support. The FR&TP Telephone support for the North American trips of first class, business class, and medallion (Platinum, Gold and Silver) customers would be carried out always by FR&TP Telephone Staff located in the USA/Canada. The differentiation could be established thru the first automatic question(s) from the 800 numbers called by the customers, or different 800 numbers could be established to serve these customers.
  - The FR&TP support of the other customers would be by FR&TP Telephone Staff located in the USA/Canada during the dayshift and redirect all customers calls to India during the USA night (from 9:00 PM to 8:00 AM EDT). The redirection of calls would be gradual according to the Time-zone; for example the Eastern USA support would be assigned to India at 9:00 PM EDT, the central USA support would be assigned to India at 9:00 PM CDT, and so on.
- ➢ Based on the figures compiled above: Cost of Operation per RCN, and ratio of number of

RCN ending up with Ticket Purchase to the total number of RCN (not included above), it was decided:

- To charge $10.00 fee per ticket for the FR&TP contacts (reservation and/or modification and of course purchasing the ticket(s)) thru the FR&TP Telephone Staff, even if the customer ended up purchasing the ticket(s) thru the Internet. This amount would cover all future contacts with ABC Airline's Telephone Staff related to the RCN. If after allocating the $10.00 fee, the number of passengers increases or decreases, new RCN(s) will be generated and the fees would be applied also to the new RCNs. These fees are not refundable (after purchasing the tickets) if the customer cancels the trip and want tickets refund (the rules governing the refund of tickets are not part of this exercise).
- Similar process would be applied for contacts with the Office Staff; however the charge is $20.00 per ticket.
- If the customer contacted the Office Staff after contacting the Telephone Staff, the charge would increase from $10.00 to $20.00 per ticket.
- The amount of the charges must be indicated to the customers at the beginning of the contact with the Agent. If the customers' request is due to FR&TP complication, misinterpretation, etc. and requires the intervention of the FR&TP staff/supervisor, the staff or the supervisor could waive this extra charge for genuine cases.
- Not to apply any additional charges for First and Business class (the cost will be part of the price of the tickets).

10.13 ABC AIRLINE'S ENTERPRISE REVITALIZATION

The Thirteenth Step involves creative thinking to overhaul the FR&TP Operation and reduce the cost.

Deliverables
The following are revitalization ideas (some of these ideas are classical) that were suggested in addition or in lieu of the improvement steps detailed in Section 10.12:

- Since the cost of FR&TP Staff is much higher than the direct revenue coming from them: $7,602,000 versus $3,450,000 per month (Ref. Sections 10.5.2 & 10.11), it is important to try to reduce this gap as much as possible.
- First, a customer on the Internet would require a Frequent Flier Number to proceed on with reservations. To assure that, it was suggested by the Marketing department to provide each customer opening a Frequent Flier account with a 2500 Frequent Flier point bonus. This would incite customers to use this Airline for traveling in order to boost their Frequent Flier Account points.
- Provide all customers on the Internet with access to the FR&TP database in order to perform Flight Reservation, Seat Assignment, and Ticket Purchasing (of course their access to the database will be limited to their own reservations and they cannot access other customers' data).
- Provide the customers each time they purchase the ticket thru the Internet with a 200 Frequent Flier points bonus.
- Since the medallion (Platinum, Gold and Silver) customers are computer and Internet

Dr. Eng. M. Naoulo

savvy, give them, temporarily (for limited time or limited number of reservations), additional Frequent Flyer Points (250-400 points) for completing their FR&TP thru the internet, thus reducing tremendously their need for Office and Telephone Staff support. Hit medallion customers with a $25.00-50.00 charge for Flight Reservation or Flight Modification or Ticket Purchasing thru the FR&TP Office and/or Telephone Staff.

The following are additional innovative revitalization ideas that were suggested:
> Relocate all FR&TP Telephone Staff to their homes and manage their telephone communication thru computer software. This will reduce the labor and facility costs.
> A radical-change idea is put for evaluation. It consists of eliminating the FR&TP service Office and Telephone Staff and keeping the FR&TP service only thru the internet. This will cut drastically the cost (the only cost left is the Hardware and Software cost and high level support for extremely complicated cases). ABC Airline's Staff at the airports and ABC Airline's Telephone Customer Service Staff can also handle these difficult cases.

The evaluation of effectiveness and impact of these suggestions on the enterprise functioning were debated. No conclusion was reached. It was decided to postpone this decision till after Step 15.

10.14 ABC AIRLINE'S TARGET APPARATUS, MACHINERY, OPERATION, ENTERPRISE ENGINEERING MODEL, & EI DATA MARTS DESIGN

The Fourteenth Step involves the design of the target Apparatus, Machinery, Operation, the Enterprise Engineering Model, and EI Data Marts.

Deliverables
If the last proposition of Section 10.13 is not adopted, the target Apparatus, Machinery, Operation, Enterprise Engineering Model, and EI Data Marts would be exactly similar to the Current Apparatus, Machinery, Enterprise Engineering Model, and EI Data Marts presented in Diagrams 10.8 and 10.9 even if the FR&TP service is confined to First and Business Class.

If the last proposition of Section 10.13 is adopted, the target Apparatus, Machinery, Operation and Enterprise Engineering Model would be used only for capturing FR&TP Operation data coming thru the Internet. The target Enterprise Engineering Data Model is shown in Diagram 10.11. This Model would be the base for possible future improvement of the Enterprise functioning. It is useful to assess the number of FR&TP Internet sessions per time interval and their distribution by the days of the weeks, months, seasons, etc. This would help in the optimization of the technical infrastructure and the load and impact of FR&TP on ABC Airline's operation.

Again it is important to note that this model represents the minimum entities and attributes to illustrate the Case Study.

Target EI Data Marts
If the last proposition of Section 10.13 is adopted, there would be no need for EI Data Marts as the Office and FR&TP staff cost is eliminated.

Dr. Eng. M. Naoulo

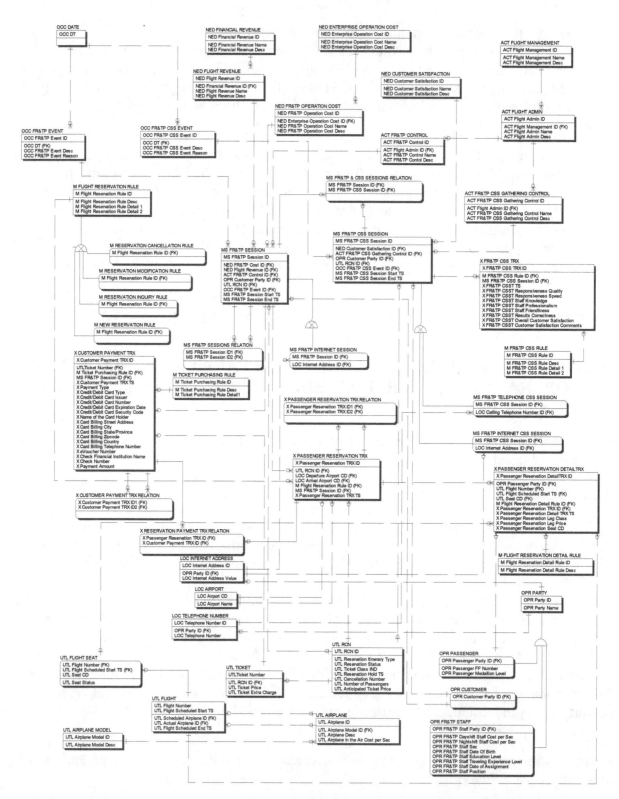

Diagram 10.11: A Concise Enterprise Engineering Model for the Target FR&TP whereas the FR&TP Service thru Office & Telephone Staff is eliminated

Dr. Eng. M. Naoulo

10.15 ABC AIRLINE'S TARGET MECHANICS PROCESSING & RESULTS GENERATION & INTERPRETATION

The Fifteenth Step involves the generation and interpretation of the results of the target Mechanics processing. Two options were considered:

Option 1

- The FR&TP Telephone support for first, business class, and medallion customers would be always by FR&TP Telephone Staff located in the USA/Canada.
- No additional charges are applied for first and business class.
- Give the medallion (Platinum, Gold and Silver) customers temporarily (for limited time) 250 Frequent Flyer Points for completing their FR&TP thru the internet.
- The FR&TP Telephone support for non-first and business class and medallion customers would be assigned to India.
- Charge the non-first and business class customers a flat $25.00 per ticket for either Flight Reservation, or Flight Modification, or Ticket Purchasing, or Ticket Refund thru FR&TP Office and/or Telephone Staff.
- Relocate all FR&TP Telephone Staff, those in USA/Canada and in India, to their homes and manage their telephone communication thru computer software. This will reduce the labor and facility costs.

Option 2

- Eliminating the FR&TP service thru Offices and Telephone Staff and keeping the FR&TP service only thru the internet. This underline a shift in the strategic business model of ABC Airline as it shifts from Full-Service to Self-Service operation that is targeting mainly Internet-savvy clientele. Other Self-Service features would accompany this strategy like the elimination of supplying foods and drinks during the flights for coach travelers, reducing the number of Flight Attendants, introducing self-check-in boosts at the Airports, reducing staff at the gates, etc.
- To kick-off this drastic change a Marketing campaign including many commercials in the TV is recommended.

The Step's Result

At the beginning of the application of any option, there would be a transition period till the customers and staff would be acquainted with the new rules of the game. The results of applying the options indicate:

Option 1

- The relocation of all FR&TP Telephone Staff into their homes would reduce the cost per RCN for the Telephone Staff located in the USA and Canada, but no significant reduction from the relocation of Indian Telephone Staff.
- The same Enterprise Engineering Model and formulas used for the generation of the current results would be used for the target results (test target data were used instead of real current data).

Dr. Eng. M. Naoulo

Deliverables
Option 1

Table 10.9 is compiled from the test database data. The cost per RCN is deduced for each staff group. It is important to note that:

- The cost per RCN for the Telephone staff as they were relocated to their homes dropped for the USA and Canadian staff by $(1.55625-1.14286)/1.55625=26.56\%$ for the dayshift operation and $(2.263158-1.53571)/2.263158=32.14\%$ for the nightshift operation while it dropped for the Indian staff by $(.957895-.88235)/.957895=7.89\%$ for the dayshift operation while increased by $(1.24444-1.071429)/1.24444=13.90\%$ for the nightshift operation. This is explained by the distractions that the Indian staff encounter while working from home.

- The overall total number of RCNs created each month (including the internet) increased from 2,900,000 to 3,100,000 while the number of RCNs handled by the Office and Telephone staff per month decreased from 3,500,000 to 2,165,000. This is due to the fact that more activities were processed by the customers thru the internet.

- The cost of operation per month decreased from 6,452,000+1,150,000 = $7,602,000 (Ref. Table 10.8) to $2,730,000+400,000 = $3,130,000 (Ref Table 10.9), while the income from extra fees for FR&TP thru Telephone or Office Agents decreased from $3,450,000 per month (Ref Section 10.5.2) to $960,000 per month. **This provides a net saving of** $(7,602,000-3,130,000)-(3,450,000-960,000) = $1,982,000 per month **($23,784,000 per year) just from applying Enterprise Engineering's Improvement and Revitalization of FR&TP Operation**.

Option 2

- Eliminating the FR&TP service Office and Telephone Staff and keeping this service only thru the internet would eliminate most of FR&TP Staff cost (ABC Airline's Staff at the airports and ABC Airline's Telephone Customer Service Staff would be impacted with additional work to handle the difficult FR&TP cases and therefore this slight additional cost should be assessed in real life exercise). Thus the cost of FR&TP staff operation was virtually eliminated

- Diagram 10.11 provides the Enterprise Engineering Model for this option.

- The total number of RCNs created each month would decrease initially as all FR&TP activities would be coming only from the internet.

Dr. Eng. M. Naoulo

	Staff Number	Staff Cost per Month	Individual Staff Cost per Month	Individual Staff Cost per Sec	Number of RCN handled per Month by the Staff	Number of RCN handled per Staff per Month	Business Offices/Home Offices Cost per Month	Business Offices Cost per Sec	Business Offices Cost per Staff per Sec	Cost/RCN
Office Staff working in the USA & Canada during dayshift	96	$540,000.00	$5,625.00	$0.009766	200000	2083.33	$100,000.00	$0.173611	$0.001808	$3.200000
Office Staff working in the USA & Canada during nightshift	34	$230,000.00	$6,764.71	$0.011744	70000	2058.82	$50,000.00	$0.086806	$0.002553	$4.000000
Telephone Staff working at Home in the USA & Canada during dayshift	433	$1,100,000.00	$2,540.42	$0.004410	1050000	2424.94	$100,000.00	$0.173611	$0.000401	$1.142860
Telephone Staff working at Home in the USA & Canada during nightshift	132	$400,000.00	$3,030.30	$0.005261	280000	2121.21	$30,000.00	$0.052083	$0.000395	$1.535710
Telephone Staff working at Home in India during dayshift	402	$240,000.00	$597.01	$0.001036	340000	845.77	$60,000.00	$0.104167	$0.000259	$0.882350
Telephone Staff working at Home in India during nightshift	288	$220,000.00	$763.89	$0.001326	225000	781.25	$60,000.00	$0.104167	$0.000362	$1.244440
TOTAL	1385	$2,730,000.00			2165000		$400,000.00			

Table 10.9: Option 1: Target FR&TP Cost

10.16 ABC AIRLINE'S ENTERPRISE ENGINEERING STRATEGIC OPERATION DECISIONS

The Sixteenth Step of the Enterprise Engineering exercise involves the evaluation of the results of the previous step and taking the appropriate Strategic Operation decisions. ABC Airline's Directors after the assessment and evaluation of the results presented to them by the Enterprise Engineers took the following path:

Option 3A
The Marketing Department looked at the results and found out that if the Telephone staff were relocated to their homes the cost of FR&TP USA and Canadian Telephone staff per RCN became only 20% higher than the cost of Indian staff per RCN (it is in fact (1.14286-0.88235)/1.14286 = 22.79% for the dayshift and (1.53571-1.24444)/1.53571=18.97% for the nightshift). Due to the high discrepancies in the Customer Satisfaction as related the performance of the USA and Canadian staff compared to the Indian staff, the Marketing Department made a strategic request to ABC Airline's top management advocating the total

Dr. Eng. M. Naoulo

elimination of the Indian staff and the reassignment of the whole FR&TP Operation to the USA and Canada. They reinforced their request by the main guiding strategy of the Enterprise: Support high class and business customers and provide them with high class services (Ref. Section 10.1). This became **Option 3A**.

The Step's Result & Deliverables

Following on Option 3A and due to the better knowledge of the Canadian staff with international travels (Ref. Section 10.11), it was decided to assign the Canadian staff with all FR&TP international travels operation.

The Marketing Department indicated that a Marketing campaign advocating that all ABC Airline's FR&TP customer support would be handled by knowledgeable and professional staff in North America who well understand the customer needs and have minimum communication problems, should be launched. The Marketing Department expects that this campaign would have enormous impact on the improvement of ABC Airline's business. The Marketing Department even envisaged the following advertising message:

"The best Class Customer Service in the Airline Industry"

The CEO indicated that the results obtained from Option 1 are good and would improve the overall operation cost. However after studying the input and suggestions for Option 3A and the input from the Marketing Department, the CEO decided to go along with Option 3A and keep Option 2 on the shelf for future re-evaluation as he/she was reluctant to proceed with this option as it requires drastic shift from the current Business Model and he/she mentioned that such drastic shift would also require the approval and backing of the Board of Directors.

The final FR&TP results are indicated in Table 10.10. Furthermore there was an additional saving of around $40,000 per month due to the elimination of the FR&TP Operation staff overhead associated with the management of the Indian branches, offices, and staff.

Note: As predicted by the Marketing Department, the Marketing campaign advocating that all ABC Airline's FR&TP customer support would be handled by knowledgeable and professional staff in North America who well understand the customer needs and have minimum communication problems had enormous impact and improvement on ABC Airline's business. The Sales increased by 12% which compensated many times the cost of the Marketing campaign and the cost difference between Options 1 and 3A.

The following table summarizes the FR&TP Operation cost per month:

	FR&TP Staff Cost per Month	FR&TP Staff Offices Cost per Month	FR&TP Staff Overhead Reduction per Month	Total per Month
Current Operation	$6,452,000	$1,150,000		$7,602,000
Target Operation Option 1	$2,730,000	$400,000		$3,130,000
Target Operation Option 3A	$2,946,860	$336,480	-$40,000	$3,243,340

Table 10.11: Comparison of FR&TP Option Costs for ABC Airline

Dr. Eng. M. Naoulo

Comparing the results of Option 3A with the goals enunciated in Section 10.3 reveals:

➤ The overall cost of the FR&TP Operations decreased by (7,602,000 − 3,243,340)/ 7,602,000 = 57.3%.

➤ The Improvement of the Customer Satisfaction is not covered here in order to keep the exercise concise. Additional effort should be put to capture the figures related to this goal and assess the results.

➤ The high level Project Management and Change Management Plans to implement these decisions are not covered here in order to keep the exercise focused on the Enterprise Engineering curriculum.

	Staff Num ber	Staff Cost per Month (including Overhead)	Individual Staff Cost per Month	Individual Staff Cost per Sec	Number of RCN handled per Month by the Staff	Number of RCN handled per Staff per Month	Business Offices/Home Offices Cost per Month	Business Offices Cost per Sec	Business Offices Cost per Staff per Sec	Cost/RCN
Office Staff working in the USA & Canada during dayshift	96	$540,000.00	$5,625.00	$0.009766	200000	2083.33	$100,000.00	$0.173611	$0.001808	$3.200000
Office Staff working in the USA & Canada during nightshift	34	$230,000.00	$6,764.71	$0.011744	70000	2058.82	$50,000.00	$0.086806	$0.002553	$4.000000
Telephone Staff working at Home in the USA & Canada during dayshift	573	$1,455,660.00	$2,540.42	$0.004410	1390000	2425.83	$132,380.00	$0.229826	$0.000401	$1.142475
Telephone Staff working at Home in the USA & Canada during nightshift	238	$721,200.00	$3,030.25	$0.005261	505000	2121.85	$54,100.00	$0.093924	$0.000395	$1.535248
TOTAL	941	$2,946,860.00			2,165,000		$336,480.00			

Table 10.10: Option 3A: Target FR&TP Cost

10.17 ABC AIRLINE'S TARGET ENTERPRISE ENGINEERING IMPLEMENTATION

The Seventeenth Step involves the development of detailed and comprehensive Project Management, Change Management, Implementation, and Operation Plans related to the chosen option. They were not included in order to keep the exercise focused on the Enterprise Engineering curriculum. Of course a complete Enterprise Engineering exercise must include these Plans.

Dr. Eng. M. Naoulo

10.18 ABC AIRLINE'S GLOBAL ENTERPRISE ENGINEERING MODEL DESIGN

The Eighteenth Step involves the identification of the objectives, scope, goals, extent, and design and development of the Global Engineering Model of ABC Airline. It includes Steps 1 thru 10 for the whole enterprise. It is out-of-scope of this Case Study.

10.19 ABC AIRLINE'S GLOBAL ENTERPRISE ENGINEERING

The Eighteenth Step involves the processing of the Global Engineering Model and improvement and revitalization of ABC Airline. It includes Steps 11 thru 17 for the whole enterprise. It is out-of-scope of this Case Study.

10.20 ABC AIRLINE'S RESOURCES HANDLING THE ENTERPRISE ENGINEERING ASSIGNMENT

The resources handling this exercise follow the recommendations and guidelines indicated in Sections 8.20 & 9.20. ABC Airline proceeded in two directions: educate many of its current staff to embrace new job descriptions and hire additional staff that is expert in Enterprise Engineering. The details of this endeavor would be customized to ABC Airline's needs and is not included here to keep the exercise focused on the Enterprise Engineering curriculum.

Dr. Eng. M. Naoulo

11. Case Study 2: XYZ Airline's FR&TP

The main guiding strategy of XYZ Airline is to **serve bargain hunting clientele and cut the cost drastically while trying to keep adequate services quality**.

This Case Study would be similar to Case Study 1 however with different strategic objectives. Thus this Case Study is elaborated to accommodate these objectives based on the effort accomplished in Case Study 1.

The approach, methodology, guidelines, model, data, etc. used here are similar to those used for Case Study 1. Also the analysis, design, and implementation of this Case Study are similar to those for ABC Airline. The differences between the two Case Studies are highlighted here.
  - ➢ **Section 11.1** is similar to Section 10.1 except the guiding strategy.
  - ➢ **Section 11.2** is similar to Section 10.2
  - ➢ **Section 11.3** is similar to 10.3 except for the following goals:
    - ▪ Decrease the overall cost of the FR&TP Operations by 50%.
    - ▪ Increase the Customer Satisfaction from the FR&TP Operations by 25%.
  - ➢ **Section 11.4** is similar to Section 10.4
  - ➢ **Section 11.5** is similar to Section 10.5
  - ➢ **Section 11.6** is similar to Section 10.6
  - ➢ **Section 11.7** is similar to Section 10.7
  - ➢ **Section 11.8** is similar to Section 10.8
  - ➢ **Section 11.9** is similar to Section 10.9
  - ➢ **Section 11.10** is similar to Section 10.10
  - ➢ **Section 11.11** is similar to Section 10.11
  - ➢ **Section 11.14** is similar to Section 10.14
  - ➢ **Section 11.15** is similar to Section 10.15
  - ➢ **Section 11.17** is similar to Section 10.17
  - ➢ **Section 11.18** is similar to Section 10.18
  - ➢ **Section 11.19** is similar to Section 10.19
  - ➢ **Section 11.20** is similar to Section 10.20.

11.12 XYZ AIRLINE'S ENTERPRISE IMPROVEMENT

The Twelfth Step involves the improvement of the FR&TP Operation based on the data gathered in Section 11.11.

Deliverables
The following improvement points were suggested:
  - ➢ Since the cost of FR&TP Operation per RCN using the Office Staff is very high vis-à-vis the cost using the Telephone Staff, it was suggested to reduce the FR&TP Office Staff by 75% thru eliminating all office locations supporting FR&TP except at the airports and further assessing the reduction of the FR&TP airports staff.
  - ➢ The comparison between the cost of FR&TP Telephone Staff per RCN in the

USA/Canada and the corresponding cost in India indicates that cost reduction will be achieved by relocating all FR&TP Telephone support to India. However the Marketing Department indicated that the Customer Satisfaction would take a hit but their objections were overruled by the Top Management.

➢ Based on the figures compiled above: Cost of Operation per RCN and ratio of number of RCN ending up with Ticket Purchase to the total number of RCN, it was decided:

▪ To charge $50.00 fee per ticket for the FR&TP contacts (reservation and/or modification and/or purchasing the ticket(s)) with the FR&TP Office Staff even if the customer ended up purchasing the ticket(s) thru the Internet. This amount would cover all future contacts with XYZ Airline's Staff related to the RCN. If after allocating the $50.00 fee, the number of passengers increases or decreases, new RCN(s) will be generated and similar fees would be applied also to the new RCNs. These fees are not refundable (after purchasing the tickets) if the customer cancels the trip and want tickets refund (the rules governing the refund of tickets are not part of this exercise).

▪ Similar process with charge of $20.00 per ticket for the FR&TP contacts (reservation and/or modification and/or purchasing the ticket(s)) with the FR&TP Telephone Staff. If the contact continued thru Office Staff, additional $30.00 fee per ticket would apply.

11.13 XYZ AIRLINE'S ENTERPRISE REVITALIZATION

Deliverables

Besides the ideas mentioned in the last paragraphs of Section 10.13 it was suggested:

➢ Eliminate completely the First and Business Class from XYZ Airline's services.
➢ Not to give any additional Frequent Flyer Points to the medallion customers for completing their FR&TP thru the internet as this is the standard procedure.
➢ Provide the possibility to the passengers to self-check-in their luggage besides checking-in their tickets.
➢ Charge the luggage of the passengers per weight. The charge is flexible and depends on the flight itinerary and gas cost.
➢ Another idea which was debatable and not implemented: it is to charge the passengers extra, varying with the flight itinerary and gas cost, if their weight including the carry-on bags exceeds a certain amount (E.g. 250 pounds) or based on the Body Mass Index.
➢ Eliminate completely the food service except for bottled water given at the boarding of the airplane.
➢ Provide free films, news, internet services, etc. and headphones to the passengers to view and listen to the movies and shows, and to hook their laptops/notebooks/etc. to the internet during the flight.

In a nutshell: whatever is not labor intensive provide it free, cut whatever is labor intensive and try to charge for whatever affects the traveling cost.

Dr. Eng. M. Naoulo

11.16 XYZ AIRLINE'S ENTERPRISE ENGINEERING STRATEGIC OPERATION DECISIONS

The Sixteenth Step of the Enterprise Engineering exercise involves the evaluation of the results of Step 15 and taking the appropriate Strategic Operation decisions. XYZ Airline's Directors after the assessment and evaluation of the results presented to them by the Enterprise Engineers took the following paths:

Option 3B

Since the cost of FR&TP USA and Canadian Office staff per RCN is very high and the cost of FR&TP USA and Canadian Telephone staff per RCN is around 20% higher than the cost of Indian staff per RCN (Ref. Section 10.16), the Top Management, in order to cut cost drastically, recommended the following strategic decisions:

➤ The total elimination of the FR&TP USA and Canadian Office staff.
➤ The total elimination of the FR&TP USA and Canadian Telephone staff and the reassignment of the whole FR&TP Telephone Operation to India. They supported their request by the main guiding strategy of the Enterprise as mentioned at the beginning of this chapter.
➤ Implementing the suggestions elaborated in Section 11.13 except the extra charge to the passengers if their weight including the carry-on bags exceeds a certain amount. The CEO indicated that this suggestion needs extra investigation and Market Research.

In order to compensate for the shortcoming of the Indian staff and forbid a hit in the Customer Satisfaction, the Marketing Department requested:

➤ Put high bar for English linguistic pronunciation on the Indian staff.
➤ Educate the Indian staff in the North American culture and ethics.

The Step's Result & Deliverables

The Marketing Department indicated that a Marketing campaign advocating that XYZ Airline is efficient, effective, and provides best prices in the market is necessary. This Department expects that this campaign would have enormous impact on the improvement of XYZ Airline's business. The Marketing Department even envisaged the following advertising message:

"The best Airline at the lowest Price"

After studying the input and suggestions for option 3B and the input from the Marketing Department, the CEO and Board of Directors decided to go along with this option.

The final FR&TP results are indicated in Table 11.1. Furthermore there was an additional saving of around $110,000 per month due to the elimination of the FR&TP Operation staff overhead associated with the management of the FR&TP US and Canadian branches, offices, and staff.

Dr. Eng. M. Naoulo

	Staff Number	Staff Cost per Month (including Overhead)	Individual Staff Cost per Month	Individual Staff Cost per Sec	Number of RCN handled per Month by the Staff	Number of RCN handled per Staff per Month	Business Offices/Home Offices Cost per Month	Business Offices Cost per Sec	Business Offices Cost per Staff per Sec	Cost/RCN
Telephone Staff working at Home in India during dayshift	750	$1,902,000.00	$2,536.00	$0.004403	1590000	2120.00	$172,000.00	$0.298611	$0.000398	$1.304403
Telephone Staff working at Home in India during nightshift	298	$900,000.00	$3,020.13	$0.005243	575000	1929.53	$68,000.00	$0.118056	$0.000396	$1.683478
TOTAL	1,048	$2,802,000.00			2,165,000		$240,000.00			

Table 11.1: Option 3B: Target FR&TP Cost

The following table summarizes the FR&TP Operation cost per month:

	FR&TP Staff Cost per Month	FR&TP Staff Offices Cost per Month	FR&TP Staff Overhead Reduction per Month	Total
Current Operation	$6,452,000	$1,150,000		$7,602,000
Target Operation Option 1	$2,730,000	$400,000		$3,130,000
Target Operation Option 3B	$2,802,000	$240,000	-$110,000.00	$2,932,000

Table 11.2: Comparison of FR&TP Costs for XYZ Airline

Note: The Marketing campaign advocating the low price had enormous impact on the Business Model and improvement of XYZ Airline's business. The Sales increased by 6% which compensated the cost of the Marketing campaign. Furthermore the FR&TP cost was additionally reduced by 3,130,000-2,932,000 (2,802,000+240,000-110,000) = $198,000 difference between options 1 and 3B.

Comparing the results of Option 3B with the goals enunciated in Section 11.3 reveals:
- ➤ The overall cost of the FR&TP Operations decreased by (7,602,000 – 2,932,000)/ 7,602,000 = 61.4%.
- ➤ Similar to what was indicated in Section 10.16; the Improvement of the Customer Satisfaction is not covered here in order to keep the exercise concise. Additional effort should be put to capture the figures related to this goal and assess the results.

Dr. Eng. M. Naoulo

12. APPENDIX A: The Interlinks of the System of Apparatus, Machinery, & Operation

The Interlinks of the System of Apparatus, Machinery, and Operation are described and detailed in this chapter. The Interactions within and across the Master Data, Mechanism, and Mechanics' in the Enterprise Engineering Model reflect the Interlinks within and across the System of Apparatus, Machinery, and Operation. These Interactions are implemented in the Entity-Relationship Diagram thru relationships. Tables 3.2 and 3.3 summarize these Interactions. The techniques handling these interactions are elaborated in Chapters 2, 3, 4, 5, 12, 13 & 14.

12.1   THE INTERLINKS WITHIN THE APPARATUS

The Apparatus Members could interlink One-to-One, One-to-Many, or Many-to-Many with other Apparatus Members or could have Recursive Interlinks:

1. <u>Within the same Apparatus Component</u>. The Apparatus Members interlink with other Apparatus Members of the same Apparatus Component. One-to-One Interlinks are Not Common. One-to-Many Interlinks could exist. Many-to-Many Interlinks should be further analyzed because the resulting associative Interlinks could be another Apparatus Member, Association of Members, or the basis for an Operation Session and/or Operation Transaction. They are handled as Many-to-Many relationships in **SAM O NAOULO** Modeling Technique and their resolution into Associative Entities is detailed in Section 13.1.

2. <u>The Apparatus Activities</u> control the Operation Sessions of the Enterprise (Ref. Section 2.2.2). The Apparatus Activities' structure follows the Decomposition Diagrams (Ref. Section 2.7). The Interlinks between Activities are to support capturing activities or activity's features that depend on other activities. This Interlinks enable more flexibility to support business specifications than allowed by the strict Decomposition Diagrams.

3. <u>Across the Apparatus Components or involving Members' Interlinks across Apparatus Components.</u> The Apparatus Members interlink with other Apparatus Members of different Apparatus Components or with Members' Interlinks across Apparatus Components. One-to-One Interlinks are Not Common. One-to-Many Interlinks could exist. Many-to-Many Interlinks should be further analyzed because the resulting associative Interlinks could be another Apparatus Member, Association of Members, or the basis for an Operation Session and/or Operation Transaction. They are handled as Many-to-Many relationships in **SAM O NAOULO** Modeling Technique and their resolution into Associative Entities is detailed in Section 13.1.

4. <u>Interlinks between the Activity Members and Members of other Apparatus Components</u> would assist capturing activities that are depending on other Apparatus Component Members.

5. <u>Interlinks between the Event Members and Members of other Apparatus Components</u> (except Activity) would assist capturing events that are depending on other Apparatus Component Members.

6. <u>Recursive Interlinks affecting the Apparatus Members</u>. One-to-One Recursive Interlinks are Not Common (some relationships provide the impression that One-to-One Recursive

Interlinks (e.g. marriage) exists, but if we consider the historic data, this interlink becomes One-to-Many and Many-to-Many. Many-to-Many Recursive Interlinks should be further analyzed because the resulting associative Interlinks could be another Apparatus Member, Association of Members, or the basis for an Operation Session and/or Operation Transaction. They are handled as Many-to-Many relationships in **SAM O NAOULO** Modeling Technique and their resolution into Associative Entities is detailed in Section 13.1.

7. Additional Restrictions on the Recursive Interlinks affecting the Apparatus Activities. Many-to-Many Recursive Interlinks affecting the Apparatus Activities are Not Common. The resulting associative Interlinks could be another Apparatus Activity or the basis for an Operation Session. They are handled as Many-to-Many relationships in **SAM O NAOULO** Modeling Technique and their resolution into Associative Entities is detailed in Section 13.1.

12.2 THE INTERLINKS WITHIN THE MACHINERY

The Machinery Procedures could interlink One-to-One, One-to-Many or Many-to-Many with other Machinery Procedures or could have Recursive Interlinks:

1. The Machinery Procedures regulate the Operation Transactions of the Enterprise (Ref. Section 2.3). The Machinery Procedures' structure follows the Decomposition Diagrams (Ref. Section 2.7). The Interlinks between Procedures are to support capturing procedures or procedure's features that are depending on other procedures. This Interlinks enable more flexibility to support business specifications than allowed by the strict Decomposition Diagrams.

2. The Machinery Procedures interlink with other Machinery Procedures. One-to-One Interlinks are Not Common. One-to-Many Interlinks could exist. Many-to-Many Interlinks should be further analyzed because the resulting associative Interlinks could be another Machinery Procedure, Association of Procedures, or the basis for an Operation Transaction. They are handled as Many-to-Many relationships in **SAM O NAOULO** Modeling Technique and their resolution into Associative Entities is detailed in Section 13.2.

3. Recursive Interlinks affecting the Machinery Procedures. One-to-One and Many-to-Many Recursive Interlinks are Not Common. One-to-Many Interlinks could exist. If a Many-to-Many Recursive Interlink is encountered, it should be further analyzed because the resulting associative Interlinks could be another Machinery Procedure or the basis for an Operation Transaction. They are handled as Many-to-Many relationships in **SAM O NAOULO** Modeling Technique and their resolution into Associative Entities is detailed in Section 13.2.

12.3 THE INTERLINKS WITHIN THE OPERATION SESSIONS

The Operation Sessions could interlink One-to-One, One-to-Many or Many-to-Many with other Operation Sessions or could have Recursive Interlinks:

1. The Operation Sessions. One-to-One Interlinks are Not Common. One-to-Many Interlinks could exist. Many-to-Many Interlinks should be further analyzed because the

resulting associative Interlinks could be another Operation Session, Association of Operation Sessions, or the basis for an Operation Transaction. They are handled as Many-to-Many relationships in **SAM O NAOULO** Modeling Technique and their resolution into Associative Entities is detailed in Section 13.3.

2. <u>Recursive Interlinks affecting the Operation Sessions</u>. One-to-One Recursive Interlinks is Not Common. One-to-Many Interlinks could exist. Many-to-Many Recursive Interlink should be further analyzed because the resulting associative Interlinks could be another Operation Session or the basis for an Operation Transaction. They are handled as Many-to-Many relationships in **SAM O NAOULO** Modeling Technique and their resolution into Associative Entities is detailed in Section 13.3.

12.4   THE INTERLINKS WITHIN THE OPERATION TRANSACTIONS

An Operation Transaction could interlink One-to-One, One-to-Many or Many-to-Many with other Operation Transactions or could have Recursive Interlinks:

1. <u>The Operation Transactions.</u> One-to-One Interlinks are Not Common. One-to-Many Interlinks could exist. Many-to-Many Interlinks should be further analyzed because the resulting associative Interlinks could be another Operation Transaction or an Association of Operation Transactions. They are handled as Many-to-Many relationships in **SAM O NAOULO** Modeling Technique and their resolution into Associative Entities is detailed in Section 13.4.

2. <u>Recursive Interlinks affecting the Operation Transactions</u>. One-to-One Recursive Interlinks is Not Common. One-to-Many Interlinks could exist. Many-to-Many Recursive Interlink should be further analyzed because the resulting associative Interlinks could be another Operation Transaction. They are handled as Many-to-Many relationships in **SAM O NAOULO** Modeling Technique and their resolution into Associative Entities is detailed in Section 13.4.

12.5   THE INTERLINKS APPARATUS – MACHINERY

It is important to remember that the Apparatus Activities (Ref. Section 2.2.2) control the Operation Sessions of the Enterprise while the Machinery Procedures (Ref. Section 2.3) regulate the Operation Transactions of the Enterprise. The Apparatus Members interlink One-to-One, One-to-Many, Many-to-One, and Many-to-Many with the Machinery Procedures.

1. One-to-One Interlinks are Not Common.
2. One-to-Many Interlinks reveal procedures that are depending on the Apparatus Members.
3. Many-to-One Interlinks reveal procedures that are dealing with many Apparatus Members. These Interlinks are treated as Many-to-Many Interlinks.
4. Many-to-Many Interlinks reveal procedures that are depending on the Apparatus Members and are dealing with many Apparatus Member Incidences. These Interlinks are decomposed and should be further analyzed because the resulting associative Interlinks could be Operation Transactions. They are handled as Many-to-Many relationships in **SAM O NAOULO** Modeling Technique and their resolution into Associative Entities is detailed in Section 13.5.
5. Direct Interlinks between Machinery Procedures and the Apparatus Activities are not

Dr. Eng. M. Naoulo

valid. Any Interlinks and dependencies between them would be thru the Operation Transactions.

12.6 THE INTERLINKS APPARATUS – OPERATION SESSIONS

The Apparatus Members interlink One-to-One, One-to-Many, Many-to-One, and Many-to-Many with the Operation Sessions.

1. One-to-One Interlinks are Not Common.
2. One-to-Many Interlinks reveal sessions that are depending on the Apparatus Members.
3. Many-to-One Interlinks reveal sessions that are dealing with many Apparatus Members. These Interlinks are treated as Many-to-Many Interlinks.
4. Many-to-Many Interlinks reveal sessions that are depending on the Apparatus Members and are dealing with many Apparatus Member Incidences. These Interlinks are decomposed and should be further analyzed because the resulting associative Interlinks could be Operation Sessions and/or Operation Transactions. They are handled as Many-to-Many relationships in **SAM O NAOULO** Modeling Technique and their resolution into Associative Entities is detailed in Section 13.6.
5. An Operation Session must interlink to at least one Member of each Apparatus Component. An Operation Session Incidence must interlink to only one Apparatus Elementary Activity Incidence (Ref. Section 2.12.1).

12.7 THE INTERLINKS APPARATUS – OPERATION TRANSACTIONS

The Apparatus Members interlink One-to-One, One-to-Many, Many-to-One, and Many-to-Many with the Operation Transactions:

1. One-to-One Interlinks are Not Common.
2. One-to-Many Interlinks reveal transactions that are depending on the Apparatus Members.
3. Many-to-One Interlinks reveal transactions that are dealing with many Apparatus Members. These Interlinks are treated as Many-to-Many Interlinks.
4. Many-to-Many Interlinks reveal transactions that are depending on the Apparatus Members and are dealing with many Apparatus Member Incidences. These Interlinks are decomposed and should be further analyzed because the resulting associative Interlinks could be Operation Transactions. They are handled as Many-to-Many relationships in **SAM O NAOULO** Modeling Technique and their resolution into Associative Entities is detailed in Section 13.7.
5. Direct Interlinks between the Operation Transactions and the Apparatus Activities are not valid. Any Interlinks and dependencies between them would be thru the Operation Sessions (Ref. Section 3.6.5).
6. Direct Interlinks between the Operation Transactions and the Apparatus Occurrence Events are not valid. Any Interlinks and dependencies between them would be thru the Operation Sessions (Ref. Section 3.6.6).

Dr. Eng. M. Naoulo

12.8 THE INTERLINKS MACHINERY – OPERATION SESSIONS

There should be no direct Interlinks between the Machinery Procedures and the Operation Sessions. All Interlinks between them will be thru the Operation Transactions. Any encountered Interlinks between the Machinery Procedures and the Operation Sessions must be further analyzed to detect any flaws (Ref. Section 13.8).

12.9 THE INTERLINKS MACHINERY – OPERATION TRANSACTIONS

A Machinery Procedure interlinks One-to-One, One-to-Many, Many-to-One, and Many-to-Many with the Operation Transactions.

1. One-to-One Interlinks are Not Common.
2. One-to-Many Interlinks reveal transactions that are depending on the Machinery Procedures.
3. Many-to-One Interlinks reveal transactions that are dealing with many Machinery Procedures. This Interlinks are treated as Many-to-Many Interlinks.
4. Many-to-Many Interlinks reveal transactions that are depending on the Machinery Procedures and are dealing with many Machinery Procedure Incidences. These Interlinks are decomposed and should be further analyzed because the resulting associative Interlinks could be Operation Transactions. They are handled as Many-to-Many relationships in **SAM O NAOULO** Modeling Technique and their resolution into Associative Entities is detailed in Section 13.9.
5. An Operation Transaction must interlink to at least one Machinery Procedure. An Operation Transaction Incidence could interlink to one or many Machinery Procedure Incidences (Ref. Section 2.12.2).

12.10 THE INTERLINKS OPERATION SESSIONS – OPERATION TRANSACTIONS

The Operation Sessions interlink One-to-One, One-to-Many, Many-to-One, and Many-to-Many with the Operation Transactions.

1. One-to-One Interlinks are Not Common.
2. One-to-Many Interlinks reveal transactions generated or modified by the Operation Sessions.
3. Many-to-One Interlinks reveal transactions that are dealing with many Operation Sessions. These Interlinks are treated as Many-to-Many Interlinks. This is because it is very often advisable to capture the history of changes affecting the transactions than to override data.
4. Many-to-Many Interlinks reveal transactions that are depending on the Operation Sessions and dealing with many Operation Session Incidences. These Interlinks are decomposed and should be further analyzed because the resulting associative Interlinks could be Operation Transactions. They are handled as Many-to-Many relationships in **SAM O NAOULO** Modeling Technique and their resolution into Associative Entities is detailed in Section 13.10.
5. An Operation Transaction must interlink to at least one Operation Session.

Dr. Eng. M. Naoulo

13. APPENDIX B: The Resolution of Relationships between the Entities of the Enterprise Engineering Model

This Appendix provides the technical details for the analysis, design and resolution of relationships between the entities of the Enterprise Engineering Model. The basics for this resolution are the 3NF technique developed in the Relational Data Modeling.

13.1 THE RESOLUTION OF RELATIONSHIPS BETWEEN ENTITIES OF THE MASTER DATA

During the design process, One-to-One, One-to-Many, and Many-to-Many relationships could be encountered either relating:

  ➤ Master Data Dimension Entities or Master Data Associative Entities of the same Master Data Dimension or Associative Entity Profile.
  ➤ Master Data Dimension Entities or Master Data Associative Entities of the same Master Data Component but different Master Data Dimension or Associative Profiles.
  ➤ Across different Master Data Components.

Also recursive relationships could exist affecting a Master Data Dimension Entity or a Master Data Associative Entity. Hereafter are the rules and resolution techniques governing the relationships between the Master Data Entities:

1. One-to-One relationship could exist between two entities within a Master Data Dimension or Associative Entity Profile. A One-to-One relationship indicates very often either the two entities are similar or one of them is a kind of subtype to the other or is the storage for additional data.
2. One-to-One relationship between entities of different Master Data Entity (Dimension or Associative) Profiles within the Master Data Component could exist in some business cases that are Not Common.
3. One-to-One relationship between entities of different Master Data Entity (Dimension or Associative) Profiles across Master Data Components, or involving Master Data Associative Entities resulting from relationships across Master Data Components could exist in some business cases that are Not Common.
4. In the case of One-to-One relationship between the Master Data Activity Entities and other Master Data Components the FK must be in the Master Data Activity Entities. That's means the Master Data Activity Entity's data is contingent on other Master Data Component Entities and not the opposite.
5. In the case of One-to-One relationship between the Master Data Occurrence Event Entities and other Master Data Components (except Activities) the FK must be in the Master Data Occurrence Event Entities. That's means the Master Data Occurrence Event Entity's data is contingent on other Master Data Component Entities and not the opposite.
6. One-to-Many relationship could exist between two entities within a Master Data Dimension or Associative Entity Profile.
7. One-to-Many relationship could exist between two entities belonging to different Master Data Entity Profiles but within the same Master Data Component.
8. One-to-Many relationship could exist between two entities belonging to two different

Master Data Components or involving Master Data Associative Entities resulting from relationships across Master Data Components.

9. One-to-Many relationships between the Master Data Activity Entities and other Master Data Components could exist. If the cardinality is many on the Master Data Activity Entities' side and one on the other Master Data Component Entity's side, the FK must be in the Master Data Activity Entities. That's means the Master Data Activity Entity's data is contingent on the other Master Data Component Entities and not the opposite. If the cardinality is one on the Master Data Activity Entities' side and many on the other Master Data Component Entity's side, this relationship is treated as many-to-many relationship and resolved as hereafter.

10. One-to-Many relationship between the Master Data Occurrence Event Entities and other Master Data Components (except Activity Component) could exist. If the cardinality is many on the Master Data Occurrence Event Entities' side and one on the other Master Data Components Entity's side, the FK must be in the Master Data Occurrence Event Entities. That's means the Master Data Occurrence Event Entity's data is contingent on the other Master Data Component Entities and not the opposite. If the cardinality is one on the Master Data Occurrence Event Entities' side and many on the other Master Data Component's side, this relationship is treated as many-to-many relationship and resolved as hereafter.

11. No Many-to-Many relationships exist between the entities of the Master Data belonging to the same Master Data Dimension or Associative Entity Profiles. If the Enterprise Engineer encounters such relationship, this would induce the need to review the analysis and assess the logic supporting this relationship. This analysis would indicate either:
    ➢ This relationship captures and reflects additional Master Data, in this case additional Master Data Entity(ies) might be needed; or
    ➢ This Associative Entity resulting from the relationship captures and reflects the Mechanics data of the functioning of the Enterprise, in this case this Associative Entity and its attributes would belong to the Mechanics Constituent and would follow the design technique pertinent to the Mechanics as detailed hereafter.

Therefore the relationships within the Profile of each Master Data Dimension or Master Data Associative Entity would contain only One-to-One or One-to-Many relationships.

12. Any Many-to-Many relationship encountered between the entities of the Master Data belonging to different Master Data Dimension or Associative Entity Profiles within the same Master Data Component, would induce the need to review the analysis and assess the logic supporting this relationship. If the analysis is genuine, this relationship should be decomposed. The analysis would indicate either:
    ➢ This relationship captures and reflects additional Master Data, in this case additional Master Data Entity(ies) might be needed; or
    ➢ The Associative Entity resulting from the relationship captures and reflects the Mechanics data of the functioning of the Enterprise, in this case this Associative Entity and its attributes would belong to the Mechanics Constituent and would follow the design technique pertinent to the Mechanics as detailed hereafter; or
    ➢ The Associative Entity resulting from the relationship captures information related to the interrelations of Master Data Dimension or Associative Entity Profiles within the same Master Data Component. This entity would have the

features of the Master Data Entities of this Component vis-à-vis the nature of the entities and their relationships with the Master Data, Mechanism, and the Mechanics Sessions and Transactions. Examples of these Many-to-Many relationships are very often encountered in UTL PRODUCT.

➢ Otherwise the Enterprise Engineers should detect any flaws in the analysis and design.

13. Any Many-to-Many relationship encountered between the entities of the Master Data across Master Data Components (none is Activity or Occurrence Event) or involving Master Data Associative Entities resulting from relationships across Master Data Components (none is Activity or Occurrence Event) would induce the need to review the analysis and assess the logic supporting this relationship. If the analysis is genuine, this relationship should be decomposed. The analysis would indicate either:

➢ This relationship captures and reflects additional Master Data, in this case additional Master Data Entity(ies) might be needed; or

➢ This Associative Entity captures and reflects the Mechanics data of the functioning of the Enterprise, in this case this Associative Entity and its attributes would belong to the Mechanics Constituent and would follow the design technique pertinent to the Mechanics as detailed hereafter; or

➢ This Associative Entity captures information related to the interrelations of Master Data Dimensions or Associative Entities across Master Data Component. This entity would have the features of the Master Data Entities vis-à-vis the nature of the entities and their relationships with the Master Data, Mechanism, and the Mechanics Sessions and Transactions.

➢ Otherwise the Enterprise Engineers should detect any flaws in the analysis and design.

14. Any Many-to-Many relationship encountered between:

➢ Master Data Activity Entities, or

➢ Involving Master Data Activity Entity(ies), or

➢ Involving Master Data Activity Associative Entity(ies) resulting from relationships across Master Data Components

should be analyzed. If the analysis is genuine, this relationship should be decomposed. The analysis would indicate either:

➢ This relationship captures and reflects additional Master Data Activity(ies), in this case additional Master Data Activity Entity(ies) might be needed; or

➢ This Associative Entity resulting from the relationship captures and reflects the Mechanics data of the functioning of the Enterprise, in this case the Associative Entity and its attributes would belong to the Mechanics Constituent and would follow the design technique pertinent to the Mechanics as detailed hereafter; or

➢ This Associative Entity resulting from the relationship captures information related to the interrelations of Master Data Activity Entities with different Master Data Components. It is a Master Data Activity Associative Entity and this entity would have the features of the Master Data Activity Entities vis-à-vis the nature of the entities and their relationships with the Master Data, Mechanism, and the Mechanics Sessions and Transactions. The Master Data Activity Associative Entities which directly interact with the Operation Sessions are also denoted as

Dr. Eng. M. Naoulo

Elementary Activities.

➢ Otherwise the Enterprise Engineers should detect any flaws in the analysis and design.

15. Any Many-to-Many relationship encountered between:

➢ Master Data Occurrence Event Entities, or

➢ Involving Master Data Occurrence Event Entity(ies) but not Master Data Activity Entity(ies), or

➢ Involving Master Data Occurrence Event Associative Entities resulting from relationships across Master Data Components (none is Activity)

should be analyzed. If the analysis is genuine, this relationship should be decomposed. The analysis would indicate either:

➢ This relationship captures and reflects additional Master Data Occurrence Event(s), in this case additional Master Data Occurrence Event Entity(ies) might be needed; or

➢ This Associative Entity resulting from the relationship captures and reflects the Mechanics data of the functioning of the Enterprise, in this case the Associative Entity and its attributes would belong to the Mechanics Constituent and would follow the design technique pertinent to the Mechanics as detailed hereafter; or

➢ The Associative Entity resulting from the relationship captures information related to the interrelations of Master Data Occurrence Event Entities with different Master Data Components (except Activities). It is a Master Data Occurrence Event Associative Entity and this entity would have the features of the Master Data Occurrence Event Entities vis-à-vis the nature of the entities and their relationships with the Master Data, Mechanism, and the Mechanics Sessions and Transactions.

➢ Otherwise the Enterprise Engineers should detect any flaws in the analysis and design.

16. The entities of the Mechanism or Mechanics could be related to the Master Data Associative Entities. In this case the Master Data Component Dimensions involved in the Master Data Associative Entities would be reflected in these Mechanism or Mechanics Entities.

17. One-to-One recursive convoluted relationship affecting a Master Data Entity is Not Common. This case, if it exists, could be solved thru a Foreign Key between the entity and itself.

18. One-to-Many recursive convoluted relationship affecting a Master Data Entity could exist. It is solved thru a Foreign Key between the entity and itself.

19. Many-to-Many recursive convoluted relationship affecting a Master Data Entity could exist. It is solved thru a Master Data Associative Entity. Examples of these Many-to-Many recursive convoluted relationship are often encountered in UTL PRODUCT or LOC REGION.

20. Many-to-Many recursive convoluted relationship affecting a Master Data Activity Dimension are Not Common.

21. The FK(s) in the Master Data Entities would represent the relations to other Master Data Entities.

Dr. Eng. M. Naoulo

Best of Practice directions would help in the illustration and visualization of the Master Data Associative Entities and their attributes. These directions are similar to those indicated for the Master Data (Ref. Section 3.3). Furthermore:

1. The Master Data Associative Entity could have as Primary Keys (PK) the concatenation of the PK of the entities associated in this Associative Entity (the relationships are identifying) or use Surrogate Keys (SK) (the relationships are not identifying). It is advisable to use, in the logical model, identifying relationships for all relationships associating the Master Data Associative Entities. This would imply the propagation of the Master Data keys involved in a Master Data Associative Entity into other Master Data Associative Entities (if this Master Data Associative Entity is identifying to other Master Data Associative Entities) and to the Mechanism, Mechanics Session and Transaction Entities therefore simplifying the understanding and the validation of the Model. The use of Surrogate Keys in the physical model is possible – and sometimes advisable – for performance needs.

2. The name of the Master Data Associative Entities resulting within a Master Data Component and the attributes of these entities shall start with the same letters of this Component.

3. The color of the Master Data Associative Entities resulting within a Master Data Components would be the same color as indicated by to the Master Data Component (Ref. Section 3.3).

4. The name of the Master Data Associative Entities resulting across the Master Data Components and the attributes of these entities that are not FK to other Master Data Entities shall start with the letter **A**.

5. The color of the Master Data Associative Entities resulting across the Master Data Components would be medium blue.

6. The name of the Master Data Associative Entities involving Master Data Activity Entities shall start with the letters **ACT** and they would have the features of the Master Data Activity Entities and their color is dark blue as the Master Data Activity Entities.

7. The name of the Master Data Associative Entities involving Master Data Occurrence Event Entities, and not involving Master Data Activity Entities, shall start with the letters **OCC** and they would have the features of the Master Data Occurrence Event Entities and their color is red as the Master Data Occurrence Event Entities.

8. The order of the attributes of the Master Data Associative Entities is the same as in Section 3.3.

13.2 THE RESOLUTION OF RELATIONSHIPS BETWEEN ENTITIES OF THE MECHANISM

During the design process, One-to-One, One-to-Many, and Many-to-Many relationships could be encountered either relating Mechanism Procedure (Non-associative or Associative) Entities within the same Procedure Profile or across different Procedure Profiles. Also recursive relationships could exist affecting a Mechanism Procedure Entity or a Mechanism Procedure Associative Entity. Hereafter are the rules and resolution techniques governing the relationships between the Mechanism Procedure Entities:

1. One-to-One relationship could exist between two entities within a Mechanism Procedure

Entity Profile. A One-to-One relationship indicates very often either the two entities are similar or one of them is a kind of subtype to the other or is the storage for additional data.

2. One-to-One relationship between entities of different Mechanism Procedure Entity Profiles could exist in some business cases that are Not Common.

3. One-to-Many relationship could exist between two entities within a Mechanism Procedure Entity Profile or between two entities belonging to different Mechanism Procedure Entity Profiles.

4. No Many-to-Many relationships exist between the entities of the Mechanism belonging to the same Mechanism Procedure Entity Profile. If the Enterprise Engineer encounters such relationship, this would induce the need to review the analysis and assess the logic supporting this relationship. This analysis would indicate either:

   ➤ This relationship captures and reflects additional Mechanism Procedure data, in this case additional Mechanism Procedure Entity(ies) might be needed; or

   ➤ This Associative Entity resulting from the relationship captures and reflects the Mechanics Transaction data of the functioning of the Enterprise, in this case this Associative Entity and its attributes would belong to the Mechanics Transactions Domain and would follow the design technique pertinent to the Mechanics Transactions as detailed hereafter.

Therefore the relationships within the Profile of each Mechanism Procedure Entity would contain only One-to-One or One-to-Many relationships.

5. Any Many-to-Many relationships encountered between the entities of the Mechanism belonging to different Mechanism Procedure Profiles would induce the need to review the analysis and assess the logic supporting this relationship. If the analysis is genuine, this relationship should be decomposed. The analysis would indicate either:

   ➤ This relationship captures and reflects additional Mechanism Procedure data, in this case additional Mechanism Procedure Entity(ies) might be needed; or

   ➤ This Associative Entity resulting from the relationship captures and reflects the Mechanics Transaction data of the functioning of the Enterprise, in this case this Associative Entity and its attributes would belong to the Mechanics Transactions Domain and would follow the design technique pertinent to the Mechanics Transactions as detailed hereafter; or

   ➤ This Associative Entity resulting from the relationship captures information related to the interrelations of Mechanism Procedures. This entity would have the features of the Mechanism Procedure Entities vis-à-vis the nature of the entities and their relationships with the Master Data, Mechanism, and the Mechanics Sessions and Transactions. The Mechanism Procedure Associative Entities which directly interact with the Operation Transactions are also denoted as Elementary Procedures.

   ➤ Otherwise the Enterprise Engineers should detect any flaws in the analysis and design.

6. One-to-One recursive convoluted relationship affecting a Mechanism Procedure Entity is Not Common. This case, if it exists, could be solved thru a Foreign Key between the entity and itself.

7. One-to-Many recursive convoluted relationship affecting a Mechanism Procedure Entity

Dr. Eng. M. Naoulo

could exist. It is solved thru a Foreign Key between the entity and itself.

8. Many-to-Many recursive convoluted relationship affecting a Mechanism Procedure Entity is Not Common.

9. The FK(s) in the Mechanism Procedure Entities would represent the relationships to other Mechanism Procedure Entities and Master Data Entities.

Best of Practice directions would help in the illustration and visualization of the Mechanism Associative Entities and their attributes. These directions are similar to those indicated for the Mechanism (Ref. Section 3.4). Furthermore:

1. The Mechanism Procedure Associative Entity could have as Primary Keys (PK) the concatenation of the PK of the entities associated in this Associative Entity (the relationships are identifying) or use Surrogate Keys (SK) (the relationships are not identifying). It is advisable to use, in the logical model, identifying relationships for all relationships associating the Mechanism Procedure Associative Entities. This would imply the propagation of the Master Data and Mechanism keys involved in a Mechanism Procedure Associative Entity into other Mechanism Procedure Associative Entities (if this Mechanism Procedure Associative Entity is identifying to other Mechanism Procedure Associative Entities) and to the Mechanics Transaction Entities therefore simplifying the understanding and the validation of the Model. The use of Surrogate Keys in the physical model is possible – and sometimes advisable – for performance needs.

2. The name of the Mechanism Procedure Associative Entities and the attributes of these entities shall start with the letter **M**.

3. The color of the Mechanism Procedure Associative Entities would be the same color used for the Mechanism Entities (Ref. Section 3.4).

4. The order of the attributes of the Mechanism Procedure Associative Entities is the same as in Section 3.4.

13.3 THE RESOLUTION OF RELATIONSHIPS BETWEEN ENTITIES OF THE MECHANICS SESSIONS

During the design process, One-to-One, One-to-Many, and Many-to-Many relationships could be encountered either relating the Mechanics Session (Non-associative or Associative) Entities within the same Session Profile or across different Session Profiles. Also recursive relationships could exist affecting a Mechanics Session Entity or a Mechanics Session Associative Entity. Hereafter are the rules and resolution techniques governing the relationships between the Mechanics Session Entities:

1. One-to-One relationship could exist between two entities within a Mechanics Session Entity Profile. A One-to-One relationship indicates very often either the two entities are similar or one of them is a kind of subtype to the other or is the storage for additional data.

2. One-to-One relationship between entities of different Mechanics Session Entity Profiles could exist in some business cases that are Not Common.

3. One-to-Many relationship could exist between two entities within a Mechanics Session Entity Profile or between two entities belonging to different Mechanics Session Entity Profiles.

Dr. Eng. M. Naoulo

4. No Many-to-Many relationships exist between the entities of the Mechanics belonging to the same Mechanics Session Entity Profile. If the Enterprise Engineer encounters such relationship, this would induce the need to review the analysis and assess the logic supporting this relationship. This analysis would indicate either:
   - ➤ This relationship captures and reflects additional Mechanics Session data, in this case additional Mechanics Session Entity(ies) might be needed; or
   - ➤ This Associative Entity resulting from the relationship captures and reflects the Mechanics Transaction data of the functioning of the Enterprise, in this case this Associative Entity and its attributes would belong to the Mechanics Transactions Domain and would follow the design technique pertinent to the Mechanics Transactions as detailed hereafter.

   Therefore the relationships within the Profile of each Mechanics Session Entity would contain only One-to-One or One-to-Many relationships.

5. Any Many-to-Many relationship encountered between the entities of the Mechanics Sessions belonging to different Mechanics Session Profiles would induce the need to review the analysis and assess the logic supporting this relationship. If the analysis is genuine, this relationship should be decomposed. The analysis would indicate either:
   - ➤ This relationship captures and reflects additional Mechanics Session Data, in this case additional Mechanics Session Entity(ies) might be needed; or
   - ➤ This Associative Entity resulting from the relationship captures and reflects the Mechanics Transaction data of the functioning of the Enterprise, in this case this Associative Entity and its attributes would belong to the Mechanics Transactions Domain and would follow the design technique pertinent to the Mechanics Transactions as detailed hereafter; or
   - ➤ This Associative Entity resulting from the relationship captures information related to the interrelations of Mechanics Sessions. This entity would have the features of the Mechanics Session Entities vis-à-vis the nature of the entities and their relationships with the Master Data, Mechanism, and the Mechanics Sessions and Transactions.
   - ➤ Otherwise the Enterprise Engineers should detect any flaws in the analysis and design.

6. One-to-One recursive convoluted relationship affecting a Mechanics Session Entity is Not Common. This case, if it exists, could be solved thru a Foreign Key between the entity and itself.

7. One-to-Many recursive convoluted relationship affecting a Mechanics Session Entity could exist. It is solved thru a Foreign Key between the entity and itself.

8. Many-to-Many recursive convoluted relationship affecting a Mechanics Session Entity could exist. It is solved thru a Mechanics Session Associative Entity.

9. A main Mechanics Session Entity could have sub-sessions.

10. The FK(s) in the Mechanics Session Entities would represent the relationships to other Mechanics Session Entities and Master Data Entities.

Best of Practice directions would help in the illustration and visualization of the Mechanics Session Associative Entities and their attributes. These directions are similar to those indicated for the Mechanics Sessions (Ref. Section 3.5). Furthermore:

Dr. Eng. M. Naoulo

1. The PK of the Mechanics Session Associative Entity will be a concatenation of the PK of the Mechanics Session Entities associated in this Associative Entity (the relationships are identifying). The use of Surrogate Keys (non-identifying relationships) in the physical model is possible – and sometimes advisable – for performance needs.
2. The name of the Mechanics Session Associative Entities and the attributes of these entities shall start with the letters **MS**.
3. The name of the Mechanics Session Associative Entities would end with the words **SESSIONS RELATION**.
4. The color of the Mechanics Session Associative Entities would be the same color used for the Mechanics Session Entities (Ref. Section 3.5).
5. The order of the attributes of the Mechanics Session Associative Entities is the same as in Section 3.5.

13.4 THE RESOLUTION OF RELATIONSHIPS BETWEEN ENTITIES OF THE MECHANICS TRANSACTIONS

During the design process, One-to-One, One-to-Many, and Many-to-Many relationships could be encountered relating the Mechanics Transaction (Non-associative or Associative) Entities within the same Transaction Profile or across different Transaction Profiles. Also recursive relationships could exist affecting a Mechanics Transaction Entity or a Mechanics Transaction Associative Entity. Hereafter are the rules and resolution techniques governing the relationships between the Mechanics Transaction Entities:

1. One-to-One relationship could exist between two entities within a Mechanics Transaction Entity Profile. A One-to-One relationship indicates very often either the two entities are similar or one of them is a kind of subtype to the other or is the storage for additional data.
2. One-to-One relationship between entities of different Mechanics Transaction Entity Profiles could exist in some business cases that are Not Common.
3. One-to-Many relationship could exist between two entities within a Mechanics Transaction Entity Profile or between two entities belonging to different Mechanics Transaction Entity Profiles.
4. No Many-to-Many relationships exist between the entities of the Mechanics belonging to the same Mechanics Transaction Entity Profile. If the Enterprise Engineer encounters such relationship, this would induce the need to review the analysis and assess the logic supporting this relationship. This analysis could indicate that this relationship captures and reflects additional Mechanics Transaction data; in this case additional Mechanics Transaction Entity(ies) would be needed. The relationships within the Profile of each Mechanics Transaction would contain only One-to-One or One-to-Many relationships.
5. Any Many-to-Many relationship encountered between the entities of the Mechanics Transactions belonging to different Mechanics Transaction profiles would induce the need to review the analysis and assess the logic supporting this relationship. If the analysis is genuine, this relationship should be decomposed. The analysis would indicate either:
   ➢ This This relationship captures and reflects additional Mechanics Transactions data, in this case additional Mechanics Transaction Entity(ies) might be needed;

Dr. Eng. M. Naoulo

or
> This Associative Entity captures information related to the interrelations of Mechanics Transactions. This entity would have the features of the Mechanics Transaction Entities vis-à-vis the nature of the entities and their relationships with the Master Data, Mechanism, and the Mechanics Sessions and Transactions.
> Otherwise the Enterprise Engineers should detect any flaws in the analysis and design.

6. One-to-One recursive convoluted relationship affecting a Mechanics Transaction Entity is Not Common. This case, if it exists, could be solved thru a Foreign Key between the entity and itself.

7. One-to-Many recursive convoluted relationship affecting a Mechanics Transaction Entity could exist. It is solved thru a Foreign Key between the entity and itself.

8. Many-to-Many recursive convoluted relationship affecting a Mechanics Transaction entity could exist. It is solved thru a Mechanics Transaction Associative Entity. This is very common for capturing whole records of every Transaction instance's change when there are transactional data modifications (Ref. Section 3.7.4).

9. The FK(s) in the Mechanics Transaction Entities would represent the relationships to other Mechanics Transaction Entities, Mechanism Procedure Entities, Mechanics Session Entities, and Master Data Entities.

Best of Practice directions would help in the illustration and visualization of the Mechanics Transaction Associative Entities and their attributes. These directions are similar to those indicated for the Mechanics Transactions (Ref. Section 3.6). Furthermore:

1. The PK of the Mechanics Transaction Associative Entity will be a concatenation of the PK of the Mechanics Transaction Entities associated in this Associative Entity (the relationships are identifying). The use of Surrogate Keys (non-identifying relationships) in the physical model is possible – and sometimes advisable – for performance needs.

2. The name of the Mechanics Transaction Associative Entities and the attributes of these entities shall start with the letter **X**.

3. The name of the Mechanics Transaction Associative Entities would end with the word **TRX RELATION**.

4. The color of the Mechanics Transaction Associative Entities would be the same color used for the Mechanics Transaction Entities (Ref. Section 3.6).

5. The order of the attributes of the Mechanics Transaction Associative Entities is the same as in Section 3.6.

13.5 THE RESOLUTION OF RELATIONSHIPS BETWEEN THE MASTER DATA & THE MECHANISM ENTITIES

The Interaction of the Master Data Entities and the Mechanism Procedure Entities would reflect in the Enterprise Engineering Model the Interlink between the Apparatus and the Machinery Procedures. During the design process, One-to-One, One-to-Many, Many-to-One, and Many-to-Many relationships could be encountered relating the Master Data Entities (Dimension or Associative) with the Mechanism Procedure (Non-associative or Associative) Entities. Hereafter are the rules and resolution techniques governing these relationships:

Dr. Eng. M. Naoulo

1. The majority of relationships are One-to-Many from the Master Data Entities to the Mechanism Procedure Entities.

2. Relationships relating Master Data Activity Entities or Master Data Associative Entities that associate Master Data Activity Entity(ies) and the Mechanism Procedure Entities are Not Valid.

3. One-to-One relationships relating the Master Data Entities and the Mechanism Procedure Entities could exist in some business cases that are Not Common. The Mechanism Procedure Entity's data is contingent on the Master Data Entities and not the opposite. Therefore the FKs must be in the Mechanism Procedure Entities and would represent their relationships to the Master Data Entities.

4. One-to-Many relationships from the Master Data Entities to the Mechanism Procedure Entities could exist. The FKs are in the Mechanism Procedure Entities and would represent their relationships to the Master Data Entities.

5. Many-to-One relationships from the Master Data Entities to the Mechanism Procedure Entities could exist. These relationships are treated as Many-to-Many relationships and resolved as hereafter.

6. No Many-to-One relationship encountered from the Master Data Occurrence Event Entities to the Mechanism Procedure Entities.

7. Any Many-to-Many relationship encountered between the Master Data Entities (except Activities or Occurrence Events) and the Mechanism Procedure Entities would induce the need to review the analysis and assess the logic supporting this relationship. If the analysis is genuine, this relationship should be decomposed. The analysis would indicate either:

   ➢ The need for additional relationships between the Master Data Entities and the Mechanism Procedure Entities, these relationships should be established; or

   ➢ The Associative Entity resulting from the relationship captures and reflects the Mechanics data of the functioning of the Enterprise, in this case this Associative Entity and its attributes would belong to the Mechanics Constituent and would follow the design technique pertinent to the Mechanics as detailed hereafter; or

   ➢ The Associative Entity resulting from the relationship captures information related to the interrelations of Master Data Dimension or Associative Entities with the Mechanism Procedure Entities. It is a Mechanism Procedure Associative Entity. This entity would have the features of the Mechanism Procedure Entities vis-à-vis the nature of the entities and their relationships with the Master Data, Mechanism, and the Mechanics Sessions and Transactions.

   ➢ Otherwise the Enterprise Engineers should detect any flaws in the analysis and design.

8. No Many-to-Many relationship encountered between the Master Data Occurrence Event Entities and the Mechanism Procedure Entities.

9. The Mechanism Procedure Entities could be related to as many Master Data Entities as needed by the business.

10. The FK(s) in the Mechanism Procedure Associative Entities would represent the relationships to other Mechanism Procedure Entities and the Master Data Entities.

The Best of Practice directions for these Mechanism Associative Entities are the same Best of

Dr. Eng. M. Naoulo

Practice directions indicated in Section 13.2.

13.6 THE RESOLUTION OF RELATIONSHIPS BETWEEN THE MASTER DATA & THE MECHANICS SESSION ENTITIES

The Interaction of the Master Data Entities and the Mechanics Session Entities would reflect in the Enterprise Engineering Model the Interlink between the Apparatus and the Operation Sessions. During the design process, One-to-One, One-to-Many, Many-to-One, and Many-to-Many relationships could be encountered relating the Master Data Entities (Dimension or Associative) with the Mechanics Session (Non-associative or Associative) Entities. Hereafter are the rules and resolution techniques governing these relationships:

1. The majority of relationships are One-to-Many from the Master Data Entities to the Mechanics Session Entities.

2. One-to-One relationships relating the Master Data Entities and the Mechanics Session Entities could exist in some business cases that are Not Common. The Mechanics Session Entity's data is contingent on the Master Data Entities and not the opposite. Therefore the FKs must be in the Mechanics Session Entities and would represent their relationships to the Master Data Entities.

3. One-to-Many relationships from the Master Data Entities to the Mechanics Session Entities could exist. The FKs are in the Mechanics Session Entities and would represent their relationships to the Master Data Entities.

4. Many-to-One relationships from the Master Data Entities to the Mechanics Session Entities could exist. These relationships are treated as Many-to-Many relationships and resolved as hereafter.

5. Any Many-to-Many relationship encountered between the Master Data Entities and the Mechanics Session Entities would induce the need to review the analysis and assess the logic supporting this relationship. If the analysis is genuine, this relationship should be decomposed. The analysis would indicate either:

   ➢ The need for additional relationships between the Master Data Entities and the Mechanics Session Entities, these relationships should be established; or

   ➢ The Associative Entity resulting from the relationship captures and reflects the Mechanics Transaction data of the functioning of the Enterprise, in this case this Associative Entity and its attributes would belong to the Mechanics Transactions Domain and would follow the design technique pertinent to the Mechanics Transactions as detailed hereafter; or this relationship would direct to the Mechanics Transactions Domain and would follow the design technique pertinent to the Mechanics Transactions as detailed hereafter; or

   ➢ The Associative Entity resulting from the relationship captures information related to the interrelations of Master Data Dimension or Associative Entities with the Mechanics Session Entities. It is a Mechanics Session Associative Entity. This entity would have the features of the Mechanics Session Entities vis-à-vis the nature of the entities and their relationships with the Master Data, Mechanism, and the Mechanics Sessions and Transactions.

   ➢ Otherwise the Enterprise Engineers should detect any flaws in the analysis and design.

6. The Mechanics Session Entities (including subtypes if any) could be related to as many Master Data Entities as needed by the business (except as indicated by the next rules).

7. Each Operation Session must interlink at least one Member of each Apparatus Component and therefore each Mechanics Session Entity (or the Session Entity and its subtypes) must be related to at least one Master Data Dimension (directly or thru Master Data Associative Entities) of each Master Data Component.

8. The Mechanics Session Entity must be related to at least one Elementary Activity Entity. The Mechanics Session subtypes must not be related to the Elementary Activity Entities.

9. The Mechanics Session Associative Entities cannot be related to the Master Data Activities or Occurrence Events.

10. An Instance of the Mechanics Session Entity must be related to only one Instance of an Elementary Activity Entity.

11. The Mechanics Session Entity must be related to at least one Occurrence Event as the Event triggers the Mechanics Session.

12. An Instance of the Mechanics Session Entity must be related to only one Instance of an Occurrence Event Entity

13. The FK(s) in the Mechanics Session Associative Entities would represent the relationships to other Mechanics Session Entities and the Master Data Entities.

The Best of Practice directions for these Mechanics Session Associative Entities are the same Best of Practice directions indicated in Section 13.3.

13.7 THE RESOLUTION OF RELATIONSHIPS BETWEEN THE MASTER DATA & THE MECHANICS TRANSACTION ENTITIES

The Interaction of the Master Data Entities and the Mechanics Transaction Entities would reflect in the Enterprise Engineering Model the Interlink between the Apparatus and the Operation Transactions. During the design process, One-to-One, One-to-Many, Many-to-One, and Many-to-Many relationships could be encountered relating the Master Data Entities (Dimension or Associative) with the Mechanics Transaction (Non-associative or Associative) Entities. Hereafter are the rules and resolution techniques governing these relationships:

1. The majority of relationships are One-to-Many from the Master Data Entities to the Mechanics Transaction Entities.

2. The Mechanics Transaction Entities must not be directly linked to the Master Data Activity Entities. All relationships between them are thru the Mechanics Session Entities.

3. The Mechanics Transaction Entities must not be directly linked to the Master Data Occurrence Event Entities.

4. One-to-One relationships relating the Master Data Entities and the Mechanics Transaction Entities could exist in some business cases that are Not Common. The Mechanics Transaction Entity's data is contingent on the Master Data Entities and not the opposite. Therefore the FKs must be in the Mechanics Transaction Entities and would represent their relationships to the Master Data Entities.

5. One-to-Many relationships from the Master Data Entities to the Mechanics Transaction Entities could exist. The FKs are in the Mechanics Transaction Entities and would represent their relationships to the Master Data Entities.

Dr. Eng. M. Naoulo

6. Many-to-One relationships relating the Master Data Entities to the Mechanics Transaction Entities could exist. These relationships are treated as Many-to-Many relationships and resolved as hereafter.

7. Any Many-to-Many relationship encountered between the Master Data Entities (other than Activities or Occurrence Events) and the Mechanics Transaction Entities would induce the need to review the analysis and assess the logic supporting this relationship. If the analysis is genuine, this relationship should be decomposed. The analysis would indicate either:

    ➢ The need for additional relationships between the Master Data Entities and the Mechanics Transaction Entities, these relationships should be established; or

    ➢ The Associative Entity resulting from the relationship captures information related to the interrelations of Master Data Dimension or Associative Entities with the Mechanics Transaction Entities. It is a Mechanics Transaction Associative Entity. This entity would have the features of the Mechanics Transaction Entities vis-à-vis the nature of the entities and their relationships with the Master Data, Mechanism, and the Mechanics Sessions and Transactions.

    ➢ Otherwise the Enterprise Engineers should detect any flaws in the analysis and design.

8. No relationships between the Master Data Activity Entities and the Mechanics Transaction Entities (Ref. Section 3.6.5 & 12.7.6).

9. No relationships between the Master Data Occurrence Event Entities and the Mechanics Transaction Entities (Ref. Section 3.6.6 & 12.7.7).

10. The Mechanics Transaction Entities could be related to as many Master Data Entities as needed by the business (except as indicated above).

11. The FK(s) in the Mechanics Transaction Associative Entities would represent the relationships to other Mechanics Transaction Entities, Mechanics Session Entities, Mechanism Procedure Entities, and the Master Data Entities.

The Best of Practice directions for these Mechanics Transaction Associative Entities are the same Best of Practice directions indicated in Section 13.4.

13.8 THE RESOLUTION OF RELATIONSHIPS BETWEEN THE MECHANISM & THE MECHANICS SESSION ENTITIES

No relationships between the Mechanism Procedure Entities and the Mechanics Session Entities.

13.9 THE RESOLUTION OF RELATIONSHIPS BETWEEN THE MECHANISM & THE MECHANICS TRANSACTION ENTITIES

The Interaction of the Mechanism Procedure Entities and the Mechanics Transaction Entities would reflect in the Enterprise Engineering Model the Interlink between the Machinery Procedures and the Operation Transactions. During the design process, One-to-One, One-to-Many, Many-to-One, and Many-to-Many relationships could be encountered relating the Mechanism Procedure (Non-associative or Associative) Entities (they must be Elementary

Procedures) with the Mechanics Transaction (Non-associative or Associative) Entities. Hereafter are the rules and resolution techniques governing these relationships:

1. The majority of relationships are One-to-Many from the Mechanism Procedure Entities to the Mechanics Transaction Entities.
2. One-to-One relationships relating the Mechanism Procedure Entities and the Mechanics Transaction Entities could exist in some business cases that are Not Common. The Mechanics Transaction Entity's data is contingent on the Mechanism Procedure Entities and not the opposite. Therefore the FKs must be in the Mechanics Transaction Entities and would represent their relationships to the Mechanism Procedure Entities.
3. One-to-Many relationships from the Mechanism Procedure Entities to the Mechanics Transaction Entities could exist. The FKs are in the Mechanics Transaction Entities and would represent their relationship to the Mechanism Procedure Entities.
4. Many-to-One relationships relating the Mechanism Procedure Entities to the Mechanics Transaction Entities could exist. These relationships are treated as Many-to-Many relationships and resolved as hereafter.
5. Any Many-to-Many relationship encountered between the Mechanism Procedure Entities and the Mechanics Transaction Entities would induce the need to review the analysis and assess the logic supporting this relationship. If the analysis is genuine, this relationship should be decomposed. The analysis would indicate either:
   - The need for additional relationships between the Mechanism Procedure Entities and the Mechanics Transaction Entities, these relationships should be established; or
   - The Associative Entity resulting from the relationship captures information related to the interrelations of Mechanism Procedure Entities with the Mechanics Transaction Entities. It is a Mechanics Transaction Associative Entity. This entity would have the features of the Mechanics Transaction Entities vis-à-vis the nature of the entities and their relationships with the Master Data, Mechanism, and the Mechanics Sessions and Transactions.
   - Otherwise the Enterprise Engineers should detect any flaws in the analysis and design.
6. The Mechanics Transaction Entities could be related to as many Mechanism Procedures Entities as needed by the business.
7. The Mechanics Transaction Entity must be related to at least one Mechanism Elementary Procedure Entity.
8. The FK(s) in the Mechanics Transaction Associative Entities would represent the relationships to other Mechanics Transaction Entities, Mechanics Session Entities, Mechanism Procedure Entities, and the Master Data Entities.

The Best of Practice directions for these Mechanics Transaction Associative Entities are the same directions indicated in Section 13.4.

13.10 THE RESOLUTION OF RELATIONSHIPS BETWEEN THE MECHANICS SESSION & THE MECHANICS TRANSACTION ENTITIES

Dr. Eng. M. Naoulo

The Interaction of the Mechanics Session Entities and the Mechanics Transaction Entities would reflect in the Enterprise Engineering Model the Interlink between the Operation Sessions and the Operation Transactions. During the design process, One-to-One, One-to-Many, Many-to-One, and Many-to-Many relationships could be encountered relating the Mechanics Session (Non-associative) Entities with the Mechanics Transaction (Non-associative) Entities. Hereafter are the rules and resolution techniques governing these relationships:

1. The majority of relationships are One-to-Many from the Mechanics Session Entities to the Mechanics Transaction Entities.

2. One-to-One relationships relating the Mechanics Session Entities and the Mechanics Transaction Entities could exist in some business cases that are Not Common. The Mechanics Transaction Entity's data is contingent on the Mechanics Session Entities and not the opposite. The FKs are in the Mechanics Transaction Entities and would represent their relationships to the Mechanics Sessions.

3. One-to-Many relationships from the Mechanics Session Entities to the Mechanics Transaction Entities could exist. The FKs are in the Mechanics Transaction Entities and would represent their relationships to the Mechanics Sessions.

4. Many-to-One relationships relating the Mechanics Session Entities to the Mechanics Transaction Entities could exist. These relationships are treated as Many-to-Many relationships and resolved as hereafter.

5. Any Many-to-Many relationship encountered between the Mechanics Session Entities and the Mechanics Transaction Entities would induce the need to review the analysis and assess the logic supporting this relationship. If the analysis is genuine, this relationship should be decomposed. The analysis would indicate either:
   - The need for additional relationships between the Mechanics Session Entities and the Mechanics Transaction Entities, these relationships should be established; or
   - The Associative Entity resulting from the relationship captures information related to the interrelations of Mechanics Session Entities with the Mechanics Transaction Entities. It is a Mechanics Transaction Associative Entity. This entity would have the features of the Mechanics Transaction Entities vis-à-vis the nature of the entities and their relationships with the Master Data, Mechanism, and the Mechanics Sessions and Transactions. In many cases this entity would capture the historical data related to the changes affecting the Transactions.
   - Otherwise the Enterprise Engineers should detect any flaws in the analysis and design.

6. The Mechanics Transaction Entities could be related to as many Mechanics Session Entities as needed by the business and vice-versa.

7. An Operation Transaction Incidence is created in the Enterprise by one Operation Session Incidence, modified by zero, one, or many Operation Session Incidences, and deleted by one Operation Session Incidence. This is reflected in the Enterprise Engineering Model by a Mechanics Transaction Instance that is generated by one Mechanics Session Instance, updated by zero, one, or many Mechanics Session Instances, and deleted or marked as deleted by one Mechanics Session Instance. Therefore each Operation Transaction must interlink to at least one Operation Session and each Mechanics Transaction Entity must be related to at least one Mechanics Session Entity or its subtypes.

8. The Mechanics Session Associative Entities cannot be related to the Mechanics Transactions.
9. The Mechanics Transaction Associative Entities cannot be related to the Mechanics Sessions.

The Best of Practice directions for these Mechanics Transaction Associative Entities are the same directions indicated in Section 13.4.

13.11 SUMMARY OF RESOLUTION OF MANY-TO-MANY RELATIONSHIPS

No Many-to-Many relationships should remain in the logical Enterprise Engineering Model. All these Many-to-Many relationships are resolved as per the techniques detailed in this chapter. The following table summarizes the resolution of the Many-to-Many relationships between Entities belonging to the same or different Enterprise Engineering Constituents.

From Constituent or Component or Domain	To Constituent or Component or Domain	Resulting Associative Entities	Features of the Resulting Associative Entities	Reference
Master Data other than Activities or Occurrence Events	Master Data other than Activities or Occurrence Events	➢ Master Data Associative Entities ➢ Mechanics Session Associative Entities ➢ Mechanics Transaction Associative Entities	➢ Would have the features of the Master Data Entities ➢ Would have the features of the Mechanics Session Entities ➢ Would have the features of the Mechanics Transaction Entities	13.1.11, 13.1.12, & 13.1.13
Master Data Activities	Master Data	➢ Master Data Activity Associative Entities ➢ Mechanics Session Associative Entities ➢ Mechanics Transaction Associative Entities	➢ Would have the features of the Master Data Activity Entities ➢ Would have the features of the Mechanics Session Entities ➢ Would have the features of the Mechanics Transaction Entities	13.1.9, 13.1.14, & 13.1.20

Dr. Eng. M. Naoulo

Master Data Occurrence Events	Master Data other than Activities	➢ Master Data Occurrence Event Associative Entities	➢ Would have the features of the Master Data Occurrence Events Entities	13.1.10 & 13.1.15
		➢ Mechanics Session Associative Entities	➢ Would have the features of the Mechanics Session Entities	
		➢ Mechanics Transaction Associative Entities	➢ Would have the features of the Mechanics Transaction Entities	
Mechanism Procedures	Mechanism Procedures	➢ Mechanism Procedure Associative Entities	➢ Would have the features of the Mechanism Procedure Entities	13.2.4 & 13.2.5
		➢ Mechanics Transaction Associative Entities	➢ Would have the features of the Mechanics Transaction Entities	
Mechanics Sessions	Mechanics Sessions	➢ Mechanics Session Associative Entities	➢ Would have the features of the Mechanics Session Entities	13.3.4 & 13.3.5
		➢ Mechanics Transaction Associative Entities	➢ Would have the features of the Mechanics Transaction Entities	
Mechanics Transactions	Mechanics Transactions	➢ Mechanics Transaction Associative Entities	➢ Would have the features of the Mechanics Transaction Entities	13.4.4 & 13.4.5
Master Data other than Activities or Occurrence Events	Mechanism Procedures	➢ Mechanism Procedure Associative Entities	➢ Would have the features of the Mechanism Procedure Entities	13.5.5 & 13.5.7
		➢ Mechanics Transaction Associative Entities	➢ Would have the features of the Mechanics Transaction Entities	

Dr. Eng. M. Naoulo

Master Data Activities	Mechanism Procedures	No Relations		13.5.2
Master Data Occurrence Events	Mechanism Procedures	No Many-to-One Relationships & No Many-to-Many Relationships		13.5.6 & 13.5.8
Master Data	Mechanics Sessions	➤ Mechanics Session Associative Entities	➤ Would have the features of the Mechanics Session Entities	13.6.4 & 13.6.5
		➤ Mechanics Transaction Associative Entities	➤ Would have the features of the Mechanics Transaction Entities	
Master Data other than Activities or Occurrence Events	Mechanics Transactions	Mechanics Transaction Associative Entities	➤ Would have the features of the Mechanics Transaction Entities	13.7.6 & 13.7.7
Master Data Activities	Mechanics Transactions	No Relations		13.7.8
Master Data Occurrence Events	Mechanics Transactions	No Relations		13.7.9
Mechanism Procedures	Mechanics Sessions	No Relations		13.8
Mechanism Procedures	Mechanics Transactions	➤ Mechanics Transaction Associative Entities	➤ Would have the features of the Mechanics Transaction Entities	13.9.4 & 13.9.5
Mechanics Sessions	Mechanics Transactions	➤ Mechanics Transaction Associative Entities	➤ Would have the features of the Mechanics Transaction Entities	13.10.4 & 13.10.5

Table 13.1 The Resolution of Many-to-Many Relationships

Dr. Eng. M. Naoulo

14. APPENDIX C: Enterprise Engineering Model's Associative Entities

The analysis of Enterprise Engineering uncovers many Associative Entities. The techniques used for the analysis and design of these entities are detailed in Chapters 2, 12, & 13. This chapter provides more in-depth assessment of these entities and summarizes their destination realm.

The source and destination realms of Associative Entities are:

	Source Realm of the Associative Entities	Destination Realm of the Associative Entities (Where the Associative Entities belong)	Reference
1	The Associative Entities within the Master Data Constituent	Master Data or Mechanics Constituents	Sections 12.1 & 13.1
2	The Associative Entities within the Mechanism Constituent	Mechanism Constituent or Mechanics Transactions Domain	Sections 12.2 & 13.2
3	The Associative Entities within the Mechanics Sessions Domain	Mechanics Constituent	Sections 12.3 & 13.3
4	The Associative Entities within the Mechanics Transactions Domain	Mechanics Transactions Domain	Sections 12.4 & 13.4
5	The Associative Entities between the Master Data and the Mechanism	Mechanism Constituent or Mechanics Transactions Domain	Sections 12.5 & 13.5
6	The Associative Entities between the Master Data and the Mechanics Sessions	Mechanics Constituent	Sections 12.6 & 13.6
7	The Associative Entities between the Master Data and the Mechanics Transactions	Mechanics Transactions Domain	Sections 12.7 & 13.7
8	The Associative Entities between the Mechanism and the Mechanics Sessions	No Associative Entities	Sections 12.8 & 13.8
9	The Associative Entities between the Mechanism and the Mechanics Transactions	Mechanics Transactions Domain	Sections 12.9 & 13.9
10	The Associative Entities between the Mechanics Sessions and the Mechanics Transactions	Mechanics Transactions Domain	Sections 12.10 & 13.10

Table 14.1: The Source & Destination Realms of Associative Entities within the Enterprise Engineering Model

The nature and behavior of the Associative Entities would be the same as the nature and behavior of the entities of the destination realms indicated in the 3rd column of Table 14.1. It is important to note that the Master Data Entities (associative and non-associative) constitute the "parental" side of the relationships between the Master Data and other constituents of the Enterprise Engineering.

Furthermore there are restrictions on the Interaction of Associative Entities with other entities. Table 14.2 indicates these restrictions.

	Source Realm of the Associative Entities	Destination Realm of the Associative Entity	Restrictions
1	Master Data Constituent	Master Data Constituent	Similar to Non-Associative Master Data Entities
2	Mechanism Constituent	Mechanism Constituent	Similar to Non-Associative Mechanism Entities
3	Mechanics Sessions Domain	Mechanics Sessions Domain	Similar to Non-Associative Mechanics Session Entities
4	Mechanics Transactions Domain	Mechanics Transactions Domain	Similar to Non-Associative Mechanics Transaction Entities
5	Master Data Constituent	Mechanism Constituent	Similar to Non-Associative Mechanism Constituent Entities
6	Master Data Constituent	Mechanics Constituent	Similar to Non-Associative Mechanics Constituent Entities. Furthermore No Relations from the Master Data Entities involving Activities or Events to the Mechanics Session Associative Entities
7	Master Data Constituent	Mechanics Transactions Domain	Similar to Non-Associative Mechanics Transaction Entities
8	Mechanism Constituent	Mechanics Sessions Domain	No Relations
9	Mechanism Constituent	Mechanics Transactions Domain	Similar to Non-Associative Mechanics Transaction Entities

Dr. Eng. M. Naoulo

10	Mechanics Sessions Domain	Mechanics Transactions Domain	Similar to Non-Associative Mechanics Transaction Entities. Furthermore No Relations from the Mechanics Session Entities to the Mechanics Transaction Associative Entities

Table 14.2: Restrictions on the Interaction of Associative Entities

14.1 MASTER DATA ASSOCIATIVE ENTITIES

Table 14.1 indicates that the only Enterprise Engineering Associative Entities which destination realm might be the Master Data Constituent are those that have their sources within this constituent. Table 3.2 provides an outline of the Many-to-Many relationships between the entities of the Master Data. Section 13.1 provides detailed approach to analyze the resolution of these Many-to-Many relationships which might end up with the creation of Master Data Associative Entities.

14.2 RULES CORRELATED WITH THE MASTER DATA ASSOCIATIVE ENTITIES

A Master Data Associative Entity associates at least two parent Master Data Entities (in the case of Master Data Associative Entity resolving recursive relationships these two parent entities are the same). The key of the Master Data Associative Entity is a concatenated key that includes the keys of the parent(s) Master Data Entities. If a Surrogate Key is used for a Master Data Associative Entity, the keys of the parent Master Data Entities would form part of Alternate key(s).

The Mechanics Session or Transaction Entities or Mechanism Procedure Entities related to these Master Data Associative Entities would be related to the parent Master Data Dimension Entities thru these Associative Entities. Of course the Mechanics Session or Transaction Entities or Mechanism Procedure Entities could also be related directly to any Master Data Entity. The relationships of the Mechanics Session or Transaction Entities or Mechanism Procedure Entities to the Master Data Associative Entities would be part of the Enterprise engineering Model satisfying the rules enunciated in Section 3.10.

14.3 EXAMPLES OF MASTER DATA ASSOCIATIVE ENTITIES

Diagram 14.1 shows two Master Data Associative Entities:
  ➤ **A FR&TP OFFICE STAFF** indicates the office(s) where the FR&TP staff works.

  Note: In the design of this model, the entity **A FR&TP OFFICE STAFF COST** could

Dr. Eng. M. Naoulo

be related directly into the entities **LOC BUSINESS OFFICE** and **OPR FR&TP STAFF** as the case of **A FR&TP TELEPHONE STAFF COST** instead of its relation to **A FR&TP OFFICE STAFF,** however this design was chosen for two reasons:

- The entity **A FR&TP OFFICE STAFF** is needed to indicate the assignment of the Office Staff to the different offices including the main Office.
- To show a case of associative entity related to another associative entity.

➤ **A FLIGHT OPERATION IN AIRPORT COST** incorporates the cost of operation of a specific Airplane at a specific Airport. It provides the cost of airplane operation while stationing in the airport for boarding and un-boarding of passengers. This is needed for analyzing the operation cost of the Airline fleet (it is outside the Case Studies 1 & 2).

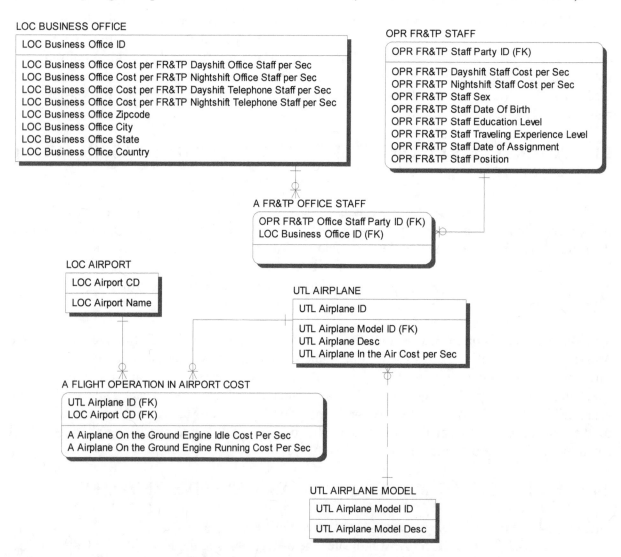

Diagram 14.1: Example of Master Data Associative Entities not involving Activities

---

Dr. Eng. M. Naoulo

Diagram 14.2b shows two Master Data Activity Associative Entities that are reflecting extreme settings (This model represents a business case that is outside the Case Studies 1 & 2):

➤ **ACT CLASS GIVING CONTROL** incorporates the Session controls pertinent to giving a Class by a specific Teacher for a specific Curriculum Course using a specific Textbook in a specific Class Room.

➤ **ACT CLASS ATTENDANCE CONTROL** incorporates the Session controls pertinent to attending a Class by a specific Student where this Class is given by a specific Teacher for a specific Curriculum Course a using specific Textbook in a specific Class Room. Of course these settings are extreme and in ordinary environment the rules would not require such details, constraints, and restrictions.

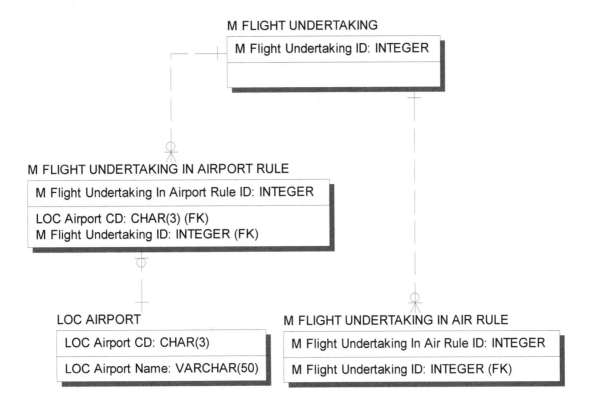

Diagram 14.2a: Example of a Mechanism Procedure Associative Entity

Dr. Eng. M. Naoulo

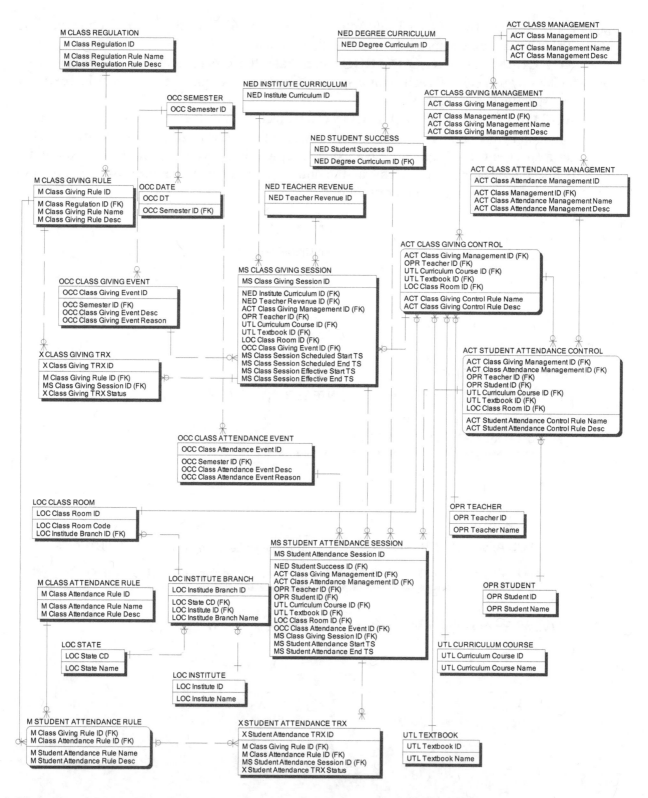

Diagram 14.2b: Example of Master Data Activity Associative Entities & Mechanism Procedure Associative Entity

Dr. Eng. M. Naoulo

14.4 MECHANISM PROCEDURE ASSOCIATIVE ENTITIES

Table 14.1 indicates that the only Enterprise Engineering Associative Entities which destination realm might be the Mechanism Constituent are those that have their sources within this constituent and those that have their sources from the association of the Master Data and the Mechanism. Table 3.2 provides an outline of the Many-to-Many relationships between the entities of the Mechanism Procedure. Table 3.3 provides an outline of the Many-to-Many relationships between the entities of the Master Data and the entities of the Mechanism Procedures. Sections 13.2 & 13.5 provide detailed approach to analyze the resolution of these Many-to-Many relationships which might end up with the creation of Mechanism Procedure Associative Entities.

14.5 RULES CORRELATED WITH THE MECHANISM PROCEDURE ASSOCIATIVE ENTITIES

A Mechanism Procedure Associative Entity associates at least two parent Mechanism Procedure Entities (in the case of Mechanism Procedure Associative Entity resolving recursive relationships these entities are the same) or at least one parent Mechanism Procedure Entity and one parent Master Data Entity. The key of the Mechanism Procedure Associative Entity is a concatenated key that includes the keys of the parent(s) Mechanism Procedure and - if applicable - the keys of the parent(s) Master Data Entities. If a Surrogate Key is used for a Mechanism Procedure Associative Entity, the keys of the parent Mechanism Procedure Entities and the keys of the parent Master Data Entities would form part of the Alternate key(s); Diagram 14.2a illustrates this case.

The Mechanics Transaction Entities and the Mechanism Procedure Entities related to these Mechanism Procedure Associative Entities would be related to the parent Mechanism Procedure Entity(ies) and the parent Master Data Entity(ies) thru these Associative Entities. Of course the Mechanics Transaction Entities and the Mechanism Procedure Entities could also be related directly to any Mechanism Procedure or Master Data Entity. The relationships of the Mechanics Transaction Entities or Mechanism Procedure Entities to the Mechanism Procedure Associative Entities would be part of the Enterprise engineering Model satisfying the rules enunciated in Section 3.10.

14.6 EXAMPLE OF MECHANISM PROCEDURE ASSOCIATIVE ENTITIES

Diagram 14.2b shows a Mechanism Procedure Associative Entity that is reflecting an extreme setting:
  ➢ **M STUDENT ATTENDANCE RULE** incorporates the Transaction Rules pertinent to attending a Class regulated by specific giving and attending rules.

Dr. Eng. M. Naoulo

14.7 MECHANICS SESSION ASSOCIATIVE ENTITIES

Table 14.1 indicates that the only Enterprise Engineering Associative Entities which destination realm might be the Mechanics Sessions Domain are those that have their sources:
  ➢ Within this Domain
  ➢ Within the Master Data Constituent
  ➢ From the association of the Master Data and the Mechanics Sessions.

Table 3.2 provides an outline of the Many-to-Many relationships between the entities of the Mechanics Sessions and between the entities of the Master Data. Table 3.3 provides an outline of the Many-to-Many relationships between the Entities of the Master Data and the entities of the Mechanics Sessions. Sections 13.3 & 13.6 provide detailed approach to analyze the resolution of these Many-to-Many relationships which might end up with the creation of Mechanics Session Associative Entities.

14.8 RULES CORRELATED WITH THE MECHANICS SESSION ASSOCIATIVE ENTITIES

A Mechanics Session Associative Entity associates at least two parent Mechanics Session Entities (in the case of Mechanics Session Associative Entity resolving recursive relationships these entities are the same) or at least one parent Mechanics Session Entity and one parent Master Data Entity. The key of the Mechanics Session Associative Entity is a concatenated key that includes the keys of the parent(s) Mechanics Session and - if applicable - the keys of the parent(s) Master Data Entities. If a Surrogate Key is used for a Mechanics Session Associative Entity, the keys of the parent Mechanics Session Entities and the keys of the parent Master Data Entities would form part of the Alternate key(s).

The Mechanics Session and Transaction Entities related to these Mechanics Session Associative Entities would be related to the parent Mechanics Session Entity(ies) and the parent Master Data Entity(ies) thru these Associative Entities. Of course the Mechanics Session Entities and the Mechanics Transaction Entities could also be related directly to any Master Data Entity. The relationships of the Mechanics Session Entities or Mechanics Transaction Entities to the Mechanics Session Associative Entities would be part of the Enterprise engineering Model satisfying the rules enunciated in Section 3.10.

14.9 EXAMPLE OF MECHANICS SESSION ASSOCIATIVE ENTITIES

Diagram 14.3 shows two Mechanics Session Associative Entities:
  ➢ **MS FR&TP SESSIONS RELATION** incorporates the relationships between the FR&TP Sessions.
  ➢ **MS FR&TP & CSS SESSIONS RELATION** incorporates the relationships between the FR&TP Sessions and the FR&TP Customer Satisfaction Survey Sessions.

Dr. Eng. M. Naoulo

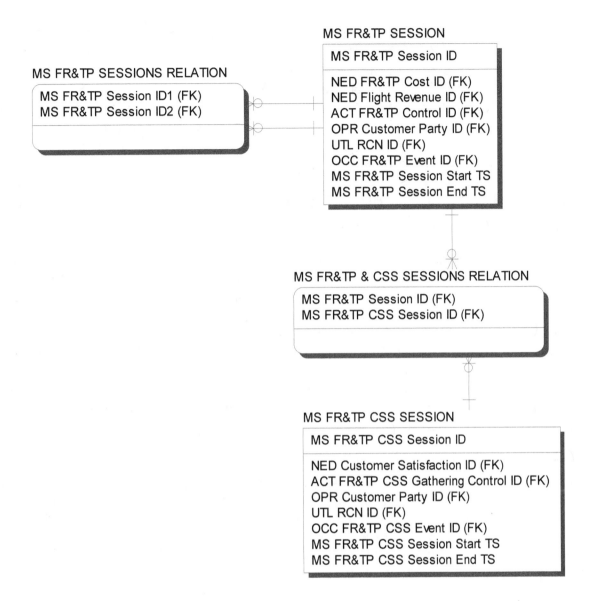

Diagram 14.3: Example of Mechanics Session Associative Entities

14.10 MECHANICS TRANSACTION ASSOCIATIVE ENTITIES

Table 14.1 indicates that the Enterprise Engineering Associative Entities which destination realm is the Mechanics Transactions Domain are those that have their sources:
  ➢ Within this Domain
  ➢ Within the Master Data Constituent
  ➢ Within the Mechanism Constituent
  ➢ Within the Mechanics Sessions Domain
  ➢ From the association of the Master Data and the Mechanism
  ➢ From the association of the Master Data and the Mechanics Sessions
  ➢ From the association of the Master Data and the Mechanics Transactions
  ➢ From the association of the Mechanism and the Mechanics Transactions

Dr. Eng. M. Naoulo

➢ From the association of the Mechanics Sessions and the Mechanics Transactions.

Table 3.2 provides an outline of the Many-to-Many relationships between the entities of the Mechanics Transactions. Table 3.3 provides an outline of the Many-to-Many relationships between the entities of the Master Data, Mechanism Procedures, and Mechanics Sessions with the Mechanics Transactions. Sections 13.4, 13.7, 13.9, & 13.10 provide detailed approach to analyze the resolution of these Many-to-Many relationships which might end up with the creation of Mechanics Transaction Associative Entities.

14.11 RULES CORRELATED WITH THE MECHANICS TRANSACTION ASSOCIATIVE ENTITIES

A Mechanics Transaction Associative Entity associates at least two parent Mechanics Transaction Entities (in the case of Mechanics Transaction Associative Entity resolving recursive relationships these entities are the same) or at least one parent Mechanics Transaction Entity and one parent Master Data or Mechanism Procedure or Mechanics Session Entity. The key of the Mechanics Transaction Associative Entity is a concatenated key that includes the keys of the parent(s) Mechanics Transaction and – if applicable – the keys of the parent(s) Master Data and/or Mechanism Procedure and/or Mechanics Session Entities. If a Surrogate Key is used for a Mechanics Transaction Associative Entity, the keys of the parent Mechanics Transaction Entities and the keys of the parent Master Data, Mechanism Procedure, and Mechanics Session Entities would form part of the Alternate key(s).

The Mechanics Transaction Entities related to these Mechanics Transaction Associative Entities would be related to the parent Mechanics Transaction Entity(ies) and the parent Master Data, Mechanism Procedures, and Mechanics Sessions Entity(ies) thru these Associative Entities. Of course the Mechanics Transaction Entities could also be related directly to any Master Data, or Mechanism Procedure, or Mechanics Session, or Mechanics Transaction Entities. The relationships of the Mechanics Transaction Entities to the Mechanics Transaction Associative Entities would be part of the Enterprise engineering Model solution satisfying the rules enunciated in Section 3.10.

14.12 EXAMPLE OF MECHANICS TRANSACTION ASSOCIATIVE ENTITIES

Diagram 14.4 shows three Mechanics Transaction Associative Entities:
➢ **X PASSENGER RESERVATION TRX RELATION** incorporates the relationships between the FR&TP Passenger Reservation Transactions.
➢ **X CUSTOMER PAYMENT TRX RELATION** incorporates the relationships between the FR&TP Customer Payment Transactions.
➢ **X RESERVATION PAYMENT TRX RELATION** incorporates the relationships between the FR&TP Passenger Reservation Transactions and the FR&TP Customer Payment Transactions.

Dr. Eng. M. Naoulo

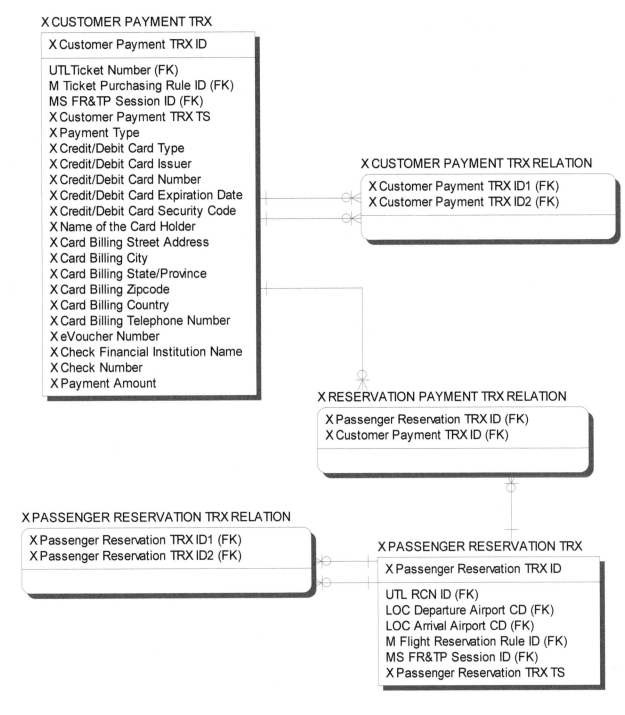

Diagram 14.4: Example of Mechanics Transaction Associative Entities

15. APPENDIX D: Transactional Data Models

The Transactional Data Model could be derived from the Enterprise Engineering Model. To accomplish this, two approaches to get the Transactional Data Model are presented. These approaches were applied on the Case Study 1 (additional info could be found in Section 4.3):

- Removing the Mechanics Session attributes from the Enterprise Engineering Model. Diagram 15.1 provides the Transactional Data Model resulting from applying this action on Diagram 10.8. The changes affecting the Enterprise Engineering Model are minimal. All relationships are kept intact.
- Removing from the Enterprise Engineering Model the Mechanism, the Mechanics Sessions, and the Master Data associated with the functioning of the enterprise: in the majority of cases Needs and Activities and the Master Data (Associative and Non-associative) Entities and attributes related to the cost and Occurrence Events. Also reallocate most of the relationships (some of these relationships might not be needed in OLTP) that relate the Mechanics Sessions and the Mechanism Procedures to the Master Data to relate the Mechanics Transactions directly to the Master Data. This is the Information Engineering Data Model used in OLTP. Diagram 15.2 provides the Transactional Data Model resulting from applying this action on Diagram 10.8.

These diagrams could be used as base for Business Intelligence.

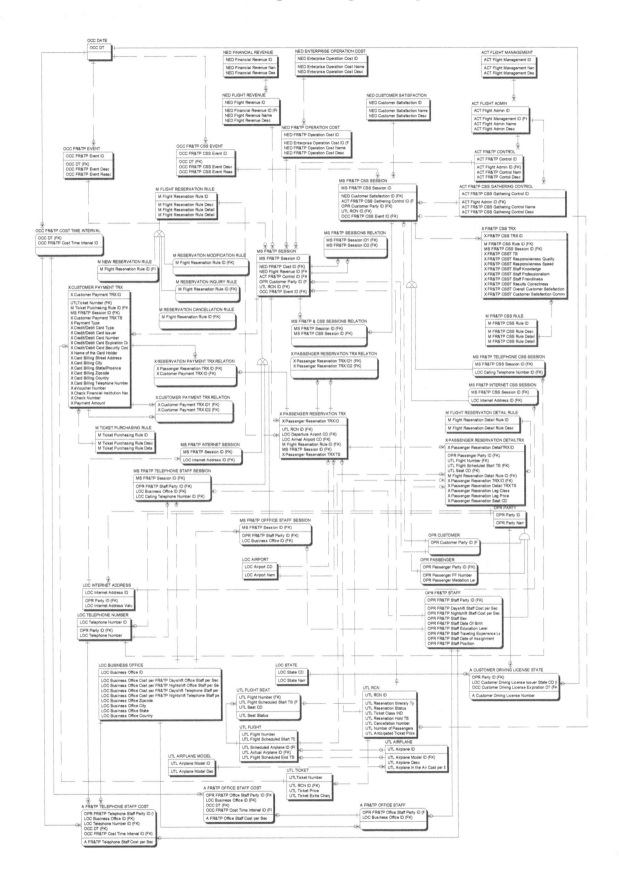

Dr. Eng. M. Naoulo

Diagram 15.1: Transactional Data Model derived from Diagram 10.8

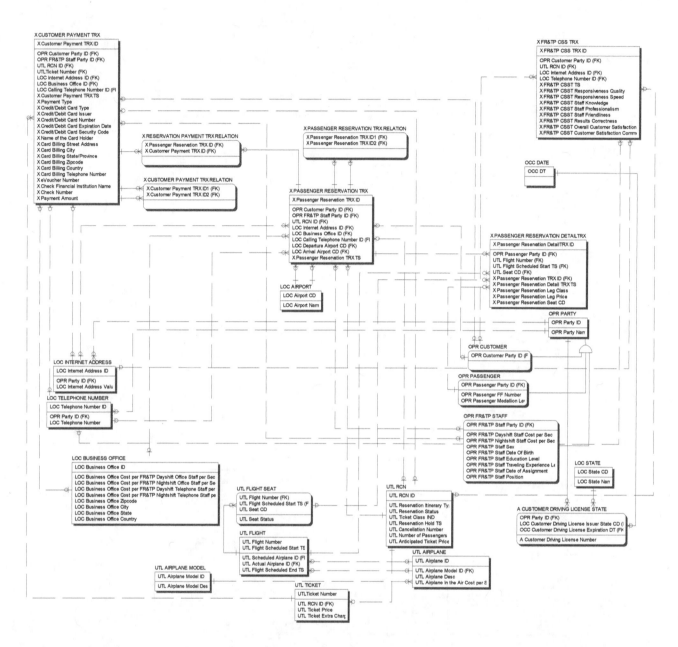

Diagram 15.2: Information Engineering OLTP Data Model derived from Diagram 10.8

Dr. Eng. M. Naoulo

16. Glossary & Index

Term	Section	Definition
Apparatus	2.1 & 2.2	The Apparatus includes the main players and objects that intervene in the operation of Enterprises. It is represented in the Enterprise Engineering Model by the Master Data.
Apparatus Activity	2.2.2	The Apparatus Activity controls the Operation Sessions. It is part of the Apparatus and answers the question HOW the Enterprise functions.
Apparatus Component	2.2	The Apparatus includes six components: Needs, Activities, Operators, Utilities, Locations, and Occurrences that answer the six questions related to the Enterprise Functioning: WHY, HOW, WHO, WHAT, WHERE, and WHEN. The Apparatus Component is composed of Apparatus Members.
Apparatus Location	2.2.5	The Apparatus Location could be a physical one: Building, Surgery Operation Room, etc. and could be virtual one; Telephone Number, URL, etc. The Apparatus Location answers the question WHERE the Enterprise functions or operates.
Apparatus Member	2.2	An Apparatus Member is a building block of the Apparatus about which information is needed and gathered.
Apparatus Need	2.2.1	The Apparatus Need indicates the reasons behind the functioning of the Enterprise. It incorporates the business requirements to be satisfied by the Enterprise functioning. It answers the question WHY the Enterprise functions.
Apparatus Occurrence	2.2.6	The Apparatus Occurrences include the date, time, time intervals, chronological periods, and the Events. It answers the question WHEN the sessions or when the transactions occurred.
Apparatus Operator	2.2.3	The Apparatus Operators designate the representatives and agents involved in the Operation. The Apparatus Operator could be a physical one: Customer, etc., and could be virtual one: Computer System, etc. It answers the question WHO the Enterprise deals with.
Apparatus Utility	2.2.4	The Apparatus Utilities include all the materiel and materials that the Enterprise uses to function. The Apparatus Utility could be physical ingredients: supply, commodity, Spare Part, Lottery Ticket, etc. and could be virtual one: Airline Flight, Taxi Ride, etc. It answers the question WHAT are the ingredients of the Sessions and Transactions.

Dr. Eng. M. Naoulo

Business Function	2.2.2	Main undertaking of an Enterprise: Manufacturing, Services, Material Handling, Information Processing, Development, Marketing, etc.
Business Intelligence	4.2	Business Intelligence aims to evaluate the Operation of the enterprise thru historical and current assessment of the enterprise's Transactional Data and provides their analysis.
Business Intelligence Data Marts	4.	The Business Intelligence Data Marts constitute the base for the classical Data Warehousing's Online Analytical Processing (OLAP) and provide query and reporting covering the historical aggregation of transactional features of the Enterprise.
Business Intelligence Dimension	4.4.1	The BI Dimension Entities include descriptive non-transactional data and non-process data. Their structure follows two schemas: Star Schema and Snowflake Schema.
Business Intelligence Fact	4.4.2	The BI Fact Entities include transactional data and Foreign Keys. Their structure is based on a central entity (the Fact entity) surrounded by Dimension entities.
Business Model	7.4	The Business Model represents various aspects of business, including its purpose, offerings, strategies, infrastructure, organizational structures, trading practices, and operational processes and policies.
Central Data Repository	6.	The Central Data Repository stores the integrated and consolidated Master Data and ultimately the Mechanism and Mechanics Transactional and Process Data.
Decomposition Diagram	2.7	Function decomposition is the breakdown of the activities of the enterprise into progressively greater detail [5].
Elementary Activity	2.2.2	The Activity directly interacting with the Operation Sessions is denoted by Elementary Activity. It is very often the lowest level of Activities.
Elementary Procedure	2.3	The Procedure directly interacting with the Operation Transactions is denoted by Elementary Procedure. It is very often the lowest level of Procedures.
Enterprise Constituent	2.1	The Enterprise's Information has three constituents that interlink to enable the functioning of the Enterprise: The Apparatus, the Machinery, and the Operation.
Enterprise Data Architecture	6.	The Enterprise Data Architecture involves Master, Transactional, and Process Data and comprises: ➢ Design the overall Enterprise Data Architecture including the Central Data Repository and ODS. ➢ Design the Business Intelligence Data Marts responding to the BI Analytical requirements and needs.

		➢ Design the Enterprise Intelligence Data Marts responding to the EI Analytical requirements and needs.
		➢ Extraction, transformation, loading, and storing the data in the Data Marts.
		➢ Design and development of query and reporting technical milieu to generate comprehensible results responding to the Analytical needs.
Enterprise Data Framework	2.	The Enterprise Data Framework lists and describes the structure of the Enterprise building blocks that contribute and participate in the construction and implementation of the Enterprise Data Architecture and Enterprise Engineering.
Enterprise Data Management	1.3	The Enterprise Data Management includes: ➢ Design, distribution, structure, modeling techniques, integration, metadata and data dictionary, consolidation, matching, referential integrity, propagation, mapping, links and relations, conversion, synchronization, Extraction, Transformation, and Loading (ETL and ELT), traceability, lineage, and standards of the enterprise data. ➢ Data governance, quality assurance (completeness, validity, consistency, timeliness/freshness, accuracy/precision, reliability, availability, and uniqueness), collection, aggregation, security, profiling, cleansing, stewardship, storage, archiving, and backup and recovery of the enterprise data.
Enterprise Engineering	7.2 & 7.4	The meticulous application of IT modeling principles to design and develop an Enterprise Engineering Framework and its Enterprise Engineering Model, reflecting the structures, apparatus, processes, machinery procedures, and operation, and their interlinks, and to proceed the current Model with full cognizance of its design; or to forecast their behavior under specific operating conditions; in order to assess and improve the performance of these enterprises. The Enterprise Engineering curriculum details a comprehensive approach for analyzing the functioning of Enterprises and includes Framework, Methodology, Guidelines, and Deliverables, and Modeling Techniques which provide the enterprises with the instruments to empower them to improve their performance and contribute to accomplish their objectives.

Dr. Eng. M. Naoulo

Enterprise Engineering Model	7.4	The Enterprise Engineering Model represents the operational aspects of the Enterprises and their relations to the Enterprise's needs. It provides is a blueprint of current/future enterprise's operative. It provides a clear and concise technical infrastructure reflecting and illustrating the Enterprises' functioning and representing and measuring their operations. The processing of this model reflects the execution of the Enterprise Engineering System of Apparatus, Machinery, and Operation (SAM O NAOULO) and underlines the strengths, weaknesses, efficiency, and performance of the Enterprise's operation.
Enterprise Intelligence	4. & 4.2	Enterprise Intelligence aims to analyze the performance of the enterprise thru historical, current, and predictive assessment of the enterprise's operation. It is dealing with Process Data and provides their analysis.
Enterprise Intelligence Data Marts	4.	The Enterprise Intelligence Data Marts constitute the base for the enterprise's improvement and revitalization and provide query and reporting covering the historical aggregation of sessions' features to illustrate the operation of the Enterprise.
Enterprise Intelligence Dimension	4.6.1	The EI Dimension Entities include descriptive non-transactional and non-process data. Their structure follows two schemas: Star Schema and Snowflake Schema.
Enterprise Intelligence Fact	4.6.2	The EI Fact Entities include process data and Foreign Keys. Their structure is based on a central entity (the Fact entity) surrounded by Dimension entities.
Enterprise's Operation Improvement	8.12	The Enterprise's Operation Improvement is realized thru the analysis of the processing and then the optimization of the **SAM O NAOULO** Enterprise Engineering Model representing the business functions.
Enterprise's Operation Revitalization	8.13	The Enterprise's Operation Revitalization is realized thru the redesign of the **SAM O NAOULO** Enterprise Engineering Model representing the business functions.
Event	2.2.6	An Event is a happening that triggers one or many Operation Sessions.
External Data	2.2.8	External Data is Master Data that is defined and controlled by external organizations.
Interaction	2.11	The Interactions between the Master Data, Mechanism, and Mechanics represent in the Enterprise Engineering Model the Interlinks between the Apparatus, Machinery, and Operation. They are illustrated thru relationships in the Enterprise Engineering Model Entity-Relationship Diagram.
Interlinks	2.6	The Interlinks denote the connections between and within the building blocks of the Enterprise Constituents.

Dr. Eng. M. Naoulo

Machinery	2.1 & 2.3	The Enterprise Machinery embodies the Procedures that encompass the Enterprise internal and external rules and regulations, guidelines, techniques, etc. governing the Operation Transactions of the Enterprise. It is represented in the Enterprise Engineering Model by the Mechanism.
Machinery Procedure	2.3	The Machinery Procedures encompass the rules and regulations governing the Operation Transactions.
Master Data	2.8.1	The Master Data represents the Apparatus in the Enterprise Engineering Model.
Master Data Activity Associative Entity	13.1.14	The Master Data Activity Associative Entity resulting from the Many-to-Many relationship encountered between the Master Data Activity Entities, or involving Master Data Activity Entity(ies), or involving Master Data Activity Associative Entity(ies) resulting from relationships across Master Data Components, or Many-to-Many recursive convoluted relationships affecting the Master Data Activity Entities. This entity would have the features of the Master Data Activity Entities vis-à-vis the nature of the entities and their relationships with the Master Data, Mechanism, and the Mechanics Sessions and Transactions.
Master Data Associative Entity	13.1.13	The Master Data Associative Entity resulting from the Many-to-Many relationship encountered between · the entities of the Master Data across Master Data Components (none is Activity or Occurrence Event) or involving Master Data Associative Entities resulting from relationships across Master Data Components (none is Activity or Occurrence Event), or Many-to-Many recursive convoluted relationships affecting the Master Data Entities. This entity would have the features of the Master Data Entities vis-à-vis the nature of the entities and their relationships with the Master Data, Mechanism, and the Mechanics Sessions and Transactions.

Master Data Occurrence Event Associative Entity	13.1.15	The Master Data Associative Entity resulting from the Many-to-Many relationship encountered between the Master Data Occurrence Event Entities, or involving Master Data Occurrence Event Entity(ies) but not Master Data Activity Entity(ies), or involving Master Data Occurrence Event Associative Entities resulting from relationships across Master Data Components (none is Activity), or Many-to-Many recursive convoluted relationships affecting the Master Data Occurrence Event Entities. This entity would have the features of the Master Data Occurrence Event Entities vis-à-vis the nature of the entities and their relationships with the Master Data, Mechanism, and the Mechanics Sessions and Transactions
Master Data Component	2.8.1	The Master Data Component represents in the Enterprise Engineering Model the Apparatus Component.
Master Data Dimension	2.8.1	A Master Data Dimension represents in the Enterprise Engineering Model an Apparatus Member.
Master Data Dimension Profile	2.8.1	The Master Data Dimension Profile is a group of entities that completely represent the Apparatus Member. It holds the detail data about a Master Data Dimension. It is illustrated in the Enterprise Engineering Model's Entity-Relationship Diagram by a set of entities and their relationships.
MDM Consolidation Hub	6.3.3, Table 6.1 & Diagram 6.4	The MDM Consolidation Hub holds all the Master Data. The Legacy Systems will be the Data Entry point for all Master, Transactional, and Process Data. These systems will update the MDM Consolidation Hub with Master Data either real-time or near real-time or batch. The MDM Consolidation Hub will feedback its data to update the Legacy Systems either real-time or near real-time or batch.
MDM Consolidation Repository	6.3.2, Table 6.1 & Diagram 6.3	The MDM Consolidation Repository holds all the Master Data. The Legacy Systems will be the Data Entry point for all Master, Transactional, and Process Data. These systems will update the MDM Consolidation Repository with Master Data either real-time or near real-time or batch. No Data Feedback from the MDM Consolidation Repository to the Legacy Systems.

Dr. Eng. M. Naoulo

MDM Master Data Hub	6.3.5, Table 6.1 & Diagram 6.6	The MDM Master Data Hub holds all the Master Data. The Legacy Systems will be a Data Entry point for Master Data and all Transactional and Process Data. The Master Data could also be entered directly into the MDM Master Data Hub. The Legacy Systems will update the MDM Master Data Hub with Master Data either real-time or near real-time or batch. The MDM Master Data Hub will feedback its data to update the Legacy Systems either real-time or near real-time or batch.
MDM Master Data Repository	6.3.4, Table 6.1 & Diagram 6.5	The MDM Master Data Repository holds all the Master Data. The Legacy Systems will be a Data Entry point for Master and all Transactional and Process Data. The Master Data could also be entered directly into the MDM Master Data Repository. The Legacy Systems will update the MDM Master Data Repository with Master Data either real-time or near real-time or batch. No Data Feedback from the MDM Master Data Repository to the Legacy Systems.
MDM Registry Repository	6.3.1, Table 6.1 & Diagram 6.2	The MDM Registry Repository holds only main data about the Master Data and links to the Legacy Systems for additional Master Data retrieval. The Legacy Systems will be the Data Entry point for all Master, Transactional, and Process Data. These systems will update the MDM Registry Repository with part of the Master Data either real-time or near real-time or batch. No Data Feedback from the MDM Registry Repository to the Legacy Systems.
Mechanics	2.8.3	The Mechanics represents in the Enterprise Engineering Model the Enterprise Operation. It includes two domains: the Mechanics Sessions and the Mechanics Transactions.
Mechanics Session	2.8.3.1	A Mechanics Session represents Session in the Enterprise Engineering Model an Operation Session.
Mechanics Session Associative Entity	13.3.5, 13.6.5, & 13.1.12	The Mechanics Session Associative Entity resulting from the Many-to-Many relationship encountered between the entities of the Mechanics Sessions, or between the entities of the Master Data, or between the Master Data Entities and the Mechanics Session Entities, or Many-to-Many recursive convoluted relationships affecting the Mechanics Session Entities. This entity would have the features of the Mechanics Session Entities vis-à-vis the nature of the entities and their relationships with the Master Data, Mechanism, and the Mechanics Sessions and Transactions.
Mechanics Session Instance	2.4.1 & 2.8.3.1	A Mechanics Session Instance represents in the Enterprise Engineering Model an Operation Session Incidence.

Mechanics Session Profile	2.8.3.1	The Mechanics Session Profile is a group of entities that completely represent the Operation Session. It holds the detail data about a Mechanics Session. It is illustrated in the Enterprise Engineering Model Entity-Relationship Diagram by a set of entities and their relationships.
Mechanics Transaction	2.8.3.2	The Mechanics Transaction represents the Operation Transaction in the Enterprise Engineering Model.
Mechanics Transaction Associative Entity	13.1.12, 13.2.5, 13.3.5, 13.4.5, 13.5.7, 13.6.5, 13.7.7, 13.9.5, & 13.10.5	The Mechanics Transaction Associative Entity resulting from the Many-to-Many relationship encountered between: ➤ The entities of the Master Data, or ➤ The entities of the Mechanism, or ➤ The entities of the Mechanics Sessions, or ➤ The entities of the Mechanics Transactions, or ➤ The Master Data Entities (except Activities or Occurrence Events) and the Mechanism Procedures, or ➤ The Master Data Entities (except Activities or Occurrence Events) and the Mechanics Sessions, or ➤ The Master Data Entities (except Activities or Occurrence Events) and the Mechanics Transactions, or ➤ The Mechanism and the Mechanics Transactions, or ➤ the Mechanics Session and the Mechanics Transactions, or ➤ Recursive convoluted relationships affecting the Mechanics Transaction Entities. This entity would have the features of the Mechanics Transaction Entities vis-à-vis the nature of the entities and their relationships with the Master Data, Mechanism, and the Mechanics Sessions and Transactions.
Mechanics Transaction Instance	2.4.2 & 2.8.3.2	The Mechanics Transaction Instance represents in the Enterprise Engineering Model the Operation Transaction Incidence.
Mechanics Transaction Profile	2.8.3.2	The Mechanics Transaction Profile is a group of entities that completely represent the Operation Transaction. It holds the detail data about a Mechanics Transaction. It is illustrated in the Enterprise Engineering Model Entity-Relationship Diagram by a set of entities and their relationships.
Mechanism	2.8.2	The Mechanism represents in the Enterprise Engineering Model the Enterprise Machinery.
Mechanism Procedure	2.8.2	A Mechanism Procedure represents in the Enterprise Engineering Model a Machinery Procedure.

Mechanism Procedure Associative Entity	13.2.5 & 13.5.7	The Mechanism Procedure Associative Entity resulting from the Many-to-Many relationship encountered between the entities of the Mechanism Procedures or between the Master Data Entities (except Activities or Occurrence Events) and the Mechanism Procedure Entities, or Many-to-Many recursive convoluted relationships affecting the Mechanism Procedure Entities. This entity would have the features of the Mechanism Procedure Entities vis-à-vis the nature of the entities and their relationships with the Master Data, Mechanism, and the Mechanics Sessions and Transactions.
Mechanism Procedure Profile	2.8.2	The Mechanism Procedure Profile is a group of entities that completely represent the Machinery Procedure. It holds the detail data about a Mechanism Procedure. It is illustrated in the Enterprise Engineering Model Entity-Relationship Diagram by a set of entities and their relationships.
Modifiable Data Instance	3.7	A Data Instance that can be modified or updated for business needs.
ODS	6.1, Table 6.1 & Diagram 6.1	The Legacy Systems is the Data Entry point for all Master and Transactional Data. These systems will update the ODS with Master and Transactional Data either real-time or near real-time or batch. No Data Feedback from the ODS to the Legacy Systems.
On-Line Analytical Processing (OLAP)	Table 3.1	Data Architecture Implementation Method to handle Business Intelligence Data to support Data Warehousing.
On-Line Mechanical Processing (OLMP)	3 & Table 3.1	Data Architecture Implementation Method to handle Enterprise Intelligence Data to support Enterprise Engineering.
On-Line Transactional Processing (OLTP)	Table 3.1	Data Architecture Implementation Method to handle Transactional Data to support Information Engineering.
Operation	2.1 & 2.4	The Operation comprises the Sessions and Transactions. It carries the Enterprise functioning. It is represented in the Enterprise Engineering Model by the Mechanics.
Operation Session	2.4.1	The Operation Session is triggered by an Event that takes place during the functioning of the Enterprise.

Operation Session Incidence	2.4.1	An Operation Session Incidence is an episode of an Operation Session. It occurs once and has Start and End Timestamps.
Operation Transaction	2.4.2	The Operation Transaction is generated or modified by Operation Sessions. It incorporates the transactional information of the functioning of the Enterprise.
Operation Transaction Incidence	2.4.2	An Operation Transaction Incidence is an episode of an Operation Transaction. It occurs once but could be modified many times. It has timestamp(s).
Process Consolidation Hub	6.3.7, Table 6.1 & Diagram 6.8	The Process Consolidation Hub holds all the Master, Transactional, and Process Data. The Legacy Systems will be a Data Entry point for all Data. These systems will update the Process Consolidation Hub with Master, Transactional, and Process Data either real-time or near real-time or batch. The Process Consolidation Hub will feedback its data to update the Legacy Systems either real-time or near real-time or batch.
Process Consolidation Repository	6.3.6, Table 6.1 & Diagram 6.7	The Process Consolidation Repository holds all the Master, Transactional, and Process Data. The Legacy Systems will be a Data Entry point for all Data. These systems will update the Process Consolidation Repository with Master, Transactional, and Process Data either real-time or near real-time or batch. No Data Feedback from the Process Consolidation Repository to the Legacy Systems.
Process Data	1.2 & 2.4	Data reflecting the functioning of the mechanics of the enterprises and includes the measures pertinent to their performance. It is expressing the data of the Operation Sessions.
Process Hub Stage 1	6.3.9, Table 6.1 & Diagram 6.10	The Process Consolidation Hub holds all the Master, Transactional, and Process Data. The Legacy Systems will be a Data Entry point for Master Data and all Transactional and Process Data. These systems will update the Process Hub Stage 1 with Master, Transactional, and Process Data either real-time or near real-time or batch. The Master Data could also be entered directly into the Process Hub Stage 1. The Process Hub Stage 1 will feedback its Master Data to update the Legacy Systems either real-time or near real-time or batch.

Dr. Eng. M. Naoulo

Process Hub Stage 2	6.3.11, Table 6.1 & Diagram 6.12	The Process Hub Stage 2 holds all the Master, Transactional, and Process Data. The Legacy Systems will be a Data Entry point for Master, Transactional, and Process Data. These systems will update the Process Hub Stage 2 with Master, Transactional, and Process Data either real-time or near real-time or batch. The Master, Transactional, and Process Data could also be entered directly into the Process Hub Stage 2. The Process Hub will feedback its data to update the Legacy Systems either real-time or near real-time or batch.
Process Hub Stage 3	6.3.12, Table 6.1 & Diagram 6.13	The Legacy Systems are phased out and all Data Entry for Master, Transactional, and Process Data will be carried out to update directly the Process Hub Stage 3.
Process or Business Process	2.2.2	A business process consists of a group of logically related **Activities**, actuated by **Occurrence** events, performed by internal and external **Operators**, use in-house and outside **Utilities**, performed across **Locations**, in order to provide results in support of the Enterprise's **Needs**.
Process Repository Stage 1	6.3.8, Table 6.1 & Diagram 6.9	The Process Repository Stage 1 holds all the Master, Transactional, and Process Data. The Legacy Systems will be a Data Entry point for Master, and all Transactional, and Process Data. These systems will update the Process Repository Stage 1 with Master, Transactional, and Process Data either real-time or near real-time or batch. The Master Data could also be entered directly into the Process Repository Stage 1. No Data Feedback from the Process Repository Stage 1 to the Legacy Systems.
Process Repository Stage 2	6.3.10, Table 6.1 & Diagram 6.11	The Process Repository Stage 2 holds all the Master, Transactional, and Process Data. The Legacy Systems will be a Data Entry point for Master, Transactional, and Process Data. These systems will update the Process Repository Stage 2 with Master, Transactional, and Process Data either real-time or near real-time or batch. The Master, Transactional, and Process Data could also be entered directly into the Process Repository Stage 2. No Data Feedback from the Process Repository Stage 2 to the Legacy Systems.
SAM O NAOULO Modeling Technique	3.	The Enterprise Engineering Modeling Technique used in the design of the Enterprise Engineering Model involving the Master Data, Mechanism, and Mechanics illustrating the Apparatus, Machinery, and Operation.

System of Apparatus, Machinery, & Operation: **SAM O NAOULO**	2.5	It is the Enterprise Engineering System that embodies the functioning of the Enterprises and serves analyzing it.
Transaction Consolidation Hub	6.5.2 & Table 6.1	Comparable to the Process Consolidation Hub however without the Process Data.
Transaction Consolidation Repository	6.5.2 & Table 6.1	Comparable to the Process Consolidation Repository however without the Process Data.
Transactional Data	1.2 & 2.4	Data detailing the transactions of the enterprise including the measures pertinent to the transactions. It is expressing the data of the Operation Transactions.
Transaction Hub Stage 1	6.5.2 & Table 6.1	Comparable to the Process Hub Stage 1 however without the Process Data.
Transaction Hub Stage 2	6.5.2 & Table 6.1	Comparable to the Process Hub Stage 2 however without the Process Data.
Transaction Hub Stage 3	6.5.2 & Table 6.1	Comparable to the Process Hub Stage 3 however without the Process Data.
Transaction Repository Stage 1	6.5.2 & Table 6.1	Comparable to the Process Repository Stage 1 however without the Process Data.
Transaction Repository Stage 2	6.5.2 & Table 6.1	Comparable to the Process Repository Stage 2 however without the Process Data.

Dr. Eng. M. Naoulo

References

1. Science, Volume 94, Issue 2446, pp. 456: Engineers' Council for Professional Development
2. Dr. E. F. Codd, A relational model of data for large shared data banks, Communications of the ACM, Vol. 13, Issue 6 (June 1970), Pages: 377-387.
3. C. J. Date, An Introduction to Database Systems, 6th Edition, Addison-Wesley, 1995.
4. James Martin, Managing the Data-Base Environment, Prentice-Hall International Inc., 1983.
5. James Martin, Information Engineering, Books I, II & III, Prentice Hall, Inc., 1990.
6. Clive Finkelstein, Information Engineering: Strategic Systems Development, Addison Wesley Longman Inc., 1992
7. Ivar Jacobson, Object-Oriented Software Engineering: A Use Case Driven Approach, Addison-Wesley, 1992.
8. Ivar Jacobson, Grady Booch & James Rumbaugh, The Unified Software Development Process, Addison Wesley Longman Inc., 1999.
9. W. H. Inmon, Building the Data Warehouse, 2nd Edition, John Wiley & Sons, 1996.
10. W. H. Inmon, Claudia Imhoff & Ryan Souza, Corporate Information Factory, John Wiley & Sons, 1998.
11. W. H. Inmon, Corporate Information Factory CIF DW2.0 Architecture Certification Documents, 2007.
12. William Inmon, Derek Strauss, & Genia Neushloss, DW 2.0: The Architecture for the Next Generation of Data Warehousing, Morgan Kaufmann, 2008.
13. Ralph Kimball & Margy Ross, The Data Warehouse Toolkit, 2nd Edition, John Wiley & Sons, 2002, 2003.
14. Thomas H. Davenport, Process Innovation: Reengineering Work thru Information Technology, Harvard Business School Press, 1993.
15. H. James Harrington, Business Process Improvement, McGraw-Hill Inc. 1991.
16. H. James Harrington, Total Improvement Management, The next Generation in Performance Improvement, McGraw-Hill Inc. 1995.
17. James G. Stovall, Journalism: Who, What, When, Where, Why, And How, Allyn & Bacon, 2004.
18. Allen Dreibelbis and al, Enterprise Master Data Management. An SOA Approach to Managing Core Information. IBM Press, 2008. Published by Pearson/Prentice Hall.
19. Dan Linstedt, Data Vault Overview: the next Evolution in Data Modeling. http://www.danlinstedt.com/AboutDV.php.
20. David Loshin, Master Data Management. The MK/OMG Press, 2008.
21. Alex Berson and Larry Dubov, Master Data Management and Customer Data Integration for a Global Enterprise. McGraw-Hill Osborn Media, 2007.
22. The Webster Dictionary, Houghton Mifflin Company, 1984, 1988, 1994.
23. Encyclopedia Britannica: Concise Encyclopedia, Encyclopedia Britannica Inc., 2002.
24. Mark W. Johnson, Seizing the White Space: Business Model Innovation for Growth and Renewal, Harvard Business Press, 2010.
25. Michael Hammer and Steven A. Stanton, The Reengineering Revolution, HarperCollins Books, 1995.

Dr. Eng. M. Naoulo

26. Michael Hammer & James Champy, Reengineering the Enterprise: a Manifesto for Business Revolution, HarperCollins Books, 1993.
27. Zachman, J.A. (1987), A Framework for Information Systems Architecture. IBM Systems Journal, vol. 26, no. 3, pp. 276-292.
28. Internet site: http://www.galawallpapers.net/tag/waterlily.

Dr. Eng. M. Naoulo

www.ingramcontent.com/pod-product-compliance
Lightning Source LLC
LaVergne TN
LVHW060136070326
832902LV00018B/2820